Seventh Edition

Modern English Rhetoric and Handbook

ROBERT GORRELL
University of Nevada

CHARLTON LAIRD

MARGARET URIE
University of Nevada

PRENTICE HALL, Englewood Cliffs, New Jersey 07632

Library of Congress Cataloging-in-Publication Data

```
Gorrell, Robert M.
    Modern English rhetoric and handbook / Robert Gorrell and Charlton
  Laird and Margaret Urie.
        p.    cm.
      Rev. ed. of: Modern English handbook. 6th ed. c1976.
    Includes index.
    ISBN 0-13-593872-4
    1. English language--Rhetoric.  2. English language-
  -Grammar--1950-      I. Laird, Charlton Grant, 1901-    .  II. Urie,
  Margaret, 1945-      .  III. Gorrell, Robert M.  Modern English
  handbook.  IV. Title.
  PE1408.G63  1988
  808'.042--dc19                                           87-23179
                                                              CIP
```

Editorial/production supervision and
  interior design: Jan Stephan
Cover design: Lundgren Graphics, Ltd.
Manufacturing buyer: Ray Keating

© 1988, 1976, 1972, 1967, 1962, 1956, 1953 by Prentice-Hall, Inc.
A Division of Simon & Schuster
Englewood Cliffs, New Jersey 07632

All rights reserved. No part of this book may be
reproduced, in any form or by any means,
without permission in writing from the publisher.

Printed in the United States of America

10 9 8 7 6 5 4 3 2 1

ISBN 0-13-593872-4 01

Prentice-Hall International (UK) Limited, *London*
Prentice-Hall of Australia Pty. Limited, *Sydney*
Prentice-Hall Canada Inc., *Toronto*
Prentice-Hall Hispanoamericana, S.A., *Mexico*
Prentice-Hall of India Private Limited, *New Delhi*
Prentice-Hall of Japan, Inc., *Tokyo*
Prentice-Hall of Southeast Asia Pte. Ltd., *Singapore*
Editora Prentice-Hall do Brasil, Ltda., *Rio de Janeiro*

Contents

Preface   xi

Introduction   1

    Rhetoric and the Communication Triangle   2
    Parts of the Rhetorical Process   3
    Prewriting, Writing, Revising   3
    Prewriting, Writing, Revising a Sentence   4
    Prewriting, Writing, Revising a Novel   5
    Two Students Prewriting, Writing, Revising an Essay   7
    Guides for Revision and Editing   12
    The Plan of the Book   13

GETTING AND DEVELOPING IDEAS

1. Getting Started   15

    Analysis and Synthesis   15
    Observing   16

Remembering 17
Freewriting 18
Clustering 19
Brainstorming 20
A Writer's Notebook 20
A Reader's Notebook 23
Asking Questions 24
Refining a Topic 25
Focusing: a Thesis Sentence 26
    For Study and Writing 28

2. Audience, Purpose, Voice   31

The Audience 32
The Student and the Audience 33
Purpose and Voice 34
Voice and Person 37
Consistency in Person 40
    Pers Consistency in Person 40
Tone: Attitude Toward Material and Audience 41
Appropriateness and Consistency in Tone 42
    Tone Appropriateness and Consistency in Tone 44
Consistency in Point of View and Tense 45
Tense Forms and Point of View 46
    Tense Consistency in Point of View and Tense 47
    For Study and Writing 48

3. Invention: Developing Ideas   52

General and Specific 53
Adequate and Specific Development 54
    Dev Adequate Development 56
Forms of Discourse 57
Development and Forms of Discourse 59
Strategies for Exposition: Types of Development 60
    For Study and Writing 69

ARRANGEMENT

4. Commitment and Response: The Paragraph   73

Commitment and Response 74
Commitment-Response Units 75

Paragraphing 76
 ¶ *Appropriate Paragraphing* 85
Coherence 86
Devices for Coherence 87
 Coh Coherence 90
  For Study and Writing 91

5. Organization: Analysis and Classification   95

Analysis 96
Classification 96
Coordination and Subordination 97
Using Analysis and Classification 99
Strategies for Organization 101
The Outline 104
Focusing Devices 111
Transitions 113
 Trans Transitions 115
Introductions 116
 Intro Introductions 120
Conclusions 121
 Conc Conclusions 122
  For Study and Writing 123

SENTENCE RHETORIC: WRITING GOOD SENTENCES

6. Basic Sentence Patterns   127

Grammar and Writing 127
Indicating Grammatical Relationships 128
Privilege of Occurrence 130
The Basic Sentence 130
SVC Patterns 132
Expanding SVC Patterns 133
Choosing Subjects 134
Actor-Action-Goal 135
 Subj Choice of Subject 137
The Verb 137
Choosing Verbs 138
The Complement 139
Clauses and the SVC Pattern 140

Completing the SVC Pattern: The Fragment   141
    Frag   *Fragment*   143
        For Study and Writing   144

7. Predication: Pattern Variations   147

Plausible Predication   147
    Pred   *Implausible Predication*   150
Equations with *To Be*   151
    Eq   *False Equations*   155
Consistency in Structure: Shifts   155
    Shift   *Shift in Construction*   156
Postponed Subject: Expletive   157
    Expl   *Overused Expletives*   158
The Passive   159
    Pass   *Inappropriate Passive*   162
        For Study and Writing   163

8. Combining Sentence Patterns: Coordination and Subordination   166

Coordinating Sentences and Clauses   167
Coordinating Lesser Sentence Elements   168
Parallelism and Coordination   169
    Paral   *Faulty Parallelism*   175
Adequate Subordination: Modification   175
    Sub   *Inadequate Subordination*   179
Adjective and Adverb   180
    Adj, Adv   *Misuse of Adjective or Adverb*   182
Modifiers and Word Order   182
    Mod   *Misplaced or Dangling Modifier*   188
Degrees of Modification   189
    Degree   *Inappropriate Degree of Modifier*   190
        For Study and Reference   191

9. Coherence in Sentences: Function Words, Reference, Agreement   196

Using Function Words   196
Conjunctions and Conjunctives   198
    Conj   *Misuse of Conjunction*   200
Prepositions   201
    Prep   *Misuse of Preposition*   202

Pronoun Reference   203
    Ref   Unclear Pronoun Reference   206
Word Reference   207
    WRef   Unclear Word Reference   209
Agreement   209
    Agr   Faulty Agreement   215
    For Study and Writing   216

LANGUAGE, USAGE, STYLE

10. Language and What to Know about It   **219**

The Indo-European Family   220
Indo-European Becomes English   222
Borrowing and the Word-Hoard   222
Building a Vocabulary   226
What Dictionaries Are For   230
How a Dictionary is Made   231
What a Dictionary is Good For   232
    For Study and Writing   233

11. Word Choice: Usage   **235**

Native Words and Borrowed Words   236
Accurate Word Choice   236
    W   Inaccurate Word Choice   237
How Words Mean   238
Figurative Language: Metaphor   244
Economy in Diction   246
    Wordy   Wordiness   248
Direction in Meaning   249
Trite Expressions: Clichés   250
    Trite   Trite Expressions: Clichés   250
Dialect, Usage, and Correctness   251
    Usage   Inappropriate Usage   255
    For Study and Writing   256

12. Style   **260**

Characteristics of Style   261
Sentence Length and Variety   262
Sound and Rhythm in Sentences   264
Cumulative and Periodic Sentences   265

Style and Parody   268
Fitting Style to the Occasion   270
Developing a Style: Reading   273
Developing a Natural Style   273
    For Study and Writing   275

SOME SPECIAL TYPES OF WRITING

13. Argument, Persuasion, Reasoned Writing   279

The Appeals   280
Persuasion and Ethics   280
The Basis of Argument and Persuasion: The Proposition   281
Strategies for Argument and Persuasion   282
Induction: Generalization and Evidence   287
Deduction   292
    For Study and Writing   298

14. Discussion, Examinations, Impromptu Writing, Business Letters, the Résumé   303

Discussion   304
The Examination Paper   305
Writing Examinations and Impromptu Essays   309
Letter Form and Conventions   312
Letter of Application   315
The Résumé   316
    For Study and Writing   319

15. Writing About Literature   321

Meaning: Theme   323
Voice: Point of View and Tone   325
Characterization   325
Conflict and Plot   327
Form and Technique   327
Style Analysis   328
Figurative Language and Literature   329
Comparison and Contrast   331
A Personal Response to Literature   332
Research for Writing on Literature   333
Mechanics for Writing about Literature   334
    For Study and Writing   335

16. The Investigative Paper — 338

    Choosing and Limiting a Subject   339
    Using Sources   340
    The Interview   340
    The Library: The Card Catalog   341
    Computer Searches   342
    Periodical and Newspaper Indexes   342
    Specialized Indexes   343
    Reference Books   344
    Bulletins and Pamphlets   346
    The Working Bibliography   346
    Taking and Preserving Notes   349
    Avoiding Plagiarism   354
    Writing and Revising the Paper   357
    Style in the Investigative Paper   358
    Incorporating Research in the Paper   359
    Documentation   361
    Works of Literature   364
    Endnotes   364
    Works Cited   365
    Sample Entries   367
    A Sample Paper   370
    Abbreviations and Conventions   385
        For Study and Writing   386

HANDLING CONVENTIONS

17. Punctuation — 389

    Uses of Punctuation   390
    End Punctuation: Period, Question Mark, Exclamation Mark   390
        P1 *End Punctuation*   392
    The Semicolon: Punctuation Between Independent Clauses, Fused or Run-on Sentences, Comma Fault or Comma Splice   393
        P2 Run-on, CF *Semicolon: Run-on Sentences*   395
    Commas After Introductory Modifiers   396
        P3 *Commas After Introductory Modifiers*   397
    Commas with Nonrestrictive or Parenthetical Modifiers   397
        P4 *Commas and Nonrestrictive Modifiers*   400
    Commas: Punctuation in a Series   401
        P5 *Punctuation in Series*   402
    Commas for Clarity   403
        P6 *Commas for Clarity*   404

Commas Separating Statistical Details   404
    P7 *Commas and Statistical Details*   405
Inappropriate or Excessive Commas   406
    P8 No P *Unnecessary Commas*   407
The Colon   407
    P9 *The Colon*   409
The Dash   409
    P10 Dash *Using Dashes*   410
Parentheses and Brackets   411
    P11 Parens *Parentheses and Brackets*   412
Quotation Marks: Punctuation with Quotations   412
    P12 *Punctuation With Quotations*   415
   For Study and Writing   416

18. The Writing System: Mechanics and Spelling   420

Manuscript Form   421
Spelling and Spellers   421
    Sp *Spelling*   426
Capitals   427
    Cap, lc *Capitalization*   429
Compounds, Hyphens   430
    Hy *Compounds, Hyphens*   431
Plurals   432
    P1 *Plurals*   433
Numbers   434
    Num *Numbers*   434
Apostrophes: Possessives, Contractions   435
    Apos, Poss *Possessives and Contractions*   436
Italics   437
    Ital *Italics*   438
Abbreviations   439
    Ab *Abbreviations*   440
Titles   440
    Titles *Improper Form for a Title*   441
Word Division   441
    Div *Word Division*   442
   For Study and Writing   443

Appendix A
Glossary of Usage   450

Appendix B
Revising an Essay Using the Guides to Revision   473

Preface

The habit of expression leads to the search for something to express.
HENRY ADAMS

But easy writing's curst hard reading.
RICHARD BRINSLEY SHERIDAN

The thirty-five years since the first edition of this book have seen rather remarkable developments in the teaching of English. Composition has emerged as a separate and respected academic discipline, based on the traditions of rhetoric but influenced by research in modern rhetoric and in a variety of related disciplines. Developments in linguistics, semantics, psycholinguistics, and communication theory have all been reflected in the teaching of writing, sometimes dominating approaches for a time. Enthusiasms for teaching devices or theoretical approaches have had periods of wide popularity and have often had a lasting effect on the discipline. Buzz words, current or outdated, suggest the range of these influences—guided research, free writing, transformational grammar, sentence-combining, speak-write, journal writing, protocols, revision, process, clustering, brainstorming, and so on.

A major pleasure of working on this book over the years has been the challenge of recognizing changes and developments, trying to distinguish between the significant and the superficial, trying to keep the book innovative but also sound. We have tried to incorporate significant results of research in rhetoric and composition and language. At the same time we have tried to keep the book focused on what seem to us basic principles of composing.

Interestingly, our fundamental purposes have not changed significantly over the years, in spite of many new approaches and methods that have influenced the book. The seventh edition is based on the following beliefs.

1. The study of writing develops skill in communication, particularly valuable for participation in modern society. But it also provides a means for creative and satisfying self-expression.

2. As Henry Adams has said, "The habit of expression leads to the search for something to express." Writing and the study of writing encourage intellectual growth.

3. Writing can be taught and can be learned. There is, of course, no one way to learn to be a great writer, but there are principles and procedures that can help writers to improve.

4. Writing can improve most through practice, discovering and applying positive principles rather than attempting to learn negative rules for correction.

5. Good writing grows from creative thinking and is a process of recurring prewriting, writing, and revising.

6. Standard English is difficult to define, but it is the dialect favored by persons in positions of power or prestige. It is not the only useful dialect, but learning it is essential for anyone involved in important activities of today's society.

7. Usage choices are rhetorical choices, based on anticipation of their effect on a reader.

8. Learning writing is a long job, but a rewarding one.

We have therefore continued to base this book on rhetoric and linguistics and to make it a "how-to" book, a book of suggestions about how to find things to write and how to write them better. We have tried to describe the most useful rhetorical devices for clear and direct prose and to explore characteristics of language that affect good writing. We have not attempted to offer rules, either positive or negative; composition is too varied and too subtle for mechanical procedures. We have tried to show, through examples and analysis and explanation, some of the ways in which a writer can go about creating sentences and paragraphs and longer units of prose.

Although we have kept in mind the complexity and holistic quality of the composing process, we have recognized that learning requires some focus on specific techniques. We have therefore divided the book to treat composition topic by topic—into chapters, each of which concentrates on a rhetorical or linguistic principle and contains exercises and suggestions under the heading "For Study and Writing." The content of these is surveyed in the table of contents and the index. Most chapters contain also brief summaries of important rhetorical principles with the heading "Guide to Revision." An instructor may refer to these to make suggestions for revising writing, as explained in Appendix B.

Faculty members may find more detailed suggestions on our intentions and on the plan of the book, as well as suggestions for teaching and comments on the exercises, in the *Teacher's Manual*, available from the publisher.

As in preparing other editions, we have become indebted to many for help—to the publisher, to students, to teachers on our own and other campuses who have been generous with time and suggestions. We are grateful for criticism and comments from William Lutz, Rutgers University at Camden; Harry Brent, Bernard R. Baruch College; Raymond MacKenzie, Mankato State University; Edward Kline, University of Notre Dame; and Michael Keene, University of Tennessee. We have benefited from editorial advice and help from William H. Oliver and Phil Miller and from the imaginative and careful editing of Jan Stephan. We are grateful to many students who have allowed us to use examples of their writing and who have helped us experience the pleasures of teaching writing. Before his death in 1984 Charlton Laird made many suggestions for this edition and his wisdom and learning still pervade the book.

Robert Gorrell
Margaret Urie

Introduction

> *She was long deaf to all the sufferings of her lovers till one day, at a neighbouring fair, the rhetoric of John the hostler, with a new straw hat and a pint of wine, made a second conquest over her.*
> HENRY FIELDING, *Joseph Andrews*

> *I see writing as a job of experiment. It's like any discovery job; you don't know what's going to happen until you try it.*
> WILLIAM STAFFORD

> *It is foolish to suppose that you can teach anybody to write, but it is equally foolish to suppose that you cannot teach people a great deal about writing.*
> ROLFE HUMPHRIES

This is intended as a very practical book, because rhetoric is useful, for everything from John the hostler's courting in *Joseph Andrews* to the conduct of the most important affairs of our society. The book is designed to help you write better, to give you hints and advice and practice for cultivating a useful skill. Because writing, in spite of the tremendous technical development of media for speech communication, is still basic to most of the serious activities of the modern world. Skill with the written language can greatly increase your chances of success in almost any endeavor—social service, teaching, marketing, engineering, medicine, law, computer science, business, diplomacy. To say that language is power is trite, but the fact remains.

This book is also intended as a guide to an important pleasure—the pleasure of self-expression and discovery. That is, writing is an important practical tool, but writing is also an art. And the satisfaction of creating, of feeling something come to life and take shape as words appear on paper, is one of the important experiences of life. Good writing is not easy, but it offers great satisfaction to the writer.

There is, of course, no one way to write—which is why writing is both difficult and exciting. Different circumstances and different audiences may require different approaches. Sometimes ideas come quickly, especially when you are writing about a subject you know well. But often you have to dig; for example, when you write on an assigned topic for a class or a job. But though there is no one way to write, no sure-fire formula, there are principles or techniques that work frequently enough to be worth studying—and they will make your writing more pleasurable. These make up the discipline of rhetoric, one of civilization's oldest studies.

RHETORIC AND THE COMMUNICATION TRIANGLE

Rhetoric is the art or discipline that studies the use of language to inform or persuade or influence a reader or an audience. Since the fifth century B.C., rhetoric has been a central discipline in education. Through the centuries, principles and procedures have been developed and discarded, rediscovered and modified, but the discipline has continued to offer help to people working to improve their writing.

Rhetorical principles grow from observing how writing works, as the following diagram describes:

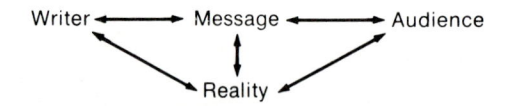

```
        Writer ←――――→ Message ←――――→ Audience
                  ↖        ↕        ↗
                         Reality
```

This is called a communication triangle. It will serve as well for other media as for writing—television commercials, films, gestures—but here we are looking at it primarily as the basis of communication through written language.

At first glance, the diagram may look simple, but it has many implications. If you are writing something, you are at the left-hand corner of the triangle. What you have in mind—the reality you are concerned with—is at the bottom corner of the triangle. The message itself, what you are producing, is in the middle of the triangle. It is directed toward an audience, the right-hand corner.

But you will notice that the arrows run both ways. You, as writer, are acting. You are expressing your personality, your insight, your experience, your ability to perceive. You are also interacting with all the other parts of the triangle at once. You are getting something from reality, which influences your message, a reflection of reality. At the same time, you are thinking of your audience. Describing your biology course, you would compose different messages for your lab instructor, for your younger sister, or for a cab driver. The audience is affected by the message, by its own sense of reality, and even by you, the writer. The audience will view the message in one way if it believes the writer is an honest, sensible, well-informed person, in a different way if it believes the writer to be boastful or uninformed.

PARTS OF THE RHETORICAL PROCESS

Learning any complicated skill creates a dilemma. Where do you start? How do you learn everything at once? As a writer trying to learn, you are like a nonswimmer tossed into the water after your first swimming lesson. You have to do more than one thing at the start to keep from drowning. You can't practice your kick and forget about breathing.

As a writer, you need to turn out a finished product; you can't concentrate exclusively on sentence structure and forget about organizing ideas into logical sequences. But as a shortcut, a practical approach, it makes sense to break a complicated subject into smaller, more manageable parts. There are different ways to think about parts of the writing process, though all of them are somewhat artificial. One division, used in classical rhetoric for centuries, identifies three parts of the rhetorical process as (1) invention or discovery, (2) arrangement or organization, and (3) style. Invention or discovery is the finding of material, of arguments or evidence to support an idea. Arrangement concerns the order or plan for putting ideas together. Style is a broad concept including matters such as word choice, sentence structure, and usage.

PREWRITING, WRITING, REVISING

Another way to think about writing is similar to the classical divisions. If we think for a minute about how we write, we can isolate three sorts of things we do. We have to do some thinking, we have to formulate that thinking in words, and we constantly change our minds about what we are saying. These three activities—prewriting or thinking, writing or putting ideas down in words, and revising—are going on all the time when we write.

Prewriting can include a variety of activities. It may stretch over years and continue even after the writing is done. It may send us to a library or on a field trip, or it may require us to sit down and concentrate. Writing occurs when we get ready to put words on paper, and it involves attention to what is labeled arrangement as a part of rhetoric. Revision goes on all through the process, and it should be distinguished from what, in this book, we call editing. Revision requires rethinking and rewriting, looking critically at each draft for possible improvements or changes. Revision is a basic part of the writing process. Editing, on the other hand, means checking for mechanical errors, including spelling and punctuation.

These activities do not occur in any sequence. The importance of each will vary for different writers and different subjects and different circumstances. Sometimes a piece of writing develops easily and may need little revision. But sometimes even a single sentence requires extensive involvement of all three approaches.

PREWRITING, WRITING, REVISING A SENTENCE

Let's look at what you might go through to put together a single simple sentence. You have recently seen a violent film, and you have a notion that you want to make a statement about violence in movies. You're concerned, but you haven't really thought much about it. Still you start with something in your mind: "There's too much violence in movies these days." You don't bother to write that down, because you're not sure you believe it, and you realize that it's too general to mean much anyway. So you try to be a little more precise; you're revising, even though nothing has been put on paper. You ask yourself whether you object to all violence, and decide that some violence may be justified. But you do object to violence exploited as mere sensationalism, violence that has nothing to do with the plot of the film. Then you think more sharply about what this sort of violence does to movies. Does it make them duller? Does it make them trite? Does it increase the chances of crime among children? You keep speculating, but you finally write down a sentence:

> Many movies are cheapened by violence exploited only as sensationalism.

You have a sentence. It is clear, and it says something worth developing; but as you look at it, you wonder if you can clarify or strengthen it. For one thing, you notice that you have not specified any kind of movies, and you think you want to emphasize the popular movies you have seen recently. You also realize that you can make the sentence more direct by using *violence*, your main concern, as the subject. You try a revision.

> Violence, introduced only for its sensational appeal, cheapens many popular movies.

You are a long way from developing your idea completely, but you have a statement that expresses your thought.

Obviously, every sentence that gets written does not require this conscious back-and-forth thinking-writing-revising procedure. Much of the thinking may be complete and ready for expression in words. And much of this process occurs almost automatically, at least after practice. But something like this—or often something more elaborate—goes on during the composing process.

PREWRITING, WRITING, REVISING A NOVEL

On a much larger scale, we can see how this process operates over years of preparation and work and reworking. Walter Van Tilburg Clark's novel *The Oxbow Incident* is a story about three innocent men hanged as cattle thieves by a posse made up of other innocent men and one woman, most of whom thought they were doing the right thing. It is a "Western," with cowboys and sheriffs and gun play, but a Western with a difference. The book has sold millions of copies and was made into a successful film, often rerun on television. It first appeared in 1940, but it had been growing many years before that.

It began when Clark was a boy growing up in Reno, Nevada, then a relatively small community. All around were the relics of mining booms, with old prospectors on the local skid row, and ghost towns; there were cattle ranches with working cowboys; there were gambling houses and brothels. Young Clark was entranced with these people. He liked them, studied them, and learned to see the world through their eyes, to feel it through their hands.

This was prewriting, and since Clark wanted to write, he knew it. He was writing from this prewriting, always scribbling about the people around him in poems and short stories, most of which have been burned because he thought they were no good. And these early writings were also prewriting, although Clark probably was not planning consciously for an eventual novel like *The Oxbow Incident*.

Talking to a college class later, Clark recalled incidents from these early days. He told how, driving home after a day in the mountains, he had stopped at a roadside shack for a beer. A huge-muscled woman called Ma ran the place, serving hamburgers and beer—and the sheriff probably never asked what else she served. But a new road was coming through; the place had been condemned and was closing up. An old truck was pulled up near the door ready to haul off some of the furnishings, and some of Ma's men friends were contemplating the huge cook stove Ma had used to fry hamburgers, wondering how to load it. When Clark asked for beer, Ma said she had shut up shop; and as if to put an end to the conversation, she laid her two great hands on the jutting top of the stove, and as Clark told the story, "gave it the knee," and heaved it into the truck.

Clark never used the incident in a story, but it was prewriting of a sort. When he needed a woman to ride with the posse in *The Oxbow Incident*, a woman powerful enough in character as well as brawn to become a steely but moral leader of the men, he dredged up the beer-and-hamburger woman and made her into Ma Grier.

Thus Clark's living was prewriting. So was his reading. Among the books he encountered as a young man was Cervantes's *Don Quixote*, which started out to be a satire of the silly knighthood romances of its day. Clark was delighted with it and related it to his other reading. He had become irked at the romances of his own time, the Westerns about gun-toting sheriffs and cowpunchers, always noble and always victorious, and heroines who survived the frontier without ever getting a curl misplaced.

So he wrote, or at least started to write, a spoof of Westerns. But while he was writing he was still observing the world around him. In those days the Nazi horror was growing in Germany. Clark saw that there was fascism in the United States too, that it could grow, and that the dangers and weaknesses of modern society could be revealed in the action he had planned for his book, in frontier notions of rough justice. He rewrote his story; it became much bigger than a satire on Westerns, a sort of fable of democracy.

This rewriting, however, although Clark was probably not aware of it at the time, was also prewriting to yet another version of the story. He realized that he wanted to do more than show how fascism and social crime can develop in a society, that he wanted to consider why. He had a story in which innocent men had been hanged; the truth of their innocence had come out, and dozens of people had begun to recognize that they were guilty of murder. But all the time there had been people who had known better—as there had been German contemporaries of Hitler who knew better—the narrator and his buddy, decent though somewhat naïve cowpunchers; a well-meaning but pitiable minister; an informed judge, corrupt but not hopelessly so; a highly intellectual but somewhat deranged idealist on the brink of suicide. Notably, there was a storekeeper, a courageous and somewhat philosophic cripple, literate and armed with his convictions. Why had he not been able to stop the mania and bloodlust of the mob?

For his further rewriting, Clark needed to incorporate more crowd psychology, even more speculation about the nature of good and evil—and his college courses in philosophy may have been more pertinent prewriting than he realized. Is a person good who only means well? Or must a person do well, also? Clark, of course, never attempted to answer these questions and never let them dominate his rewriting enough to turn his story into a tract. But they led him into rewriting that found added meaning in the events of his western tale. Thus, when he finally submitted his manuscript, it was the culmination of years of living, thinking, writing, and rewriting that had matured into something he wanted to say.

Clark's years of recurring considerations of his material are essentially the same as a student's activity in producing a single statement or an essay. Details vary, but the basic procedures are the same. And a writer can often profit by working consciously at some aspect of composing, realizing the value of prewriting and the need for constant revision.

TWO STUDENTS PREWRITING, WRITING, REVISING AN ESSAY

The next examples, both by students, illustrate the importance of this process. The first student, Phil Pinto, was writing an examination in a composition class. He had been given several topics, and after some thought, he decided to write an essay defining a rock concert. As he later explained, he had attended many concerts and considered himself an expert on the topic. But instead of immediately starting a draft, Phil began by jotting down ideas that popped into his head.

Kinds of rock concert watchers

locomotion, a flux, flow
current circuit
motive is to
"too cool to move"
transfixed heavy eyes
followers know lyrics (repetitious)
hard core rockers
dancers — boring ("stand theres") — singers — head shakers
transfixed immobile standstill
— wasted cases — drugs — groupies — fanatics — occasional reporters (pad out / cut?)
disciple devotee, parasite
twitchy, jerky, askew — spastic movements — choreographer — impulsive screams
cessation performance
conduct / behavior
pursuit of happiness
— concert watching
reaction to the stimulus (light, feeling, sounds)

pursuit of happy — Mine is people watching — I like to watch people in their pursuit — I noticed some like to sit in the yard & relax, some create & some like to watch a performance — athletic — a movie — a play or a concert. I especially like to watch people at a R & R concert

He quickly realized that much of this had nothing to do with the concert, but described the audience. In other words, while prewriting, Phil had shifted his main interest and found a focus for his ideas. At the same time, in the lower right-hand corner of his note sheet, he had discovered an idea for an introduction to his essay.

Still prewriting, Phil made an informal outline. From the different types of concert watchers he had listed in his first notes, he selected four that he thought he could best describe. He used them as main topics in his outline and noted specific characteristics of each type.

I. <u>Singers</u> ⟨obvious group follower, chin up, transfixed eyes⟩ knows lyrics — I'm not sure if he sings or just mouths to singers?

II. <u>Groupies</u> / fanatics ⟨twitch, jerk, twist body askew, spastic movements which no choreographer could produce, impulses, screaming bursts young girls, occasional fainting, swooning, throw flowers & admiration notes⟩

III. <u>Waste-cases</u> ⟨stand there, too cool to move, immobile, long hairs, leather, smoke pot, drink smuggled alcohol⟩

IV. <u>Dancers / headshakers</u> —
   A. Dancers — mellow, steady rhythm, flow w/ beat, slow locomotion of the arms
   B. Headshakers — head shaking, vigor, hard-core rockers violent contractions until cessation of concert

With this outline, he could see the structure of his essay. Then he wrote a purpose statement, which established his relationship as a writer to his audience and his subject—the communication triangle:

> My intended audience is anyone who has not yet watched rock-and-rollers at a concert. My voice is that of an experienced concert watcher/people watcher. My purpose is to classify and describe rock-and-roll audiences.

The statement would, of course, not appear in the essay, but it allowed Phil to clarify his goals, and he was ready to write.

Almost immediately Phil became involved in that back-and-forth process of thinking, writing, and revising simultaneously. The first draft of his paragraph on singers shows these three activities occurring:

> Always obvious to spot, because of their transfixed eyes, their upward-pointing chins, and their moving mouths, are the singers. ~~These people are driven followers, disciples to the group, I know this beca~~ I know these people are disciples to the group because they know every lyric to every song. ~~They never~~ The singers never dance or move around, they

simply stand there motionless and sing. ~~I am not sure they~~ Because of the loud music, however, ~~you e~~ I never can hear these people singing until the band asks the audience to sing along; then the singers drown out everyone else.

After the first draft was finished, Phil went over it again, not changing much of the original because of his time limit, but revising and editing for style. Finally Phil's time was up, and he turned in the completed copy.

With more time, Phil's rewriting and revising could have continued. Looking at the paper two weeks later, he might have thought of further revisions or even a different approach. But by using this technique—prewriting, writing, and revising—he was able to move from a blank sheet of paper to a respectable essay even under the pressures of time.

A second student, Susie Uramoto, had been given an assignment to write an essay about a person or event that had a special meaning in her life. Susie chose to write about her favorite uncle, who had recently died. This was a difficult topic, and Susie almost abandoned it after her first two rough drafts. However, she did her prewriting and organized her ideas and brought the following paper to class.

Starting a New Life

There have been many special moments in my life; however, the incident that will always be especially meaningful to me is when my favorite uncle became ill and died. Before he passed away, I had never thought about how precious life really is. After all, no one close to me had ever died, and the idea of death just didn't seem realistic. As a result, I was extremely lazy and developed the motto, "There's always tomorrow." In a sense, I had practically wasted a large portion of my life by simply being lazy and nonchalant. About a year ago, however, my attitude towards life changed considerably.

Last July, my uncle was diagnosed as being terminally ill, and he was given only a short time to live. Even though my parents told me what the outcome of his illness would be, I couldn't let go of the possibility that he would ultimately get better. As the days passed, however, I began to see the hands of death gradually take hold of him. At first, he began to lose a tremendous amount of weight. Then dark circles appeared under his eyes, which made his face seem empty and hollow. Finally, he became so weak and drained that he was confined to bed.

Even though he drastically deteriorated physically, his mental outlook remained amazingly healthy and positive. Not once did he show any signs of bitterness or despair. He treated each day very special and relished every moment. My uncle continued to live his days to the fullest until he died.

The experience of my uncle's illness and ultimate death is meaningful to me because it taught me a great deal. It taught me that in reality life can be taken away just as quickly as it can be given and that no one should take it for granted. Observing his tremendous courage taught me to enjoy and make the most of every day. My uncle's illness and death helped me to actually start living my life in a new perspective. Now, I have adopted a new motto, "Live life to its fullest!"

When Susie read her copy to her response group, the students were interested in the essay. They liked the use of the motto in the first and last paragraphs. They noticed that paragraph two was well developed with some concrete details. They thought the introduction was a little slow, and they noticed some bad sentences. But mostly they wanted more specific information to support the general assertions about the uncle's influence. They wanted to know more about the uncle, what he was like, what he did in those final days, and how all this changed the writer.

Susie's instructor also thought the paper needed revision and made the following comments on the draft:

It is difficult to write about a subject so close to you and an event so recent; it is hard for you to look objectively at the death and its effect on you. I think, however, that you should not abandon the subject but try looking at it from a different direction. With a sharper focus, you may be able to avoid the unsupported generalizations and provide specific development. Here are two suggestions for approaching a revision:

1. Focus on the uncle. You have details about his physical deterioration, but you could expand on his positive mental attitude. What did he do to live a full life? If you learned a lesson, what did he do that taught you?

2. Make yourself a narrator for the essay and focus on you and your reactions. You say that the experience changed you. How have you changed? Can you cite specific examples of things you do differently?

Either of these approaches—or a combination—might help you improve your paper.

With the help of these suggestions, Susie was able to stand back from her work and look at it critically. She decided to try focusing on her uncle and the effects of the death on her. She discovered that she could use specific examples of her reaction and behavior but could also retain details of her uncle's behavior. She revised to produce a better paper.

Observe and Learn

Every day when I arrived home from school, he would be waiting for me with a big gleaming smile on his face. It seemed that no matter how bad my day at school had been, he would always make everything much brighter with a few wise and kind words. My Uncle George was indeed a very wise person. He once told me that observing is the best tool for learning. I really didn't understand what he meant at the time, but I did as his life grew closer to a premature end; I became an observer. As a result, I learned something very special.

Last July my uncle was diagnosed as terminally ill and was given only a short time to live. At first, I absolutely refused to accept the diagnosis. However, as the weeks passed, I began to see the hands of death gradually take their hold. His full, healthy face started to lose its normal, glowing warmth. Instead it gradually grew very thin and pale. Dark circles began to appear under his eyes, which made them seem hollow and empty. It was apparent that the disease had physically seized him; however, it could do nothing to damage his vitality.

Nearly every day he insisted that we embark on a new adventure. He unexpectedly drove us to Lake Tahoe one afternoon, and he insisted that we rent a speed boat and race it as fast as it could go. "I have always wanted to do this!" he said. We went to San Francisco and sat on the beach as a thick blanket of fog rolled in from the bay. "Why?" I asked as I sat there on the sand and watched a broad grin appear on his face. Again, he simply replied, "I have always wanted to do this."

I continued to watch him enjoy every moment of the things that he had "always wanted to do." At first I simply thought he was crazy, but then I began to recognize the tremendous courage that he possessed. It was the courage that allowed him knowingly to ride a roller coaster for the last time. It was the courage that allowed him to continue doing things, despite knowing that it would all end soon. Somehow, I was able to see that strong courage just by observing him during the last moments of his life.

Uncle George is gone now, but his special courage lives on—in me. When it came time for me to move out of the house and go to college, I became frightened and unsure of myself. However, I began to remember my uncle and the courage he had in order to live actively the remainder of his life. I then found the courage inside me that allowed me to move on and face the many obstacles in life. "Observing is the best tool for learning," he once said, and I did, in fact, observe. As a result, I learned what it's like to possess a strong sense of courage that allows me to overcome any barrier.

The revision is still not entirely successful in making the reader understand the uncle's courage and its effect on the narrator. But it is greatly improved over the earlier draft, especially because it relies more on specific details.

Susie had an advantage over Phil because she could profit from comments by readers and look back on her essay after a period of time. Ideally, a writer should put any draft aside for a few days and then take a fresh look at the subject. Practically, it is often necessary to revise fairly promptly, and it may be useful to check the manuscript with specific questions like the following:

1. Does my paper have a central purpose and idea?
2. Does all the material focus on this central idea?
3. Is all the material relevant, or could some be cut?

4. Is the development specific? Could more or better specific illustrations be added?
5. Is the order of details clear within paragraphs and through the whole essay?
6. Are sentences clear and direct? Could any of them be improved by changing the subject?

Dozens of other questions could be asked, and you may develop some especially useful to you as you discover what you want to concentrate on to improve your writing. But the best approach to revision is to stand as far as you can from your draft and think objectively about what you've said.

GUIDES FOR REVISION AND EDITING

Novelist Vladimir Nabokov comments: "I have rewritten—often several times—every word I have ever published. My pencils outlast their erasers." As discussed above, revision occurs throughout the writing process and often produces multiple drafts. If you are working with a word processor, you may make revisions on the screen before you print a draft. But you need to look at every draft—whether it is handwritten, typed, or printed—for possible rethinking or rearranging of the entire paper.

An important part of the review of a draft is editing or checking details—spelling and mechanics, usage, typographical errors, neatness of the manuscript—and this needs to be done before submitting a final draft. Many editing changes may occur during the general revising process. With a word processor you will catch errors on the screen. Various software packages, called text editors, can help you check spelling and mechanics. Still, every draft of your paper needs a final editing, usually more than one proofreading.

Another way to go about general revising and editing is to have someone else read the manuscript. As a writer, you can become so involved with your ideas that it is hard to view your work objectively, to see its strengths or weaknesses. In classes on writing, criticisms from classmates or an instructor provide help for both revision and editing. This book is designed to make that criticism easier and to help you understand suggestions.

Throughout the book there are guides for revision to which an instructor may refer in making comments on your manuscript. These guides, for both general revision and editing, are brief summaries of longer discussions in the chapter; your instructor may refer to them with abbreviations that are listed in Appendix B. Since you will be writing essays before you have studied many of the topics in this book, that reference system will help you make suggested revisions. Appendix B explains how to use it.

THE PLAN OF THE BOOK

Revision is a main topic of this book, for it is intended to help you improve your writing, and improvement by definition involves rethinking, reworking, and rewriting. We have emphasized in the discussions above how prewriting, writing, and revising occur together all through the writing process. These elements, which parallel divisions of classical rhetoric—invention, arrangement, and style—provide the basis for the organization of this book.

We have recognized, however, that as a writer you need to know about all these topics at once, but can study and practice only one part of the process at a time. We have, therefore, organized the book to take up different parts of the composing process one at a time, realizing that you will be using all the parts as you study each one. The first chapters concern gathering ideas and details for writing—prewriting and invention. The following chapters concern arrangement and the problems of getting ideas into words, devices for making one idea stimulate another. The next parts of the book address questions of style, with methods of building sentences and techniques for choosing and controlling words. Later chapters discuss some special types of writing and conventions to be followed in writing and checked in editing.

1

Getting Started

First catch the rabbit . . .

Grandma's recipe for rabbit stew began with the obvious: "First catch the rabbit." You need more than water and an appetite to make a stew. And you need more than a pencil or an assignment to write an essay. There are many ways to catch a rabbit—hunting, trapping, tracking, or starting a colony in a hutch. There are even more ways to get ideas for writing. This chapter suggests some of them, ways of getting prewriting, writing, and revising started.

ANALYSIS AND SYNTHESIS

Any approach to writing involves thinking. According to scientists, the two spheres of the human brain govern different sorts of operations, both of which are essential to the writing process. One sphere, usually the left, governs what may be called logical and critical procedures, such as analysis. The other sphere concentrates on creative activity and emotions, wholes or synthesis. Writing, as a function of the entire brain, requires the coopera-

tion of both spheres, requires looking at both parts and wholes, for instance.
The writing process, therefore, can be viewed as a combination of analysis and synthesis, sometimes a kind of alternation between them. Analysis breaks wholes into parts, into their various elements. Synthesis works in the other direction, combining parts or units into wholes, often new wholes. For example, consider the fairly general notion we developed as a sentence in the previous chapter:

> Violence, introduced only for its sensational appeal, cheapens many popular movies.

This general idea could be developed into writing by various kinds of analysis. For example, you could break one part of the whole—popular movies—into examples of specific movies that exploit violence. Or you could sort out the types of violence you have observed.

With the opposite approach, however, you might start with parts, as you probably would have in formulating a general idea like that in the sentence. You might see a violent movie or two, single out others with violence in them, and then try to produce a synthesis of what you observed. You might produce a general comment, such as the conclusion that violence cheapens some movies.

These two ways of looking at the world, at the specific trees or at the general forest, characterize our thinking and also the writing process. In almost every section of this book we will see the two approaches working together, in finding ideas for writing, in discovering materials and developing ideas, in revising and reworking. They are basic to what rhetoricians call invention, the discoveries that may result from the following procedures.

OBSERVING

Sherlock Holmes liked to twit Dr. Watson about his failure to observe. "You see, but you do not observe," he says, after finding Watson unable to specify the number of steps in the stairs leading to his apartment. For the writer, as for the detective, observation remains one of the best ways to get writing started. Look at something, anything—a roller skate, a gum wrapper—so hard and long that you see things you had not known before. Try a dollar bill. What kind of edging does George Washington have on his jacket? How does the cut of his hair differ from the way some men wear their hair today? Is there a pyramid on the bill? If so, what is on the pyramid? Can you figure out why? What is the eagle grasping?

Observation provides the material for synthesis and analysis, for seeing both wholes and parts and relating them. Look around the room of someone you don't know very well and observe as many details as you can. What colors predominate? Are there any books? Any records? Any clothes lying about? Look at these parts and then think about whether they give you ideas about the whole, about the person who lives in the room. Or look at one of the students in your class. What can you tell about her by her clothes, by the way she asks questions, by the way she sits when the lecture seems long?

The following is the result of a professional writer's observing, seeing details and also seeing how they fit together.

> But after a while, I was glad I had seen the cars in this natural setting, which was, after all, a kind of Plato's Republic for teen-agers. Because if you watched anything at this fair very long, you kept noticing the same thing. These kids are absolutely maniacal about form. They are practically religious about it. For example, the dancers: none of them ever smiled. They stared at each other's legs and feet, concentrating. The dances had no grace about them at all, they were more in the nature of a hoedown, but everybody was concentrating to do them exactly *right*. And the bouffant kinds all had form, wild form, but form with rigid standards, one gathers. Even the boys. Their dress was prosaic—Levis, Slim Jims, sport shirts, T shirts, polo shirts—but the form was consistent: a stovepipe silhouette. And they all had the same hairstyle; some wore it long, some short, but none of them had a part; all that hair was brushed back straight from the hairline. I went by one of the guitar booths, and there was a little kid in there, about thirteen, playing the hell out of an electric guitar. The kid was named Cranston something or other. He looked like he ought to be named Kermet or Herschel; all his genes were kind of horribly Okie. Cranston was playing away and a big crowd was watching. But Cranston was slouched back with his spine bent like a sapling up against a table, looking gloriously bored. At thirteen, this kid was being fanatically cool. They all were. They were all wonderful slaves to form.
>
> Tom Wolfe, *The Kandy-Kolored, Tangerine-Flake Streamline Baby*

Wolfe observed closely—details like the boys' clothing, their hair, the slouch of Cranston's spine—but he also saw that some of the details he observed could be related, could be grouped into a whole. He had an idea for his paragraph, focused on the proposition that "they were all wonderful slaves to form." Observing and thinking about what you observe can get writing started.

REMEMBERING

Teachers sometimes suggest topics for writing such as "My First Dance," "Getting a Job," or "Life with Father." Such well-worn topics may produce well-worn writing, but topics like these can also stimulate remembering. And remembering what you have observed or thought or felt in the past can give your writing a start. Looking back even has some advantage over observing in the present, because you can observe the past more objectively, seeing implications in events that become apparent only after reflection. For instance, what may seem terribly serious when it occurs—a torn dress, a broken date, a throwing error—may seem trivial or amusing a few years later. Conversely, what seems trivial or uninteresting on the surface may, on reflection, reveal a special meaning and become a subject for writing.

For example, in the passage below, a Norwegian student explains the memories that are triggered for her by the smell of evaporated milk.

> The aroma of evaporated milk filled my kitchen, and my thoughts and feelings went back to the war; German soldiers, my mother's green dress with yellow flowers, eggs on the asphalt, and an old brown hat were my recollections. The smell of cooking with evaporated milk, a typical war product—"box milk"—stirred up memories. I very rarely have thoughts about the war, I feel no resentment toward the Germans: I only remember what happened.

Another student recalls specific details of an incident, sees significance in them, and is able to work them into an interesting paragraph.

> The evening gown hung on the rack, lifeless and formless, but when Patty put it on, at fifteen, it was transformed into the gown of an empress and she became a Grecian goddess. Her voluptuous figure filled it out admirably, incredibly to me, who at sixteen barely supported a strapless formal. It was light blue and silver chiffon, and it fell from her shoulders in soft folds. Her skin glowed, her dark hair glistened above the gown, and her Irish eyes twinkled beneath her dark lashes. Then she smiled. Rows of metal shone harshly from her teeth. She was changed again into my fifteen-year-old schoolmate, my childhood friend in her new braces and the beautiful blue gown.

FREEWRITING

An easy way not to write is to sharpen half a dozen pencils and then sit staring at paper waiting for inspiration to strike. It seldom does. One way to start is just to start, to force yourself to write whatever pops into your head just as fast as you can, without worrying about form or spelling or a grade. This technique, called freewriting, provides a way to escape the restrictions of the analytical left side of the brain and to give the right side a chance to dominate. It works like priming a pump; it gets something going. The assignment for the following was to write as fast as possible for no more than ten minutes.

> I have to write for ten minutes about anything. I don't think I can do it. Don't stop says the instructor—what a drag. Standing there in her pert little

suit, looking so organized and telling us what to do. My hand hurts. What can I write about? Think about something. Oh yes, that lemon in the fruit bowl this morning. It looked awful, old. With some mold on it, and kind of green. I bet it's sour. But I used to like lemonade, it's sweet. Lemon. Lemon. A funny word. A car can be a lemon. Or anything can be. Why pick on the lemon. Why can't a bad car be an orange. Maybe because it's sour. Lemon tree song. Jack Lemmon. Ball player named Lemon maybe. Lemmings run into the sea. People do that too. Not into the sea, but after fads. Paul with his buzz hair cut. I've never seen anything so awful. Like running into the sea. Lemons, lemmings. I'd rather see than be one. I want to be myself, an individual. This is pretty heavy stuff. Isn't it time to quit?

Most of this will probably be discarded, but it is not all useless. Mostly it records facts directly and simply, talking about real things—a teacher, a moldy lemon, Paul's haircut. It sounds honest. And there are germs for ideas here, for things to write about—a character sketch of Paul, a discussion of the connotations of the word *lemon*, even a serious discussion about peer pressure and the problems of being an individual.

CLUSTERING

Another way of putting the right side of the brain to work is sometimes called clustering. You simply pick a topic or a word and write down as rapidly as you can all the ideas you associate with it. These often come out as single words or phrases, and they continue to appear as long as new associations occur. Here's the result of one attempt, based on the word *alone*.

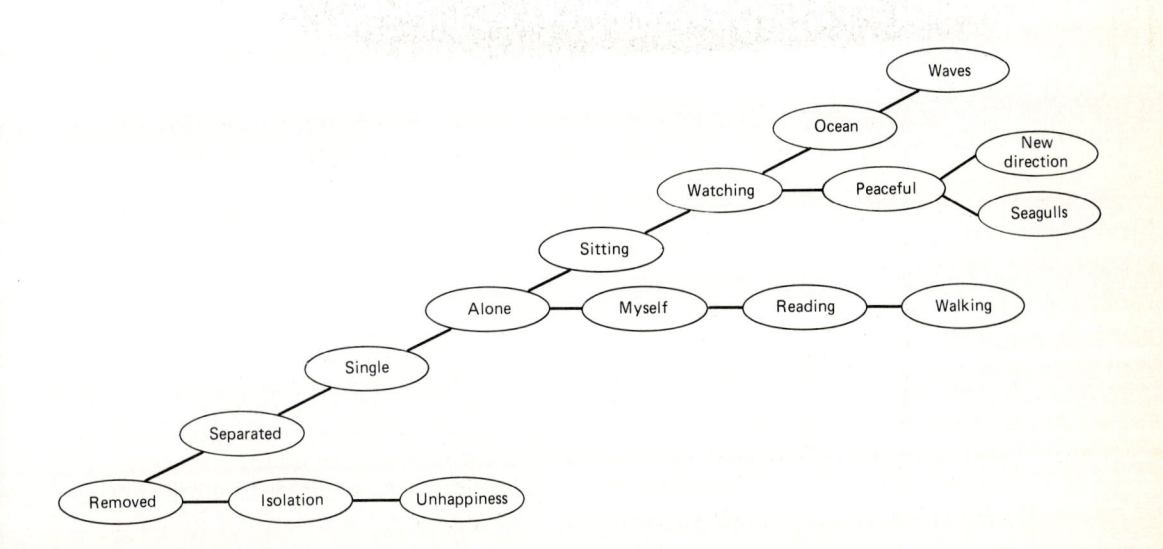

What is interesting about clustering is its twofold nature. Although it works by free association, it also organizes and arranges these associations logically, without much conscious effort by the writer. Look again at the cluster. On the left side are the writer's negative feelings about being alone. On the lower right are activities that she associates with the word, and on the upper right, her positive feelings about a specific day at the beach. The writer, however, did not consciously make this arrangement; the ideas automatically occurred in that sequence. Clustering often has this additional advantage, that it orders ideas. But essentially it is a way to discover ideas, to get ready to write. In fact, the last word written in this cluster, *seagulls*, served as an impetus for the writer to begin drafting, as we see in the following paragraph.

> A seagull goes flying, soaring high above me, alone. I am alone like the gull, sitting and watching the sky reflect its blueness into the turbulent ocean water. It is peaceful near the ocean. The sharp contrast that lies between the inactivity of my sitting and the ocean's constant ebb and flow brings me a feeling of inner peace. As the waves crash against the fine grains of sand, I reorganize my thoughts. My need to be alone resembles the seagull's need to fly. We are both in an ever constant search for some necessity of life. The seagull dives into the water and I realize how much I enjoy sitting and watching him, alone.

BRAINSTORMING

Brainstorming, much like clustering, works by free association. It is a technique often associated with the board room or the corporate office—"Let's get together at 10:00 with Jones and Smith and brainstorm the O'Neill account." But brainstorming is also a way to discover ideas, by analyzing the various parts of a topic. As with the cluster, you begin with a word, phrase, or idea and randomly list as many ideas as you can on that topic. The notes on page 21 represent the initial brainstorm written before a student began a character sketch of a friend. The notes can be organized into an outline (see chapter 5) or can provide reminders for development as the writing proceeds.

A WRITER'S NOTEBOOK

A notebook or journal provides one useful source of ideas for writing. Many professional writers keep journals, and many instructors require their students to keep them and make regular entries—a kind of orderly extension of freewriting. Keeping a notebook gives you regular practice in writing, can be fun, and can become a source of ideas for more formal writing.

To use a notebook profitably, get into the habit of making regular entries, writing something at the same time every day, just before going to

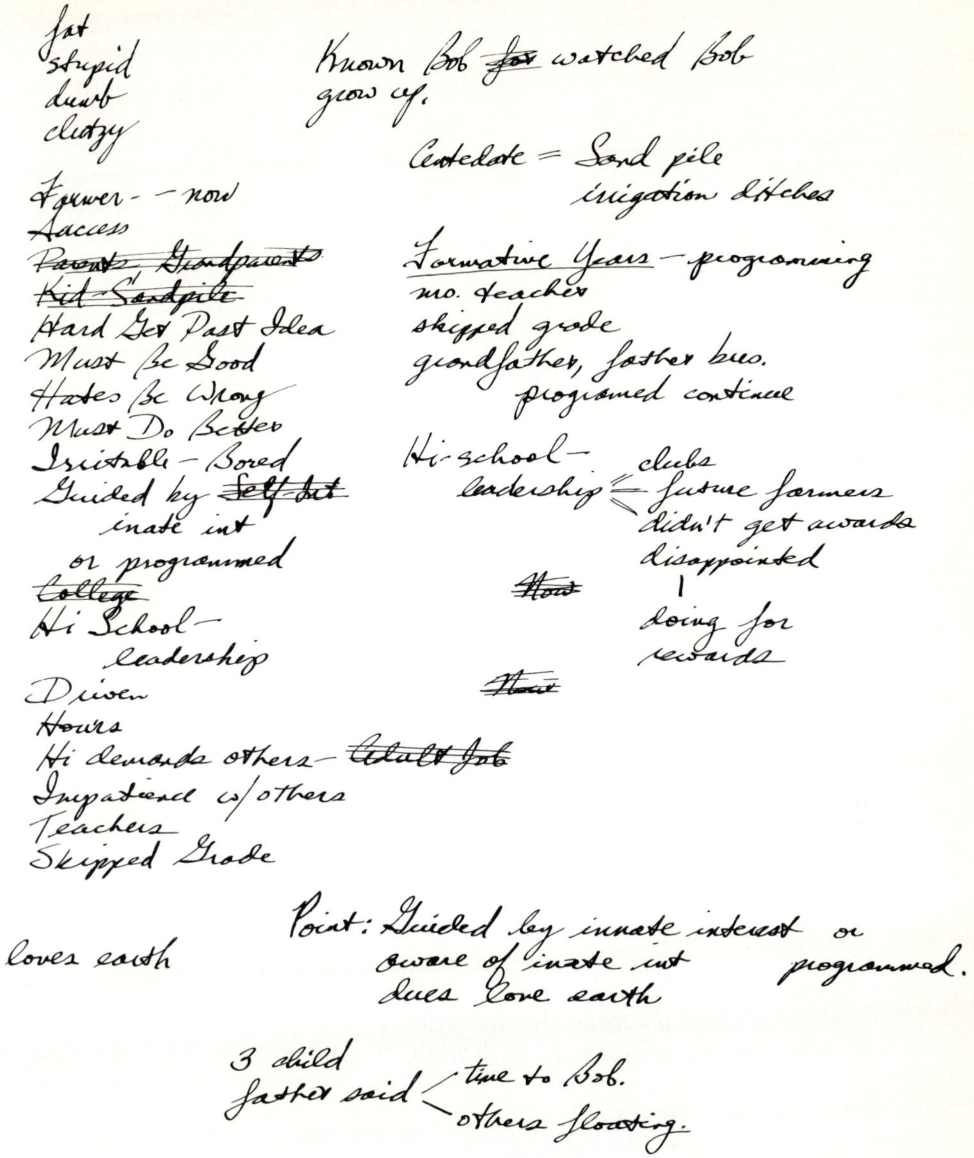

[Handwritten notes:]

jot
stupid
dumb
klutzy

Fewer — now
~~Access~~
~~Parents Grandparents~~
~~Kid Sandpile~~
Hard Get Past Idea
Must Be Good
Hates Be Wrong
Must Do Better
Irritable — Bored
Guided by ~~Self but~~
   inate int
   or programmed
~~College~~
Hi School —
   leadership
Driven
Hours
Hi demands others — ~~Adult Job~~
Impatient w/others
Teachers
Skipped Grade

Known Bob ~~for~~ watched Bob grow up.

Antedote = Sand pile
   irrigation ditches

Formative Years — programming
mo. teacher
skipped grade
grandfather, father bus.
   programed continue

Hi-school —
leadership — clubs
   future farmers
   didn't get awards
   disappointed
   ~~How~~
   doing for
   rewards
~~Hou~~

loves earth

Point: Guided by innate interest or
   aware of innate int   programmed.
   does love earth

3 child
father said — true to Bob.
   — others floating.

---

bed, for instance. You can jot down whatever comes into your mind, but thoughtful entries are more useful than routine records of getting up in the morning or going to bed at night. An entry might be a full account of an event or incident that you want to get on paper before you forget details. Or it might be rough notes to remind you of something to use later.

Novelist Joan Didion, for example, used a fragment from an old notebook. The note reads:

"That woman Estelle is partly the reason why George Sharp and I are separated today." *Dirty crepe-de-chine wrapper, hotel bar, Wilmington RR, 9:45 A.M. August Monday morning."*

Didion commented:

> Since the note is in my notebook, it presumably has some meaning to me. I study it for a long while. At first I have only the most general notion of what I was doing on an August Monday morning in the bar of the hotel across from the Pennsylvania Railroad station in Wilmington, Delaware (waiting for a train? missing one? 1960? 1961? why Wilmington?), but I do remember being there. The woman in the dirty crepe-de-Chine wrapper had come down from her room for a beer, and the bartender had heard before the reason why George Sharp and she were separated today.
>
> *On Keeping a Notebook*

Sometimes you can get more interesting or useful entries by asking yourself questions. What was the best thing I did today? Why was it the best? What did I learn that was interesting? Who was the most exciting person I met? Did any of my instructors say anything worth remembering? Did I get angry about anything? Consider the following entry from a student notebook:

> Spent all day yesterday with Al. We drove his old car into the hills and then walked. Everything was dry. Dust was flying up every step. Jeep tracks all over and beer cans and Kleenex and pieces of plastic bottles, even two miles from the highway. It was cool under the trees, and we finally found a spot with no junk around and sat and talked. Almost two hours. He's afraid he won't get a job when he graduates next year. He may be right. We were both feeling pretty low when we saw the eagle. We weren't sure what it was at first, it was so high up. I'd never seen an eagle, but Al knew what it was when it came a little closer. He said they are almost extinct around here now. He was excited, and we ran out so we could see better. He said his father shot one when Al was little. Al found it when it fell, and he said he almost got sick when he saw the bullet hole with blood staining a little ring of feathers. He said he never would go hunting with his father after that. But seeing the eagle made us both feel better, especially Al. We saw it dive once, and then it disappeared.

This entry suggests two ways that keeping a notebook helps. First, there is the writing itself; it gets something on paper. Even though the writing may be hurried, it forces thinking. As the experience is recalled, it becomes sharper. The writer has to select, and details become more important—the debris in the forest, the effect of the dead eagle on Al, and then the effect of the live one. Second, the entry could be useful for future reference. On review, the beer cans under the trees and Al's mention of the eagle as an endangered species might suggest a composition on the need for preserving the wilderness. Or recording the dust and the Jeep tracks might remind the writer of other details, that plants had been beaten down and that gullies were forming that would wash the soil away. The entry might suggest writing something about what off-road vehicles are doing to the only world we have to live in. Al's recollection of his father and the dead eagle might be the germ of a story. Remembering the flight of the eagle might suggest a poem.

A READER'S NOTEBOOK

Often the best way to get writing started is to read—an article in a magazine, a feature story in the newspaper, a chapter in a textbook. Almost always you'll run into something you disagree with or something you think should be supported or something you can relate to your own experience. An article on drugs and athletics may stimulate you to write an essay on drug tests for campus athletes. A feature story on an art show may prompt you to record your opinions on abstract art. Sometimes, just a minor comment in what you are reading may trigger an idea, remind you of something worth writing about.

One student used to write responses to her class assignments in a reader's notebook. On the right-hand page she would take class notes; on the left-hand side she would write a journal entry. She wrote the entry below after reading William Howell's "Editha," the story of the courtship of Editha and George.

> I felt sorry for George. He was manipulated by Editha, who didn't give a damn about him. She is another character I would have liked to slug. Some of these characters bring out the worst in me. That's what the author wants us to feel, I'm sure. Editha is rather repulsive to me. Of course, there are individuals in our everyday life like her. No guilt feelings for things they do to people until one day they get their just rewards. Everyone does.

This response is far from a finished essay, but it might trigger ideas for later writing—a character study of Editha, for instance, or an essay analyzing how people manipulate others.

In another notebook entry, this same student decides on a topic for a paper suggested by reading a poem.

> My second paper will be on "The Love Song of J. Alfred Prufrock." I saw something in the poem I could relate to and can use in a paper. My only problem with Eliot is why couldn't he write something original and stop borrowing so much from other writers. A person needs a guide of footnotes to get through his writings. But, all in all, I like "Prufrock" and "Hollow Men."

Both examples indicate how reading can suggest ideas for writing and how notebook entries can clarify your understanding of what you have been reading.

ASKING QUESTIONS

One way to clarify an idea, to see its implications or to discover its possibilities, is to carry on a kind of mental question-and-answer dialogue, asking yourself questions like the following.

1. *What is it?* Questions leading toward a definition or description are obvious starters. What is a butterfly or a hay baler, a wedding or a debate? A description of a butterfly would be useful for a textbook in entomology. A description of a bicycle might appear in a mail-order catalog. Asking "What is a kidnaping?" might lead to an essay on law enforcement. Thinking about an old house might produce a description of its architecture. Examination of the thing itself may lead to a workable idea, but it may also lead to further questions.

2. *Who are the people involved?* Incidents, events, institutions—almost any phenomena—have people participating in them. Who started the revolt or painted the picture or stole the bicycle? Who built the old house and who lived in it? Thinking about a person may produce an idea for a character sketch.

3. *What is it made of? What are the parts of it?* Analysis, thinking by breaking something into its parts (considered in more detail below), can be useful in prewriting as a way of generating ideas. What are the parts or components of the old house? The question might lead to a paper on the junk in the attic or on methods of framing a gable roof.

4. *Where did it come from?* A writer looking at an old house may see possibilities in a survey of its history. Applying such a question to a person might produce a biographical essay rather than a character description. In viewing an event, the question may become "What caused it?" Thinking of a fist fight between two campus leaders, a writer may reject a blow-by-blow account and survey the reasons for the squabble.

5. *What does it do? How does it work?* A process paper may emerge from such questions—a recipe for making home-brewed beer or a step-by-step account of how a generator produces electricity. Such questions may promote ideas for broader discussions—the impact of school segregation, the ways in which weather affects air pollution, how the presence of city police at campus events dampens student enthusiasm.

6. *What is it like? What does it remind me of?* The person looking at the old house may relate it to other houses and become interested in writing about architectural styles in central Ohio in the late nineteenth century. Or a student poking around in the dark looking for a candle so that he can see

to replace a blown-out fuse may remember a four-hour power failure during a storm earlier in the year. In this way he may get an idea for writing a paper to show that our society is dangerously dependent on electricity.

7. *What is its significance? How is it important?* Any phenomenon exists as part of the world around it. The writer thinking about his blown fuse arrived at his idea in part by thinking of the effects of a power blackout on transportation, on home freezers, on furnaces in steel mills, on hospital operating schedules. Shelley saw a kind of significance in the west wind that led him to write a poem on how ideas change society; Hopkins saw something in a bird to make him write a poem on religion.

REFINING A TOPIC

You may be an avid fisherman and want to write about your sport, but "Fishing" is a topic for a book, not a five-hundred-word essay. "How to Tie a Fly" might work. "American Newspapers" or even "Newspapers in This Town" needs to be limited for a short essay. "The Editorial Attitude of the Daily News Toward the University" is possible.

If you consider writing about an old house in your home town, the questions above can lead you to concentrate on its architecture, the people who live in it, its history, or its possibilities as a museum. But even these would require you to cover too much. You might narrow further to topics like "What Gables Are Good For" or "The Ghost in the Wingfield Mansion," or "How to Restore Wallpaper."

A good way to limit a topic to something you can manage in your space is to analyze, breaking a broad subject into parts and then continuing to subdivide until you get a topic you can handle. Suppose you are considering television as a general subject. It is too broad, and you know it. So you analyze and subdivide. You think of various aspects of television you might consider: production, types of programs, effects on children, financing, effects on politics; and there could be more.

You decide that you're interested in types of programs, but that's still too much. So you divide again: educational, news, dramatic, variety, talk shows, children's programs. In this list of types of programs, the topic, dramatic programs, interests you, although it can still be subdivided into situation comedies, detective stories, cowboy stories, family drama, old movies, daytime serials. You get some ideas from this listing, such as violence in the private eye series or conventional plots in westerns. But you decide it might be more fun to write about daytime serials. You analyze again into acting, production, themes and ideas, educational value—all parts of daytime serials. And as you look at this list you get an idea that might work, discussing how themes and ideas in daytime serials are related to women's place in society. The process you have followed, obviously more elaborate than you will follow all the time, might be pictured like this:

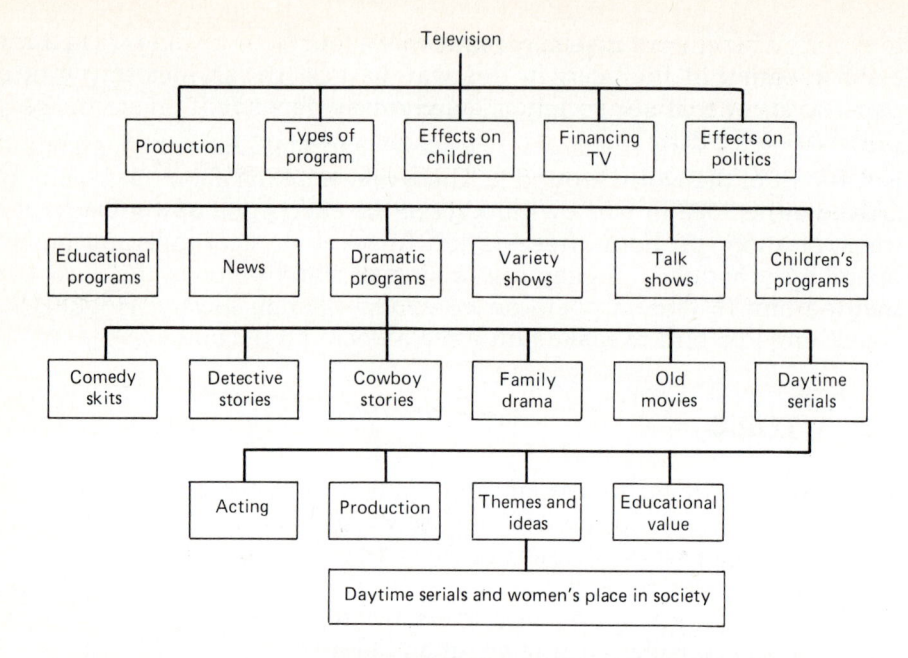

```
                          Television
         ┌──────────┬──────────┼──────────┬──────────┐
    Production  Types of  Effects on  Financing  Effects on
              program    children      TV       politics
    ┌──────────┬──────────┼──────────┬──────────┐
Educational  News   Dramatic   Variety    Talk    Children's
programs             programs   shows    shows    programs
    ┌──────────┬──────────┼──────────┬──────────┐
 Comedy   Detective  Cowboy   Family    Old      Daytime
 skits    stories   stories   drama   movies     serials
              ┌──────────┼──────────┬──────────┐
           Acting    Production  Themes and  Educational
                                   ideas       value
                     Daytime serials and women's place in society
```

This process, much simpler and less formal in actual practice, offers one way of getting at something manageable as a topic. Actually the topic is still too broad. You may want to focus on a single serial, and even then you may have to look at more soap operas in order to get your evidence. But you have moved from a general notion to something you can manage, and you can think about focusing on what you want to say.

FOCUSING: A THESIS SENTENCE

To write you need more than a topic; you need a point to make *about* a topic—a thesis. You need to interpret, take a position, defend your belief, explain your attitude, or make an argument. "Women in Professional Tennis" is a topic; "Women and men in professional tennis should receive equal pay" is a thesis. "A Visit To a Brewery" is a topic; "A visit to a brewery can provide insights into modern technology" is a thesis. In fact, you do not usually get a topic and then think of something to say about it. You pick the topic because you have thought at least generally of something you want to say about it. In narrowing the subject of television, you made each selection partly because you had ideas about a subdivision. You had your own way of looking at each subdivision; otherwise you would not have chosen it.

But your attitude toward the topic is usually not precisely formed. The whole process of writing and revising helps to clarify that attitude. And a statement of what you have to say, written out as a complete sentence, is one practical way of getting started. You may revise the statement as you proceed, or you may discard it completely, but such a statement can give your writing initial direction.

Assume you have settled on the topic "Daytime Television Serials and Women's Place in Society." You have picked it because serials you have looked at seem dedicated to preserving the status quo in relations between the sexes. You realize that you need evidence and illustrations to test your hypothesis, but you can phrase a tentative statement:

> Daytime television serials consistently express conservative attitudes toward women and their traditional roles.

You might even go farther and add to your statement some illustrations of what you mean:

> Daytime television serials consistently express reactionary attitudes toward women's roles, perpetuating the stereotype of the female chained to house and children, preoccupied with attracting a male, and contented in a man's world.

You might decide to press still further with an argument:

> Because they present unfair attitudes toward women, daytime television serials should be banned.

This kind of statement would be much harder to support. You might take a less controversial stand:

> Daytime television serials flatter the housewife by reinforcing her traditional attitudes about her status and responsibilities.

Like the others, this would require you to specify attitudes of the programs and to illustrate them. Other students might arrive at the same topic but have quite different ideas:

> Because they present many women characters in professional positions, daytime television serials are furthering the cause of women's rights.
> By sensationalizing and sentimentalizing the problems of women in their traditional roles, daytime television serials support the movement for equal rights for women.
> By putting totally insipid characters of both sexes into the traditional sexual roles, daytime television serials become an unintentional argument for change.
> The increased use of violence and fantasy in daytime television series makes them more unrealistic than they were ten years ago when they projected the myth of the happy homemaker.

Any such statement could serve as a starter, although it might never appear in the finished paper. New evidence or new thinking may change a paper from the original plan, but settling on at least a tentative statement gets the process going.

FOR STUDY AND WRITING

A. Keep a journal for a week, recording each day your observations of the people around you and the events or activities you attend. At the end of the week, look back over what you have written. Is the week well reflected in the seven entries? Which is the best? Why? Select one episode from your journal and write an account of it, using concrete description, physical details, and dialogue to make it come alive for your reader.

B. Write two entries, as for a journal, one about the most interesting class you have had thus far, and one about the dullest. For one, make the reader see the classroom and students, hear what was said, and even smell the atmosphere. For the other, analyze what happened. What made the class interesting? The subject? The manner of the instructor? The sense that you were learning something important? Or what made it dull? Did you feel that all this did not amount to much? Were you too hot or too sleepy? Did the mannerisms of the instructor bother you? Compare the two entries. Which do you think is the most effective and why? Bring them to class to read in a response group to see if the group agrees with your evaluation, or if they have any suggestions for revision.

C. Choose one of the broad topics listed below or one suggested by your instructor and write for ten minutes. After you have done this, brainstorm the same word for about the same length of time. Which technique was the most effective for you?

1. Advertising
2. Television
3. Physical fitness
4. Desserts
5. Prejudices
6. College sports
7. Snobs
8. Music
9. Pollution
10. Business

D. Look back over the freewriting and brainstorming you did in the above exercise. Choose one of the more specific words or ideas you discovered and do a cluster. After you have done this, can you come up with a limited topic you could write a short essay on? Try to formulate a thesis statement for this paper.

E. Go back to the list of broad topics in exercise C and use analysis to narrow one of them. See if you can be as elaborate as the example below. Try to formulate a thesis statement based on your analysis.

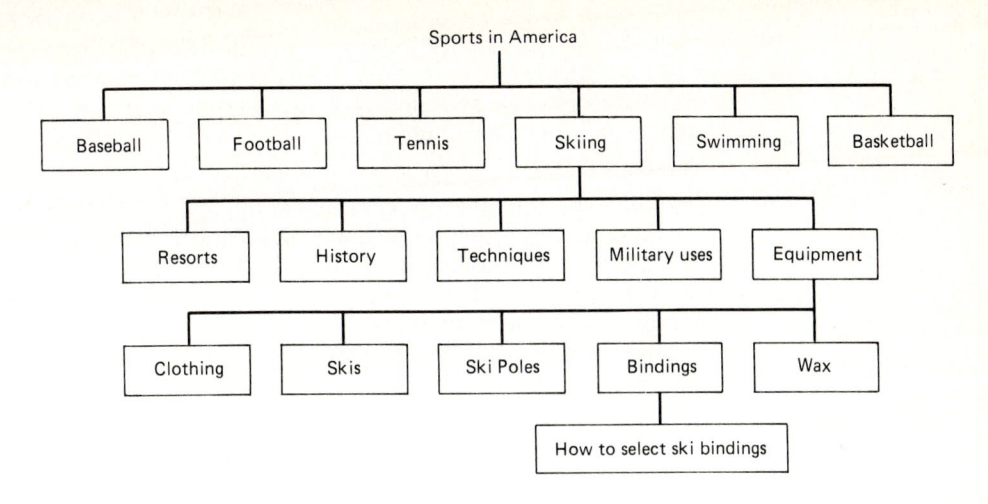

```
                          Sports in America
    ┌──────┬──────┬──────┬──────┬──────┬──────┐
 Baseball Football Tennis Skiing Swimming Basketball
                          │
              ┌──────┬────┼────┬──────┐
           Resorts History Techniques Military uses Equipment
                                              │
                    ┌──────┬──────┬──────┬──────┐
                 Clothing Skis Ski Poles Bindings Wax
                                        │
                              How to select ski bindings
```

Thesis sentence: Selecting the proper bindings for skis requires both time and knowledge.
To select the proper ski bindings is not as easy as it would seem.
Before you buy ski bindings, check with an expert.

F. Read the following topics and thesis sentences. Which are suitable for a student essay? Revise any you think are too broad or misleading.

1. *Topic* Sutpen's Mansion
   Thesis An hour wandering through the ruins of the old mansion makes one feel a sense of loss for a way of life that has disappeared from the South.

2. *Topic* Orientation
   Thesis This theme will show various problems of the freshmen at a large university and how their courses are different from high school work and something should be done to remedy the situation.

3. *Topic* Becky Thatcher's Home
   Thesis When we visited Hannibal, Missouri, we went to see it.

4. *Topic* Woodchucks as Game Animals
   Thesis Hunting woodchucks provides good sport; woodchucks are plentiful and never out of season, and properly dressed, the flesh is excellent food.

5. *Topic* Improving Bus Service
   Thesis Bus service in town could be made better, and even profitable, if the bus company would change some of the routes to fit shifts in population, adjust schedules to popular need, and teach drivers some common courtesy.

6. *Topic* Learning American History from Stamps
   Thesis Collecting American stamps is a painless but profitable way to learn the facts of American history.

7. *Topic* Making Your Own Clothes
   Thesis Making clothes requires consideration of texture and color in choosing material, selection of a suitable and practical style, patience, and a sense of humor.
8. *Topic* Ballet
   Thesis I would expect to give a brief sketch of the invention, history, and development of ballet, say something about the recent popularity of ballet in this country, the leading ballet companies, especially the New York City Ballet, and the amateur and semiprofessional groups that are growing up everywhere, very much like the little theater movement of the last generation, the ballet in movies and TV, and give some of my own opinions of ballet as an art, based on my lessons in ballet.

G. Write a paragraph describing the prewriting activities that work best for you, or new ones you would like to try. Remember these for your next writing assignment.

2

Audience, Purpose, Voice

> *I will aggravate my voice so that I will roar you as gently as any sucking dove; I will roar you an't were any nightingale.*
> WILLIAM SHAKESPEARE

Bottom, a well-meaning weaver in *A Midsummer Night's Dream*, is no writer, but he has a sense of one of the fundamental premises of writing—the implied compact among writer, material, and audience. In the play, Bottom and some other unlettered workmen plan an amateur skit involving a stage lion. One prissy fellow fears trouble. He warns that if the lion roars too terribly, the "faire ladies" will shriek, "and that were enough to hang us all." Bottom sees the solution, quoted in the passage above. He senses that the lion's voice should be modified to fit the tastes of the audience.

Although Bottom is no rhetorician, he is expressing one of the basic concepts of rhetoric—that communication involves the interplay, the cooperation, of four elements: the writer or speaker, the purpose, the subject matter, and the audience. Each of these elements affects each of the others. The writer adopts a manner and form to fulfill a purpose and to fit the audience and the material.

When you write, you are being an actor, playing a role. Even if you are trying to be completely yourself, simply to write sincerely, you are playing the role of you, writer, not speaker or thinker. And, most of the time, you are playing the role of you in different circumstances and for different purposes—you as a son or daughter writing home, you as an employee writing a report for a corporate executive, you as a supporter of a candidate for political office, you as a student answering test questions in sociology or writing an essay for an English class. These are, of course, all basically similar characters, but they are also all different in some ways. And they should be, because they are dealing with different audiences and different subject matter for different reasons.

In other words, whenever you write, you adopt what might be called a voice or persona, the "I" that says what is on the paper rather than the "I" of real life. That "I", that voice or persona, adopted to fit your purpose in writing, has certain characteristics that are related, as in the following diagram:

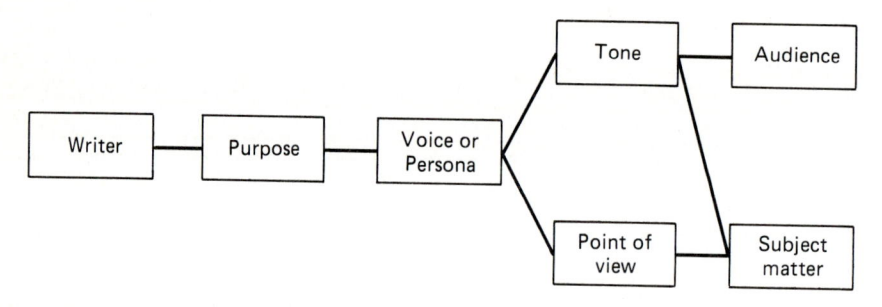

Writer → Purpose → Voice or Persona → Tone → Audience
                                    → Point of view → Subject matter

As the diagram indicates, the writer considers a purpose and then adopts a voice, assumes a role, that will help achieve that purpose. That voice is expressed in two ways: by the point of view toward the subject matter and by the tone or attitude toward the subject matter and audience. The elements in the diagram and their relationships are the subjects of the sections of this chapter.

THE AUDIENCE

Writing anticipates an audience. Whenever you put words on paper, you have to consider the possibility that someone will read them, even if it's only yourself a month later. Most of the time when you write, you can make good guesses about the most likely readers. The following are types of audience you may be addressing.

The Limited Audience Bottom had to please only a limited audience, including the "faire ladies." Theoretically, every audience is limited, at least to those who know how to read and can understand the language of the writer. Usually the potential audience is limited also by size, location, age, or interests. Teen-agers make different demands on a writer than do bankers. Readers of *Vogue, House Beautiful, Mad,* and the college newpaper have different expectations. Milton addressed *Paradise Lost* to "fit audience though few."

The Specialized Audience An in-group having special knowledge or skill may require writing of a particular sort. An engineering firm may expect technical reports to take a specified form, as a chemistry teacher may require patterned laboratory reports. Specialists may be scholars or scientists or enthusiasts for almost anything—bridge, jazz, skiing, chess, motorcycles, or horses. The writer must be prepared to give an audience the information it wants, in an acceptable style, but a specialized audience offers at least one great convenience. It is familiar with the vocabulary and information common to its subject.

The General Audience Even specialists have only general knowledge about most things. Thus most writing is addressed to a general audience, able to read and understand, and presumably interested in the ideas or interpretations of a writer. In a sense, the general audience is composed of many limited audiences, who read for interest, enjoyment, or practical knowledge. They like narrative, background information, competent prose. Anticipating the reactions of people with varied interests is never easy, but usually writing clearly and directly in standard, nontechnical language will work.

THE STUDENT AND THE AUDIENCE

In one sense, if you are a student in a composition class, you have an audience of one, your instructor. In fact, a myth persists among students that success in class depends on analyzing the instructor and then catering to his or her prejudices—the "what-does-the-teacher-want" syndrome. This procedure seldom works. Individual standards and requirements may be part of any class, but most instructors judge a paper on how well it meets the needs of a generalized audience or the specialized audience to which it is directed. Although your student writing is primarily practice, it has intrinsic value, and it should be directed to an audience, not just to an instructor. Furthermore, you are likely to exchange papers with other students and have your work considered in response groups or editing circles. Your fellow students become your audience too.

In planning your paper, you may want to ask yourself questions like the following:

1. *Who is the audience?* If you are writing a letter to your mother, you know the audience. If you are writing a letter to the student paper, you know your audience less intimately; but you still know some-

thing about it—that it may include many students, your teachers, the dean and president, and perhaps the governor and some easily irritated alumni. If you are writing a paper for class, you need to decide whether to direct it to a general or a limited audience—your teacher may specify—and then tailor it to the audience's expectations.

      2. *How intelligent, educated, informed is the audience?* If you are writing for a specialized group, you can assume its members have specialized knowledge. A physicist writing for other physicists can use technical language and forego explanations of fundamentals with which the readers will be familiar. If you are writing for a more general audience, you can assume much less. Imagine, for example, the difference for that physicist in explaining nuclear power to a fourth-grade science class, a PTA group, and a convention of scientists.

      3. *What does the audience want or need to know?* In a conversation, you can tell by watching facial expressions when you are telling more than people want to know about penguins or about your Uncle Harry's love life. When you write, you lack such gauges, but you have to try to guess, relying on what you know or can find out about the interests and backgrounds of your potential readers. A specialized audience is perhaps easier to assess than a more general one—readers of a drag-racing magazine may not read avidly an article on Platonic philosophy. On the other hand, any well-written paper with keen insights or fresh interpretations, with dramatic prose and human interest, will appeal to many members of a general audience.

PURPOSE AND VOICE

Thinking about your audience helps determine your purpose, what you hope to accomplish with the piece you are writing. You need to ask yourself why you are writing this piece. Do you want to educate or inform or inspire or amuse or annoy your audience? With your purpose in mind, you can consider the voice you will adopt. Once you begin to write, your purpose and your voice may shift—voices like masks can be changed—but you will have established a starting position.

      In the play Bottom adopts the voice of a lion to match his subject matter, but he softens his roar to the supposed needs of his audience. For other characters, Bottom offers other voices. To play Pyramus the lover he will "condole," to be a tyrant he will play "a part to tear a cat in," or to be the heroine he will "speak in a monstrous little voice." Theoretically, at least, the writer is always acting, playing a role, speaking in a voice assumed for the occasion.

      The distinction between a speaking and a writing voice has uses, although distinguishing is not always easy. In expository prose the writer usually plays the role of someone writing, using language associated with writing rather than speech. But much current exposition at least seems to imitate speech. A writer of fiction describing events objectively may adopt a voice associated with writing, but if the story is told in the first person, it may use the idioms and rhythms of speech. The writer of fiction, indeed, may assume a role quite different from real life, telling the story in the words of a narrator, a created persona, from a different position in society or a different period in history or even a different planet. J. D. Salinger wrote *The Catcher in the Rye* in the words of a teen-ager. William Faulkner in many of his stories used the voice of an itinerant sewing-machine salesman.

The writer of expository prose is less obviously an actor. The writer is not working to create a character as a narrator, but to a degree at least is playing a role, varying the choice of voice according to purpose and audience, wearing one mask to write for a group of small children and another for the readers of a scientific journal. The following passages illustrate voices writers have adopted for various subjects, audiences, and purposes.

1. The purpose of the following paragraph is obviously to sell bottles.

> The art of yesteryear comes vibrantly alive in the magnificent collection of Old Fashioned decorator decanters. Original hand-blown glass has become a prized collector's item, its direct and honest beauty bringing a classic charm to any setting. Washed by the light from a window the clear, liquid topaz, deep cobalt blue and limpid seagreen glass glows with a warm internal beauty. Among the designs in this collection are the Benjamin Franklin decanter, the Liberty Bell Medicine Bottle, the Dolphin jug and nine more just as famous. Limited editions of these decanters sell for up to $25.00 or more, and the 12 in this collection represent the most precious designs in the history of American glass making. A superb decorating collection, you'll want to order several sets as special gifts.
>
> *Advertisement*

The slightly pretentious archaism of "yesteryear" and the exaggeration of "vibrantly alive" suggest the carefully enthusiastic, confidential, soothing note familiar in the voice of the ad writer. The writer is addressing a specialized audience, potential glass collectors, and adopting the voice of a fellow enthusiast.

2. Another passage adopts a voice intended to serve the writer's purpose of criticizing conventions.

> In ten years of journalism I have covered more conventions than I care to remember. Podiatrists, theosophists, Professional Budget Finance dentists, oyster farmers, mathematicians, truckers, dry cleaners, stamp collectors, Esperantists, nudists and newspaper editors—I have seen them all, together, in vast assemblies, sloughing through the wall-to-wall of a thousand hotel lobbies (the nudists excepted) in their shimmering grey-metal

suits and Nicey Short collar white shirts with white Plasti-Coat name cards on their chests, and I have sat through their speeches and seminars (the nudists included) and attentively endured ear baths such as you wouldn't believe. . . .

Tom Wolfe, *Pause, Now, and Consider Some Tentative Conclusions About the Meaning of this Mass Perversion Called Porno-Violence: What It Is and Where It Comes From and Who Put the Hair on the Walls*

For his *Esquire* audience, Wolfe plays the role of an informal, chatty reporter. He uses contractions, tries for humor in the list of conventions and the joke on nudists, works for freshness in the diction—perhaps without total success in his metaphor "ear baths." The writer here is obviously avoiding any hint of the sweetness that pervades the advertisement above, but curiously, the voice he adopts has something in common with that of the advertisement as it presses for familiarity.

3. The purpose of the following passage is to amuse or entertain a general audience, but also to poke mild fun at ranger slide shows, and perhaps at camping in general:

There's not much night life here. You can either hang around the campground waiting for the bears to rip into the ice chests, or you can catch the ranger slide show. I caught the slide show. I can report that there's not much new in the world of ranger slide shows. The average one goes like this. . . .

Steve Rubenstein, *San Francisco Chronicle*

The voice here probably represents the writer's actual feelings, but exaggerated, for example through the repetition of "ranger slide show," for humorous effect.

4. On a similar topic, but with a totally different purpose, John McPhee opens a book with a vivid description of himself in the Alaskan countryside.

My bandanna is rolled on the diagonal and retains water fairly well. I keep it knotted around my head, and now and again dip it into the river. The water is forty-six degrees. Against the temples, it is refrigerant and relieving. This has done away with the headaches that the sun caused in days before. The Arctic sun—penetrating, intense—seems not so much to shine as to strike. Even the trickles of water that run down my T-shirt feel good. Meanwhile, the river—the clearest, purest water I have ever seen flowing over rocks—breaks the light into flashes and sends them upward into the eyes.

John McPhee, *Coming into the Country*

The voice sounds autobiographical. The persona McPhee has created seems close to the real McPhee and makes the account seem authentic. The voice suits McPhee's purpose, to make the reader see and feel the penetrating Arctic sun, the "trickles of water," the light that breaks into flashes.

5. The following passage, for a different audience and for different purposes, employs a different voice.

> Academic institutions exist for the transmission of knowledge, the pursuit of truth, the development of students, and the general well-being of society. Free inquiry and free expression are indispensable to the attainment of these goals. As members of the academic community, students should be encouraged to develop the capacity for critical judgment and to engage in a sustained and independent search for truth. Institutional procedures for achieving these purposes may vary from campus to campus, but the minimal standards of academic freedom of students outlined below are essential to any community of scholars.
> American Association of University Professors,
> *Joint Statement on Rights and Freedom of Students*

The voice here characterizes the composition of serious writers collaborating on committee prose. The writing suggests no personality at all; it is formal, careful, proper. Its purpose is to define objectively academic freedom for students. For most purposes it is not a good type of prose to imitate.

VOICE AND PERSON

One specific decision you as a writer must make is identification of the voice as person. You must decide, for example, whether you are speaking directly as yourself, in the first person, using *I*, or whether you are assuming a position somewhere outside events and looking at them in the third person, using pronouns like *he* and *she*.

To see the difference this decision can make, compare two versions of the beginning of an essay in which Juliana Johnson describes a childhood fantasy of attending a first dance. In her first version, she identifies with the character, eight-year-old Juliana:

> "May I have this dance?" The music was softly drifting across the lawn and through the air. I lifted my gloved hand and put it into his. As he led me off the chair and on to the dance floor, I caught my dress demurely with my hand. We began dancing, only it wasn't dancing; it was more like gliding and floating and often a combination of both.

In her next draft, Juliana shifts to a more objective, third-person approach:

> She would sit on the front lawn in the brown grass under the hot August sun for hours. She would sit Indian style, her hands folded in front of her;

occasionally she would lift her hand and turn her head as though she were looking at or talking to someone. Sometimes she would take a ladylike sip from an imaginary glass. Sometimes she would start dancing.

The class read both drafts, and they and Juliana decided the first-person version was more appropriate for the subject. The third-person approach did not as effectively achieve the writer's purpose of capturing a personal reminiscence. Other circumstances might have warranted a different decision.

But the decision has to be made, with the identification of the speaker clearly and consistently expressed in the choice of personal pronouns. You decide whether to speak as "I," or address "you," or speak about "he" or "she." The following list indicates most of the ways in which you can use pronouns to identify the voice you are adopting.

First Person

The writer may appear as *I* or sometimes *we*, but these pronouns may have various meanings, including:

1. *I, Straightforward* The writer tries to take the role of himself or herself speaking sincerely and directly, as in a letter home or a conversation: "I am a pacifist because I have seen the kinds of horrors that war can bring."

2. *I, as a Different I* Especially in humorous or whimsical writing, the *I* may play a role: "I am probably the only person outside Australia who is in love with a bandicoot."

3. *I, Fictional Narrator* The writer speaks through the voice of a created narrator: Melville's *Moby Dick* opens by identifying this narrator: "Call me Ishmael." Fiction produces many varieties of this voice; the *I* may be a main character or may be a barely visible outside observer.

4. *We, You and I, or Everybody* The writer may use the plural first-person form in any of several ways: to represent more than one author speaking directly, as we sometimes do in this book; to represent the writer and the reader and pretend a kind of conspiratorial arrangement; or to represent general agreement, the voice of everybody in an impersonal way, as in "We use language to express our prejudices as well as our meanings."

5. *We, Editorial, or I in Disguise* Somewhat as kings refer to themselves as *we*, a writer may use a voice in which *we* really means *I*, or perhaps a newspaper or an editorial group: "We cannot resist expressing our surprise at the secretary's response."

Second Person

You may identify yourself and your attitude by addressing an audience directly.

1. *You, Specific* Some uses of *you* attempt to establish a one-to-one informal relationship between writer and reader, as in a recipe or a set of directions or an advertisement or much persuasive or informative writing: "If you believe what the recent Gallup poll says, you will . . ." *You* sometimes addresses the reader in this book.

2. *You, General* Informally, *you* may stand for a group, as in "You who have experienced these hardships," or for people in general, as in "What you don't know won't hurt you."

Third Person

As a writer, you may try to seem entirely uninvolved, to report objectively.

1. *He, She, It, Objective* When you are reporting or describing or telling a story you can refer to characters and things without appearing as a character yourself.

2. *He, She, It, for Audience* You may refer to your audience indirectly, as this sentence does, by speaking to the reader as part of a group or by specifying interests: "the reader," "the serious student," "users of this book."

3. *He, She, It, as Stand-ins* You may give an impression of objectivity and at the same time express personal views by referring to yourself in the third person—"this reporter," "this investigator," "the editors of this book." An earlier fashion, especially for formal theses or technical reports, once condemned the use of *I* and made this device more common than it is today.

4. *One, He, Indefinite and without Gender* *One*, sometimes like *a person*, can mean anybody, including reader and writer: "What can one do to help?" This indefinite *one* is mainly formal and often sounds stuffy, especially when repeated; but English has no workable pronoun that will refer to anybody, of either sex. As a result, *he* has come to be used in two ways—as a masculine pronoun and also to mean "he or she": "The writer (or one) does what *he* can." Currently there are objections to this use of *he* as evidence of sex discrimination (see chapter 11), but substitutes like *he/she* have not gained acceptance, and *he or she* readily becomes awkward. Informally, *you* can be used as an impersonal pronoun; see above. With some restrictions, the passive voice may be used to avoid an impersonal pronoun.

CONSISTENCY IN PERSON

Pronouns refer; that is, they act as substitutes for the name of a person or thing already identified. Personal pronouns referring to the same person, therefore, ought to be consistent. If you refer to a person as *he*, it doesn't make sense to refer to him as *they* a few words later. If you start by addressing "you," it makes no sense to refer to the person as "he." Consider the following:

> If a person wants to learn, you can always find exciting classes.

The shift from *a person* to *you* in effect changes the writer's voice. Revision is not easy. Changing *you* to the allegedly impersonal *he* is clear but in violation of most publishers' style on sexism. Both pronouns could change to *you* if the change fits the context, or both the subject and the pronoun can be made plural:

> If students want to learn, they can always find exciting classes.

Often a revision to avoid the problem is the best solution:

> A student who wants to learn can always find exciting classes.

Guide to Revision   **Pers**

CONSISTENCY IN PERSON

Put pronouns in the same person and number to keep reference clear.

ORIGINAL	REVISION
When *one* is abroad, *you* will almost always find somebody who can speak *your* language. [*One* seems overly formal, and the shift to *you* shifts the person of the writer.]	When *you* are abroad, *you* will almost always find somebody who can speak *your* language. [*One* and *one's* might have been repeated or the sentence rewritten in the third-person plural.]
From our hotel room you could see the Golden Gate Bridge.	From our hotel room we could see the Golden Gate Bridge.

TONE: ATTITUDE
TOWARD MATERIAL AND AUDIENCE

Tone refers to characteristics of the writer's voice. It has much the same effect as the tone of voice in which something is spoken. "Yes," can be questioning, doubting, hesitating, acknowledging, or affirming, depending on the way it is said. In the same way, a composition can make various impressions, depending on the tone of the writer's voice. That is, tone in writing refers to whatever reveals the writer's attitude toward the subject matter and toward the audience. For example, when Juliana shifted her essay from first to third person (see p. 37), the tone changed. Her third-person voice created an objective tone and robbed the piece of the intimate, nostalgic feeling, or tone, she wanted.

Compare the following passages from two student essays, written for the same purpose and about the same idea, that some types of advertising should be discontinued:

> The general public has great faith in communications media. People tend to believe what they see and hear on television and what they read in newspapers and magazines. Advertising, therefore, that makes false claims about the values of a product or the consequences of failing to use it may cause real hardship and may eventually even harm the standing of a company.
> The current campaign, for instance, to exaggerate the horrors of underarm perspiration or oily hair seems calculated to produce some kind of shift in social values. . . .

> "Don't you want to kiss me again?" Gullible asked, quickly chewing her breath mint to get at the little drop of something it contained.
> "I can't," he said. "That no-wetness stuff you use dries me up so much it cracks my lips." He turned away, slipped on her newly waxed floor, fell down, and broke his neck.
> "I used the wrong floor wax," she said. "If I'd used the new, shinier, harder, more glasslike plastic kind, he'd have zoomed right out the front door and the police wouldn't find the body here."

The first is serious and objective, an attempt to make a reasoned statement. The second is ironic, exaggerated; it employs ridicule, reducing to absurdity the kind of advertising its author resents. The essays differ in *tone*—that is, in the attitude the writer takes toward the material and toward the reader.

Since tone reflects attitudes, it can vary almost infinitely. Compare the following brief passages on the same topic—the weather:

> What happens in this particular case—and it accounts for half our winter days—is simply that the cool ground of the wintry continent chills this moist, warm air mass—chills it just a little, not enough to change its fundamental character, and not all the way up into its upper levels, but in its bottommost layer and that only just enough to make it condense out

some of its abundant moisture in the form of visible clouds; it is quite similar to the effect of a cold window pane on the air of a well-heated, comfortable room—there is wetness and cooling right at the window, but the bulk of the room's air is not affected.

Wolfgang Langewiesche, *What Makes the Weather*

The January wind has a hundred voices. It can scream, it can bellow, it can whisper, and it can sing a lullaby. It can roar through the leafless oaks and shout down the hillside, and it can murmur in the white pines rooted among the granite ledges where lichen make strange hieroglyphics. It can whistle down a chimney and set the hearth-flames to dancing. On a sunny day it can pause in a sheltered spot and breathe a promise of spring and violets. In the cold of a lonely night it can rattle the sash and stay there muttering of ice and snowbanks and deep-frozen ponds.

Hal Borland, *The January Wind*

Clearly the pieces differ in tone. The differences grow partly from the content; but the content, the selection of materials, is determined by the writer's attitude. The first sounds informal and familiar, but is mainly objective in tone. Its purpose is to inform the reader of facts. The second, designed to convey an impression, gives a feeling about the day. To express its tone, it selects different details. Its style is more "poetic," more dependent on images.

APPROPRIATENESS AND CONSISTENCY IN TONE

A good writer selects an appropriate tone and then avoids slipping out of character. A columnist ridiculing the foibles of bargain-hunting shoppers picks one tone; a sociologist trying to explain why a juvenile delinquent may kill for fun picks another. An editorial writer for a college newspaper may discuss student membership on faculty committees as a serious requirement of a democratic society, or the writer may take an ironic approach, ridiculing the administration's fear of student influence. A writer for the audience of a metropolitan paper is more likely to treat the subject lightly. Neither writer, however, would be likely to comment humorously on an international incident that threatened war.

Situations and purposes for writing vary so widely that any "rules" for avoiding inappropriateness are dubious, but the following observations are useful.

1. *Suitability* Some shifting in tone is inevitable, but ideally a writer adopts and maintains a tone that fits a subject and an audience. What seems most natural to the writer, usually a direct, unpretentious attitude, is likely to work best. Condescension, even in writing for children, seldom works.

2. *Maturity and Taste* Student writers need to remove themselves far enough from a subject to view it with perspective and good taste. The essay that reports with a straight face that making that final basket was an earth-shaking event—"The most important moment of my life . . ."—may be unintentionally humorous. The essay that includes graphic descriptions of a weekend escapade may violate standards of good taste.

3. *Sincerity and Simplicity* Although a writer may adopt a voice, play a character as author, bad acting shows. Imitation of a style usually sounds artificial, insincere, affected, or pompous. The kind of sports writing, for example, that relies on calling a baseball a pill or the old apple sounds posed and imitative, not clever and racy. A student paper rings false when it inflates a trivial incident with an overdramatic tone—"Little did I know how this day would change my life."

4. *Objectivity and Emotion* Directness and sincerity become a virtue of style and tone, especially when a writer tries to convey emotion. As in life, buckets of tears do not measure the depth of grief, so in writing multiple superlatives do not reveal sincerity of emotion. If emotion is there, it will be conveyed best by a straight and objective presentation. Writing that tries to milk more emotion than the facts warrant is sentimental and false.

5. *Humor* Humor usually profits from a straight face. Notice, for example, the following brief excerpt from James Thurber's reminiscences:

> One day General Littlefield picked our company out of the whole regiment and tried to get it mixed up by putting it through one movement after another as fast as we could execute them: squads right, squads left, squads on right into line, squads right about, squads left front into line, etc. In about three minutes one hundred and nine men were marching in one direction and I was marching away from them at an angle of forty-five degrees, all alone. "Company, halt!" shouted General Littlefield. "That man is the only man who has it right!" I was made a corporal for my achievement.
>
> *My Life and Hard Times*

Thurber has let the humor grow from the facts. Intended humor may fail because a writer relies on overworked tricks—stale quips or slang intended to suggest a blasé style, attempts at exaggerated, thesaurus-inspired wit ("In elucidating that toothsome phenomenon characterized among the ranks of the intelligentsia as granulated cow . . ."). Just as bad is irony with a question mark to explain the joke ("The instructor started his clever? lecture"). These devices usually amuse the writer more than the reader. Genuine humor, of course, is effective.

Guide to Revision   **Tone**

APPROPRIATENESS AND CONSISTENCY IN TONE

Adopt and maintain a tone that reflects your purpose and your attitude toward your subject and your audience.

ORIGINAL

Graduation from high school is a very important event, often shaping much of a person's future career in life. It is a time of commencement, not of ending. But it also is a time when a person realizes the importance of the hard struggle that has carried him successfully through four years of heartbreaks and triumphs. When those wonderful words of congratulation ring out after the awarding of diplomas, every graduate knows a thrill that he will never forget. It is truly a wonderful moment.
[*The tone of overstatement and high seriousness is not justified by the occasion, and the passage does more to reveal the immaturity of the writer than to convince a reader.*]

When the light of day next osmosed through our hero's casement it discovered the would-be Romeo and mighty guzzler with a disturbance in that portion of his anatomy known as the cranium that was so perceptible that it resembled nothing so much as the activities of a jackhammer. In short, he was, to use the vernacular, hanging over.
[*Some readers may find this mildly amusing the first time through, but a discerning person is likely to resent a cheap attempt to show off.*]

REVISION

To the high school graduate, commencement may seem the most important event in life. The parade in white dresses and blue suits or caps and gowns, the music with all the ringing discords of which a nervous school orchestra is capable, the grim, freshly scrubbed faces, the earnest platitudes of the student orations, all convince the graduate that this is the real turning point of life. The graduate leaves, certain never to forget a moment of what has occurred, and a year later may actually remember something of it.
[*A lighter tone, with factual details replacing the overstatement, leads to a less naïve paragraph. Other approaches would have been possible.*]

Jeffrey was half awake with the pain throbbing in his temples. He fought his way under the covers, but he could not escape the sense of smothering. He tried with his right hand to block off the sunlight from the window, but he could not get things quite right. His head kept pounding, and his eyes hurt. He struggled up, dizzy and blinking.

[*The revision is not funny, but it does not sound affected, and it says much more than did the original.*]

CONSISTENCY IN POINT OF VIEW AND TENSE

As part of your rhetorical stance, you adopt a point of view in time and in space. You assume that you are in the present looking back, for example, or you assume that you are watching events or thinking about them as they occur. You select among the many tense forms of verbs to indicate the relationships in time.

Compare, for example, the following passages describing the same scene from the reign of terror that followed the French Revolution:

> The call to plunder was received with enthusiasm, and in the morning of the 25th of February a troop of women marched to the Seine and, after boarding the vessels that contained cargoes of soap, helped themselves liberally to all they required at a price fixed by themselves, that is to say, for almost nothing. Since no notice was taken of these proceedings, a far larger crowd collected at dawn of the following day and set forth on a marauding expedition to the shops. From no less than 1200 grocers the people carried off everything on which they could lay their hands—oil, sugar, candles, coffee, brandy—at first without paying, then, overcome with remorse, at the price they themselves thought proper.
>
> Nesta H. Webster, *The French Revolution*

> And now from six o'clock, this Monday morning, one perceives the Bakers' Queues unusually expanded, angrily agitating themselves. Not the Baker alone, but two Section Commissioners to help him, manage with difficulty the daily distribution of loaves. Soft-spoken, assiduous, in the early candle-light, are Baker and Commissioners: and yet the pale chill February sunrise discloses an unpromising scene. Indignant Female Patriots, partly supplied with bread, rush now to the shops, declaring they will have groceries. Groceries enough: sugar-barrels, rolled forth into the street, Patriot Citoyennes weighing it out at a just rate of elevenpence a pound; likewise coffee-chests, soap-chests, nay cinnamon and clove-chests, with *aqua-vitae* and other forms of alcohol,—at a just rate, which some do not pay; the palefaced Grocer silently wringing his hands!
>
> Thomas Carlyle, *The French Revolution*

The passages differ in many ways, but most obviously in point of view, in the position in time each author assumes. The first writer is looking back on events, describing them objectively. The second pretends to be at the scene and asks the reader to join in watching what is happening. Verbs in the first are in past tense, in the second in the present tense.

You may also need to locate yourself in space. In a formal description, or while using description as part of some other sort of writing, you need to decide where you are in relation to the scene you are describing. You may pretend you have ascended to some spot of heavenly omniscience where you can see and describe everything. Or for a sharper sense of reality, you may pretend to stand in a specific place, from which you can logically describe only what would be within your range of vision.

The reader needs to know where you are in time and space and should not be jarred by any careless or useless change. Usually you stay where you are and indicate your place in time in your choice of verbs.

TENSE FORMS AND POINT OF VIEW

The English verb system is complicated, and formal rules for using tense forms are likely to be more confusing than helpful. Furthermore, most native speakers have little difficulty with the forms so long as they remember to keep a consistent point of view. But you may want to consider some of the following conventions.

Sequence of Tenses

When events at different times are expressed in the same sentence, tense forms follow a sequence to keep the times straight. For example, if the time in the main clause is past, you can indicate that something in a subordinate sentence element occurred earlier by putting the verb in a past perfect form, using *had*.

My sister *arrived* at noon after she *had finished* eating breakfast.

The past perfect form *had finished* indicates time before the past form *arrived*. In a reverse situation, a past perfect form in the main clause usually would be followed by a past form.

My sister *had finished* all the routine correspondence before she *arrived*.

Following are other illustrations of common patterns:

I *had known* for some time that my brother *would arrive* late.
I *have known* for some time that my brother *will arrive* late.
He *knows* that my brother *has been* busy.
My sister *changed* her plans after she *returned*.
My brother *changed* his plans after he *had eaten*.
Every noon, if my sister *has arrived*, I *go* out for lunch.
We *expected* my brother *to change* his plans.
We *expected* my brother *to have changed* his plans.
If my brother *arrives* by noon, *I'll take* him to lunch.

Guide to Revision — **Tense**

CONSISTENCY IN POINT OF VIEW AND TENSE

Maintain a point of view in space and time, changing tense forms of verbs when necessary.

ORIGINAL

From my corner I could see the long platform of the subway station stretching dimly beside the tracks. A girl clicked through the turnstile and sat at once on the bench beyond the change booth. The street was empty and quiet. For a moment there was no rumble of trains, no sound of voices—a frightening silence.
[*The third sentence shifts the point of view by making the reader change position to imagine the scene.*]

REVISION

From my corner I could see the long platform of the subway station stretching dimly beside the tracks. A girl clicked through the turnstile and sat immediately on the bench beyond the change booth. For a moment there was no rumble of trains, no sound from the street above, no voice—a frightening silence.
[*The revision retains the detail of the original but presents it from the point of view already established.*]

The play begins with a scene on the castle walls of Elsinore. Horatio, a friend of Hamlet, met the soldiers who were on watch and learned from them about the ghost that had appeared. Then as the soldiers were talking, the ghost, dressed in full armor, appeared again.
[*The writer perhaps begins to think of the experience of reading or seeing the play rather than the play itself and after one sentence changes tense.*]

The play begins with a scene on the castle walls of Elsinore. Horatio, a friend of Hamlet, meets the soldiers who are on watch and learns from them about the ghost that has appeared. Then as the soldiers are talking, the ghost, dressed in full armor, appears again.
[*The revision consistently considers the play as a piece of literature still in existence that can therefore be referred to in present time.*]

FOR STUDY AND WRITING

A. Using some incident that has occurred to you recently, or some problem that has lately arisen, write three letters: (1) to a friend you knew in secondary school, who is thinking of going to college next year; (2) to one of your parents or to some older person you know; and (3) to the student newspaper. Notice the difference in tone and point of view. Can you identify a different purpose in each?

B. Read the following excerpts. Then write a statement expressing what you believe is the author's purpose and anticipated audience.

1. People all dream, whether they want to or not. Even animals dream. A cat's ears and tail sometimes twitch as if they were having a fight. Even when they are awake animals "see things," so that a cat's fur will rise on its back, for no apparent reason, as it peers into a dark cupboard. And we, too, have goose pimples when we feel frightened.

2. They're all on the telephone!
   It's the new Bell Speakerphone. It's a hands-free, group-talk, across-the room kind of telephone. About as flexible as a phone can be. Perfect for "conference" conversations. Ideal when you need both hands free for writing or filing or searching. Just right when it's more convenient for you to talk from another part of the room.

3. I once heard a swell story about Gary Cooper. The person I heard the story from did this terrific Gary Cooper imitation and it may be that when I tell you the story (which I am about to), it will lose something in print. It may lose everything, in fact. But enough. The story was that Gary Cooper was in a London restaurant at a large table of friends. He was sitting in a low chair, with his back to the rest of the room, so no one in the restaurant even knew that he was tall, much less that he was Gary Cooper. . . .

4. Resource protection is of major concern in the Pismo Dunes. The unique flora of the dunes is being severely impacted by off-highway vehicle (OHV) use, and degradation of the vegetated dunes has continued almost unabated for years. This situation has reached a critical stage and cannot be allowed to continue.

5. Dry skin? Not me, darling.
   Every inch of little me is as smooth as (well, you know what).
   Because I never, never bathe without Sardo.

After you have analyzed these for purpose and audience, read them again, noting what voice is created in each.

C. Following are some openings of novels and stories using the voice of a narrator. From these passages try to write a short characterization of each narrator, pointing out clues in the voice that create the impression you get.

1. I was getting along fine with Mama, Papa-Daddy and Uncle Rondo until my sister Stella-Rondo just separated from her husband and came back home again. Mr. Whitaker! Of course I went with Mr. Whitaker first, when he first appeared here in China Grove, taking "Pose Yourself" photos, and Stella-Rondo broke us up. Told him I was one-sided. Bigger on one side than the other, which is a deliberate, calculated falsehood: I'm the same. Stella-Rondo is exactly twelve months to the day younger than I am and for that reason she's spoiled.

2. Harry, you been jacking me up about how I been neglecting Rotary here lately, so I'm going to break down and tell you something. Now I don't want you to take this personal, Harry, because it's not meant personal at all. No siree! Not *a*-tall! But, just between you and I, Harry, I'm not going to be coming out to Rotary lunches any more. I mean I'm quitting Rotary!

3. I am Mr. Allen Frisbie's chauffeur. Allen Frisbie is a name I made up because they tell me that if I used the real name of the man I am employed by that he might take offense and start trouble though I am sure he will never see what I am writing as he does not read anything except the American Golfer but of course some of his friends might call his attention to it.

4. As I take up my pen at leisure and in complete retirement—in good health, furthermore, though tired, so tired that I shall only be able to proceed by short stages and with frequent pauses for rest—as I take up my pen, then, to commit my confessions to this patient paper in my own neat and attractive handwriting, I am assailed by a brief misgiving about the educational background I bring to an intellectual enterprise of this kind.

5. Do you reckon Tom Sawyer was satisfied after all them adventures? I mean the adventures we had down the river, and the time we set the darky Jim free and Tom got shot in the leg. No, he wasn't. It only just p'isoned him for more. That was all the effect it had.

D. Below is an excerpt from The Declaration of Independence and a "translation" in a widely different style. Write a brief comment on the kinds of changes the parodist has made. How do these changes of tone affect the writing? Indicate which version seems more dated to you and why.

> When, in the course of human events, it becomes necessary for one people to dissolve the political bonds which have connected them with another, and to assume among the powers of the earth the separate and equal station to which the laws of nature and of nature's God entitle them, a decent respect to the opinions of mankind requires that they should declare the causes which impel them to the separation.
>
> We hold these truths to be self-evident: that all men are created equal; that they are endowed by their creator with certain inalienable rights; that among these are life, liberty, and the pursuit of happiness. . . .
>
> Thomas Jefferson, *The Unanimous Declaration of the Thirteen United States of America*

> When things get so balled up that the people of a country got to cut loose from some other country, and go it on their own hook, without asking no permission from nobody, excepting maybe God Almighty, then

they ought to let everybody know why they done it, so that everybody can see they are on the level, and not trying to put nothing over on nobody.

All we got to say on this proposition is this: first, me and you is as good as anybody else, and maybe a damn sight better; second, nobody ain't got no right to take away none of our rights; third, every man has got a right to live, to come and go as he pleases, and to have a good time whichever way he likes, so long as he don't interfere with nobody else.

H. L. Mencken, *The Declaration of Independence in American*

E.
Topics	Audience	Voice
Gay Rights	*Newsweek*	concerned
Physical Fitness	*National Enquirer*	angry
The Arts in America	*Playboy*	rational
Sex Education	*Field & Stream*	sarcastic
Television Sitcoms	*Good Housekeeping*	humorous
Computer Technology	*PTA Newsletter*	knowledgeable

Choose one topic from the first column and narrow it into what could be treated in a three-page essay. Then look at the magazines listed and analyze their audiences based on possible interests of their readers, age, educational level, and knowledge of your subject. How do they differ? In what ways will a different audience affect the approach you would take in an essay? Finally, having determined the topic and audience for a proposed essay, which voice would you consider most appropriate? Try varying this several times to see how the rhetorical situation changes.

F. Revise the following passages so that the point of view and tense are consistent.

1. Students who want to get something out of their classes must do more than simply the required work. They can often get a degree by doing just the minimum, but you cannot get an education that way.

2. At the beginning of the play Romeo was very much in love with Rosalind. He seemed almost amusing as a lovesick youth. Then he meets Juliet, and at once he is madly in love with her. The sudden change was not convincing to me.

3. The motion picture *Heartburn* turned me on. It was a serious study of divorce, yet it treats the subject humorously.

4. *Huckleberry Finn* is more than a children's book. Huck, of course, is interesting to children. He was always doing something exciting. I can remember still how interested I was when I first read the book. But the novel has ideas in it that appeal also to an adult mind.

5. No matter how carefully one plans, you can always count on forgetting something.

6. When I first read the story I thought Hemingway was interested mostly in the two killers who come into the restaurant and inquire about Ole. They were revealed through their clipped speech and their attempts to bully the boys in the diner. Most of the story seems to concern them. Nick did not speak very often.

7. Too many people get so used to doing nothing, sitting around wasting time, being bored, that it becomes a way of life, and before you know it, you've gotten yourself in a rut.

G. Choose any piece of writing you have done recently and analyze it for voice. Write a short paragraph describing the voice you hear on the page. Comment how you might like to change or improve your voice in writing.

3

Invention: Developing Ideas

> *When you write, you make a point, not by subtracting as though you sharpened a pencil, but by adding.*
> JOHN ERSKINE

Classical rhetoricians called one part of the composing process invention, the process of adding, of discovering arguments or illustrations. Invention was and still is an essential part of the writing process—developing and fleshing out an idea. Typically invention involves marshaling specifics—concrete details and examples, particular facts and arguments—to support general ideas. And nonfiction writing, at least, typically develops by pushing toward greater specification, as the following brief passage does.

> Change in meaning is frequently due to ethical, or moral, considerations. A word may, as it were, go downhill, or it may rise in the world; there is no way of predicting what its career may be. *Politician* has had a downhill development in American English; in British English it is still not entirely without honor.
>
> Thomas Pyles, *The Origin and Development of the English Language*

The ideas become more specific as the writing progresses. The first sentence presents a general idea. Then the second sentence provides a specific instance of how a word may change because of ethical or moral considerations; it may go downhill. The third sentence moves to greater specificity with an illustration of such meaning change in the word *politician*.

GENERAL AND SPECIFIC

The interplay between general and specific is behind so many of the suggestions in this book that you need to be clear about the meaning of the terms. They are relative terms. Nothing is absolutely general or specific; but some things are more general or more specific than others. *Human* is more specific than *living being*; *American citizen* is more specific than *human*; *John Jones* is more specific than *American citizen*. Or compare the following examples:

> College activities are bad.
> Extracurricular activities in college are harmful to the student.
> Extracurricular activities in college prevent good academic work.
> Adrian failed Chemistry 101 because he spent too much time with the fencing team.

Each statement has been revised to be more specific than the one preceding it. And each gives the reader a more accurate impression. This is the purpose of specifying, to help the reader see or understand more precisely.

Generalizing provides one way of getting writing started, drawing a conclusion from specific instances that may become a topic. Generalizing is seeing the significance of an event or series of events, seeing a broader meaning, a pattern, a relationship, coming to your own individual way of looking at something. But even while you are generalizing, you are thinking about the specifics that support your generalization. As you proceed, you push toward greater specificity, sometimes revising your generalization, but mainly using additional details—examples, illustrations, facts—to support or clarify.

This push toward specifics, the essence of invention, is one of the most interesting parts of the writing process because it challenges the imagination. And the difference between bad writing and good writing is often the difference between a string of undeveloped generalities or judgments and writing that is adequately developed with specific instances and facts.

ADEQUATE AND SPECIFIC DEVELOPMENT

Consider the following, written by a student about his job:

> The most important reason for being employed is the check that is placed in my hands every week or two. Having money is an important asset in every person's life. And the only way to make money is to work for it. The feeling that you get knowing that you deserve the money is a good one. When you work hard for your money, you feel proud of yourself.

The writer had trouble continuing, probably because he had no more to say. He had listed his reasons for working in the form of broad generalizations, sometimes called "glittering generalities" because they sound impressive but communicate little. For example, "Having money is an important asset in every person's life" and "The feeling that you get knowing that you deserve the money is a good one" are both hard to debate; they begin by concluding. The student realized that if he were to continue he would need to develop his general ideas, his reasons for working, by discovering specific examples and details.

He began by brainstorming, searching for specific details that would support his general statements, and made the following rough notes.

> Why I liked my job—MONEY
> able to pay dad the rest of the car loan
> bought new stereo for my room
> able to visit John in New York
> extra cash on weekends—fun restaurants, blew money if I wanted to (day downtown with Sue)
> not always asking mom and dad for money
> independent feeling
> not dependent on mom and dad
> learned to plan and budget
> can stand up for myself
> can say this is mine—I earned it.
> learned to say no, not to buy what I don't need

Using these specific details, he was able to rewrite:

> The most important reason for being employed is the check that is placed in my hands every week or two. At first I thought it was just the money that mattered. Then I realized that it was the feeling of indepen-

dence and freedom that the paycheck gave me. I didn't feel like the "baby" of the family any more, and I could stand up to Mom and Dad and express an opinion. For example, when John called from New York and asked me to come out and visit, my parents said no—"It's too far, it's too expensive." But I could tell them that I wanted to go and that I'd pay the airfare myself. There was not much they could say. As I got on the plane, I felt proud of myself. This trip is mine, I said to myself, I've earned it.

This draft is more fully developed. We now know, because of the examples included, why the job and paycheck are important to the writer. Other students might have used other examples; but this piece of writing is "his"; it belongs to him alone. The third draft—his final revision—appears below. This draft begins with a more focused general statement and develops through additional specifics:

Each week when I picked up my paycheck, I was filled with a sense of pride. At first, I thought it was the money that gave me this feeling, but it was not—it was what the money provided, the sense of freedom and independence that I enjoyed. No longer did I feel like a kid in a family of grownups; no longer was I dependent on Mom and Dad. For example, when I wanted a new stereo, I didn't have to plead with Dad. I merely saved the money and bought one. When my friend John called and asked me to visit him in New York City over Easter vacation, I immediately said yes, because I could afford it. Now when I look at my stereo, when I think about my trip to New York, or whenever I make a purchase, I can say with pride, "This is mine. I've earned it."

In another example, a student paper sets out to convince the reader that living in the dorm is less expensive than living off campus:

First of all, on-campus housing is cheaper than off-campus. In the dorm you have only two initial payments that you must make. One is for the room itself and the other is for food. Off campus you are always paying for food, rent, power, and other important subsidies.

Again the passage is only a series of unsubstantiated assertions. It says that dormitory living is less expensive, but it provides no evidence. The writer needs to search out concrete details, to interview students living on and off campus, to get facts from the housing office, to do research. The student might ask himself: How much does a dorm room cost? Is there a difference if one shares a room or lives alone? What is the cost of a typical off-campus apartment? How much is a meal ticket? How much does an apartment resident spend on utilities and food each month? What are the "other subsidies" at the end of the paragraph?

A reader wants to be shown, not just told. And instructors often make a distinction between writing which relies only on general statements ("The movie was bad"; "Abortion is immoral") and writing that shows or

Guide to Revision

Dev

ADEQUATE DEVELOPMENT

Recast generalizations that can't be supported; then supply specifics to illustrate or support.

ORIGINAL	REVISION
College education is much too expensive in America, and it is getting worse every day. Many deserving students either have to postpone college indefinitely or to work so much of the time that they neglect their studies. If democracy is to survive, the government must provide some method for enabling more capable students to get college educations. Scholarship awards are unfair because they put a premium on memory and mental ability and not on character and need. If our country is to survive, something must be done about this problem.	The cost of a college education in the United States has more than doubled in the last fifteen years. A young man can no longer save enough from his paper route and a job mowing lawns to see him through four years at a university. In most colleges and universities tuition and fees have more than doubled. The textbook that cost $5.00 a few years ago is likely to cost from $10.00 to $20.00 now. Inflated food prices have affected college cafeterias, and even the soft drink or cup of coffee that used to provide recreation for a quarter is now seventy-five cents or a dollar.

demonstrates, making its point through specifics. For example, a class was asked to take a silly generalization, "The bug was awesome," and translate it into showing writing. Many specific bugs were produced; one appears in the following:

> The bug was awesome—yellow and transparent, similar to a dried piece of fingernail that has sat in the windowsill for days. Six spiny legs emerged from underneath its oval body, each working in harmony with the other to facilitate its travel. Sporadically-placed black specks covered its head and back, and two long antennae protruded from its forehead, although one was broken three-fourths of the way up. Its mandibles were moist, protruding from its mouth, chewing nervously on a small piece of white matter.

Whether you are describing a large bug or arguing about the inequities of a new tax reform bill, the principle is the same—writing needs to be developed so that the reader is shown, not just told. There are many ways in which specific facts and details can be used to develop writing so that the reader is shown. They can be classified broadly as forms of discourse.

FORMS OF DISCOURSE

Writing can develop in many ways, but traditionally discourse has been thought of in four types or forms: narration, description, exposition, and argumentation. These are not sharp divisions, but they are useful because they suggest different ways of approaching a subject, as the following demonstrate.

Narration

Narration tells a story, recounts a sequence of events. The events may be real, as in a newspaper account or history, or they may be imaginary, as in a novel. Usually events are recorded in the order in which they occur, chronologically, as in the following:

> As I approached an intersection, I noticed a blue car entering the highway from the left. I did not slow down because I was in the outside or right-hand lane, and I assumed the driver of the blue car would take the inside lane. Suddenly I realized that he had no intention of doing so, that he was swinging wide to my lane. "This is it!" I thought, and I jumped on the brake. My car swerved a bit, then righted crazily, the tires screeching on the pavement. In spite of my seat belt I was catapulted against the steering wheel. My car caromed off the guard rail, but slowed so abruptly that I gave the blue car only a slight bump.

The account starts at the beginning of the incident and reports the events in sequence.

Description

Description presents a picture, usually with the writer taking a point of view in space and telling what can be seen.

> Standing on the top of the hill, I could see the entire intersection spread out like a huge wheel with bent and irregular spokes. Only two cars were visible. On the wide highway, just south of the intersection, was a small red sports car, with the top down and a single occupant. Coming in from the west, swinging wide toward the outside lane, was a lumbering old blue sedan, with a badly battered rear fender. The sun gleamed on the pavement, making the black surface look wet, and flashed in the windshields of the converging cars.

The description here is relatively objective, focusing on the incident at one particular time and reporting factually what the writer sees—the red car, the blue car, the battered rear fender, the sun on the pavement. But even here the writer interprets, and like most descriptions this is partly subjective: the comparison to a wheel, the "lumbering" sedan, the "wet" look of the pavement. Often description makes its primary appeal to the senses, attempting to convey to a reader the feelings of the observer of the scene.

Exposition

Exposition exposes—explains, analyzes, interprets. It tries to make something understandable. Following is an expository comment on the incident at the intersection.

> According to police records, the commonest accident on four-lane highways results from illegal left turns into the wrong lane. Let us assume that the driver is entering the highway from the west and expects to turn north. He should wait until the southbound lanes are clear, cross them, and turn into the left-hand lane of the two going north. Some drivers, however, perhaps feeling that they should use the outside lane unless they are passing, swing wide to the right-hand lane. If there is oncoming northbound traffic, there may well be an accident.

The account explains, tells how and why bad left turns cause accidents on four-lane highways. Much college writing will be expository, writing term papers and answers to examination questions that require explanation and analysis.

Argumentation

Argumentation is intended to urge a belief or conviction on readers, to change an attitude.

> Having spent a summer driving four-lane highways, I can assure you that whoever teaches courses in driving should give more attention to the dangers of the left-hand turn. A driver entering from the left and turning left should take the first lane legally open to him. If he swings wide and takes any but the nearest lane, he is courting a collision with an oncoming car, whose driver expects him to obey the law and take the left-hand lane of those going his direction. This is an easy rule to follow, but many drivers are not aware of it, or ignore it. They should at least be told about it.

The passage uses some exposition to clarify points, but mainly it musters reasons or evidence to support the contention that driving courses should pay more attention to left turns. Argumentation attempts to change a reader's mind.

DEVELOPMENT AND FORMS OF DISCOURSE

There are other ways of classifying forms or modes of discourse, and not every type of writing fits readily into one of the traditional classes discussed above. A direct expression of feeling, for example, may seem different from any of these.

The important thing to observe here is how all these forms work together and how each one may serve as development of another. Narrative, for example, is almost always useful to flesh out exposition or argument, and it usually includes passages of description. You need to command all four modes in order to work successfully with any one. Consider the opening of a student essay prepared to meet an assignment in exposition. The writer's purpose was primarily expository, to discuss an agricultural inspection station, known locally as the bug station, which she passed on her way to school. But throughout her exposition she uses other forms of discourse—especially narration and description—to support her main purpose.

Good! There's Stead. No more traffic signals between here and home. No more interruptions except the turnoff at Hallelujah Junction. God, I love this drive. So I spend two hours a day driving back and forth. Everyone at work thinks I am crazy to do it, but they don't understand what it was like spending almost that much time over the last twenty years on the southern California freeways: bumper-to-bumper traffic, eye-watering smog, endless billboards, sterile city buildings. Compared to that, this drive is heaven. . . .

Today, the hills and valleys are all dressed in the breathtaking green of spring, but I also remember the joy of finding them last fall in yellows and oranges and browns. And in winter, cloaked in white. Today the sky is a brilliant blue, and the clouds look like floating feathers. Sometimes it is grey, and the clouds lie across the hills like a comforter lying across a bed. Now, instead of watching cars and billboards, I can watch hawks playing on air currents, herds of grazing deer, and red-coated coyotes scurrying across the highway or through the fields. Humm. Just around that bend ahead is one sight I didn't always appreciate—the bug station.

When construction of the bug station began, I was curious. I speculated daily as to what possible purpose might be served by that little square shack. When I found out that it was a check stop for fruit flies and gypsy moths, I was angry. My pleasant drive was going to be cut in half. As it turned out, bug station was the perfect name for it. Every day I had to stop, and every day the officer on duty bugged me with the same old question—"Just coming from town, Ma'am?" All I had to do was say "yes" or nod my head, and he waved me on through. How did he know I wasn't lying? The interruption to my daily reverie was as annoying as the pests it was supposed to control. Too bad, I thought, that I can't control this pest with a fly swatter or some bug spray. What a nuisance. . . .

Jeanne Verdeyen

The essay continues, explaining the bug station through the eyes and actions and feelings of the narrator. The blending of forms of discourse and the use of specific details make the essay sound authentic.

STRATEGIES FOR EXPOSITION: TYPES OF DEVELOPMENT

Much of your writing will be expository, and there are many places to look for material to develop an essay—for specifics, details, evidence. You can, for instance, use any of the approaches outlined in chapter 1 for getting started—asking questions, drawing on experience, reading, remembering. Or you may get ideas by thinking about different sorts of material that are available—considering sources for concrete, specific details. Here are a few of the most useful methods of development:

Instances, Examples, Illustrations

One sure-fire way to develop an idea is to mention a number of particular instances that illustrate or support it. Assume that you want to make the following statement:

> The houses on our block represent the worst characteristics of modern tract-house architecture.

The sentence introduces at least two general topics—the houses in the block and your ideas about architecture. You can develop these with particulars, like those in the following sentence. In other words, you can show the reader what you mean, not merely declare a generalization without support.

> The new house on the corner has a picture window with a view of a neighbor's clothesline and garbage cans, shutters that were never intended to work and are nailed to the siding, and a heating system that keeps the living room at 85 degrees but sends no heat to the bathroom. The house next to that . . .

You could follow with more illustrations from the individual houses. Or you might approach from a different point of view, looking at the impression made by the block as a whole. A sentence following that opening statement might read:

Invention: Developing Ideas   61

> Viewed from the street, the houses are identical, except that the doors of the two-car garages are painted in different bright colors.

You could go on with additional observations.

The following selection is even more obviously just a list of examples, with an opening sentence telling us what the writer is going to do, introducing the list.

> The foregoing are particularly striking examples, but hundreds of others could be cited. We find generalization in such everyday words as *picture*, once restricted, as the etymology would suggest (compare: the Picts, "painted ones"), to a *painted* representation of something seen, but now applicable to photography, crayon drawing, and so forth; *butcher*, who once slew one animal only, the goat (French *bouc*); the verb *sail*, which has been transferred to steam navigation, just as *drive* has been transferred to self-propelled vehicles. . . .
>
> Stuart Robertson and Frederic G. Cassidy,
> *The Development of Modern English*

The statement to be developed had apparently appeared earlier in the discussion—that some words have become more generalized in their meaning. And then the writer mentions five specific words, showing how each has become more general.

The next example opens with a statement that does not dictate the structure but introduces two topics—the evening and the crowds.

> It was early evening of a day in the late fall and the Winesburg County Fair had brought crowds of country people into town. The day had been clear and the night came on warm and pleasant. On the Trunion Pike, where the road after it left town stretched away between berry fields now covered with dry brown leaves, the dust from passing wagons arose in clouds. Children, curled into little balls, slept on the straw scattered on wagon beds. Their hair was full of dust and their fingers black and sticky. The dust rolled away over the fields and the departing sun set it ablaze with colors.
>
> Sherwood Anderson, *Winesburg, Ohio*

The second sentence provides specific instances of the first topic, the evening. The next sentence combines more details about the evening with a specific comment about the crowd, the wagons. The fourth and fifth sentences continue with specifics about the crowd, and then the final sentence returns to the evening.

In the following, James Baldwin opens with an accumulation of details, which argue why the projects in Harlem are hated by those who live there:

> The projects are hideous, of course, there being a law, apparently respected throughout the world, that popular housing shall be as cheerless as a prison. They are lumped all over Harlem, colorless, bleak, high, and revolting. The wide windows look out on Harlem's invincible and indescribable squalor: the Park Avenue railroad tracks, around which, about forty years ago, the present dark community began; the unrehabilitated houses, bowed down, it would seem, under the great weight of frustration and bitterness they contain; the dark, the ominous school houses from which the child may emerge maimed, blinded, hooked or enraged for life; and the churches, churches, block upon block of churches, niched in the walls like cannons in the walls of a fortress.
>
> *Notes of a Native Son*

When you can handle easily this one type of development—framing a statement that is not so broad that it stops discussion, and then finding details to support it—you are well on your way to good writing.

Extended Incident, Example, Illustration

Instead of offering a series of instances, you may want to develop a point by telling a story or recounting a single incident in some detail. Exposition becomes clearer and more convincing when it can be illustrated by narrative and description. In the following a student uses an extended illustration to show how left-handed people are discriminated against.

> One of the best places to see how lefties are being ignored is in the schools. I remember when I was in first grade and it was time to decorate the classroom with paper cut-outs of Santa Claus. We each had been given a mimeographed Santa and told to color it. When we were done, we were to cut it out and mount our picture on a piece of colored construction paper with our names printed below. My coloring was fine, probably all outside the lines, but Santa looked terrific to me. Then I asked the teacher for some left-handed scissors. Instead of scissors, I received a blank stare and an admonition to go back to my desk and do my work. Dejected, I sat down and tried to tear out my Santa Claus and paste him on the paper. He looked ugly and ragged. I crumbled him up. I didn't want him hanging in the room with my name below his jagged face.

Professional writer Joan Didion uses the same technique, an extended illustration, to analyze the general concept "morality."

> Here are some particulars. At midnight last night, on the road from Las Vegas to Death Valley Junction, a car hit a shoulder and turned over. The driver, very young and apparently drunk, was killed instantly. His girl was found alive but bleeding internally, deep in shock. I talked this afternoon to the nurse who had driven the girl to the nearest doctor, 185 miles across the floor of the Valley and three ranges of lethal mountain road. The

nurse explained that her husband, a talc miner, had stayed on the highway with the boy's body until the coroner could get over the mountains from Bishop at dawn today. "You can't just leave a body on the highway," she said. "It's immoral."

Didion continues, "It was one instance in which I did not distrust the word [*immoral*], because she meant something quite specific." Although the general concept is important, often its meaning can best be conveyed through an incident, example, or illustration.

A narrated incident can be especially useful in getting an expository essay started, as in the following opening of an essay on movie director Francis Coppola and his studio.

> Underneath the flashing neon signs, next to the cumbersome camera equipment, Gene Kelly is offering advice, "Cut the legs out of that bit," he says. "The public will never know it's gone." Dressed in a navy blue sweater, checkered slacks, and a sporting cap, Kelly looks as if someone has plucked him off the putting green and dropped him onto the set of a movie musical. While cast and crew wait for scene 106, take 22 of *One from the Heart* to commence, Kelly confers on a dance combination with choreographer Kenny Ortega. Ortega is four decades Kelly's junior and wearing black leather pants, a high-fashion black T-shirt with wrap-around zipper, and bright red socks. Past these unlikely collaborators walks a high-heeled showgirl with a button pinned to her scant, sequin-speckled costume. It reads: "I believe in Francis C."

The opening tells what is happening on the set, what Gene Kelly says and wears, and ties into the subject of the essay only in the last sentence with the showgirl's button introducing Coppola. After this narrative opening, the next paragraph begins "Welcome to Zoetrope Studios," and the essay proceeds with an expository discussion of the movie industry and Coppola's role in it.

Definition

You can use definition in writing both as a device for development and as a way to keep your logic clear, to be sure that everyone understands how you are using your terms. W. H. Auden develops part of a discussion of detective stories with definitions.

> The vulgar definition, "a Whodunit," is correct. The basic formula is this: a murder occurs; many are suspected; all but one suspect, who is the murderer, are eliminated; the murderer is arrested or dies.
> This definition excludes:
> (1) studies of murderers whose guilt is known, e.g., *Malice Aforethought*. There are borderline cases in which the murderer is known and

there are no false suspects, but the proof is lacking, e.g., many of the stories of Freeman Wills Crofts. Most of these are permissible.

(2) thrillers, spy stories, stories of master crooks, etc., when the identification of the criminal is subordinate to the defeat of his criminal designs.

The Guilty Vicarage

The definition lists characteristics that distinguish whodunits from other stories and then cites examples of what a whodunit is not. It is a variation on the standard logical definition (see chapter 13) in which you put something into a class and then distinguish it from other members of the class: A triangle is a plane figure (class) with three sides (differentiation).

In developing writing, definitions are likely to be less formal and often more extensive, defining a complex idea by listing many of its characteristics. In parodying the traditional logical definition, one student defines a type of male on campus as "the wolf."

> Let's start with the genus called the wolf, the male who is always on the prowl for his next victim. Some girls dread the wolf and will do everything they can to avoid him, but others find him exciting. It can be fun to flirt with danger. However, dangerous is exactly what the wolf is. Being in the majority, his habitat is everywhere, except maybe the library. And he is always easy to spot. The typical wolf wears an all-American football jersey or a fraternity sweatshirt. He swaggers when he walks and has a high opinion of himself. Unfortunately, he does not have the same opinion of females. He is full of guile and difficult to escape. His sweet words often drip off his tongue like honey. But beware. The wolf may wear sheep's clothing; nevertheless, he is still a wolf.

Or Edward Abbey uses a definition of a wilderness to support an argument for conservation:

> No doubt about it, the presence of bear, especially grizzly bear, adds a spicy titillation to a stroll in the woods. My bear-loving friend Peacock goes so far as to define wilderness as a place and only a place where one enjoys the opportunity of being attacked by a dangerous wild animal. Any place that lacks GRIZ, or lions or tigers, or a rhino or two, is not, in his opinion worthy of the name "wilderness." A good definition, worthy of serious consideration. A wild place without dangers is an absurdity, although I realize that danger creates administrative problems for park and forest managers. But we must not allow our national parks and national forests to be degraded to the status of mere public playgrounds. Open to all, yes of course. But—*Enter at your own risk.*
>
> *The Journey Home*

The definition is not scientific, but it serves to make a point about national parks and forests.

Cause and Effect

People clarify their thinking by speculating about causes and results, and you can use the same strategy to develop writing. The following lists the causes for an observed effect.

> The Yellow or Silver Pine is more frequently overturned than any other tree on the Sierra, because its leaves and branches form the largest mass in proportion to its height, while in many places it is planted sparsely, leaving long, open lanes, through which storms may enter with full force. Furthermore, because it is distributed along the lower portion of the range, which was the first to be left bare on the breaking up of the ice-sheet at the close of the glacial winter, the soil it is growing upon has been longer exposed to postglacial weathering, and consequently is in a more crumbling, decayed condition than the fresher soils farther up the range, and therefore offers a less secure anchorage for the roots.
>
> John Muir, *The Passes of the Sierra*

The passage opens with an assertion that the Yellow Pine is most frequently overturned, an effect, and then explains why, the cause.

The following passage works from the other direction, enumerating effects the telephone has had on our lives.

> What has the telephone done to us, or for us, in the hundred years of its existence? A few effects suggest themselves at once. It has saved lives by getting rapid word of illness, injury, or famine from remote places. By joining with the elevator to make possible the multistory residence or office building, it has made possible—for better or worse—the modern city. By bringing about a quantum leap in the speed and ease with which information moves from place to place, it has greatly accelerated the rate of scientific and technological change and growth in industry. Beyond doubt it has crippled if not killed the ancient art of letter writing. . . .
>
> John Brooks, *The Telephone*

The paragraph continues to describe specific ways in which the telephone has affected society.

Analogy

Analogy is a special kind of illustration in which a writer draws a parallel, explaining something relatively unknown by comparing it to something familiar. To explain the rotation of the earth to a child, we might use a rubber ball or a top. For example, Michael Arlen develops the idea of what it is like to take an airplane trip by comparing it to watching television:

> A few days ago, while seated snugly in an airplane seat on my way back to New York from Chicago, with a drink in front of me, last week's copy of *Sports Illustrated* on my lap, the soothing hum of the engines wash-

ing over my ears, and with the memory of the hectic taxi ride to the airport and wretched traffic jams and ticket-counter chaos already receding in my brain, it occurred to me that a rather striking similarity existed between the situation I found myself in then, flying in a modern airliner, and what I've often felt as I watch television. To begin with, both experiences are largely passive experiences.

Prufrock Aloft; Prufrock Before the Television Set

Process Analysis

If you have ever followed a recipe or assembled a child's toy from directions, you are aware of development by analyzing a process. Such analysis can be complex—explaining how to fly an airplane or how to administer CPR to a heart attack victim. In technical writing, process analysis is frequently used to explain a complicated mechanism or machine. In business, a flowchart is a visual representation of process analysis—a description of how the organization functions.

The ability to write a clear and accurate description of a process is not easy. In the following, Lewis Thomas, relying on a bit of analogy, explains the process by which slime molds form into larger organisms.

> The phenomenon of separate animals joining up to form an organism is not unique in insects. Slime-mold cells do it all the time, of course, in each life cycle. At first they are single amebocytes swimming around, eating bacteria, aloof from each other, untouching, voting Republican. Then, a bell sounds, and acrasin is released by special cells toward which the others converge in stellate ranks, touch, fuse together, and construct the slug, solid as a trout. A splendid stalk is raised, with a fruiting body on top, and out of this comes the next generation of amebocytes, ready to swim across the same moist ground, solitary and ambitious.
>
> *The Lives of a Cell*

Classification

In developing an idea by process analysis, you usually arrange ideas in a spatial pattern or a time sequence. In developing an idea by classification, you analyze a general topic by grouping specifics according to type. Classification, in fact, is basic in most plans for organizing writing (see chapter 5). Writer Donald Hall, in discussing how we read, identifies four ways of reading. Robert Brustein, writing about horror movies, classifies them into three major categories that he calls the Mad Doctor, the Atomic Beast, and the Interplanetary Monster. Or John Ruskin uses classification to develop a complex philosophical argument about the way human beings think as poets.

And thus, in full, there are four classes: the men who feel nothing, and therefore see truly; the men who feel strongly, think weakly, and see untruly (second order of poets); the men who feel strongly, think strongly, and see truly (first order of poets); and the men who, strong as human creatures can be, are yet submitted to influences stronger than they, and see in a sort untruly, because what they see is inconceivably above them. This last is the usual condition of prophetic inspiration.

Of the Pathetic Fallacy

Or Terence McLaughlin, a leading authority on pollution, develops a discussion of the word *dirt* first by defining it and then by categorizing the variety of ways in which people view it:

Dirt is evidence of the imperfections of life, a constant reminder of change and decay. It is the dark side of all human activities—because it is only in our judgements that things are dirty: there is no such material as *absolute* dirt. Earth, in the garden, is a valuable support and nourishment for plants, and gardeners often run it through their fingers lovingly; earth on the carpet is dirt. A pile of dung, to the dung-beetle, is food and shelter for a large family; a pile of dung, to the Public Health Inspector, is a Nuisance. Soup in a plate, before we eat it, is food; the traces we leave on the plate imperceptibly become dirt. Lipstick on a girl's lips may make her boyfriend more anxious to touch them with his own lips; lipstick on a cup will probably make him refuse to touch it.

Dirt

Comparison and Contrast

Writing can also develop by enumerating similarities or differences. The following paragraph compares legends of the North and South to make a point about the Civil War.

But there is another side to the War and one that it would be wrong to ignore or minimize—the side of glory. There was glory enough for each side. The North has its legends (true legends) as well as the South. There is the desperate and fruitless courage of Fredericksburg; there is the rush by Missionary Ridge; there are the heroic stories of units like the 20th Maine at Gettysburg; there is Sheridan riding on to the field at Cedar Creek and turning the tide of battle like Desaix at Marengo. There is most impressive of all, the disciplined and despairing advance at Cold Harbor. Here is glory. But whether the South has more glory than the North or not (I think it has), it needs it more and, as is right, cherishes it more. It cherishes the fame of the most Plutarchian (and greatest) American soldier, "Marse Robert." It cherishes or should cherish, with Pickett's attack, the memory of

Hood's men advancing to their doom at Franklin. And for the individual heroic actions, their name is legion. It should remember with pride, not that there were so few under arms to surrender with Lee or Johnston, but that there were still so many.

D. W. Brogan, *A Fresh Appraisal of the Civil War*

The first three sentences introduce a topic, that there was glory in the war for both sides. Then the paragraph breaks into two parts listing particulars.

Another passage is developed by citing differences. For example, historian John Mack Faragher discovered essential differences of style between the diaries of pioneer women and men.

> Differences between the worlds of men and women are reflected in the emigrant diaries. Despite similarity in content, there was a notable difference in the style of men's and women's writing. Women usually wrote with a pervasive personal presence, most often using the first person. "I am now sitting on a hill side on a stone, a little distant from the camp," Rebecca Ketcham wrote in her diary late one afternoon. "After I commenced writing Mrs. Dix called to me to come to her to see a beautiful bunch of verbena she had found. I went and looked about with her a little, then sat down again to my writing. . . ." Men, on the contrary, typically employed the more impersonal "we." Sometimes the referent of this pronoun is hard to specify, shifting with the context. Usually the "we" most clearly referred to the men as a group.
>
> [May 4, 1851] We traveled 16 miles this day over very hilly road.
>
> [May 6] This day we left camp at 8 o'clock and traveled 12 miles, camped where we found but little wood and poor water.
>
> *Women and Men on the Overland Trail*

Comparison or contrast, like all other strategies mentioned here, can also provide the structure of an extended introduction or an entire essay, as the following opening paragraphs of an article on basketball show.

> Basketball is the city game. Its battlegrounds are strips of asphalt between tattered wire fences or crumbling buildings; its rhythms grow from the uneven thump of a ball against hard surfaces. It demands no open spaces or lush backyards or elaborate equipment. It doesn't even require specified numbers of players; a one-on-one confrontation in a playground can be as memorable as a full-scale organized game. Basketball is the game for young athletes without cars or allowances—the game in which the drama and action are intensified by its confined spaces and chaotic surroundings.
>
> Every American sport directs itself in a general way toward certain segments of American life. Baseball is basically a slow, pastoral experience, offering a tableau of athletes against a green background, providing moments of action amid longer periods allowed for contemplation of the spectacle. In its relaxed, unhurried way, it is exactly what it claims to be—the national "pastime" rather than an intense, sustained game crammed with

action. Born in a rural age, its appeal still lies largely in its offer of an untroubled island where, for a few hours, a pitcher tugging at his pants leg can seem to be the most important thing in a fan's life.

Football's attraction is more contemporary. Its violence is in tune with the times, and its well-mapped strategic war games invite fans to become generals, plotting and second-guessing along with their warriors on the fields. With its action compressed in a fairly small area and its formations and patterns relatively easy to interpret, football is the ideal television spectacle. Other sports have similar, if smaller, primary audiences. Golf and tennis belong first to country-club members, horse racing to an enduring breed of gamblers, auto racing to Middle Americans who thrive on its violent roaring machines and death-defying risks. But basketball belongs to the cities—and New York, from its asphalt playgrounds to the huge modern arena that houses the professional basketball champions of the world, is the most active, dedicated basketball city of all.

Pete Axthelm, *The City Game*

The selection develops three paragraphs to make the contrast—one describing basketball, one baseball, and one football and other sports, with a final sentence in the third paragraph returning to basketball, which the rest of the article discusses.

Obviously these are not the only ways of developing an idea in writing. Aristotle, centuries ago, put together a long list of topics as aids to invention, places where one could look for arguments and illustrations. And there are no right or wrong ways to proceed; no formulas to ensure a successful essay. But the forms of discourse and strategies for development discussed here provide opportunities. They offer suggestions from which you can select to suit your purpose and your subject matter.

FOR STUDY AND WRITING

A. Look at the cover of a book, a drawing on a box of cereal, or a favorite poster in your room and list as many specific details as you can. Or take a piece of candy or popcorn and describe it, using all five senses. Make notes on your observations and write a descriptive paragraph.

B. Go to a busy place on campus—the union or the library or a residence hall—and note what you see, the people who are there, what they are wearing and doing, even snatches of conversation. Based on your observations, can you draw any generalizations about those who frequent this spot or about the spot itself? Using any pattern of exposition, write a paragraph demonstrating what you observed.

C. Below are listed some sentences which make a statement by *telling* the reader, not *showing*, what was intended. Using each as the first sentence of your writing, develop with concrete details. Compare yours with others in the class to see how they vary.

1. I often associate colors with particular things.
2. Some television programs are worth watching.
3. Comic strips often express political and social concerns.
4. I still remember many of our favorite childhood games.
5. Slang can be expressive and clever.

In the next two sentences, write a story or incident that illustrates each.

1. It is not always wise—or economical—to purchase a "bargain."
2. Practical jokes often have a serious side.

D. Rearrange the roughly synonymous expressions in each of the following groups in order of their specificity, with the most general first and the most specific last.

1.
   a. dark outfit
   b. Mary's black jersey ensemble
   c. wearing apparel
   d. garment contrived for the purpose of covering the female figure
2.
   a. drum
   b. musical instrument
   c. percussion instrument
   d. band instrument
3.
   a. It was a lovely scene.
   b. The western sky was deep blue-green with feathered gold spots where the sun broke through.
   c. The sky was bright-colored and lovely.
   d. The greenish western sky was mottled with gold spots.
4.
   a. Dogs used by hunters for flushing and retrieving water fowl.
   b. Modern breeds of dogs.
   c. Labrador retrievers.
   d. Hunting dogs.
5.
   a. Nike-Hercules missile.
   b. Modern weapon for defense.
   c. Weapon for defense against enemy aircraft.
   d. Surface-to-air missile.
6.
   a. The three major composers of the post-Romantic revolution are like the three brothers in the fairy tale who set off in different

                directions, follow divergent paths, and after sundry adventures arrive at much the same destination.

        b. The three major composers of the post-Romantic revolution used different methods and different procedures to achieve their ends but finally achieved new types of music.

        c. The three major composers of the post-Romantic period sought to move away from what they considered the sterility of nineteenth-century music—Schöenberg through mathematics, Bartók through ethnography, Stravinsky through history.

        d. The changes that characterize the post-Romantic revolution in music came about through varying influences on composition.

7.   a. The sculpture sat in the Museum of Modern Art garden, impressive for its unusual materials and its effective symbolism, combining mass and void in a complex symphony of light and shadow.

        b. Reuben Nakian's sculpture *The Rape of Lucrece,* in the Museum of Modern Art garden, is two interacting abstract figures constructed of variously shaped, movable plates of sheet metal mounted on a framework of black pipe.

        c. Nakian's sculpture in the Museum of Modern Art garden is a complex construction of metal sheets mounted in different planes, on which light and shadow play.

        d. The sculpture in the garden was exciting and moving because of the sculptor's unusual approach to his subject and his skillful handling of materials.

E. A classmate has asked for help on the following paragraph. Read it and make suggestions for revision. Then write a revision yourself based on the original.

        In a residence hall you'll meet a lot of new people, and you will have things to do in your spare time. At the beginning of the semester, everyone is looking for a friend. Many times your roommate becomes your best friend. Everyone is a community with at least one common purpose, going to school. Hall governments sponsor activities regularly. Movies are shown weekly and various activities are offered to the student. There are, of course, parties, which help you cope with your classes.

F. Read the thesis sentences below and indicate what method of development—comparison/contrast, definition, etc.—you expect. Some sentences may have several possible answers, so be able to justify yours.

    1. In Faulkner's fiction, two characters—Flem Snopes and Miss Emily Grierson—seem opposites; however, in their selfishness and single-mindedness, they are almost identical.

    2. The effects of lowering the legal drinking age to eighteen in our state are not known, but some can be assumed.

3. Watching television is like taking a trip on an airplane; you sit passively while life goes on around you.
4. After observing my classmates, I have discovered that there are several methods of preparing for exams.
5. It is said that experience is the best teacher.
6. The term "historical romance" has different meanings to different people.
7. I thought cross-country skiing looked easy until I tried to learn one sunny Tuesday afternoon.
8. Although I consider myself a "city kid," I treasure my memories of a summer spent in a small mountain town of 200 people.
9. Why is the sky blue? I will tell you.
10. Once you have been bitten by the travel bug, you'll never be content to stay home again.

G. Choose a general topic that you are familiar with, for example a sport or hobby you enjoy or a subject in school you have studied. Write about a humorous or embarrassing incident on this topic. Then write a set of paragraphs developing the *same* single topic, using the different patterns of development explained in this chapter: example, definition, cause and effect, analogy, process analysis, classification, and comparison and contrast. Judge which method does the job best.

4

Commitment and Response: The Paragraph

> *Life is just one damned thing after another.*
> FRANK WARD O'MALLEY
>
> *A paragraph is a mindful.*
> OLD TEXTBOOK

Writing, also, is just one thing after another. It is one letter, one word, one sentence, one paragraph after another. It is a sequence, a continuity, a flow. Writing is a series of decisions, mostly automatic, about what should come next.

To some extent, these decisions, especially as they concern individual words, are regulated by characteristics of the language. The order of modifiers preceding a noun, for instance, is established firmly enough to eliminate many choices. If it is to modify *book, the green* cannot be followed by *only* but can be by *music*. The order for these words is set grammatically: *the only green music book*. But most decisions, especially those concerning units longer than a word or two, are the writer's, and they are made to guide the readers' thoughts, to move their understanding from one point to another.

COMMITMENT AND RESPONSE

The flow or continuity of ideas in prose may be viewed as a series of commitments and responses. Whenever, for instance, you put a sentence on paper, you make a commitment to go ahead in some ways but not in others. You establish expectancies in your reader that limit what you are going to say next. And when you frame your next sentence, you respond in some way to the commitment you have made before. Suppose, for example, you start with this sentence from a recent autobiographical piece.

> I used to love to get into the thick of crowds.

You could think of hundreds of sentences that might follow, but you would probably go on with one of the following four types of response.

1. *Repetition*   You could say the same thing in different words.

> Moving along in a crush of pulsing humanity was one of my greatest pleasures.

The sentence adds a detail or two, but it provides little development. Too frequently a response that repeats only postpones getting something said.

2. *Diversion*   You could change directions.

> More recently, however, I find myself mistrustful and frightened in even a small group of strangers, with my hand automatically hovering near my billfold.

As *however* signals, this sentence shifts the discussion to a new topic, from the writer's love of crowds in the past to his fear of them in the present.

3. *Return; Further Generalization*   You could, assuming that the original sentence is one of several listing early interests of the writer, move to another generalization.

> It was these interests and enthusiasms that influenced me to join the circus.

This sentence refers to an earlier passage and commits the writer to develop a related idea.

4. *Specification*   You could write sentences to make key ideas of the sentence more specific.

> I felt enlarged, recharged, much as I did when climbing on a mountainside.
> I loved the subway rush hour, the crush at ticket windows, the squeeze of New Year's Eve on Forty-second Street, or the night street market in Boston.

The first sentence responds to the verb of the original sentence, *used to love;* the second specifies crowds. These represent the most common kind of response, the most useful kind of development, moving thought ahead by making it more specific. The second sentence, incidentally, is the one the author used.

Clear prose proceeds in this way, with each sentence pointing to what is to follow and also responding to what has preceded it.

COMMITMENT-RESPONSE UNITS

Chunks of writing, like chunks of thought, tend to form into units, segments of what a writer wants to say about a subject. At its simplest, a unit may be as small as a brief sentence. *Birds sing* includes a commitment in the topic *birds* and a response about birds in the comment *sing*. But usually a commitment elicits a fuller response, a sentence or a number of sentences. The last response described above, for instance, specification, combines with the commitment to form a unit that could be extended. On the other hand, the second or third type described above, a diversion or a shift to a new generalization, usually begins a new unit. The following passage contains two commitment-response units, the second introduced by a diversion from the original commitment.

> [1] At the moment, as for many years past, the chances to see silent comedy are rare. [2] There is a smattering of it on television—too often treated as something quaintly archaic, to be laughed at, not with. [3] Some two hundred comedies—long and short—can be rented for home projection. [4] And a lucky minority has access to the comedies in the collection of New York's Museum of Modern Art, which is still incomplete but which is probably the best in the world.
>
> [5] In the near future, however, something of this lost art will return to regular theaters. [6] A thick straw in the wind is the big business now being done by a series of revivals of W. C. Fields's memorable movies, a kind of comedy more akin to the old silent variety than anything which is being made today. [7] Mack Sennett now is preparing a sort of potpourri variety show called *Down Memory Lane* made up out of his old movies, featuring people like Fields and Bing Crosby when they were movie beginners, but including also interludes from the silents. [8] Harold Lloyd has re-released *Movie Crazy*, a talkie, and plans to revive four of his best silent comedies (*Grandma's Boy, Safety Last, Speedy,* and *The Freshman*). [9] Buster Keaton hopes to make at feature length, with a minimum of dialogue, two of the funniest short comedies ever made, one about a porous homemade boat and one about a prefabricated house.
>
> James Agee, *Agee on Film*

The passage opens with a general statement committing the writer to justify or illustrate the idea that chances to see silent comedy are rare. Sentence 2 responds with specification, and sentences 3 and 4 continue with the same kind of response. Sentence 5 changes the pattern, responding to sentence 4 with a diversion, signaled by *however*. Then sentences 6 to 9 respond again with specification, four examples of coming events.

Of course not all writing proceeds in exactly this way. Commitment-response units may be a single sentence or may be sequences longer than those in the Agee selection. Narrative writing may be an almost continuous chronological sequence, one event after another. But one good way to develop a composition is to write a sentence that seems worth writing and then respond to its commitment with specification until the idea is fully developed. Then a diversion or a further generalization can begin a new unit.

PARAGRAPHING

Paragraph division, marked by indention, is a device for organizing commitment-response units. A paragraph may mark the limits of a single unit. Or a paragraph may combine two or more related units. The Agee selection above was originally printed as a single paragraph, pulling two units together, although it could plausibly have been printed as two.

When you write, you create or generate paragraphs with a kind of double process—discovery and construction. You may simply write in sequences, with one sentence following another so that each responds to the commitment of whatever precedes it. These sequences fall naturally into units that can be set off by indention to emphasize that they are related. You discover paragraphs as you write. Or, using the other part of the double process, you may start with a paragraph pattern in mind and may choose and order sentences to fill that pattern. You write step by step, sentence by sentence, but you construct your paragraph according to plan.

To see how this combination of processes works to produce a paragraph, assume that you have done the prewriting for a paper entitled "Women's Rights at the University" and have made some progress in the writing. You have decided that your purpose is to argue that the treatment of women on the campus is unfair. You have been talking about rules, have written all you want to write about them, and you respond to your final sentence on rules with a diversion, turning to a new topic.

> Although some of these rules may be justified because they reflect attitudes of society, no such rationalization can explain why the university should favor men in supporting extracurricular activities.

The sentence makes a commitment that could evoke more than one response. You could explain why this discrimination is not justified or turn the discussion in a new direction, but most obviously you might respond by specifying. The sentence suggests that you support the main assertion, that the university favors men's extracurricular activities, and you move toward specific examples to prove the point.

> For example, nobody can justify the university's apparent unfair solicitude for the social life of the male.

You might, of course, have gone directly to specific instances, but the sentence above would take a useful intermediate step, leading to a list of particulars:

> There is a men's lounge in the Union Building, but no women's lounge. Of the organizations officially recognized by the university, eight are exclusively for men, two for women. Four of these organizations have permanent offices in the Union; neither of the women's organizations has been given any space. The two new dormitories built last year, with large living rooms, study rooms, and even kitchen facilities, have both been assigned to men; women remain in the old dormitories with inadequate space for social activities.

As you write the last of these sentences, you realize that someone might offer arguments to oppose it. You forestall objections by additional explanation:

> The new dormitories, of course, were needed to relieve overcrowding in the old men's dorms; but at least one of the new buildings might have been given to women, with men taking over one of the old women's dorms to get necessary space.

After this sentence, you feel that you have amply illustrated the bias favoring male social life, and you respond with a diversion:

> Discrimination is even more obvious in the support given to athletics.

The shift toward a new direction is partly signaled by *even more obvious*. And the new sentence clearly commits the writer to respond with further specification.

    The result of this sentence-by-sentence writing is a sequence of related ideas that can readily be indented as a paragraph—or possibly as two paragraphs with a break before the final sentence. The paragraph would turn out as the following, printed here with levels of specification indicated by indention and small numbers.

> [1]Although some of these rules may be justified because they reflect attitudes of society, no such rationalization can explain why the university should favor men in supporting extracurricular activities.
>> [2]For example, nobody can justify the university's apparent unfair solicitude for the social life of the male.
>>> [3]There is a men's lounge in the Union Building, but no women's lounge.

³Of the organizations officially recognized by the university, eight are exclusively for men, two for women.
³Four of these organizations have permanent offices in the Union; neither of the women's organizations has been assigned any space.
³The two new dormitories built last year, with large living rooms, study rooms, and even kitchen facilities, have both been assigned to men; women remain in the old dormitories with inadequate space for social activities.
⁴The new dormitories, of course, were needed to relieve overcrowding in the old men's dorms, but at least one of the new buildings might have been given to women, with men taking over one of the old women's dormitories to get necessary space.
²Discrimination is even more obvious in the support given athletics.
³Although the university has ample facilities for extensive athletic activities, intercollegiate competition has first call on all of them, and this is exclusively for men.
³Women are allowed to use the swimming pool one night a week—unless the swimming team needs it for practice or a meet.
³Women almost never have access to the fieldhouse or the gymnasium.
³There is an extensive program of intramural athletics for men, but women presumably get enough exercise walking to classes.

The passage illustrates how sequences of commitments and responses fall into units and generate paragraphs.

The Topic Sentence

In the examples above, all the units focus on the first sentence that makes a commitment for the entire unit. The Agee selection, as mentioned before, opens by asserting generally that "the chances to see silent comedy are rare," committing the rest of the unit to show that this is true. Such a sentence, introducing or summarizing a subject, and often defining the direction of a sequence of sentences, is called a topic sentence. It may govern a paragraph, a single unit within a paragraph, or even a group of paragraphs. It is the easiest device for unifying a paragraph.

Since a topic sentence introduces a new topic or a new subtopic, it links what has preceded with what is to follow. It also establishes the new direction for the paragraph, sometimes indicating how the paragraph will be structured. Consider the following:

Nineteenth-century writers admired this culture for two chief reasons: because it was beautiful, and because it was not Christian. They saw their own civilization as squalid and greedy; they praised the Greeks and Romans as noble and spiritual. They felt contemporary Christianity to be mean, ugly, and repressive; they admired the cults of antiquity as free, strong, and graceful. Looking at the soot-laden sky, pierced by factory chimneys and neo-Gothic steeples, they exclaimed

> Great God! I'd rather be
> A Pagan suckled in a creed outworn.
>
> Gilbert Highet, *The Classical Tradition*

The opening sentence is precise, directing the paragraph to be more specific about the two reasons, "it was beautiful" and "it was not Christian." Furthermore, the sentence makes a transition by referring to "this culture." Highet might have written:

> In this connection it is interesting to note that earlier periods exerted a certain charm over many of the more sensitive spirits of the nineteenth century and that among the reasons for this charm were the differences between theirs and an earlier day. They saw in their own civilization . . .

As a topic sentence this could have been worse. It provides a transition, "In this connection," and it would permit the writer to say almost anything. But it is clearly a worse topic sentence than Highet's, just because it is less exact, less precise. It tells the reader too little. It does not restrict the paragraph to those ideas that are to be its content.

Highet might have begun his paragraph in another way:

> Nineteenth-century writers resented living under a soot-laden sky. They resented the growing ugliness of an industrial society. They disliked the factory chimneys that thrust up everywhere, and not only the factories but the neo-Gothic spires, which suggested that the Christianity of the day, like the industry, was ugly. They saw in their own civilization . . .

Again, he did not, and the reason is obvious. He would have provided the reader no transition from previous material. And he would have begun with specifics, without telling the reader why to pay attention to these details.

The Standard Expository Paragraph

Although paragraphs tend to create themselves as one sentence leads to another, some patterns emerge so often that you need to be aware of them. You can take a shortcut to building paragraphs by thinking in terms of what might be called the standard paragraph, a workhorse pattern with many uses. It is built with the type of development emphasized in chapter 3, the use of specific details, and at its simplest it is a single commitment-response unit, a topic sentence followed by a series of particulars. The following illustrates the pattern:

> His folks talked like other folks in the neighborhood. They called themselves "pore" people. A man learned in books was "eddicated." What was certain was "sartin." The syllables came through the nose; "joints" were "j'ints"; fruit "spiled" instead of spoiling; in cornplanting time they

"drapped" the seeds. They went on errands and "brung" things back. Their dogs "follered" the coons. Flannel was "flannen," a bandanna a "banddanner," a chimney a "chimbly," a shadow a "shadder," and mosquitoes plain "skeeters." They "gethered" crops. A creek was a "crick," a cover a "kiver."

Carl Sandburg, *Abraham Lincoln: The Prairie Years*

In the following passage a student uses the same general scheme to describe a high school teacher.

> When I read the essay, "The Teacher as Dragon" by Anna Tuttle Villegas, I was amazed at how much the Dragon Lady reminded me of my sophomore English teacher. She was an amorphous mass of humanity, with sagging wrinkles as far as the eye could see. She wore the same "inevitable thick spectacles," which seemed to magnify her gaze to an ice-cold death stare; you could feel it passing through you like needles of ice, but you wouldn't dare look up and meet it for fear of turning to stone. Her typical attire consisted of a pale green dress (which looked like a clipper ship sail), pink socks, and purple tennis shoes. Before class would start, when everyone was still socializing, you could hear her walking down the hallway toward the class. Boom! Boom! Boom! Echo! Echo! Echo! It sounded like the Jolly Green Giant stomping through a gymnasium. The clamor rose above the din of thirty talking students; dead silence soon followed.

The first sentence commits the writer to show why the Dragon Lady reminded him of his teacher; the remainder of the paragraph musters specifics to illustrate.

Other variations are possible, and in some the simple pattern of topic sentence plus specification may become obscured. Consider the following comments of a reporter sharing the routine of a New York detective.

> Traveling about with a detective, it strikes me, is like being in a mild accident or a fistfight. You feel fine while it's going on, even elated, and the shock of what has happened—or worse, what might have happened—doesn't set in until a bit later. I enjoyed John's company, and since writers are actors too, mimics, role-players of a kind, I felt a little detectivelike myself for the next few days, looking people over more carefully and attributing the very worst possible motives to their behavior. As for John himself, I was able somehow to block out the fact that he carried a loaded gun at all times and indeed was paid, when the circumstances fit, to blow people's heads off with it.

Bruce Jay Friedman, "Lessons of the Street"

The paragraph is a single commitment-response unit, but the opening topic sentence leads to four sentences making different comments about how the writer felt in the company of the detective.

Another variation on this pattern opens with a topic statement, restates the topic more specifically, and then adds a particular example or illustration to reinforce the first sentence. The following student paragraph uses this pattern.

> I have often given my prints, in frames, to my friends, believing they will see what I see in them, that they will appreciate that part of me within the frame. Most do. There are a few, however, who do not see what I present to them. Once I went to a friend's house, a friend to whom I had presented a print in a frame, only to find that the frame was now holding a photograph instead of my print. I looked about the house for the print, but found it nowhere. All that was important to this person was the usefulness of the frame. Much later, I saw my print's final resting place—in a closet crumpled under some old tennis shoes.

The pattern may vary in still another way to include two or more units held together by a topic sentence, as in the following comment on middle-class public interest groups.

> [1] Most of all, members of these groups have a determination to make their presence felt. [2] It was not always thus. [3] "In the old-style service groups, the Boy Scouts and 'friends of the hospital,' " says Carl Clark, "the volunteers weren't really trusted. [4] They were used to carrying out policies that were set by the leadership. [5] It was fine for a Gray Lady to read to a wounded soldier in the hospital, but it wasn't fine for her to ask, 'Why is that soldier lying there all this time without an operation?' [6] In the new public interest groups, people ask questions like that, and they care about the answers." [7] Further, they become impatient with anything short of what they see as direct action to solve a problem. [8] "The people we get don't want study groups or lectures anymore," says Ken Smith of Common Cause. [9] "They say, 'Tell us how to get so-and-so's vote on an issue.' "
>
> Roger M. Williams, "The Rise of Middle Class Activism: Fighting 'City Hall' "

The main topic, that members of these groups want to "make their presence felt," is developed by contrasting past and present. The paragraph breaks into two parts, in a pattern that might be analyzed as follows:

Topic:	[1] Members of groups have determination to make presence felt.
Subtopic 1:	[2] It was not always thus.
Development:	[3]–[5] Volunteers not trusted, expected to follow leadership, not to ask serious questions.
Subtopic 2:	[6] In new groups people ask serious questions.
Development:	[7]–[9] People also want answers to the questions that will lead to direct action.

Conventional Paragraphing

On occasion, paragraphing may be conventional, an arbitrary breaking up of a passage to make it look more readable or provide emphasis. Newspaper stories are conventionally divided into paragraphs of a sentence or two, almost mechanically, so that only a few lines in the narrow columns appear without a break. Some modern writers, using a journalistic style, set off almost every sentence with indention. For example, Marya Mannes uses journalistic indentions in the following, although it is actually in the pattern of a single standard paragraph:

> A French philosopher, Joseph de Maistre, observed that "every individual or national degeneration is immediately revealed by a directly proportional degradation in language."
> He would find further evidence in a nationwide survey made three years ago to find out how well Johnny can write. It was based on uniform writing exercises administered to 86,000 children aged 9, 13 and 17 in 2,500 schools in every section of the country, and to nearly 8,000 young adults.
> Herewith some findings:
> Nine-year-old Americans show almost no command of the basic writing mechanics of grammar, vocabulary, spelling, sentence structure and punctuation.
> Even the best of the 17-year-olds seldom displayed any flair or facility by moving beyond commonplace language.
> Only four or five people in the whole assessment, the survey found, had a really good command of the English language. They could write adequate business letters and personal notes, but their writing usually "lacked imagination, vitality and detail."
>
> Marya Mannes, "Style: The Decline Of"

The first four sentences, set off as three paragraphs, introduce and develop the topic. They funnel the general topic—that national degeneration is shown in a degradation of language—toward a single illustration, a survey of children's writing. Then four sentences, in three paragraphs, cite particular findings of the survey. Thus the page looks different, with more indentions, but the paragraph pattern is the same.

Another convention helps writers distinguish speakers in reports of dialogue. Indention introduces every speaker and every change in speakers:

> "Good evening. It's a cold night," said Holmes.
> The salesman nodded, and shot a questioning glance at my companion.
> "Sold out of geese, I see," continued Holmes, pointing at the bare slabs of marble.
> "Let you have 500 tomorrow morning."
> "That's no good."

Appropriate Paragraphing

Although a topic sentence and a series of supporting details may fall naturally into a pattern, collection of more varied kinds of information may require conscious organization. Especially in revision you may need to reorder the sequences of sentences and may find it profitable to work them into a standard pattern. Compare, for example, a first draft and a revision of a comment on a student election:

> George McDermott is likely to win the election as president of the Associated Students. He is both a quarterback and an actor, and he has support from organizations all over the campus. Meanwhile, some candidates for offices are running unopposed or are opposed by candidates who have little support. The widest interest in the election is being drawn by the races for the three vacant seats in the Student Senate. Many campaigners believe that the election of even one candidate for the Senate supported by the Associated Resident Halls Party will assure the decline or abolishment of football at State University. The reasons for this belief are complicated and will later require some analysis. Meanwhile, Nancy Jenkins and Dorothy Cochran are leading a lively field of candidates for the presidency of AWS. That race is attracting no attention off the campus, and very little on the campus, though the question of who is to be elected to the Student Senate has become a statewide issue. The other contests, except for the race for the Student Senate, are sideshows. None of the freshman candidates, for instance, is well known or widely supported. But the Senate race has raised questions of such interest and has stimulated so much electioneering that billboard space is getting scarce on the campus, with placards plastered all the way from the president's gate to the back door of the Aggie Greenhouse.

Although sentences follow one another without notable confusion, the paragraph reads like a string of notes. The writer has listed details but has done little to show what the evidence means. The following revision provides an overall topic sentence and orders the material into two units. Each unit is introduced by a subtopic sentence, making a commitment followed by specification. The paragraph is printed with indentions and small numbers to mark levels of specification.

> [1]Interest in the State University elections this year centers on the race for three vacant seats in the Student Senate.
>   [2]The other contests are likely to be sideshows.
>   [3]George McDermott, known as both an actor and a quarterback, has support from so many organizations that his election as president of the Associated Students is practically conceded.
>   [3]Some candidates for other class offices are running unopposed, and others are attracting little attention.
>   [4]None of the freshman candidates, for instance, are well known or widely supported.
>   [3]For the presidency of AWS, Nancy Jenkins and Dorothy Cochran are

leading a lively field of candidates, but the race is attracting no attention off campus and relatively little on campus.
[2]The election of three members to the Senate, on the other hand, has become a question of interest throughout the state and has led to so much electioneering that placards are plastered all the way from the president's gate to the back door of the Aggie Greenhouse.

The first sentence takes from the original version what seems to be the main idea, the interest in the senate election. The second sentence is a diversion, but it supports the topic sentence negatively, opening a discussion of why nonsenate races lack interest. Then a series of specifications supports this subtopic until a diversion in the seventh sentence returns to the topic sentence and introduces a new unit on the senate races. The final sentence also provides a transition to the next unit.

Unity in Paragraphs

Paragraphing is flexible in English. As we have seen, a paragraph may be a single commitment-response unit or several units. Or it may be a long unit divided into subunits. But if the writing is to be clear, the units need to be related in such a way that the reader can understand the relationship; that is, they must have unity or focus. The purpose of organizing material into units is to help the reader organize ideas. Usually this can best be achieved by keeping the ideas focused on a central topic and avoiding the inclusion of irrelevant material. The following paragraph suffers from a lack of unity:

>Good strategy is essential to success. When I used to watch my high school football team play back in Mountain View, I used to think this a lot. I was trying to plan my future then, and my parents wanted me to go into the family business. I wanted to be an artist though. There's nothing I like better than to paint a picture of some beautiful landscape or person. I think that art is important because it gives us a different way of looking at things. Anyway, football is a sport that's a lot like life: you have first downs and touchdowns, the outcome of the game depends on strategy, and sometimes the quarterback is sacked. But I thought that if I could plan it just right, I could convince my parents to send me to art school. Even if you lose the game, that's not the whole season.

The opening sentence could serve as a topic sentence, and it seems to commit the writer to provide material in support of the importance of good strategy. Instead it wanders off with autobiographical details, the importance of art, and clichés about football, which do not appear related to the main idea. The paragraph needs a new start with ideas developed in commitment-response sequences. For example, the writer could take the first idea and write a unified paragraph:

>One day as I watched my high school football team, I realized that a good strategy is essential to success in life—not only in football. In football the

outcome of the game depends on how well you plan, how you create the first downs that lead to the eventual touchdown. In life, you do much the same. You plan the small steps that lead to the desired outcome—the touchdown and then final victory.

Guide to Revision ¶

APPROPRIATE PARAGRAPHING

Revise choppy or disorganized writing into paragraph patterns that clarify relationships between commitment-response units.

ORIGINAL

In the suburbs and on the highways of many large American cities, young men are killing themselves by the thousands.
    Many of the accidents could be avoided if a little common sense were used. When a boy gets behind the steering wheel of a car, the first thing he thinks of is how fast he can go.
    Speed is the reason for so many deaths. The teen-ager does not seem to realize that his car is dangerous if it is not used sensibly.
    There is another reason for a large number of teen-age automobile accidents.
    This is the playing of games with cars. These senseless games kill hundreds of teenagers every year.
    The most popular game is "Chicken." Two or more cars . . .
[*The body of the theme concerns the game mentioned in the last sentence, but the preceding matter is broken into what appear as five paragraphs. This passage is not well planned or closely knit, but such plan as it has is obscured by the meaningless indentions.*]

REVISION

On the highways in and around many large American cities, young men are killing themselves by the thousands in automobile accidents that could be avoided by the use of a little common sense. First, young drivers must learn to be sensible about speed. When a boy gets behind a steering wheel, the first thing he thinks of is how fast he can go. He does not seem to realize that his car is dangerous if it is not used sensibly. Second, young drivers must learn some sense about the senseless games played with cars, which kill hundreds of teen-agers each year.
    The most popular game is "Chicken." Two or more cars . . .
[*Five paragraphs have been combined into one, but the revision has involved more than removing the indentions. For example, the first two sentences have become a single sentence, with its elements subordinated. And three sentences have become a single sentence to close the paragraph. The remark of the original about common sense has been exploited to provide unity.*]

COHERENCE

One result of the revision of the paragraph above is that relationships among the ideas are clearer. The paragraph seems to hang together; one sentence flows from another. We say that the parts *cohere*. The following contrast provides another illustration of the importance of coherence. Consider first a list of sentences about the American opossum.

> The opossum has survived in definitely hostile surroundings for 70 million years.
> The opossum is small; it can easily find hiding places.
> The opossum can always find a little food, while big animals starve.
> The individual opossum is not very delicate; it can stand severe punishment.
> It "plays 'possum" when it gets into trouble.
> It can go without food for a long time.
> Many different things are food to an opossum.
> Traits of the opossum have a high survival value.
> The opossum is a survivor from the Age of Reptiles.

These sentences, in this order, do not produce a clear paragraph. There is no sense of coherence, no help for the reader in knowing how the bits of information are related. But a professional writer was able to form this information into a successful paragraph.

> The reasons our opossum has survived in definitely hostile surroundings for 70 million years are evident. One is his small size: small animals always find hiding places, they always find a little food, where the big ones starve. Another of its assets was its astounding fecundity: if local catastrophes left only a few survivors, it did not take long to re-establish a thriving population. Also the individual opossum is not exactly delicate: it can stand severe punishment—during which it "plays 'possum" and then scampers away—and it can go without food for a considerable time. Finally, a great many different things are "food" to an opossum. Each of these traits has a high survival value, and their combination has presented the United States with a survivor from the Age of Reptiles.
> Willy Ley, *The Lungfish and the Unicorn*

The paragraph differs from the list largely because it has coherence; the elements hang together. The coherence grows in part from aids to writing that we have already discussed. The paragraph begins with a topic sentence that provides a focus—why the opossum has survived so long. It then develops with an orderly series of specific responses to the opening commitment—its small size, its fecundity, its hardiness, and its ability to eat almost anything. In addition, the paragraph provides transitional words—*one, another, also, finally*—that help the reader see how sentences are related, how one idea follows another, how the passage is organized. Ideas "track"; the paragraph has continuity.

DEVICES FOR COHERENCE

Devices for coherence and continuity can clarify the movement of thought through a paragraph, guiding the reader through the sequence of commitments and responses. Often, of course, coherence develops almost automatically as a writer concentrates on a subject; but frequently, especially in revision, conscious attention to devices like the following can improve prose.

Repetition of Key Ideas

Repeated references to central ideas may bind parts of a passage together. Notice how a central idea echoes through the following:

> In time of peace in the modern world, if one is thoughtful and careful, it is rather more difficult to be killed or maimed in the outland places of the globe than it is in the streets of our great cities, but the atavistic urge toward danger persists and its satisfaction is called adventure. However, your adventurer feels no gratification in crossing Market Street in San Francisco against the traffic. Instead, he will go to a good deal of trouble and expense to get himself killed in the South Seas. (In reputedly rough water, he will go in a canoe; he will expose his tolerant and uninoculated blood to strange viruses.) This is adventure. It is possible that his ancestor, wearying of the humdrum attacks of the saber-tooth longed for the good old days of pterodactyl and triceratops.
>
> John Steinbeck and Edward F. Ricketts, *Sea of Cortez*

A reference to killing, danger, or adventure occurs in every sentence and holds the passage together.

Continuing a Subject

Repetition of a subject from sentence to sentence promotes coherence.

> The heroes who pushed the frontier constantly westward were rough men, with gargantuan appetites and little refinement, men who did prodigiously hard physical labor. They are epitomized in such folk characters as Paul Bunyan, Ben Hardin (Davy Crockett's mythical companion who had taken mermaids for concubines), and Mike Fink. Their idea of play was the rough-and-tumble brawl, in which they brought to perfection the manly arts of biting, butting, scratching, and gouging. Their ways of life were indeed not modest; neither were their opinions of themselves; neither was their language.
>
> Thomas Pyles, *Words and Ways of American English*

The passage carries through a single subject, *heroes*, designated by the synonym *men* and referred to in a series of pronouns, *who*, *they*, and *their*.

Word Order and Coherence

The links between sentences, the structural indicators of the commitment-response patterns of ideas, can be reinforced through word order. The following two sentences are linked, even though the subjects differ, because the subjects appear in the same relative place in each:

> An old man stood in front of the monkey cage excitedly throwing peanuts at a score of begging arms. A small boy only a few feet away sat with his face buried in a comic book.

The repetition of word order sharpens the contrast between the two main actions. On the other hand, variations from usual word order may provide bridges, carrying special emphasis from one sentence to another.

> In front of the monkey cage stood an old man, excitedly throwing peanuts at a score of begging arms. A few feet away sat a small boy, his face buried in a comic book.

The shift in order throws emphasis on the location, heightens the contrast in the actions by stressing the nearness of the two persons, and helps link the sentences through the repetition of the reversed pattern. There is some loss of continuity when the word order pattern is not repeated, as in the following:

> In front of the monkey cage stood an old man, excitedly throwing peanuts at a score of begging arms. A small boy only a few feet away sat with his face buried in a comic book.

Transitional Words and Coherence

Transitional words can clarify order. The following are some of the more useful transitional terms:

> To mark an addition or continuation: *and, furthermore, next, moreover, in addition, again, also, likewise, similarly, finally, second*
>
> To introduce or to emphasize a contrast or alternative: *but, or, nor, still, however, nevertheless, on the contrary, on the other hand, conversely*
>
> To mark a conclusion: *therefore, thus, then, in conclusion, consequently, as a result, in other words, accordingly*
>
> To introduce an illustration or example: *thus, for example, for instance, that is, namely*

Others indicate shifts of time or introduce clauses; almost all connectives can provide transitions. Overuse of transitional expressions makes stiff prose; careful use of them helps make clear prose. For example, look again at the paragraph about the opossum on page 86. Notice that the first sentence is cast as the topic sentence, "reasons our opossum has survived," and each sentence after that is introduced by a transitional word and repeated word order. Or notice the use of transitional words and a repeated pattern in a student's essay arguing against capital punishment.

> Some argue that capital punishment deters capital crime. *However,* there is no proof that the state's taking of a human life is a deterrent to murder or other capital crimes. *In fact,* some studies have found that states which have abolished capital punishment have lower murder rates than states which have retained it ("Capital Punishment," 158). *Still* other comparisons show that no unusual increase results when a state abolishes capital punishment. *Further,* statistics point to no discernible difference in the murder rates between states which have capital punishment and those that do not (Shapiro). *Taken together,* these studies suggest that capital punishment fails as a deterrent.

Guide to Revision   **Coh**

COHERENCE

Revise, using devices such as repetition, continuing a subject, parallel order, or transitional words to make ideas flow smoothly.

ORIGINAL

Modern scholars now agree that the ancestor of the Romance languages is not now much taught in our schools. It was Vulgar Latin, which is usually taught today only in graduate schools. The kind of language that was written by Virgil and Cicero is the kind that is usually taught both in high school and in college, but it is not the kind from which French or any other language of that sort has come. In English we have words from the language of the Romans, and some of those words did come from the language written by famous Romans. However, what are called Romance languages did not. The working men were the ones who determined the language in the various countries that had been conquered by Caesar and other classical generals. Church Latin is still spoken but is not much taught. Vulgar Latin is made up of words spoken by the common people, or *vulgus*. [*This paragraph is confused, partly because of faulty order, but partly also because sentences are not linked by synonyms and repeated words. Three ideas run parallel in the paragraph: the kinds of Latin, the descent of the Romance language, the teaching of Latin in the schools. These ideas should be distinct but should also be tied together.*]

REVISION

The modern Romance languages come from Latin, but not from the Latin usually taught in the schools. There are several Latins, including Classical Latin, Church Latin, and Vulgar Latin. Of these three divisions of the Latin language, Classical Latin is about the only one taught now. Church Latin is still spoken but is seldom taught to undergraduates. Vulgar Latin is taught only in a few graduate schools. Yet Vulgar Latin is the one that all modern Romance languages came from—Italian, French, Spanish, Portuguese, and Romanic. Classical Latin has accounted for words borrowed by these languages, as it accounted for words borrowed by English, but all scholars now agree that the Romance languages did not come from the classical speech of Virgil and Cicero. French and Italian and Spanish came from the Latin speakers who were working in France and Italy and Spain, the soldiers, the merchants, the laboring men, that is, the *vulgus*, whose speech is known as Vulgar Latin.
[*The three ideas are carried through the paragraph by repetition of such words as Latin, and the general use of such synonyms and partial synonyms as "Vulgar Latin" and "the classical speech of Virgil and Cicero."*]

However connects the second sentence to the first and shifts to an opposite view. *In fact* introduces a specific example of this opposing point of view. *Still* indicates that another, and similar, example will follow, as does *further* introducing the next sentence. In the last sentence, *taken together* indicates that the writer is making a summary statement about the issue. Try reading the paragraph without these transitional words and notice the loss in coherence. The student has gained additional coherence by continuing a subject—*some studies, other comparisons, statistics,* and *these studies*—and repeating a sentence pattern. We follow her reasoning because she has carefully structured her paragraph.

FOR STUDY AND WRITING

A. Following are sentences from paragraphs about language, each followed by four alternative succeeding sentences. Indicate which of the alternatives makes an adequate response to the commitment of each sentence, and indicate which would not move the development ahead. One alternative in each group appeared in the original paragraph, but frequently more than one of the alternatives would be a suitable second sentence.

1. Of course there are many ways of making sound.
   L. M. Myers, *The Roots of Modern English*
   a. Most of these, however, are not suitable to the production of language.
   b. Crickets rub their legs together and ruffed grouse drum on hollow logs, but neither method seems to permit much variety.
   c. Variations in pitch depend on the frequency of vibrations of the sound waves.
   d. Sounds are the basis of human speech; communication is possible because different sounds are arbitrarily given different symbolic significances.
2. Loan words not only alter their meaning in the course of the borrowing process, but they are equally liable to change after they have become a naturalized part of the English language.
   Albert H. Marckwardt, *American English*
   a. A loan word is a word borrowed from another language.
   b. Examples include even words adopted in the seventeenth century from American Indian languages.

c. Borrowing accounts for much of the rapid expansion of the vocabulary of the English language, and especially for the growth of American English.

d. *Powwow,* one of the very early American Indian adoptions, originally bore its etymological meaning of priest or medicine man.

3. There is practically no limit to the number of social affinities revealed in differences of language.

Dwight Bolinger, *Aspects of Language*

a. Many of these social distinctions, however, produce only insignificant language differences.

b. The bases of social class distinctions in America differ, of course, from those in many other countries.

c. To age, sex, occupation, and occasion, it would be necessary to add religion, politics, lodge affiliation, preference as to sports or amusements, and any other circumstances under which people meet and speak.

d. Language differences are of many kinds, but among the most interesting are those that distinguish geographical dialects.

4. The era of discovery and exploration brought new knowledge about the languages of the world.

John B. Carroll, *The Study of Language*

a. Travelers and missionaries wrote grammars and dictionaries of languages they found in Africa, America, and other parts of the world.

b. There are certainly more than two thousand different languages in existence throughout the world today.

c. Much of this knowledge was inaccurate, based on hasty descriptions and colored by prejudices and misconceptions, but it stimulated the kinds of speculation that led to modern linguistics.

d. Using this language, however, required ingenuity and imagination.

B. The following groups of sentences are taken from published paragraphs but not in their original order. In each group, one sentence states the main topic, and the others present subordinate ideas. Rearrange them so that the main idea is stated first and the subordinate ideas grouped after it. Then decide whether this order seems to be the most logical for the sentences within their paragraphs.

1. a. All our energies ought to be going into the attempt to get world attention for this objective, so that a framework will be created within which sources of income will not depend on voluntary offerings or payments, any more than individual citizens may decide when, how, and if their taxes are to be paid.

   b. The United Nations is not a country club for privileged members who have access to the facilities so long as they keep up their dues.

c. The United Nations is, or should be, a world constitutional body with complete jurisdiction in those matters concerning the common safety of the world's peoples.

Norman Cousins

2. a. However, the Chinese are a proud people.
    b. They are not partial to foreigners, and they are thoroughly confident of the superiority of their age-old culture.
    c. They have not yet recovered from the wounds and indignities which the Western world unjustly and arrogantly inflicted upon them during the last century.

James S. Duncan

3. a. *Huckleberry Finn* deals directly with the virtue and depravity of man's heart.
    b. *Tom Sawyer* has the truth of honesty—what it says about things and feelings is never false and always both adequate and beautiful.
    c. It is more intense truth, fiercer and more complex.
    d. The truth of *Huckleberry Finn* is of a different kind from that of *Tom Sawyer*.

Lionel Trilling

C. Consider the following sequences of sentences. Which provide good transitions? Which are inadequate and why? Revise any that are weak or vague.

1. The dean concluded by saying that whether educators like it or not, college students today are primarily interested in getting jobs. My father said that when he came to the University the emphasis was on becoming cultured men and women.
2. Drug addiction on campuses is quite different from the same problem as it appears in secondary schools. First, let us consider the rash of drug addiction in junior and senior high schools.
3. Everybody had left by midnight, and we went to bed. I put the coffee on and started to mix batter for pancakes.
4. The poll to assess student sentiment showed overwhelming enthusiasm for the proposed Student Union Association. They decided I should be chairman of the membership drive committee.
5. Here with a view of the mountains on three sides and the tiny creek near the center of the area was a perfect site for the new school. The site was nearly fifty miles from a sizable town. Supplies and help would be a problem. Building costs would be high.
6. Interpreting local news, therefore, is perhaps the most important single function of the college newspaper. National affairs should be of interest to college students and college journalists.
7. Thus for a century or two, the natives of Southeast Asia have associated extortion, brutality, and bad manners with white men. They are making

white men pay—all white men, from whatever country they come and whatever their previous connection with Asia—for the mistakes and crimes of a few.

D. Rewrite the following paragraphs, attempting to improve the continuity from sentence to sentence:

1. What to wear was a very important problem to me. Blue was the color which my mother considered most flattering to me, but I liked red. I was only in the seventh grade. It was very hard for me to find a formal that fit me. Dress designers apparently did not take sufficient account of the special problems of seventh-graders. Many dresses, both blue and red, were presented. I did not seem to have curves in the right places. When I did find a suitable dress, the alterations turned out to be more complicated than making the dress could have been.

2. *(The following is a rewrite of a review of a book about the "bad old days" a century or so ago.)*
   A lot of alcohol was consumed. A number of drugs were consumed, too. There were quite a lot of immigrants, and these immigrant groups had traditions of drinking. This is all according to the historian Bettman. Patented elixirs were sold at fairs, and some were even prescribed by doctors, and these nostrums were mainly alcohol mixed with other drugs. The veterans of the Civil War, like the veterans of more recent wars, came home hooked on drugs. This, also, Bettman reports. The favorite drug was laudanum. Mothers who were living in the 1880's—most of them, it is said—gave their babies baby sirup that was spiked with morphine, and somewhat later, in 1898 to be exact, the same pharmaceutical house that gave the world aspirin marketed a cough medicine that contained heroin.

E. Use the thesis sentences in Exercise F, chapter 3, as topic sentences and develop each into a unified paragraph.

5

Organization: Analysis and Classification

Order is heaven's first law.
ALEXANDER POPE

To write is to disarrange the dictionary.
JEAN COCTEAU

Writing, as we observed in the preceding chapter, can be thought of as a kind of linear progression. One thing leads to another. A commitment activates a response which becomes a commitment for another response, and so on. Ideas group themselves into units, fall into order, into a series.

Writing, however, can also be thought of as a process of putting these units of thought into orderly patterns to show how they are related. Words and sentences are arranged in a sequence; but also, especially in any piece of discourse longer than a short paragraph, they are arranged in a kind of hierarchy, a system based on ranking or classifying. A major purpose of a composition is to establish some individual relationships among ideas. To accomplish this purpose, the composition is arranged into a pattern, to establish a central structure and fit parts to it. Analysis and classification are basic processes—actually different aspects of the same process—in making this arrangement, in bringing order out of chaos.

ANALYSIS

We have already observed how analysis, dividing wholes into parts, can be useful in limiting a topic (chapter 1). Analysis is also a way of establishing an organizational pattern for a piece of writing. A main topic can be analyzed into parts, each of which becomes a main section of the paper. And each of these parts may be analyzed into its parts, which become the material of the section.

Obviously all your essays will not require a scientific analysis to dictate an organization. But analysis can help. Suppose you decide to write a paper on what you consider unwise or unfair practices in an office where you worked. Analyzing informally you could think of the main types of bad practices you want to discuss—for instance, inequitable salaries, sex discrimination, favoritism, a lack of any grievance procedure, poor leadership at the management level. Such a list might not be a complete analysis, but it would work as a start for your organization, with each topic a main section of the paper. You might find, of course, that some of the divisions overlap or that some others exist, and you would modify your plan accordingly.

CLASSIFICATION

Analysis divides things into parts; classification puts the parts into groups. If, for instance, you established the main sections for your paper on office practices, a next step would be to group the details you remembered about what happened into each of these sections. You would classify one set of details under poor leadership by the management, another set under sex discrimination. With analysis and classification working together, you would have a scheme for putting all your material in order.

Classification brings likes together and distinguishes them from unlikes. Like analyses, however, classifications can be made on different bases. As a simple example, consider the following items: fire truck, bluebird, violet, yellow convertible, goldfinch, poinsettia, sunflower, blue bicycle, cardinal. They can obviously be classified by kind.

Vehicles	**Birds**	**Flowers**
fire truck	bluebird	violet
yellow convertible	goldfinch	poinsettia
blue bicycle	cardinal	sunflower

But the same objects can be classified on the basis of color:

Red	Blue	Yellow
fire truck	blue bicycle	yellow convertible
cardinal	bluebird	goldfinch
poinsettia	violet	sunflower

The students in a classroom can be classified by the registrar as freshmen, sophomores, juniors, and seniors; by a minister as Baptists, Roman Catholics, Episcopalians, Methodists; by the instructor as A students, B students, C students; by the football coach as potential spectators, potential halfbacks, potential linemen. The purposes of the classifier determine the basis for the classification.

But items should be classified on only one basis at a time. It is not useful to classify apples as green, yellow, red, small, and winter; the bases for classification—color, size, time of ripening—differ, and the classes overlap. Such cross classification can confuse the organization of a paper. Consider the following introduction:

> Between 1932 and 1936 the government of the United States created a number of temporary bureaus and agencies. Why were some of the supposedly temporary agencies accepted permanently? I shall consider four groups of agencies: agricultural agencies, financial agencies, agencies established after 1936, and agencies that exist today.

The first two classes are established on the basis of the business of the agencies, the third on time of establishment, and the fourth on permanence of the agency. The classes overlap. The following suggests a revision of the final sentence that establishes classes on the same basis:

> I shall consider the agencies in four groups: those abandoned after a short trial, those replaced by other agencies, those abandoned because their purpose was accomplished, and those still in existence.

The new classification, based on the permanence of the agencies, is more consistent with the purpose proposed for the paper.

COORDINATION AND SUBORDINATION

In writing, the results of analysis and classification are reflected in two related structural devices, coordination and subordination. They depend on nothing inherent in ideas or things themselves, but they indicate relationships we want to give to ideas. *Ham and eggs,* to take a simple example, may be coordinated in the sentence "He ate ham and scrambled eggs." The two are put into a coordinate pattern; that is, they are presented in such a way that the reader finds them bearing the same—an equal—relationship to the rest of the sentence. *And* is the most common signal of coordination.

Nothing in the nature of the two foods requires this sort of relationship, and the sentence, with equal logic, might be "He ate eggs scrambled with ham," in which *ham* is subordinate to *eggs*, or "He ate ham garnished with scrambled eggs," in which *eggs* is subordinate. In the second and third sentences, ham and eggs are not coordinated; they are not listed as two items of equal rank, independent of each other. One is subordinate to the other, not because one is less important, but because the writer wants to talk about them differently—about eggs as they are prepared in a particular way involving ham, or about ham as it is served along with eggs.

The organization of a piece of writing depends on these concepts of coordination and subordination. The parts of a topic discovered by analysis are put into a structure that makes them subordinate to the main topic, but often coordinate with one another. The items classified into one of these sections are made subordinate to the main topic of the section. The indentions in the printing of the following indicate this pattern of coordination and subordination.

> [1]The English language is spoken or read by the largest number of people in the world, for historical, political, and economic reasons;
> [1]but it may also be true that it owes something of its wide appeal to qualities and characteristics inherent in itself.
>> [2]What are these characteristic features which outstand in making the English language what it is, which give it its individuality and make it of this worldwide significance?
>> [2]Some of the more obvious of these are the following:
>>> [3]First and most important is its extraordinarily receptive and adaptable heterogeneousness—the varied ease and readiness with which it has taken to itself material from almost everywhere in the world and has made the new elements of language its own.
>>>> [4]English, which when the Anglo-Saxons first conquered England in the fifth and sixth centuries was almost a "pure" or unmixed language—which could make new words for new ideas from its own compounded elements and had hardly any foreign words—has become the most "mixed" of languages, having received throughout its history all kinds of foreign elements with ease and assimilated them all to its own character.
>>>> [4]Though its copiousness of vocabulary is outstanding, it is its amazing variety and heterogeneousness which is even more striking;
>>>> [4]and this general receptiveness to new elements has contributed to making it a suitable and attractive vehicle in so many parts of the world.
>>> [3]A second outstanding characteristic of English is . . .

The opening sentence, with two coordinate parts, is at level 1. It is a topic statement, or thesis, for the entire essay, and other sentences are subordinate to it. At level 2 are sentences that expand the topic of the first sentence, and sentences at level 3, which introduce "these characteristic features" of the language, are subordinate to them. Three sentences at a fourth level of subordination provide instances of the "heterogeneousness" introduced in the level-3 sentence. The opening sentence of the next paragraph is back at level 3, introducing a second characteristic and coordinate with the sentence introducing the first. Each of the following paragraphs of the essay begins with a coordinate level-3 sentence introducing third, fourth, and fifth characteristics of the language.

USING ANALYSIS AND CLASSIFICATION

If we return to the paragraph on strategy in chapter 4 (p. 84), we can see how analysis and classification can work together to organize ideas. The paragraph as originally written was unsuccessful because it lacked coherence, but the student who wrote it was able to produce an acceptable paper by relating and reorganizing the material it contained. As he analyzed his original paragraph, he saw four different, but possibly related, ideas:

1. Good strategy is essential to success.
2. Good strategy is essential to football.
3. I want to be an artist, but my parents want me to go into the family business.
4. If I apply strategy to my parents, maybe they will let me go to art school.

After thinking about what he wanted to say, he realized that these could be revised into four coordinate ideas. These could be arranged chronologically to describe how he convinced his parents to send him to art school. The ideas he discovered through this second analysis were:

1. A thesis: Strategy is important in life just as it is in football (original ideas 1 and 2).
2. Example: My decision to apply strategy to convince my parents to send me to art school (original idea 4).
3. The first step: How I convinced my parents that art is important to me (expansion of ideas 3 and 4).
4. The next step: The actual strategy I used (expansion of idea 4).

The student then could classify specifics under each of the general statements, or topic sentences, which illustrated his thesis or main idea—that strategy is important in life. For example, under idea 3, he needed to show the reader how he actually convinced his parents of the importance of art in his life. What did he do? What concrete instances did he use? He chose an example from his original paragraph, "for me there is nothing more enjoyable than painting a beautiful landscape or person," and added the idea that art can change one's perspective on life.

Following his general plan, he wrote his first draft. As he reread it, however, he realized that paragraph 3 contained two coordinate ideas—the enjoyment art gave him and the educational value of art—both of which could be expanded:

> 1. First, I had to convince them that art was important to me. The family business was okay, but I wanted them to understand that for me there is nothing more enjoyable than painting a picture of some beautiful landscape or a person. 2. Art can also give us a different perspective. For example, when I saw the painting of Mountain View, I saw it in a new light.

During his next revision, he divided that paragraph into two coordinate parts, added more illustrations, polished the copy, and submitted the following draft:

The Art of Strategy and The Strategy of Art

One day as I watched my high school football team, I realized that a good strategy is essential to success in life—not just in football. In football the outcome of the game depends on how well you plan, how you create the first downs that lead to the eventual touchdown. In life, you do much the same. You plan the small steps that lead to the desired outcome—the touchdown and then final victory.

I was able to apply this strategy when I realized that I wanted to go to art school. My parents had always wanted me to stay home and go into the family business, and I agreed until my senior year. Then I realized that I wanted to be an artist—at least I wanted to try—and I knew I would have to marshall my strategy to convince my parents to allow me to attend art school for a year, then maybe another, until I could demonstrate to them that I could succeed in this career.

First, I had to convince them that art was important to me. The family business was important, too, but I wanted them to understand that for me there is nothing more enjoyable than painting a picture of a beautiful landscape or a person. I have often lost myself for hours in the hills behind our house trying to capture the different shades of the sunset as the sun slipped behind the hill.

Art is important, too, because it gives us a different perspective. I once saw a painting of my hometown. I had never noticed how quiet and peaceful—how right—the town looked, tucked into the surrounding hills. I could see the harmony of the natural landscape and the man-made city. I could appreciate the way the town followed the meandering river that ran through the heart of our valley. It made me see Mountain View in a whole new way.

So I began my strategy, my campaign, to convince my parents of my perspective. I casually left half-finished pictures propped on chairs around the house. I dropped small mentions of art shows and exhibits into my conversation. I urged them to attend a traveling art show visiting our town. And finally, I invited them to the high school art show. Touchdown. When they saw the first-place blue ribbon attached to my painting of our old barn, dappled in late afternoon sunshine, they were convinced. I was allowed to enroll in art school for one year.

But the final victory is not mine yet; now my real work has begun.

Through analysis and classification and a series of revisions, a disconnected paragraph has become a plausibly organized paper.

STRATEGIES FOR ORGANIZATION

Through the revisions, this student paper has also developed an arrangement of its main ideas into a sequence, describing steps in his campaign to influence his parents in the order in which they occurred. This chronological pattern is one of the most useful in writing, but it is not the only one. The following are common organizational strategies that can be used in both writing and revising.

Chronological Organization

In the following sentences, order shows a relationship in time:

> A yellow convertible flashed by the billboard and screamed around the curve. A traffic policeman wheeled his motorcycle from its hiding place and roared into the highway.

Because one sentence precedes the other, the reader assumes that the event it describes precedes the other event. Reversing the order of the sentences would reverse the order of events and save a fine for the driver of the convertible.

Any record of happenings can almost always be planned around related times—often by the simple procedure of putting first things first, as in the following description of Mary Stuart's preparation for execution:

> She laid her crucifix on her chair. The chief executioner took it as a perquisite, but was ordered instantly to lay it down. The lawn veil was lifted carefully off, not to disturb the hair, and was hung upon the rail. The

black robe was next removed. Below it was a petticoat of crimson velvet. The black jacket followed, and under the jacket was a bodice of crimson satin. One of her ladies handed her a pair of crimson sleeves, with which she hastily covered her arms; and thus she stood on the black scaffold with the black figures all around her, blood-red from head to foot.

James Anthony Froude, History of England

In technical or commercial writing, chronology may provide the best way of tracing the successive actions in a process—how to do something or how something is made or how it works.

Spatial Organization

Order can show relationship in space as well as in time. Describing a scene, a writer can arrange details as they meet the eye.

> The ship turned sharply and steamed slowly in. It was a great landlocked harbour big enough to hold a fleet of battleships; and all around it rose, high and steep, the green hills. Near the entrance, getting such breeze as blew from the sea, stood the governor's house in a garden. The Stars and Stripes dangled languidly from a flag staff.

W. Somerset Maugham, "Rain"

A writer may clarify order in space with words like those italicized in the following:

> *On* the shelving bank of the river, *among* the slimy stones of a causeway—not the special causeway of the Six Jolly Fellowships, which had a landing place of its own, but another, a little *removed* and very *near* to the old windmill which was the denounced man's dwelling-place—were a few boats; some, moored and already beginning to float; others, hauled up *above* the reach of the tide. *Under* one of these latter Eugene's companion disappeared.

Charles Dickens, Our Mutual Friend

Ascending or Descending Order

Writing may follow an order of importance or emphasis, either ascending or descending. A newspaper reporter goes from the most newsworthy events or results to the least newsworthy, knowing that many readers do not bother to read all of a news account. A teacher, however, may start with the easiest part of an explanation and work toward the harder parts. Anyone trying to change people's opinions may use the order of climax, from the least interesting to the most interesting, from the least damaging to the most damaging. The pattern may govern the organization of an entire essay or any segment of it, and the order reflects the writer's purpose. In the following passage the statements move toward the sweeping claim of the final summary:

> It's hardly an accident that Robert Frost coupled poetry and power. For he saw poetry as the means of saving power from itself. When power leads man toward arrogance, poetry reminds him of his limitations. When power narrows the areas of man's concern, poetry reminds him of the richness and diversity of his existence. When power corrupts, poetry cleanses.
> John F. Kennedy, *Dedication of the Robert Frost Library*

The relatively specific second and third sentences lead to a broader generalization in the fourth sentence that becomes a kind of climax.

Logical Organization

Much expository writing must reveal complicated relationships that can be loosely described as "logical"—such as cause and effect, conclusion and reasons, comparison or contrast, or the steps in a chain of reasoning (see chapter 13). Sometimes, in fact, organization is logical in relatively strict senses. Commander X receives unexpected reinforcements just at the time the river freezes over between him and his enemy, and his scouts report that the opposing forces have been decimated by a plague. Commander X decides to attack. The organization of a description of this decision is clearly that of cause to effect. Conversely, consider the situation of a householder who discovers water leaking into his living room. The leak is an effect; what is the cause? He checks the flashing of the chimney, the calking around nails, the flue, and the concrete cap on the chimney. All seem to be in order. Then he remembers that although the chimney is built of porous blocks it has never been waterproofed. He concludes that the chimney needs waterproofing. The order here is that of effect back to cause.

In the following, Thomas Jefferson is urging a young student friend of his to examine the claims of truth made by different religions.

> For example, in the book of Joshua, we are told, the sun stood still several hours. Were we to read that fact in Livy or Tacitus, we should class it with their showers of blood, speaking of statues, beasts, etc. But it is said, that the writer of that book was inspired. Examine, therefore, candidly, what evidence there is of his having been inspired. The pretension is entitled to inquiry, because millions believe it. On the other hand, you are astronomer enough to know how contrary it is to the law of nature that a body revolving on its axis, as the earth does, should have stopped, should not, by that sudden stoppage, have prostrated animals, trees, buildings, and should after a certain time have resumed its revolutions, and that without a second general prostration. Is this arrest of the earth's motion, or the evidence which affirms it, most within the law of probabilities?
> Thomas Jefferson, *Letter to Peter Carr*

Jefferson orders his idea logically. He states a proposition, breaks it into parts, and presents evidence that moves toward a conclusion.

THE OUTLINE

One useful device for organizing any extended piece of prose is the outline. It can be used to establish levels of coordination and subordination and to provide a blueprint for keeping relationships clear and consistent. Often, as in planning the paper on "The Art of Strategy," (p. 100), rough scribbled notes are the only outline necessary, but frequently a carefully prepared outline, using a standard form, can be helpful in at least three ways: (1) as a method of planning a paper—as a device for prewriting; (2) as a way of checking the organization of a draft—a device for revision; (3) as a way of analyzing, summarizing, or taking notes. The first two of these are considered here.

Suppose, for example, that you continue with the topic proposed in chapter 4, "Rights of Women at the University." You can, of course, just start writing. That procedure may work, especially if you have had a good deal of experience in writing and have thought about the topic. If, however, you have trouble getting ideas in order, a more systematic approach may help. A start, as indicated in the advice on prewriting, is to formulate a tentative thesis statement: "At the University women do not have rights and privileges equal to those of the men."

As a next step you might try some free writing or jot down at random any ideas on the subject that occur to you (see chapter 1), producing a list like the following:

1. Discriminating regulations on student housing
2. Antifeminine bias in the student court
3. The paragraph in the University Catalog concerning equal rights for all students
4. Women in student-body offices
5. Men's lounge in Union Building, but no women's lounge
6. As many women on campus as men
7. Women not willing to assert their rights
8. Lack of courses on women's literature, women in history, etc.
9. Swimming-pool privileges
10. Prejudice against women in textbooks
11. Intercollegiate athletics
12. College women just as responsible as college men
13. Attitudes of parents
14. The time Anne Wilkins was expelled but the boy who was equally guilty was not
15. Married women students

16. Women not interested in student government
17. Gymnasium and athletic facilities
18. Modern women taking equal responsibilities in the world
19. Military service of women
20. Courses biased toward male accomplishments
21. Regulation of fraternities and sororities
22. Preponderance of males on the faculty

From rough notes like these you can develop a plan, working with analysis and classification. You can analyze the subject, thinking of possible main subdivisions you might want to discuss—social discrimination, differences in curriculum, athletic distinctions, and so on. You can also look over your notes for items that belong together, that might be put into classes under broader headings. Items 11 and 17 could be put together as concerned with athletic facilities. And item 5 could be included in this group by broadening the heading to something like "inequalities in university facilities." Some items seem, on further examination, to be irrelevant, but most of them could be grouped into classes that might look like the following:

Social Discrimination Against Women

1. Discriminating regulations on student housing
2. Antifeminine bias in the student court
14. The time Anne Wilkins was expelled but the boy who was equally guilty was not (possible introduction as example of social discrimination)
21. Regulation of fraternities and sororities

Inequalities In University Facilities

5. Men's lounge in Union Building, but no women's lounge
9. Swimming-pool privileges
11. Intercollegiate athletics
17. Gymnasium and athletic facilities

Curricular Bias Toward Males

8. Lack of courses in women's subjects
10. Prejudice against women in textbooks
20. Courses biased toward male accomplishments
22. Preponderance of males on the faculty

Reasons Why There Should Be Equality

3. The statement in the University Catalog
6. As many women on campus as men
12. College women just as responsible as college men
18. Modern women taking equal responsibilities in the world
19. Military service of women

Causes For Inequalities

7. Women not willing to assert their rights
16. Women not interested in student government

Tradition in colleges and world
Prevalence of men in administration and on faculties
Old prejudices against educating women
[*The writer adds new items.*]

The classifications themselves provide a kind of outline, but they also reveal that some notes and some classes need to be pruned in order to focus the paper on the main idea. Reasons and causes are relevant, but they would greatly expand the scope of the paper. Thus you decide to limit yourself to two coordinate main headings that are aspects of the original purpose, to show that discrimination exists:

I. Discrimination in social attitudes
II. Inequalities in university facilities

Form of the Outline

Various schemes can arrange notes to show classification; one combines numbers and letters and indention:

MAIN IDEA (THESIS): _____
    I. _____
        A. _____
            1. _____
            2. _____
        B. _____
    II. _____
        A. _____
        B. _____

1. _____
    a. _____
        (1) _____
        (2) _____
    b. _____
2. _____
    a. _____
    b. _____
C. _____

When this pattern is used formally, a number of conventions are observed:

1. Coordinate items are made parallel in form.
2. Subdivisions are elements of the topics they divide.
3. Single subdivisions are avoided as illogical; you cannot divide something into one.
4. Topics are as specific as possible; broad headings like "reasons" or "incidents" only postpone thinking.

Using this scheme you might produce a formal outline for the paper on "Rights of Women" like the following:

MAIN IDEA (THESIS): At State University, women do not have rights and privileges equal to those of men.

INTRODUCTION: Use the statement in the University Catalog that all students have equal rights and privileges and point out that the paper will show the statement to be misleading.   [*A detail from the writer's first thoughts about the topic seems a possible introduction; a reminder may be handy.*]

  I. Social discrimination against women
    A. Differences in regulations   [*The writer sees a need to subdivide the first main topic.*]
      1. Housing
      2. Sororities' rules—stricter than those for fraternities   [*The writer does not make an illogical separate subdivision of the expansion of A.2.*]

B. Differences in application of rules
     1. Mary Wilkins story   *[The writer is again reminded of a possible use for a detail—the Mary Wilkins story.]*
     2. Student court
        a. Male membership on court
        b. Record of biased decisions
     3. Administrative and faculty attitudes   *[Details earlier classified differently are regrouped to be applied in a different way.]*
        a. Small number of women on faculty
        b. Tradition of "protecting" women
        c. Influence of parental pressure
II. Inequalities in university facilities. (Possible transition pointing out that above rules can be justified on ground that they are for students' "own good" but that other inequalities cannot.)   *[A lengthy note for future use records an idea that occurs to the writer as the outline develops.]*

  A. Social facilities
     1. Lack of meeting places for women's organizations
     2. Lack of a room comparable to the men's lounge in the Union Building   *[Coordination of topics is indicated by parallel form.]*
  B. Athletic facilities
     1. Lack of women's sports comparable to men's intercollegiate athletic program
     2. Lack of equal swimming-pool privileges
     3. Restriction on women's use of gymnasium

CONCLUSION: Use idea that there are as many women on the campus as men, that they will have equal responsibilities in later life, and that they should have equal rights and privileges in college. [*A possible conclusion is suggested by another of the groups of details rejected in preparing the body of the outline.*]

The outline is more elaborate than most papers would require. But even an outline this thorough should be a guide, not a tyrant. You will change your mind as you write, think of new material and new ways of relating it. The outline is a preliminary sketch, a record of prewriting, constantly subject to revision or neglect.

The Sentence Outline

Outlines like the example above, with items stated as topics, are adequate for most purposes. However, many writers prefer a sentence outline, finding it more precise. In a sentence outline, every topic is presented as a complete sentence. The outline above would begin as follows:

INTRODUCTION: The University Catalog includes the statement that all students have equal rights, but this statement is not true because of differences in regulations and their application and in facilities provided by the university.
  I. Women are discriminated against by rules and the application of rules.
      A. Regulations on social life are not the same for men and women.
          1. Women are more restricted than men by housing regulations.
          2. Rules governing sororities are stricter than those for fraternities.

The Outline and Revision

Although outlining is usually associated with planning, it also provides an aid to critical reading or a device for testing the organization of a paper in revision. The following versions of an essay suggest how outlining can direct profitable revision:

Original

A word not only indicates an object but can also suggest an emotional meaning. The essence of poetry depends upon words that arouse the emotions of the reader. An experiment may be conducted to prove how much

Revision

A word not only "means"; it conveys emotion. If we refer to a dog as a *mongrel*, we objectively define his pedigree, but we also reveal an attitude toward the dog.
    The emotional meanings

words mean in poetry. Replace the emotionally filled words with neutral ones, and all the poetic value will be knocked out of the poem by the change. Politicians are apt at changing the public's opinion merely by the use of words. *Bolshevik, Fascist, reactionary, revolutionary* are examples of emotional words used by politicians. Emotional words find their place in poetry but are out of place in modern science where exact thinking is required. Scientists want only the facts. They do not want to be swayed by words, only facts. This type of straight scientific thinking results in new discoveries. Science has worked hard ridding their books and discussions of emotional words; politics should do the same. The use of emotional words makes it hard for us to think straight in national and social problems. If clear unemotional words were used by people in the government, it would benefit our civilization. People would then be able to form their opinions by facts, not words.

Emotion-filled words are used not only by politicians but also by critics. By the use of words a critic can sway the public opinion against a writer, simply because he does not like the work.

We need to be careful not to form opinions on emotionally filled words.

[*The student essay printed above contains inaccuracies. Worse, it lacks any clear plan. An attempt to* of words are useful, especially if the writer's purpose is to sway opinion. Poetry, for example, depends on words that arouse the emotions of the reader, as we can demonstrate if we replace the emotion-filled words of a poem with neutral ones; all the poetic value will be knocked out of the poem by the change.

Emotional words have their place in poetry, but they are misleading when we are concerned with facts rather than attitudes. Scientists, for example, want facts; they do not want to be swayed by words. They have worked to rid their books and discussion of emotional words, and by straight scientific thinking have made important discoveries. Politicians have not done the same. They are apt at changing the public's opinion merely by the use of such emotional words as *Bolshevik, Fascist, reactionary,* or *revolutionary*. They prevent straight thinking about national and social problems. If people in the government would use clear, unemotional words, we could form opinions on facts, not words, and society would benefit.

Emotional words can present a danger as well as an advantage, and we need to be careful not to form opinions on them.

[*The essay is still undeveloped, in spite of the addition of an illustration or two. But it does come nearer than the original to showing how ideas are related. The revision involved first of all a new outline:*

outline the theme reveals its weakness, for a meaningful outline proves to be almost impossible. An attempt might look like this:

INTRODUCTION: Words have emotional as well as denotative meaning.

I. Importance of emotional words to poetry
II. Use of emotional words by politicians
III. Avoidance of emotional words by scientists
IV. Danger of emotional words in politics
V. Use of emotional words by critics

CONCLUSION: We need to be careful in using emotion-filled words.

Topic II is out of order. The outline reveals the lack of classification of material and the failure to subordinate minor to major topics.]

THESIS: Emotion-filled words are a handicap to scientific thinking.

INTRODUCTION: Words not only "mean"; they convey emotions.

I. Usefulness of emotional words
   A. Usefulness in swaying opinions
   B. Usefulness in poetry
II. Dangers of emotional words
   A. Use in science
   B. Use in politics

CONCLUSION: We should avoid using emotion-filled words to form opinions.

The new outline classifies topics under two main headings and organizes the paper around a central idea. It changes the illogical order revealed by the original outline. The writing follows the outline, corrects the obvious errors in accuracy, revises many of the sentences, and leaves out the undeveloped and nonessential example of the critic.]

The outline is a guide, a way of planning an organization and keeping materials in order. And a writer can help readers see that organization, keeping them on the track by using focusing devices, maintaining clear transitions, and providing appropriate introductions and conclusions.

FOCUSING DEVICES

Motion picture directors planning crowd scenes face problems like those of writers. They are attempting to picture a large number of details in such a way that they will make a unified impression. They may provide views from a distance to present the over-all scene, and then turn the cameras to details, to pictures of people and smaller segments of the scene. Almost always they help the audience keep these more concentrated scenes in order by focusing attention on some central object. A tree or a building or an important character becomes a focal point, and the camera swings back to it and then away from it so that the audience can keep the great mass of details in order by relating them to this point of focus.

Writers, like cameramen, may tie their work together by using a detail as a focal point. Watch, for example, the binoculars in the following opening paragraphs of a novel:

> A man with binoculars. That is how it began: with a man standing by the side of the road, on a crest overlooking a small Arizona town, on a winter night.
>
> Lieutenant Roger Shawn must have found the binoculars difficult. The metal would be cold, and he would be clumsy in his fur parka and heavy gloves. His breath, hissing out into the moonlit air, would have fogged the lenses. He would be forced to pause to wipe them frequently, using a stubby gloved finger.
>
> He could not have known the futility of this action. Binoculars were worthless to see into that town and uncover its secrets. He would have been astonished to learn that the men who finally succeeded used instruments a million times more powerful than binoculars.
>
> There is something sad, foolish, and human in the image of Shawn leaning against a boulder, propping his arms on it, and holding the binoculars to his eyes. Though cumbersome, the binoculars would at least feel comfortable and familiar in his hands. It would be one of the last familiar sensations before his death.
>
> Michael Crichton, *The Andromeda Strain*

The novelist focuses the reader's attention, using field glasses as a point of reference to unify the passage. But the binoculars also have a more complex function. Lieutenant Shawn is looking at a town where most of the inhabitants have been struck dead by a microscopic intruder from outer space, brought back by an artificial satellite and called the Andromeda strain. The opening paragraphs use the binoculars to anticipate this story, to introduce its theme, its main idea. In the first paragraph the binoculars are simply mentioned; the man has them. In the second they become part of the immediate practical problems of the lieutenant; the metal is cold and the lenses frost. In the third paragraph, however, the binoculars acquire significance in contrast to the electronic microscope with which in the novel scientists detect the Andromeda strain threatening the human race. In the fourth paragraph the binoculars suggest even more pointedly some basic topics of the novel: the ignorance of human beings about the universe, their helplessness when confronted with unknown sorts of disaster, the role of science in the modern world.

Devices of this sort risk seeming artificial, but they can be useful even in shorter pieces of writing and without assuming the symbolic function they have in Crichton's novel. For example, a student paper describing a vacation trip gains coherence by recurring references to an engine knock that becomes more distracting as the miles pass. Another paper, arguing for a beautification project for a city, uses a jungle of wires and light poles as a point of reference.

TRANSITIONS

In chapter 4 we observed that, within paragraphs, words and phrases usually give the reader enough guidance to follow a thought. Longer pieces of writing may require sentences or even paragraphs of transition to mark turns in the trail. In a longer essay, for example, one writer uses this short, rather formal transitional paragraph to move from one section of the paper to another.

> So much, then, by way of proof that the method of establishing laws in science is exactly the same as that pursued in common life. Let us now turn to another matter (though really it is but another phase of the same question), and that is, the method by which, from the relations of certain phenomena, we prove that some stand in the position of causes toward the others.
>
> Thomas Henry Huxley, "Darwiniana"

The paragraph uses one sentence to summarize what has preceded and another to announce what is to follow. Usually, however, even in a long paper, transitions, shifts from one part of a discussion to another, are handled in topic sentences of paragraphs (see chapter 4). The following passages from a longer essay show how topic sentences and transitional paragraphs may provide a map of a composition's organization:

In all the medical schools of London a notice is posted over the door leading to the dissecting room forbidding strangers to enter. I propose, however, to push the door open and ask the reader to accompany me within. . . . We propose to watch them [the students] at work. Each student is at his allotted part, and if we observe them in turn we shall, in an hour or less, obtain an idea of the main tissues and structures which enter into the composition of the human body.	[These passages appear in the opening paragraph, which serves as an introduction showing the reader the overall purpose of the essay and the writer's plan for achieving it—by observing the students as they dissect. The paragraph commits the writer to describe the "main tissues and structures" of the human body.]
By good fortune a dissection is in progress in front of the	[The second paragraph locates the reader near the first student.]

wrist, which displays, amongst other structures the radial artery. . . .

Lying side by side with the sinews of the wrist there is another cord. . . . It is the median nerve. . . . [*The third paragraph opens with a sentence linking the preceding topic, "sinews of the wrist," with a new one, "the median nerve."*]

We propose to observe the dissector as he traces the radial artery to the heart. . . .

Before leaving the dissection we have been surveying it will be well to see one of those marvelously contrived structures known as a joint. . . . [*The reader is led to another stage in this dissection and is also warned of a change to come.*]

We have surveyed the anatomy at the wrist in some detail and with a very distinct purpose. . . . [*A summary or transitional paragraph marks the end of this episode; the reader is led to a turn in the trail.*]

We now propose to transfer our attention for a short time to two students who are uncovering the parts in front of the neck between the chin and breastbone or sternum. . . . [*The writer indicates a major shift to a new dissection.*]

Our time with the students in the dissection room has almost expired; there remains only a moment to glance at a dissection which is exposing the important organs which are enclosed within the thorax and abdomen. . . . [*The writer marks another turn and also prepares the reader for the end of the trail.*]

Our cursory visit to the dissecting room has not been in vain if the reader has realized how complex the structure of the human body really is, and how necessary it is that those who have to cure its disorders should try to understand the intricacy of its mechanism. . . . [*Transitional materials have kept the reader informed of the author's subsidiary commitments as these have developed. The conclusion reminds the reader of the purpose of the discussion, of the writer's overriding commitment.*]

Sir Arthur Keith, "Man: A History of the Human Body"

Organization: Analysis and Classification 115

Guide to Revision **Trans**

TRANSITIONS

Revise to provide an adequate transition, when appropriate framing a better topic sentence or providing a transitional paragraph.

ORIGINAL

. . . *Derring-do* is an example of a meaning that has developed from misunderstanding, the original being something like "He was one of few daring do it."

    Edward Sapir, in his book, *Language* makes use of the English words *foot* and *feet* to illustrate linguistic change, what he calls drift.

[This transition is clumsy. Concluding and topic sentences would smooth it out, but since this is a turning point in the discussion, a transitional paragraph like that in the revision is useful. The writer is discussing two books on language. In the section with which the passage above opens, he has said that the first of the books is concerned with stories about odd words. He is now ready to turn to a more penetrating book by Sapir.]

REVISION

. . . *Derring-do* is an example of a meaning that has developed from misunderstanding, the original being something like "He was one of few daring do it."

    Thus, the first of the two books under discussion is mainly concerned with telling engaging stories about the origin or growth of odd words. The second, Edward Sapir's *Language*, is quite different. Sapir studies words—common words more than odd ones—to try to understand the nature and working of language.

    Take, for example, his illustrations for his theory of linguistic change of the sort he calls drift. He starts with the common English words *foot* and *feet*, and by tracing these to such early forms as *foti* in Gothic . . .

    The essay includes even more guides to its general pattern than have been excerpted here, but these samples, most of them opening sentences of paragraphs, illustrate the importance of such aids, outlining the complete essay:

    MAIN IDEA: A visit to the dissecting room reveals the complexity of the human body and the importance of studying it.

I. The anatomy at the wrist: the first dissection
   A. The radial artery
   B. The median nerve
   C. Tracing the radial artery to the heart
   D. The joint
II. The parts in front of the neck
III. Organs within the thorax and abdomen

The reader can follow clearly and easily because the writer has revealed his outline step by step.

INTRODUCTIONS

An introduction is essential to clear organization because it introduces, gives the reader a notion of what the paper is about. It arouses the reader's interest, limits the topic, and sets the tone of the piece. It should reveal clearly its relation to the main ideas of the paper and should be in proportion, not half as long as the body of the paper. And an introduction should not apologize. To meet all these requirements is not easy, but an effective introduction is often the most important part of a paper. Getting a good start can help both a writer and a reader see where they are going.

Every introduction needs to be individual, but consideration of the following types of introduction may help get a paper started.

1. *Statement of Proposition*   Often a direct statement of the proposition to be defended provides a good introduction.

The Growing Power of Admen

America's advertising industry is moving into a commanding role in our society. Its executives are becoming masters of our economic destiny, the engineers behind some of our most successful political campaigns. . . .
               Vance Packard

[Here Packard begins with his general thesis, continues with general illustrations, and goes on to more specific evidence. Sometimes the statement of the main idea that has evolved as part of prewriting can be adapted for this kind of introduction.]

2. *Presentation of Factual Background*   A common and successful opening offers factual statements to provide justification, background, or the reason for a thesis.

What Every Writer Must Learn

The teaching of writing has become practically a profession by now. There is hardly a college in the land that does not offer at least one course in "creative writing" (whatever that is) by some "teacher of writing" (whoever he is). There are, moreover, at least fifty annual writers' conferences now functioning among us with something like fifty degrees of competence. And there seems to be no way of counting the number of literary counselors, good and bad, who are prepared to promise that they can teach a writer what he needs to know.

John Ciardi

[*The introduction continues, after this opening, to assert that writing requires inventiveness and then to consider six ways in which the writer's talents for creation may be realized. The introductory sentence does not state the main idea, but opens a brief summary of the facts that make the essay's subject worth writing about.*]

3. *Questions to Isolate a Problem* Opening a paper with a series of questions that lead to the main topic can be effective.

Force and Freedom

Can there be a moral basis for freedom in a world of force? This is one of the ugly questions that disturb many intelligent people at this moment. Can we reconcile the doctrine of military force—the idea of killing men in war—with a moral purpose? As a matter of history, freedom has often emerged from the successful use of force; yet we abominate war as intensely as we love freedom. How are we to resolve this paradox?

James Bryant Conant

[*A series of questions leads to the basic problem of the paper: the relationship between force and freedom. The first question is the main one Conant will try to answer, with the other questions expressing subordinate parts of it. Sometimes opening with a question can make a paper sound more oratorical than is appropriate.*]

4. *Analysis* The introduction may divide the subject into its parts and indicate which parts will have emphasis.

Prospects in the Arts and Sciences

The words "prospects in the arts and sciences" mean two quite different things to me. One is prophecy: What will the scientists discover and the painters paint, what new forms will alter music, what parts of experience will newly yield to objective description? The other meaning is that of a view: What do we see when we look at the world today and compare it with the past? I am not a prophet; and I cannot very well speak to the first subject, though in many ways I should like to. I shall try to speak to the second, . . .

      J. Robert Oppenheimer

[*The introduction is an excellent model of the careful analytic opening. It divides the topic into two parts, "prophecy" and "view," announces that it will consider only the second of these, and tells the reader why. The device gives Oppenheimer a means of limiting his subject but at the same time shows that he is aware of more aspects of the subject than the one he chooses to discuss.*]

5. *Statement of View the Writer Is to Oppose* Describing a popular opinion the writer thinks is erroneous, or commenting on earlier writings or a person the writer disagrees with is another way to begin. This device gains the interest that always attaches to an argument and at the same time defines the writer's own stand by its opposite.

Has the Education Industry Lost Its Nerve?

The leaders of many so-called education companies, especially those formed through marriages of electronics and publishing, seem to be losing confidence in the premise that technology can change education. Having eagerly embraced that enticing proposition a few years ago, and having since discovered that it is more difficult to consummate than they expected, some now appear ready to abandon it.

      Robert W. Locke

[*The introduction, relying on a figurative comparison with matrimony, suggests that the educational conglomerates have become disillusioned. This statement prepares for (1) a survey of the disillusionment and (2) development of the idea that times have now changed enough to make a cautious development of new devices and techniques both useful and profitable.*]

6. *Justification or Explanation* The writer may have been an eyewitness to an important event, or have done exhaustive research, or conducted controlled experiments. Many research papers begin with a presentation that allows the reader to judge the validity of the material presented.

Thomas Couture

My first meeting with Couture, who became one of my best and dearest friends, was odd and characteristic. It was in 1834; I was not yet one and twenty, and had just arrived from the United States, well provided for in the way of courage and determination, with a stock of youthful illusions, and very little besides.
George P. A. Healy

[The introduction has the easy grace of familiar narration. It also lets the reader know that the writer is speaking on the basis of long and intimate acquaintance with his subject.]

7. A Relevant Incident, a Striking Illustration, an Anecdote An account of something that has happened can catch the reader's interest and also lead into the main topic of a composition.

A Pig from Jersey

Among those who passed through the general clinic of Lenox Hill Hospital, at Seventy-sixth Street and Park Avenue, on Monday morning, April 6, 1942, was a forty-year-old Yorkville dishwasher whom I will call Herman Sauer. His complaint, like his occupation, was an undistinguished one. He had a stomach ache.
Berton Roueche

[The incident, which the writer develops in detail, not only introduces the discussion of a disease, trichinosis, but serves as a unifying thread running through the entire essay. Notice the details that make it convincing. This kind of introduction must be clearly related to the main idea.]

8. A Quotation A quotation may serve as a starting point because it illustrates the main idea to be presented.

The Uses of Flexibility

Thackeray wrote, "The wicked are wicked, no doubt, and they go astray and they fall,

[Fulbright goes on to discuss the dangers of inflexible and intolerant attitudes growing from the

and they come by their deserts; but who can tell the mischief which the very virtuous do?"

J. William Fulbright

purest of motives. The quotation illustrates his main idea.]

9. *Short, Emphatic Sentence*   Sometimes plunging right in is the best way to start. A short sentence grabs the reader's attention:

It was her eyes. They were always staring at me, making me uneasy, always letting me know that she was one step ahead of me. She knew what I was thinking before I did. I was eleven, I guess, and in the sixth grade. She was seventeen and had been my babysitter ever since I could remember. Her name was Margo.

Guide to Revision   Intro

INTRODUCTIONS

Revise the introduction so that it presents the subject, is connected to the main idea, is in proportion, and is not merely an apology.

ORIGINAL

Proper Feeding Of Cattle

[*The main idea of the paper is that scientific feeding of cattle has improved the entire beef industry.*]
This has always interested me, and I have noticed the growing importance of the cattle industry in all parts of the country. Not only has the quality of American beef improved in recent years, but the raising of beef cattle has spread throughout the nation.
    The first requirement of proper feeding for beef cattle is . . .
[This *refers to a title that may be changed or lost; thus the introduction is not independent.*]

REVISION

Proper Feeding Of Cattle

The American beef industry has shown important developments in recent years. Not only has cattle raising been introduced in areas formerly thought unsuitable; at the same time the quality of beef has improved. The progress is due primarily to the introduction of scientific feeding.
    The first requirement of . . .
[*The revision omits superfluous, confusing material and tells what the paper is about; it introduces. It is also independent, avoiding reliance on the title.*]

CONCLUSIONS

A conclusion concludes; that is, it gives the reader some notion of where the essay has gone, what its purpose has been. A conclusion should be interesting when possible, for it offers the writer a last chance to engage the reader, to be convincing and make a point. Like the introduction, a conclusion should be in proportion and should be clearly related to the ideas of the paper.

The following are examples of some of the kinds of conclusions that work.

1. Restatement of Main Idea Modern exposition tends to conclude with a restatement of the main idea of the composition. This is usually not a formal summary, but a fresh presentation of the idea.

The Illusion of the Two Cultures

Today we hold a stone, the heavy stone of power. We must perceive beyond it, however, by the aid of the artistic imagination, those humane insights and understandings which alone can lighten our burden and enable us to shape ourselves, rather than the stone, into the forms which great art has anticipated.

Loren Eiseley

[*A scientist uses a prehistoric, shaped stone as a unifying device for his essay (compare Crichton's use of binoculars in* The Andromeda Strain, *mentioned at the beginning of the chapter) and turns his conclusion about it, emphasizing his point that the artistic and the practical can work together.*]

2. A Supplementary Comment A writer may reinforce the argument by adding a new but related observation, which serves to emphasize what the essay has said.

Walt Whitman: He Had His Nerve

Let me finish by mentioning another quality of Whitman's—a quality, delightful to me, that I have said nothing of. If some day a tourist notices, among the ruins of New York City, a copy of *Leaves of Grass*, and stops and picks it up and reads some lines in it, she will be able to say to herself: "how very American! If he and his country

[*The essay has discussed a variety of aspects of Whitman's poetry. The final comment, although technically presenting a new quality, actually epitomizes the attitude of the essay.*]

had not existed, it would have been possible to imagine them."
Randall Jarrell

3. Statement of Importance, Plea for Change A conclusion can suggest the importance of what has been presented and may also make a plea for a change of attitude or for specific action.

Moonlight and Poison Ivy

Better marriage relations in this country await an extensive revaluation of our attitude towards life and living. If our values are shabby and our attitudes adolescent, how can American marriage, made in our image, be anything but a monumental failure?
David Cohn

[*An essay on the weaknesses of our attitudes toward marriage ends by suggesting that we change and by pointing out the necessity for change.*]

Guide to Revision **Conc**

CONCLUSIONS

Revise the conclusion so that it rounds out the composition logically.

ORIGINAL

[*The body of the paper presents examples of commercialism in college football.*]
On Saturday afternoon in the crowded stadium twenty-two young men are preparing for careers in a very lucrative profession. May the best team win.
[*The conclusion includes one point from the paper but does not express the main idea. And the final sentence is irrelevant.*]

REVISION

The twenty-two men on that field may be on the way to lucrative careers, but they are really demonstrating that college football has become so commercialized that it is no longer related to education.
[*The revision focuses on the opinion that the examples in the paper have been intended to emphasize.*]

4. Repetition of Key Expression Specific reference to a word or phrase important early in the paper, especially to a focusing device, can round out a paper smoothly.

> I tilted my head back with a sigh of joyful relief and stared again at the bright lights; this time the insects were dancing.

[A student paper uses the insects in the stadium lights as a focusing device in an essay on a baseball game. The conclusion echoes the introduction and other references.]

FOR STUDY AND WRITING

A. Go through your purse or pockets or look at the books in your room, and see if you can classify your personal items or your books, using a common quality as a basis. Go back to the writing you did after observing students in a particular area of campus. Can you establish any basis of classification?

B. Indicate one item in each of the following classifications that is inconsistent because it has not been classified on the same basis as the other items:

1. Causes for water pollution: industrial waste, pesticides, untreated garbage, inadequate government regulations, refuse from boats
2. Pictures: oil, landscape, watercolor, pastel, tempera
3. Books: novels, collections of poems, collections of short stories, leather-bound books, collections of plays, histories, textbooks
4. Dresses: evening dresses, afternoon dresses, sports dresses, cotton dresses, dinner dresses
5. Criminals: burglars, murderers, incorrigibles, arsonists, embezzlers
6. Stylistic qualities of a poem: alliteration, rhyme, meter, consistency, stanzaic pattern

C. Which of the types of organization or combination of organizational plans described in this chapter would work best for each of the following compositions? Explain your choice.

1. A survey covering the past ten years of attempts to get a factory to stop polluting a lake
2. A pamphlet explaining to incoming students what they should do during orientation week and registration

3. A description of the library building intended to help new students find their way in it
4. An essay for a campus magazine advocating the inclusion of students in the membership of all faculty committees dealing with the hiring, tenure, and salaries of faculty members
5. A report on discrimination in housing in your city presenting the results of two surveys, one a questionnaire to real estate companies asking for statements of their policies, the other a house-to-house canvass of minority students attempting to rent
6. A report for a physics course on a laboratory experiment on the speed of falling bodies
7. A report to a club on a national convention to which you have been the club's delegate
8. A letter to the editor of the campus newspaper protesting an editorial in a previous issue on the grounds that the editorial contained a number of factual errors

D. This paragraph is less clear than it should be, largely because material has not been classified and presented in an organized pattern. Several bases for classification are possible, one of them suggested in the first sentence. Select a suitable basis, and then on separate paper list details used in the paragraph, grouping them into appropriate classes. Prepare an informal outline and revise the paragraph, using the system of classification you have worked out.

Australia's three best known animals all have unusual characteristics. The long, powerful tail of the kangaroo is an example. Another is the curious duck bill of the platypus. The kangaroo can use its tail as a third support when sitting up. It carries its young in a pouch. The koala bear is also marsupial. The platypus, however, lays eggs and suckles its young, combining characteristics of animal, bird, and fish. The koala does not drink, but obtains all the moisture it needs from the juices of gum leaves. The kangaroo feeds principally on grass but has a taste for cultivated crops. The platypus has a six-inch tail not unlike that of a beaver, a furry body, a duck-like bill, and webbed feet ending in claws. The koala sleeps in a tree during the day and wakes as much as it ever does at night. Female koalas are habitual kidnappers and steal one another's babies whenever they can. The platypus hunts its food in rivers and creeks. The koala is a small, soft, furry bear, weighing only about twenty pounds.

E. Below are beginning paragraphs, with the sentences that follow them, taken from papers discussing various sorts of courses. Comment specifically on the appropriateness of each as an introduction.

1. I went to high school in the heyday of the free school and the open classroom. There were no assignments, and students did what they wanted to. True, there were books and magazines and movie equipment and stuff around, and the teachers were helpful and encouraged us to do things. There were even classes if you wanted to go to them, and sometimes some of us did.

Now there has been a revolution in my high school, and I realize I was shortchanged, cheated out of an education.

2. In this theme I shall consider action-oriented courses.

   Action-oriented courses have both advantages and disadvantages.

3. Not being a member of the faculty, or the administration, or the student committee that has been investigating the relevance of the new or the old courses, I do not have much information about this subject, but I will write about it as well as I can.

   I am sure, however, that drastic changes are needed.

4. When my older brother came to the university, the word *relevance* was not much used in regard to courses, but he soon found out what irrelevance can be. He took a course in English in which he learned how to spell and punctuate and to parse sentences, but he had already won a spelling contest and he had been parsing ever since the sixth grade. He failed a course in trigonometry, but what he needed, if he was to take over his father's business, was some accounting. If the courses he registered for in Spanish, history, and art appreciation meant anything in his life, he did not know what it was.

   When I arrived things had changed a little, but not much.

5. Like a good many of my friends, I came to the university because I could not get a good job, and I did not know what else to do. I am having a good time, and that is all right, but a good time isn't everything.

   That gets me to my subject, because I have been thinking about the courses I have been taking.

F. Below are concluding paragraphs taken from papers having the same general subject as those in E., above, the role of various courses in collegiate curricula. Comment on the appropriateness of each as a conclusion.

1. [*The paper surveys five courses the student is registered for and tries to examine each of them to see what the relevance for the student may be.*]

   The fifth course I am taking is called "Introduction to Home Economics." It meets three times a week, but one class is a kind of laboratory and lasts from one to four P.M. The instructor is quite jolly, and I like her a lot.

2. [*The paper argues that students should be allowed to elect courses like anatomy and surveying if they expect to have use for them, but that all required courses should stimulate students, not provide organized information.*]

   The courses I am taking are dull, dull, dull! I cut class and I don't read the assignments. After all, why should I?

3. [*The paper contrasts a course given in an ethnic studies program on the role of emancipated slaves in the American Civil War and a course given in the department of history on the same struggle.*]

I learned more about mankind and the nature of civilization from my history professor, but I learned more about what history means in men's lives from the ethnic studies course.

4. [*The paper describes several courses the writer took in an ethnic studies program. The writer found them repetitious, vague, and lacking in content.*]

As a result of my experience with ethnic studies, I have concluded that I want two things out of college: to learn how to think and to learn facts to think with. I need no course to "turn me on"; until I can turn myself on I have no business in college.

6

Basic Sentence Patterns

> *The congruent and harmonious fitting of parts in a sentence hath almost the fastening and force of knitting and connexion: As in stones well squar'd, which will rise strong a great way without mortar.*
> BEN JONSON

If you want to build a stone wall, with or without mortar, you pick suitable stones, cut them to the shape you want, and set them where they fit. Ben Jonson, who was a bricklayer before he became one of England's great poets and playwrights, saw the practical parallel with writing. However mysterious the process of composition may be, the act of writing is obvious enough; you pick words and fit them together in sentences.

GRAMMAR AND WRITING

In spite of its popular reputation, grammar need not be a rack for torturing the young. Infants start learning sentence patterns as they babble, and within a few years they have learned all the grammar that is likely to be much good to them. Grammar describes how a language works. *Grammar* refers to the forms that words or other linguistic units take and to the patterns in which these units are habitually ordered. All native speakers of a language know its grammar. Without it they could not understand or be understood. To use grammar to improve writing, we need only become aware of what we all know and have known since childhood.

Using our native awareness of grammar can seem more complicated than it is, partly because the word *grammar* is variously used. In one popular variation, *grammar* refers to what students of language mean by *usage*, linguistic good manners. In this sense, "ain't" or "she don't" is banished as "bad grammar" or "ungrammatical." Actually both expressions are grammatical, in the sense in which we have used *grammar* above, because they fit regular patterns of the language. Whether these terms are appropriate in a given context—and frequently they are not—is another question, considered as *usage* in chapter 11.

When we study a grammar, we study how a language works. When we look at rhetoric, we study how to make language work well. Grammar is the anatomy of a language. Rhetoric is more like medicine and physical education; it shows how to help the body function, how to use it. Grammar is like the rules of a game, rhetoric like the strategies for playing it. Rhetoric is concerned with making choices among available grammatical alternatives. Because this book is intended to help writers write, we are mainly concerned with rhetoric, with effects, with strategies.

But to develop strategies you must know the rules of the game. You cannot choose the best plays if you do not know what plays are possible. To decide which sentence pattern will work best, you must know what patterns you can choose from. A writer tries to anticipate effects and to build sentences to get a result. Accordingly, we shall consider grammar insofar as it has practical value in helping a writer do the job. This and the following chapters treat the rhetoric of the sentence, discussing ways of constructing sentences to do the work for which they are intended.

INDICATING GRAMMATICAL RELATIONSHIPS

Language conveys ideas in two ways: through the meanings associated with individual words and through the way those words are related. That is, a sentence has both semantic meaning—what the individual words say—and grammatical meaning—how the individual words affect one another, how they are related.

Consider the following group of words, arranged in alphabetical order: *car, collapse, front, just, of, old, postman, the, the, tree*. Although you know the meaning of each individual word, the string makes no sense. The signs of meaning are there, but the signs of grammar are missing. When the signs of grammar are added, the group of words becomes a sentence:

The old tree had collapsed just in front of the postman's car.

Three kinds of signals have been added to the string of words to reveal grammatical relationships, to show how the words fit together. First, a few words have been changed internally, have acquired endings that indicate how they are used. *Collapse* becomes *collapsed*, with the *-d* ending indicating past time. And *postman* gains an ending, *-'s,* to indicate possession. Second, *had* is inserted before *collapsed*. It has almost no meaning in the usual sense; rather it is a function word, revealing grammar, specifying time along with the *-d* ending. Finally, the words have been rearranged, and the order shows us who or what is acting and on what. Simply by changing the order, we could change what happened:

The postman's old car had collapsed just in front of the tree.

These three kinds of signals—internal changes or inflection, the use of function words, and word order—reveal grammar in English.

The first of these, inflection, was extensive in Latin and Greek and Old English, and many modern languages continue to rely on inflection, especially the addition of endings. A few inflectional changes survive in modern English— *-ed, -ing,* and other endings for verbs; form differences like *he, her,* and *him,* to show how pronouns are used; form differences for the verb *to be;* or the use of *s* to indicate plural. These are probably the least important ways of revealing grammar in English; but since they are less common than other devices, they often cause the most trouble.

As the use of endings has declined in the development of English, function words have become more important. Different uses for the verb, for instance, are shown mainly by words like *is* or *have* or *were*, which have little meaning themselves but show something about the use and meaning of other words. *She was flying, She had been flying,* or *She must have been about to go flying* use the *-ing* ending but differ in meaning mainly because of the use of function words. Chapter 9 discusses function words in more detail.

As suggested by the examples above, word order has become the most important grammatical device in English. The basic structure of the sentence, for example, which is indicated in Latin by inflection, is clarified in English by word order. A schoolbook Latin sentence uses three common words—*puella* meaning "girl," *agricola* meaning "farmer," and *amat* meaning "loves." "Agricola puellam amat" says that the farmer loves the girl. "Agricolam puella amat," changing two endings but keeping the same word order, says that the girl loves the farmer. English can change the meaning, the sense of the basic sentence pattern, by simply shifting the positions of *farmer* and *girl*.

Another way to observe how we recognize signals of grammar is to consider a group of nonsense syllables like the following from *Through the Looking Glass:*

The slithy toves did gyre and gimble.

We don't know what this says, because we don't know what the "words" mean, but we understand the grammar. We assume that *slithy* describes *toves*, mainly because of the *-y* ending, which makes it sound like a modifying word. From the function word *did*, we understand that *gyre* and *gimble* are verbs. And, most important, we know what does what: that toves, whatever they may be, gyre and gimble, whatever that is.

PRIVILEGE OF OCCURRENCE

One characteristic of languages that affects their grammar is sometimes called "privilege of occurrence." That is, some words or phrases are "privileged" for certain uses but not for others. For example, *apple* or *banker* can appear as a subject, but not as a verb. You can't apple anything. On the other hand, *is* and *exaggerate* cannot be used as the subject of a sentence but do work as verbs. *Violently* and *hopeful* and *the* do not fit in either subject or verb positions but can be used to modify other expressions.

Traditional grammar classifies expressions into parts of speech, partly on the basis of how they can and can't be used: nouns, pronouns, verbs, adjectives, adverbs, prepositions, conjunctions, and particles including interjections. These parts of speech can be defined in various ways, none of them totally satisfactory, but for practical purposes they can be distinguished by the ways they are characteristically used in a sentence. For example, a noun is a word that can fit in the blank in a test frame like "The _____ seemed ready," or an adjective can fit in "the _____ house."

English is an unusually flexible language, and many words can have more than one function, can work as more than one part of speech. *Fast*, to take a common example, can be an adjective or an adverb and, with a different meaning, a noun or verb. Furthermore, words easily shift from one function to another. *Cow* is normally thought of as a noun, but notice the following:

The foreman tried to *cow* the women workers.
The road to the old mine was only a *cow* path.

Because of this flexibility, we usually have little trouble fitting expressions to their standard uses. But a writer needs to be aware of how privilege of occurrence affects the patterns of the basic English sentence.

THE BASIC SENTENCE

An English sentence is a string of words, but not a random string. The words are ordered as variations on a few set patterns, and words fit into positions where they have privilege of occurrence. To see how this works, we can think of a sentence as a series of variously shaped bins or pigeonholes or slots, as follows:

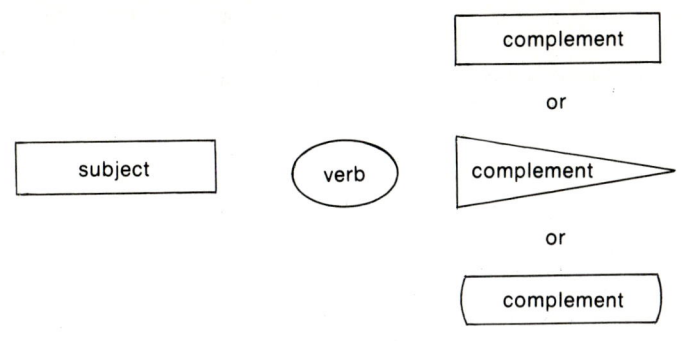

[subject] [verb] [complement]
or
[complement]
or
[complement]

Fillers with appropriate shapes could be used to fit into these slots. Assume that we have the following:

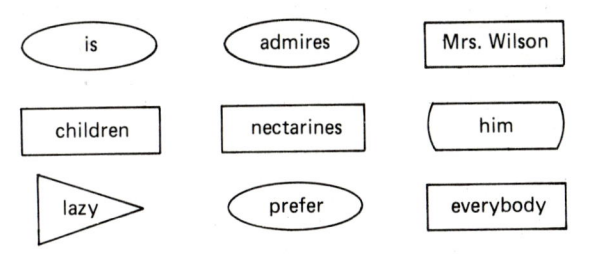

is   admires   Mrs. Wilson
children   nectarines   him
lazy   prefer   everybody

The shapes of these blocks indicate that their words have privilege of occurrence in the slots with the same shape. Inserting them in the slots of the pattern could produce the following simple sentences:

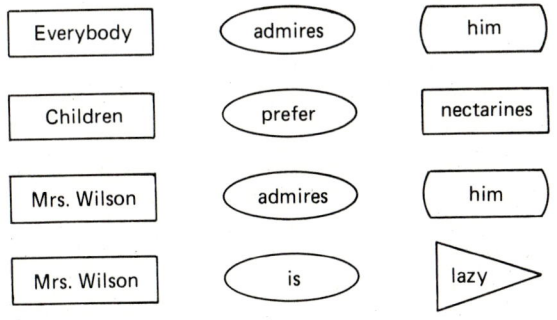

Everybody   admires   him
Children   prefer   nectarines
Mrs. Wilson   admires   him
Mrs. Wilson   is   lazy

Some words—nouns like *Mrs. Wilson, nectarines,* and *children*—will fit either the subject slot or one of the complement slots, but others can be used in only one of the slots. *Him* would not fit the subject slot nor *nectarines* the verb slot. To make such a scheme apply to more complex sentences would require more shapes, but more could be provided:

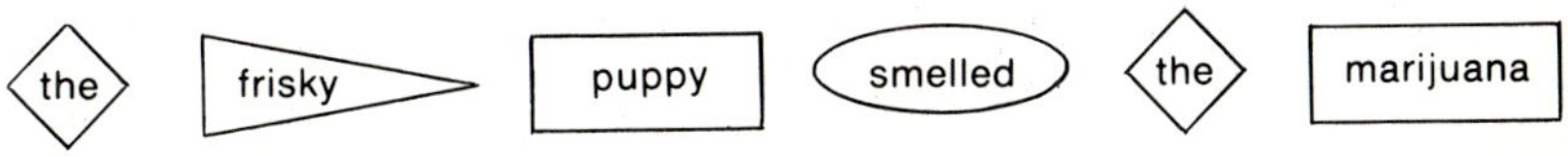

the   frisky   puppy   smelled   the   marijuana

The scheme is an oversimplification, but it suggests how an English sentence grows, through the working together of three elements: subject, verb, and complement. These form the basic framework of English sentences, which we shall refer to as the SVC pattern. It is the basis, also, of more complicated sentences, as the following passage demonstrates. Subjects, verbs, and complements are italicized:

> *Government* in America *has* always *regarded* the *operation* of industry as a purely private function. To return to an earlier example, even the *newest-biggest* of all governmental agencies, born in the early days of the Atomic age and the Fair Deal—the AEC—*operates* its vast, complex, "monopolistic," and largely secret *domain* through private industrial contractors. But *business has* yet *to show* a comparably broad and tolerant *understanding* of the legitimate domain of government. In fact, some *sections of* the community *could not do better than follow,* in this regard, Dr. Johnson's *advice,* and *clear* their *minds* of cant and prejudiced misinformation, not to say the downright nonsense about "governmental dictatorship," and, of course, "creeping Socialism" that all too often, as a species of businessman's groupthink, takes the place of responsible consideration of the proper functions of government in free society.
>
> Adlai Stevenson, *My Faith in Democratic Capitalism*

Each of the four fairly long sentences of the paragraph has as its framework an SVC pattern:

Subject	Verb	Complement
1. Government	has regarded	operation
2. newest-biggest	operates	domain
3. business	has to show	understanding
4. sections	could not do better than follow	advice
	clear	minds

SVC PATTERNS

The basic SVC framework may appear in any of five patterns, as follows:

1. | **Subject** | **Verb** |
|---|---|
| Fish | swim. |
| Blue | fades. |

2. | **Subject** | **Verb** | **Object Complement** |
|---|---|---|
| Maxine | broke | her engagement. |
| Jack | threw | Evelyn the orchid. |

	The children	consider	her stupid.
	The voters	made	him an ex-president.
3.	**Subject**	**Linking Verb**	**Predicate Nominative**
	The moon	was	a ship.
	The pumpkin	became	a coach.
4.	**Subject**	**Linking Verb**	**Adjective**
	Life	is	real.
	The coat	felt	warm.
5.	**Subject**	**Linking Verb**	**Adverb of Place**
	Nobody	was	there.

The patterns are the common variations on the slots shown above, differing only because different sorts of verbs and complements are available. With some verbs no complement is needed (1), and with linking verbs the complement can be a noun (3), an adjective (4), or an adverb of place (5).

EXPANDING SVC PATTERNS

Most experienced writers find few uses for sentences as simple as "Fish swim," but one writer did produce "Most fish of which we have any record, either contemporary or geologic, swim with the digestive organs downward." The precise grammatical rules by which "Fish swim" can generate a longer sentence are the materials of modern grammars; in general the processes involved are the following:

1. *Using Word Groups* Groups of words as well as single words can function as any of the main parts of the SVC pattern. The complement, especially, is frequently a word group.

> Jack hated *washing the car.*
> Jerry learned *how to retouch the photographs.*
> The new boss promised *that nobody would be fired.*
> *Where you hid the bottle* is not my concern.
> The meeting *should be starting* now.

In the first three sentences the italicized word group serves as a complement, in the fourth as a subject, in the last as a verb.

2. Combination or Coordination Words or groups of words can be combined or coordinated to serve as any of the main parts of the pattern.

> *Music* and *poetry* can open *hearts* but not *purses*.
> The children *ran out the door* and *jumped on their bicycles*.
> They knew *what they wanted* and *what they could get*.

In the first example *music* and *poetry* are joined by *and* as the subject, and *hearts* and *purses* are joined as compound object complements. In the second, two predicates, verb-complement combinations, are joined by *and*. In the third, two word groups are joined as object complements. Furthermore, complete patterns can be joined to develop complicated sentences.

>   S   V   C   S   V   C
> Tam O'Shanter sang a sonnet, but his wife made him change his tune.

Possibilities for combining patterns and parts of patterns are almost infinite.

3. Subordination Any part of the sentence pattern can be modified by a word or group of words subordinated to it.

>   S   V
> When it is exposed to strong sunlight, blue often fades to a dull gray.

The basic pattern is "blue fades"; the beginning word group modifies the whole pattern and *often* and *to a dull gray* modify the verb *fades*. For the last two of these processes, coordination and subordination, see chapter 8.

CHOOSING SUBJECTS

We recognize a subject in English mainly from its position, at the beginning of the SVC sequence, except in a few inverted patterns. The order is so nearly standard in English that we identify it even without anything that can be called words, as in "The quigquig obled a biscum." We know at once, because it is preceded by the determiner *The*, that *quigquig* is a symbol like *girl* or *wind* and not a word like *off*. From its position we assume that *quigquig* is the subject and that it obled the biscum.
    Most frequently subjects are what modern grammarians call *noun phrases*, composed of a pronoun or a noun and its modifiers. "Saleswomen" or "the saleswoman" or "the new saleswoman with the plastic wig" may be a noun phrase working as a subject. Various verbal constructions may serve as subjects. They include clauses, which themselves include subjects and verbs, and are usually distinguished by an introductory word like *that, how, what, whether, whoever*. (*Whoever* broke the vase fled.)

English grammar being what it is, the first word in a sentence that can be the subject automatically becomes the subject, whether the writer wants it to or not, unless he or she does something to keep it from being the subject. Consider, for example, one student trying to write a sentence on why he came to college. The first word that comes to mind is *reason*, and he writes it down as a start. As soon as he does, he restricts what is to follow. He cannot easily use a verb like *growls* or *objects* or *admires*, but is almost committed to *is* or a verb like it:

> The reason why I came to college is because, there being a law you have to have a degree for a license in the field of embalming in this state, which is my goal in life.

This, of course, is not a sentence at all. The writer's troubles began when he chose to begin with the relatively abstract word. He might have chosen another abstraction: "My desire to meet the state requirements for an embalming license . . ." He would have had a somewhat larger group of verbs to select from—*cause* or *make* or *influence,* as well as *is*—but he would still have been likely to write an indirect and perhaps wordy sentence. In conversation, if the student had been asked why he came to college, he probably would have stayed out of trouble. He might have said something like "I want to be a mortician" or "I need a degree so I can get a mortician's license." He would have chosen the actor as the subject and produced a straightforward, clear sentence.

ACTOR-ACTION-GOAL

The principle of choosing the actor as the subject applies most readily to statements about events or acts. If a pencil drops off the table, someone may say "The pencil dropped" or "The pencil fell on the floor," picking the actor for the subject and using the verb to specify what the actor did. Writers of fiction draft most of their sentences so that someone or something does, says, or is something. This choice of subject does not necessarily follow the order of our thoughts. Often we detect actions before actors. When we see something fall, we may be aware of the falling but not identify the pencil till we see it bounce. We might as logically start with the action and go on to the actor, as some languages regularly do, and perhaps say something like "The falling of the pencil occurred." But whether we like it or not, English conveys ideas most directly by putting the name of the actor in the subject slot whenever possible. The subject-verb-complement formula most frequently expresses actor-action-goal.

Even when writers of factual, expository prose have to deal in abstractions, they often take advantage of the actor-action-goal pattern. The following passage illustrates how a scholarly topic may be discussed mainly in sentences with the actor as subject:

Two sages of a later day actually preached that the independent growth of American English was not only immoral but a sheer illusion. They were Richard Grant White, for long the most widely read writer upon language questions, and Thomas R. Lounsbury, for thirty-five years professor of English language and literature in the Sheffield Scientific School at Yale. White's "Words and Their Uses" (1872) and his "Everyday English" (1880) were mines of erudition. Lounsbury effectively attacked the follies of the grammarians; his two books "The Standard of Usage in English" and "The Standard of Pronunciation in English," not to mention his excellent "History of the English Language" and his numerous magazine articles, showed a sound knowledge of the early history of the language, and an admirable spirit of free inquiry. But when these laborious scholars turned from English proper to American English, they tried to deny its existence altogether, and to support that denial brought a critical method that was anything but scientific.

H. L. Mencken and Raven I. McDavid, Jr.,
The American Language

A less skillful writer might have been tempted to start sentences differently, to begin the first one, for example, with "A major contribution to the study of . . ." or "The attitude of two sages of a later day. . . ." The resulting sentences would have been less direct and less clear.

Since a sentence begins to take shape the moment a possible subject is put on paper, the following suggestions may forestall verbal quagmires.

1. *Prefer actors as subject* On the whole, make the subject the actor, if there is one. That is, use as the grammatical subject, the actual subject, whoever or whatever is doing something. Prefer, for example, "The mechanic repaired the car" to "The car was repaired by the mechanic." The mechanic, not the car, is the actor.

2. *Avoid abstract subjects* Whenever possible, prefer concrete specific subjects to abstract or general ones. Especially treacherous are abstract words that usually must be followed by *is* or *was*—words like *reason*, *aspect*, *explanation*, *conclusion*, *situation*, and *attitude*.

3. *Consider the verb* Choose the subject in light of the verb that is to follow it; usually a concrete, precise subject will permit the choosing of an appropriate verb. Avoid overuse of forms of *to be*; try for a more precise verb.

4. *Rewrite for clarity* If you have trouble completing a sentence, try finding a new subject and starting over. Or if a finished sentence sounds awkward or roundabout, try rewriting it with a new subject.

> **Guide to Revision**   **Subj**
>
> # CHOICE OF SUBJECT
>
> *Select a new subject and revise the sentence, preferably with a verb other than* to be.
>
> | ORIGINAL | REVISION |
> |---|---|
> | The important thing is that shifting your weight is necessary on a turn if the centrifugal force is to be accommodated for. [*The abstract subject leads to a clumsy construction.*] | You must shift your weight to accommodate for the centrifugal force developed in the turn. [*With a pronoun as the subject the sentence becomes simpler and clear.*] |
> | The reason for Gary's wanting to major in molecular physics was because of his interest in a graduate degree in rocket engineering. | Gary wanted to major in molecular physics as preparation for a graduate degree in rocket engineering. |

THE VERB

The second part of the SVC, the verb, is the focal point of the comment about the topic. It is the engine that brings the sentence to life and gets it moving forward.

1. *Intransitive* An intransitive verb has no complement. It does not *transfer* or *transmit* meaning. Along with modifiers, it can complete the comment on the topic. It appears in sentences based on SVC pattern 1.

She *sang*.

In spite of her incipient laryngitis, the drafty old barn in which she was asked to perform, and the handicap of a foreign audience, she *sang* very well, reaching high C with scarcely a suggestion of a squeak.

2. Transitive The transitive verb takes at least one object complement. Pattern 2 sentences use transitive verbs.

The car *turned* the corner.

Johnny *gave* his mother a green apple.

3. Linking A linking verb, usually some form of *to be*, carries little meaning but links a subject with a subject complement. Linking verbs appear in patterns 3, 4, and 5.

The big car *was* a gas hog.

The milk *turned* sour.

Linking verbs are primarily function or relationship words, doing more to show how other words are related than to carry meaning. *Was* joins *big car* and *gas hog*, a subject complement that restates the subject. *Turned* joins *milk* with a complement, *sour*, that modifies *milk*.

Notice that *turned* appears in all three groups, with some change of meaning in its different uses. Most verbs can function as either transitive or intransitive, and some may also serve as linking verbs (*seem, appear, look, get, become, feel, taste, smell, sound*). *Turned* can function also in sentences like the following:

The car *turned over*.

The cook *turned off* the gas.

The verbs in these sentences are called *separable suffix verbs* or *merged verbs*. Compare the following:

Frankie *looked* over the transom.

Frankie *looked over* the contract.

In the first, *looked* can be thought of as the verb with "over the transom" telling where Frankie looked. In the second, the contract is not a barrier over which Frankie cast her glance. *Look over* has become a merged verb, and a single synonym like *examined* might be substituted for it.

CHOOSING VERBS

Even with a good subject, an inadequate verb will weaken a sentence. Consider "Johnny is a dropout." The sentence begins with the actor as subject, but *is* does little more than fill the sentence pattern and link *Johnny* and *dropout*. If the writer has no more to say, the sentence is adequate; but usually a writer has more to say. He could go on with the same pattern: "Johnny is a dropout. He was the owner of a convertible. It was new. But he was in a wreck with it." This sounds wordy and immature largely because verbs carry none of the meaning. Compare "Johnny, a dropout, wrecked his new convertible." With an expressive verb, *wrecked*, for the main predication, *is* and *was* can be dropped and *dropout* and *new* can be subordinated (see chapter 8).

A writer can often improve a paper by checking every use of a form of the verb *to be* and trying to revise by using a more precise verb. Furthermore, sensitive choice of verbs permits subtle distinctions. In the example above, the devastation to Johnny's car could be altered by changing *wrecked* to *scratched, dented, crumpled, smashed,* or *demolished.* Some writers quoting material overuse the verb *state,* when they might gain at once variety and exactness by judicious use of synonyms like *write, declare, assert, imply, infer, admit, insist, concede, suggest, explain, postulate, amplify, propose, conclude, reveal, doubt, argue, point out, wonder if, question whether, add,* or *continue.* Usually the more specific and concrete the verb, the more forceful and clear the sentence will be. Compare:

He was unhappy.   He wept.

THE COMPLEMENT

Complements are not always easy to define or to distinguish from complex verbs, but in general they are of two sorts, the *object complement* and the *subject complement*.

The *object complement* (in pattern 2 sentences) completes the verb by introducing the name of something that is not the subject and that receives the predication of the verb:

Tam O'Shanter saw a *witch*.
He admired her short *skirt*.
His wife made *it* an *issue*.
She gave *Tam* some *advice*.

Object complements are highly varied, and a complete analysis of them is not easy. For instance, in the sentences "Mary made a cake" and "The cake made Jimmie sick," the cake, clearly, did not make Jimmie in the same sense that Mary made the cake. Fortunately, the student need not distinguish different sorts of object complements in order to write vigorous sentences.

The *subject complement* completes predication but also elaborates or modifies the idea expressed in the subject. One type of subject complement, known as a *predicate nominative* or *predicate noun* (pattern 3 sentences), may give another name for the subject, mention a class that includes the subject, or include the subject in a group and sharpen our understanding of it:

> Tam O'Shanter was a *Scotsman*.
>
> He was an old *soak*.

A second type of subject complement (pattern 4 sentences) acts as a modifier, specifying a quality or characteristic of the subject:

> Tam seemed *thirsty*.
>
> He was *drunk* every Saturday night.

Often this type of subject complement is called a *predicate adjective*.

The distinction between object and subject complements has practical importance in usage because pronouns used as subject complements traditionally take the subjective or nominative form.

>   S   V C
> The *person* they're talking about is *I*.
>   S   V C
> The real *winner* is *she*.
> S V C
> It was *I* who brought you the message.

Informally and in speech, however, objective forms are common: "It's me."

CLAUSES AND THE SVC PATTERN

Word groups that contain a subject and a verb, SVC patterns, are called clauses. A clause that can stand alone as a sentence is called independent. An independent clause may be a complete sentence or may be joined with other clauses in a more complex sentence. Following are examples of independent clauses:

> Horses eat hay.
>
> Towering genius disdains a beaten path.
>
> Pure truth cannot be assimilated by the crowd; it must be communicated by contagion.

The third sentence contains two independent clauses, with subject and verb *truth cannot be assimilated* and *it must be communicated*.

Sometimes, however, a clause is introduced by a function word like *when* or *although* or *if* (see chapter 9) which makes it dependent or subordinate. The following combines two clauses, but only the second is independent:

Until you have become a brother to everyone, brotherhood will not come to pass.

The first clause, introduced by *until*, is dependent.

COMPLETING THE SVC PATTERN: THE FRAGMENT

A complete English sentence must have at least one independent clause containing the two main elements of the basic SVC pattern, a subject and a verb. Anything punctuated as a sentence—beginning with a capital letter and ending with a period—and not containing an independent clause with a subject and verb, is only a fragment of a sentence, and usually is a serious writing error.

Fragments, of course, sometimes work. Often in conversation and sometimes in writing, parts of the basic sentence are not expressed; they are understood from the context. They are incomplete in form, but they can stand independently in their contexts and are punctuated as sentences. Among the most common are exclamations, like "Oh, wonderful!" or "Incredible!" or "Good morning," and replies to questions, like "No," "Yes," or "Of course." Also used in both speaking and writing is the command, in which no subject is expressed: "Go wash the dishes" or "Let sleeping dogs lie." Our feeling for usual word order is so firm, moreover, that other types of incomplete sentences can make complete statements in context. "How old are you?" might be answered by the complete sentence "I am twenty years old," but the incomplete sentence "Twenty" is more likely. "Years old" can be omitted because we habitually state ages in years (we would specify two decades), and "I am" can be omitted because it is so obvious a part of the regular word order that the question implies it.

A paragraph from Thomas Wolfe's *Of Time and the River* illustrates a modern writer's use of the incomplete sentence, punctuated like a complete sentence and making a statement:

> The coming on of the great earth, the new lands, the enchanted city, the approach, so smoky, blind and stifled, to the ancient web, the old grimed thrilling barricades of Boston. The streets and buildings that slid past that day with such a haunting strange familiarity, the mighty engine steaming to its halt, and the great trainshed dense with smoke and acrid with its smell and full of the slow pantings of a dozen engines, now passive as great cats, the mighty station with the ceaseless throngings of its illimitable life, and all of the murmurous, remote and mighty sounds of time forever held there in the station, together with a tart and nasal voice, a hand'sbreadth off that said: "There's hahdly time, but try it if you want."

Such sentences are incomplete as grammatical units because they omit an essential element, subject or verb, but they may work, because basic word order has become standard in English. We anticipate missing elements, and in successful incomplete sentences we automatically supply them. The writer establishes a pattern that helps the reader perceive unexpressed thoughts. The incomplete sentences in the Wolfe paragraph above are subjects. The reader can understand what the writer means to say about these subjects—that they are observed or were part of an experience.

Except in reports of conversation, however, the incomplete sentence seldom works. Usually a fragment indicates that a writer is careless or doesn't understand the basic structure of the English sentence. The most common types of unwarranted incomplete sentences are the following:

1. Patterns Lacking a Verb The writer of the following sequence punctuated as sentences two groups of words that have no verb:

> Looking out toward the horizon, she saw only the old cabin in which Mary had been born. A single cottonwood with most of its branches dying. The apparently boundless expanse of sunburned prairie.

The last two groups of words are not sentences, but they could be incorporated as complements in the sentence:

> Looking out toward the horizon, she saw only the old cabin in which Mary had been born, a single cottonwood with most of its branches dying, and the apparently boundless expanse of sunburned prairie.

2. Verbal Mistaken for a Verb An *-ing* or *-ed* form of a verb, unless it is part of a complete verb, will not complete an SVC pattern. Consider:

> A communist government attempts to distribute the products of industry equally. It often restricts individual liberty, however. The system requiring careful control of the means of production.

Requiring in the final word group functions as a modifier, not a verb. A verb, *requires*, could be supplied to produce a sentence:

> The system requires careful control of the means of production.

The three short sentences, however, don't clearly relate ideas, and a revision combining the word groups works better:

> A communist government attempts to distribute the products of industry equally; but since the system requires careful state control of the means of production, it often restricts individual liberty.

3. Dependent Clause as Sentence An SVC pattern may be introduced by a word like *because* or *after* or *if* which makes it dependent, not

Basic Sentence Patterns

> *Guide to Revision:*   **Frag**
>
> ## FRAGMENT
>
> *Rewrite, completing an incomplete sentence pattern or combining a fragment with another sentence.*
>
> | ORIGINAL | REVISION |
> |---|---|
> | The actor strapped his ankle to his thigh. In this manner giving the impression he had only one leg. [*The second group of words contains no verb.* Giving *could work as part of a verb like* was giving, *but alone it cannot fill the verb slot.*] | The actor strapped his ankle to his thigh to give the impression he had only one leg. [*Joining the fragment to the existing sentence is the best solution.*] |
> | He failed the course in physics. Either because of laziness or because of stupidity. [*The final group of words fills no basic sentence pattern. The writer probably only mispunctuated, having meant something like (1). The writer could revise also by adding a verb (2) or by making the subordination clearer (3).*] | (1) He failed the course in physics, either because of laziness or because of stupidity.
 (2) He failed the course in physics. Either laziness or stupidity was his trouble.
 (3) Because of either laziness or stupidity, he failed the course in physics. |

able to stand alone as a sentence. The second word group in the following is a fragment:

> In the morning, Thoreau was released from jail. Although he still refused to pay the tax.

Although makes its clause dependent. It could simply be omitted to make the group of words grammatically a sentence, but combining is a better solution:

> Although he still refused to pay the tax, Thoreau was released from jail in the morning.

Other words which may introduce dependent clauses include: *when, whenever, before, while, during, that, which, until, since* (see chapter 9).

FOR STUDY AND WRITING

A. Revise each of the following sentences by choosing a new subject and following it with a verb other than a form of *to be*. If you remember to put the actor in the subject position, you should have no trouble. For example, the revision of the first sentence might read: "Every young person should have some self-confidence."

1. Something any young person should have is some self-confidence.
2. By promising everybody everything they might ever want was the system by which it was her hope that she would be victorious in the election.
3. The result John hoped to achieve was frightening the girls by holding the skull on a stick outside their window.
4. The reason for the confusion of the people with the new regulations was the ambiguous way in which they were written.
5. The influence that he had over his wife was only in regard to her political attitudes.
6. The way in which he taught his daughter to swim was by throwing her into the middle of the lake without her water wings.
7. Realizing that society had more important goals than producing wealth was the guiding force in Mary's decision to start a cooperative community.
8. Because he was stalking her calf was why Bryan was chased by the moose.
9. The information that we needed to discredit the first witness was from an old man who had seen the accident occur.
10. The method by which the fence was built by the new gardener was by the use of plum saplings planted and twisted so that they would grow together.

B. Brainstorm on several of the following verbs to see how many concrete and specific action verbs you can discover: *said, walked, saw, asked, laughed, cried*. Remember this technique for your next writing assignment.

C. The passage below contains a number of fragments used as sentences. Revise the passage to make the fragments complete sentences or to combine the fragments with other sentences.

Catherine II, called Catherine the Great, came to the throne of Russia in 1762. Her reign being the most notable of those that followed the long rule of Peter the Great. Although she was not a Russian by birth, Catherine remained on the Russian throne for thirty-four years. Since she was a German princess whose marriage to Peter III had been arranged by Frederick the Great. Peter III being half-insane when he took the throne. Catherine, a despot who wished to be regarded as an "enlightened" despot like Frederick II of Prussia, more concerned with maintaining prestige than spreading culture through her country. She continued some of the work of Peter the Great, ruling the country firmly and strengthening the central authority by administrative reorganization. Divisions of the government under appointed governors and vice-governors, all responsible to the tsarina. A church dependent for its property and power on the desires of the central authority. By maintaining a strong foreign policy and striking her rivals when they were weak, she established the international position of the Russian empire. A war against the Ottoman Empire, 1768–1774, was highly successful. Which led to navigation rights for Russian ships and added considerably to Russian territory. Poland, weakened by internal strife, and easily preyed upon by surrounding empires. By 1795 Poland had virtually ceased to exist as an independent state. Her territory partitioned among Austria, Prussia, and Russia. With Catherine getting the lion's share. Catherine's internal policies did bring about a number of reforms. The establishment, for example, of schools and academies. Reform, however, being carefully regulated. In order to prevent genuine enlightenment of the masses that might weaken the position of the aristocracy.

D. Sentences developed from the different patterns have different uses. The following paragraphs have been rewritten—often distorted—by changing sentences from one pattern to another, so that patterns with linking verbs predominate. Rewrite each paragraph, changing sentences to subject-verb or subject-verb-object patterns whenever you think you can make the writing more direct.

1. [1] My father was as unmechanical a man as ever lived, and the gasoline engine was a complete mystery to him. [2] Sometimes as far as he went was to lift the hood and stare at the engine, or maybe it was to reach in and wiggle a wire to see whether it would wiggle. [3] But mostly his procedure was to confine himself to kicking the tires. [4] It was never clear to me, and I doubt that it was clear to him, what he expected to learn from this, but he was very serious and professional about it. [5] His attitude was that of thumping a patient's chest. [6] It is a wonder to me that he never placed a stethoscope to the casing or stuck a fever thermometer down the valve stem.

2. [1] The fact that courses are the means by which information is made available to students is one reason for there being textbooks. [2] Knowing where you are going in a class is easier for both student and teacher if there is a textbook available to them. [3] That is, to make the point briefly we could say that a textbook helps to show where the course is going and that it provides a kind of record to how the teacher and the class are getting on.

[4] A lot of people are going to have their feelings hurt by this statement, especially those teachers that are liberal and progressive, who are the same ones who deplore there being any kind of prescription in teaching, and who may also have various reasons for not wanting textbooks, perhaps partly because of the name, textbook, because the word *text* has echoes of scripture and authority.

3. [1] The great migratory wave in American life is from country to city. [2] What happens to tens of thousands of children is that they are swept up in this wave and transplanted from a rural variety of poverty to the more oppressive urban ghetto. [3] Something from which they suffer is what social scientists call "cultural shock." [4] Little conception of what happens in cities or even what they look like is the rule for such children. [5] Trips to and around the city, routine for more privileged children, are the instruments whereby it is possible to help equalize the impoverished child's knowledge of modern realities.

E. Go through a draft you have written and circle all the forms of *to be*. Then replace these with active verbs, and see if this improves your prose. You may need to make other changes too.

F. Analyze the sentences in an essay you have written recently, underlining subject, verbs, and complements in the main patterns of each. Which of the main patterns appear most frequently? Try changing any of the sentences you can to another pattern, and decide whether the original or the revision is better.

7

Predication: Pattern Variations

You can't put a square peg in a round hole.

I got into my bones the essential structure of the normal British sentence—which is a noble thing.
WINSTON CHURCHILL

A subject, a verb, and often a complement form the backbone, the essential structure, of a sentence. If the backbone, the basic SVC pattern, is to be strong enough to support the rest of the sentence, the parts of the pattern must work together. This working together, expressing what a subject does or is, is called *predication*. And for clear predication we must fill the slots of basic SVC patterns wisely—square pegs in square slots—and vary patterns only for a purpose.

PLAUSIBLE PREDICATION

Pegs can have too many corners for round holes. As discussed in chapter 6, only certain sorts of words have privilege of occurrence in the main slots of the SVC pattern—nouns in the subject and complement positions, verbs as verbs. But privilege of occurrence depends also on meaning. And sometimes words that seem at first glance to have the right shapes will not fit because their meanings do not make sense together. Consider:

> The prejudice ambushed inconsequentials.
> The lampshade promised Albert.
> Any person meant the failure.

Nobody is likely to write such absurdities, but the following sentence was committed to paper:

> Any person ill on the day of that first performance would have meant the failure of the entire summer theater.

Embedded in the longer sentence, the basic pattern, "any person meant the failure," does not parade its lack of sense. The reader can guess at what the writer intended, but essentially the longer sentence is as illogical as the shorter one above. The writer has not produced a plausible predication, has not built the sentence on a framework with a compatible subject, verb, and complement. The writer probably meant:

> The illness of any member of the cast on the day of that first performance would have led to the failure of the entire summer theater.

"Illness would have led to failure" as the SVC core at least makes sense, but the sentence remains awkward. Compare:

> If any member of the cast had been ill on the day of that first performance, the entire summer theater would have failed.

A better subject leads to a better verb. Consider a similar sentence:

> The basis for the continuing unrest, which was partly misunderstanding and partly understanding too well what our motives were, held little hope among our representatives for success in negotiating new treaties.

At first glance the words seem to communicate; they sound like a sentence. But they communicate only confusion because the basic pattern is confused: "The basis held little hope." The subject, verb, and complement do not make sense together, even though the length of the sentence momentarily obscures the confusion. With a new subject and verb the sentence comes nearer sense:

> Our representatives had little hope of negotiating new treaties because of the continuing unrest, based partly on misunderstanding our motives and partly on understanding them too well.

Obviously not all possible subjects, verbs, and complements make sense in combinations. The possible subjects for *sparkle* are numerous, but they are also limited; *gold, eyes,* and *hair* would work, and metaphorically even *wit* and *conversation,* but *clamor, participation, sneeze,* and *appetite* are not likely. Various kinds of nouns point toward certain sorts of verbs. For example, animate nouns (*boy, dog, captain*) can be followed by verbs that will not work with inanimate nouns (*book, opinion, cup*). You can say "The boy is swimming" or "The dog barks," but not "The opinion is swimming" or "The cup barks." A few structures warrant special notice.

The Forgotten Subject

If you temporarily lose sight of your subject, probably thinking of what you mean rather than what you write, absurdities like the following appear:

> If present trends continue, by next year the applicants who want to be considered for the benefits of free advanced education will have doubled.
>
> Many people may find homes there and expand into towns.

Isolating the basic patterns from which the two sentences derive, "applicants double" and "people expand," reveals the absurdity—with applicants splitting like amoebas and people becoming balloons. Revision would require a new basic pattern:

> If present trends continue, by next year the number of applicants for free advanced education will have doubled.
>
> Many people may find homes there and start developing towns.

The Verb Influenced by a Modifier

Predication becomes implausible if you pick a verb that would logically follow a modifier but does not fit with the subject. Consider:

> The setting of this picturesque little town was filled with a colorful history.

The sentence is confused in more ways than one, but incompatibility of the subject and predicate is central. The town, mentioned as part of a modifier, can be "filled with a colorful history," but the setting, used as the subject, cannot be. The sentence could be revised as follows:

> This picturesque little town has a colorful history.

It as Dummy Subject

It, when used as a substitute for the subject, may encourage illogical predication. Consider:

Guide to Revision **Pred**

IMPLAUSIBLE PREDICATION

Revise so that main parts of sentence patterns—subjects, verbs, and complements—are compatible in meaning.

ORIGINAL

My mother being unable to resist installment buying meant the difference between a comfortable existence and constant fear of poverty.
[*Mother makes no sense as a subject for* meant. *The subject probably intended is buried as a modifier.*]

The lack of a proper diet and work as heavy as lumbering demanded a man with a strong body.
[*The second part of the compound subject fits logically with the verb, but the first does not.*]

Perhaps there are omissions that should have been included.
[*Even though the verb should have been included is in a subordinate clause, it must make sense with* omissions, *represented by* that.]

He managed during his life to defy all the traditional qualities of an outstanding politician.
[*"To defy qualities" makes no sense.*]

REVISION

My mother's inability to resist installment buying meant the difference between a comfortable existence and constant fear of poverty.
[*Not* mother, *but* mother's inability *was probably intended as the subject.*]

Work as heavy as lumbering, carried on without a proper diet, demanded a man with a strong body.
[*The main subject is selected and the inappropriate idea becomes a modifier.*]

(1) Perhaps there are omissions that should have been remedied.
(2) Perhaps material has been omitted that should have been included.
[*The second revision is clearer.*]

He managed during his life to defy all the traditions associated with success in politics.

> With a knowledge of the history of words it will enable a student to read with keener understanding.

Insertion of the vague *it* confuses the predication to "it would enable." The writer might have used either of two available subjects, "knowledge" or "student," to produce revisions like:

> Knowledge of the history of words will enable a student to read with keener understanding.
>
> With a knowledge of the history of words, a student can read with keener understanding.

The Implausible Object

In the following, the choice of an unsuitable object produces a confused metaphor:

> Economists are still piecing together the overall situation.

The metaphor implied by the verb *piecing together* aggravates the disorder here so that *situation* cannot logically follow it as an object; you cannot piece together a situation. If the metaphor is to be retained the sentence might read:

> Economists are still piecing together the overall picture.

Or the trite metaphor could be abandoned.

> Economists do not yet understand what happened.

Hidden Objects

In the following sentence, a passive structure disguises a similar inconsistency between a verb and its complement:

> They let the discussion continue until after midnight in order that a consensus might be garnered.

Extraction of the basic pattern behind the final clause, "they garnered a consensus," exposes the awkwardness.

EQUATIONS WITH *TO BE*

The verb *to be*—which appears in forms like *am, is, are, was, were, be, being,* or *been*—is the verbal workhorse of the language. But it is deceptively handy—a trickster conning unwary writers into talking nonsense, partly because its uses are so varied. It may carry some meaning, as in "To be or not to be" and "Whatever is, is right," where it can mean *to exist*. It may imply definition or classification (Music is an art), supply a name (This is John), connect a subject with a modifier (The apple is ripe), or act as part of another verb (The picture is being made now). In all these the *to be* means very little; it mainly joins or links other meanings. Used in this way, to link a subject and a complement, the verb *to be* almost always implies some kind of identity.

Sentences developed from patterns with *to be* need not, of course, be mathematical equations; life is not literally a dream. But a sentence in the form of an equation must link ideas that can plausibly be identified with each other. Abstractions in either the subject or complement position are especially treacherous:

> Ranching is an idea that has always attracted me.

Ranching is not an "idea"; the implausible equation spoils the sentence. The equation could easily be improved:

> Ranching is a profession that has always attracted me.

A better revision eliminates the equation, shifting to a different sentence pattern:

> Ranching has always attracted me.

Even a difference in number between the subject and the complement may make an equation sound illogical:

> The problem for the students was the instructor's many personal anecdotes, which distracted them.

The sentence is awkward mainly because the singular subject, *problem*, is linked with the plural complement, *anecdotes*. Changing the pattern solves the problem:

> The instructor's personal anecdotes distracted the students.

A few variations on equation problems warrant special attention.

False Equations with Modifiers for Complements

The only pattern with a linking verb that does not equate the subject with a complement is pattern 5, in which an adverb indicating place occupies the complement slot: "The moon was over his left shoulder." In sentences with this pattern the adverb seems to modify both subject and verb, and the construction is clear. But other kinds of modifiers—*quickly, prominently, with abandon, whenever he was ready*—will not work in a pattern 5 sentence. When they are put into the complement slot, they become ambiguous because they act as if they should equate with the subject or modify it; that is, they look like pattern 3 or 4 sentences. Consider:

> The method of holding a club that some golfers find produces the longest drives is with the hands locked together.

The sentence derives from "method is with the hands locked." The adverb of manner, "with the hands locked," will work neither as a subject complement nor as an adverb of place. The pattern is not characteristic of the language. As usual, choosing a different subject, the actor, begins the best revision:

> Some golfers find that they can make longer drives if they grip the club with locked hands.

Or consider:

> The way Mary wore her clothes was with an air of sophistication.

The sentence is based on an implausible equation. Compare a direct sentence:

> Mary wore her clothes with an air of sophistication.

"Is because," "Is when"

One variation on the dubious equation uses in the complement slot a clause beginning with words like *when, why, where,* or *because,* which traditionally introduce modifying clauses. Such equations abound in conversation and can even be found in carefully written prose. But they can become ludicrous, and even if they are clear in meaning they may irk logical minds that like their equations to equate. Here are samples:

> Radicalism is when you jump to conclusions.
> The study of mathematics is where I get my lowest grades.
> The reason Johnson wrote *Rasselas* was because he needed money for his mother's funeral.

None of these presents much danger of serious misunderstanding, but the equations are hardly precise. Whatever radicalism may be, it is not time, and study is not a place. *That,* not *because,* is the standard introduction for a noun clause. Sentences of this sort are almost always wordier and less precise than more direct constructions.

> Radicalism usually involves jumping to conclusions.
> I get my lowest grades in mathematics.
> Johnson wrote *Rasselas* because he needed money for his mother's funeral.

Such constructions can have uses, as in the witticism, "Summer is when parents pack up their troubles and send them off to camp," but in general, clauses relying on *is when, is where, is why,* and *is because* are best revised.

Equations in Frame Sentences

In most of the sentences we have considered, the main predication, the SVC, has carried the important part of the meaning of the sentence. Consider, however, the following:

> The most important thing to remember is that nobody has ever reached the peak without oxygen tanks.
> The first matter to consider is how far we can go without letting the administration express its attitude.
> I think that somebody must have picked the lock and taken the examinations.

Each of these sentences has a standard basic pattern, subject-verb-complement, with the complement slot filled by a clause. But the three subjects, *thing, matter,* and *I,* are not what the sentences mainly concern, and the verbs *is* and *think* do not embody significant assertions. In each sentence the complement makes the important comment. The basic pattern works only as a kind of "frame" to present the idea in the complement.

Such sentences are useful, especially in introductions and transitions. Context may require them, to carry on a subject or to provide special emphasis, as in the following, which use a possible object to construct a frame:

> Algebra was the only course John studied last year.
> This quarrel with his son was now his only regret.

Both of these, however, are indirect and carry the hazards of the *to be* sentence, with its need for a logical equation. Often the more direct sentence, with the actor as subject, can improve the writing:

> John studied only algebra last year.
> Now he regretted only this quarrel with his son.

Guide to Revision   Eq

FALSE EQUATIONS

Revise to avoid an implausible equation of subject with subject complement. Usually the best solution is to change the basic sentence pattern, shifting from "to be" to a different verb.

ORIGINAL	REVISION
The only knowledge I have had about horses is living on a farm and raising them. [Knowledge *is not* living.]	The only knowledge I have of horses comes from living on a farm and raising them. [*Changing the verb makes the sentence logical.*]
The only uniform I have been issued was in camp last August. [*The sentence is unclear because* was *links no complement with* uniform. *Either supply a complement (1) or change the verb (2).*]	(1) The only uniform I have been issued is the one I received in camp last August. (2) I have been issued only one uniform, which I received in camp last August.
A syllogism is where you use a major and minor premise to get a logical answer. [*A syllogism is not a place.*]	In a syllogism, you use a major and minor premise to obtain a logical answer.

CONSISTENCY IN STRUCTURE: SHIFTS

Since an English sentence develops from one of the basic patterns, predication is clear only when you follow a pattern consistently. If you begin with one pattern in mind, then forget and shift to a different one, inevitably you produce something other than sense. Consider.

> For information concerning almost any event that is too minor to be found in periodical articles may be located through *The New York Times Index.*

The writer apparently started the sentence with a subject in mind, perhaps *you* or *one;* but by the end of the long modifier, any sense of a pattern was lost. The "sentence" never acquired a subject. The writer might have followed the original structure, supplying a subject:

> For information concerning almost any event too minor to be found in periodical articles, the research worker can use *The New York Times Index*.

With a new subject, the sentence works better:

> *The New York Times Index* includes information about almost any event too minor to be reported in periodicals.

The same sort of forgetfulness can weaken continuity and produce confusion by shifting patterns unnecessarily from clause to clause. Consider the following:

> We packed the baskets of food and the seven children into the old car, and a very pleasant afternoon at the lake was enjoyed by everyone.

Guide to Revision — **Shift**

SHIFT IN CONSTRUCTION

Revise to avoid shifted structures, either shifts within the basic pattern of a sentence or illogical shifts in pattern from one sentence or clause to another.

ORIGINAL

Any passage that pleased him he tried to write something in the same style.
[*What promises to be the subject*, passage, *never becomes one.*]

After the textbook had been mastered, she had no trouble with chemistry.
[*The impersonal passive construction shifts awkwardly to the active.*]

REVISION

(1) Any passage that pleased him was likely to become the model for a composition in the same style.
(2) He would imitate any passage that pleased him.

After she had mastered the textbook, she had no trouble with chemistry.
[*Both structures are now active.*]

The sentence shifts from a regular subject-verb-complement pattern in the first clause to a passive variation of it in the second clause. Maintaining the first pattern produces a more direct sentence:

> We packed the baskets of food and the seven children into the old car and enjoyed a pleasant afternoon at the lake.

POSTPONED SUBJECT: EXPLETIVE

Most English sentences work best with the standard SVC order. For some purposes, however, the parts of the basic pattern may be rearranged. The pattern "The children are happy" readily changes to "Are the children happy?" to ask a question. In another variation, the first element of the SVC pattern, the subject, moves to a position later in the sentence. Consider:

> It is simply impossible to exhaust the variety of significant change in linguistic growth: there is no conceivable direction in which a transfer may not be made; there is no assignable distance to which a word may not wander from its primitive meaning.
>   William Dwight Whitney, *Language and the Study of Language*

In each of these three patterns, *it* or *there* serves as an expletive. That is, in each clause *it* or *there* fills the subject slot, although it is not a noun and carries no meaning, serving mainly as a function word to fill the sentence pattern. The ideas being talked about, the usual material for the subject, appear in the complement position after *is*.

This sentence is unusual in the book from which it is taken; Whitney relies mainly on subject-verb-complement sentences. Here, however, he has good reasons for the variations: reasons that will appear if we consider the following main uses of the expletive sentence.

1. *To Provide a Simple Predication* The expletive provides a simple means of saying that something exists, as in "There are two reasons for doubting his word" and "There will be time for one more question." These ideas could be expressed in other ways, as in "We could find two reasons . . ." and "Two reasons are apparent . . . ," but for most purposes such devices would offer no improvement. For simple purposes like identification, expletives may provide the smoothest, most economical structure. Expletive sentences of this sort frequently appear as topic sentences: "There were three good reasons for preferring the safer course."

2. *To Permit a Parallel Structure* Expletives permit the writer to assemble parallel details, especially materials too complicated to serve well in the subject, which usually should be followed by a verb without much intervening matter. Whitney used the structure to give parallel form to parallel ideas, "no conceivable direction in which," and "no assignable distance to which."

3. To Promote Continuity The expletive variation can provide continuity from clause to clause or give special emphasis. The following example illustrates:

> There is no such thing in America as an independent press, unless it is in the country towns. You know it and I know it. There is not one of you who dare to write his honest opinions, and if you did you know beforehand they would never appear in print.
>
> John Swinton, *"Five-Minute Talk"*

The final sentence could easily have been phrased in the SVC pattern: "Not one of you dares. . . ." By making the sentence parallel with the first sentence, however, the writer expedites the flow of thought.

Except for these purposes, the expletive pattern seldom helps. The construction is by its nature roundabout. Often it is wordy, and it obscures

---

Guide to Revision   **Expl**

OVERUSED EXPLETIVES

Revise to remove expletives and to restore the subject-verb order.

ORIGINAL	REVISION
There was a long argument, and then we decided to push on. It was soon agreed among us, however, that we had made a mistake. Within an hour all our patrols were pinned down by sniper and mortar fire. It was obvious that we should have stayed at the base camp. [*The needlessly inverted sentences slow and obscure the passage.*]	After a long argument we decided to push on. Soon, however, we agreed that we had made a mistake. Within an hour all our patrols were pinned down by sniper and mortar fire. Obviously, we should have stayed at the base camp. [*Normal order strengthens and shortens the passage.*]

the parts of the sentence that are potentially strongest, the subject and the main verb. Consider, for example, "It is a fact that it is hard to get people to see that there is a lot of sport in snowshoeing." The sentence limps along mainly because so many subjects are needlessly postponed. Compare "Although few people know it, snowshoeing can be a rewarding sport." Another example, "It is required that you complete Form 16-B before you can be admitted," omits the actor from the sentence. The bewildered form-filler has no idea who requires this, who is responsible—state law, federal government, divine fiat.

THE PASSIVE

Another variation in predication preserves the SVC order but shifts the actor to the complement slot. Usually an agent or actor is named in the first position of the SVC pattern; we need to know whom or what we are talking about. Sometimes, however, the agent or actor is less important than the action or the result. The actor may be unknown or should not be mentioned; or continuity may require that some word other than the name of the actor appear first. The passive construction provides for such variations. Compare:

> The rebels fired the first shot.
> The first shot was fired by the rebels.

In the first, the more direct sentence, the actor, *rebels*, is the subject, with *shot* as object. The second reverses the pattern. The verb is made passive by adding a form of the verb *to be* as a function word, *was fired*. *Shot* becomes the subject in the passive sentence. Either pattern would work, of course, depending on the context and the emphasis desired. Compare the following, however:

> In June somebody completed the new road.
> The new road was completed in June.

The second sentence omits the subject *somebody*, and for most purposes this passive sentence would be preferable to the active. The useless subject *somebody* can be omitted.

Passive constructions are frequently misused and overused, especially in business, institutional, and scientific writing. Apparently the writer hopes to lend a more formal, objective quality to the writing. Actually the passive weakens the prose and produces flabby writing. Compare:

> The experiments on the fruit fly's adaptability to environmental changes were carried out by a team of researchers.

A research team experimented on the fruit fly's adaptability to environmental change.

Coordination of financial planning was agreed upon by the corporation's board of directors.

The corporation's board of directors agreed to coordinate financial planning.

Inversion through use of the passive construction throws stress on the receiver of the action, draws attention away from the actor-action pattern, and may produce roundabout sentences like the following:

The lake where the meetings of our gang are held is reached by an old road that was found by me when I was hidden there by the kidnappers.

Two of the passives in the sentence may be justified, but revising at least two of them strengthens the sentence:

The lake where our gang holds its meetings can be reached by an old road that I found when I was hidden there by the kidnappers.

Whenever an actor is named, it usually works best in the subject slot. Like the expletive sentence, however, the passive sentence has important uses:

1. When an Actor Is Not Known A historian writes, "The world of St. Paul was steeped in guilt and wretchedness." He does not know who steeped it; the agent, even if it could be determined, would be much too complicated for expression in a single sentence. Or consider "Nations that have lost their moral self-respect are easily conquered." This generalization does not depend on who conquers these nations; no one actor could be specified.

2. When There Are Reasons for Not Naming the Actor Assume we wish to mention the publication of a book in 1623, but we have no reason to name the publisher. If we use the subject-verb-object pattern, we are faced with something like "A person or persons whom we do not wish to mention just now published the book in 1623." We can solve the problem by saying "The book was published in 1623." There may even be legal reasons for not specifying an actor. A newspaper reporter might be telling the truth by writing "John A. Scrogum murdered Joseph Meek at 7:45 this morning in the Hot Spot Lunch." This statement is libelous. Accordingly, the reporter would probably write something like "Joseph Meek was shot and killed at 7:45 this morning in the Hot Spot Lunch." With the actor removed, the statement is legally publishable.

3. *For Stylistic Reasons, Especially for the Following Purposes:*

a. To provide continuity by maintaining the same subject in a sequence of sentences.

> The new student-body president gained immediate support when he proposed a campaign to clean up the campus. He was severely criticized, however, by the student senate committee when he suggested that the campaign should be financed with student-body funds.

Using *he* as the subject of the second sentence continues the subject. Using *committee*, the actor, as the subject would break the continuity.

b. To give special prominence to the receiver of the action.

> An investigation was authorized by the legislature an hour after the protest march began.

c. To avoid inserting extensive material between a subject and verb.

> The chairman of the committee, who was known for ruthlessness in smirching the reputations of innocent witnesses and for cleverness in beclouding the issue by witticisms and innuendoes, opened the hearing.

The long modifier interrupts the basic sentence pattern, separating the subject, *chairman*, from the verb, *opened*. Compare:

> The hearing was opened by the chairman of the committee, who was known for ruthlessness in smirching the reputation of innocent witnesses and for cleverness in beclouding the issue by witticisms and innuendoes.

The revision, with a passive construction, keeps subject and verb together. Except in these special situations, the passive usually weakens English prose. In the following, most of the verbs are passive:

> Zoroaster's spirit was rapidly caught by the Persians. A voice that was recognized by them as speaking truth was responded to eagerly by a people uncorrupted by luxury. They have been called the Puritans of the Old World. Never, it is said, was idolatry hated by any people as it was by them, and for the simple reason that lies were hated by them.

Compare this passage with the original:

> The Persians caught rapidly Zoroaster's spirit. Uncorrupted by luxury, they responded eagerly to a voice which they recognized as speaking truth to

them. They have been called the Puritans of the Old World. Never any people, it is said, hated idolatry as they hated it, and for the simple reason that they hated lies.

James Anthony Froude, *Calvinism*

Guide to Revision **Pass**

INAPPROPRIATE PASSIVE

Strengthen sentences by replacing unwarranted passives with subject-verb-complement structures.

ORIGINAL

That there were many difficulties whereby women were unable to use the new union lounge was the attitude that was stated by the first speaker. It was her contention that women were resented in the lounge by the men students and that this resentment was clearly made known by the men in their actions. A different point of view was introduced by the second speaker, by whom it was stated that the reason for the inability of the women to make full use of the lounge was caused by the attitude of the women themselves. The views expressed by this speaker were the objects of sharp criticism from the other members of the panel.

The trouble was caused by John's insistence that he begin.
[*Nothing here warrants departing from normal order. The actor-action elements are present and important.*]

REVISION

The first speaker insisted that women were unable to use the new union lounge because men students resented having women there and made their resentment clearly known. The second speaker introduced a new point of view, that women were unable to make full use of the lounge because of their own attitude. The other members of the panel sharply criticized the views of this speaker.
[*The original has many weaknesses, but basic to most of them is overuse of unwarranted passives. The revision still needs development, but it improves the passage, mainly by recasting sentences in the actor-action pattern.*]

(1) John's insistence that he begin caused the trouble.
(2) John caused the trouble by insisting that he begin.

Froude's version keeps the actor-action pattern everywhere but in the third sentence and the parenthetical "it is said" of the fourth—in which the subjects of the action are unknown.

FOR STUDY AND WRITING

A. The sentences below contain faulty predication; that is, the basic sentence in each is illogical. Point out the main SVC in each sentence, analyze relationships, and revise each sentence so that the subject, verb, and complement work together.

1. The reason for our delay in prompt processing of this application is caused by staff shortages.
2. As soon as they are corrected these disadvantages will improve the club a great deal.
3. The sidewalk, being old and broken in many places, made our progress slow.
4. My mother objected to everybody whom I associated.
5. A parrot can be stroked on the chest, but anywhere else usually costs the admirer a sore finger.
6. The friends that you make often result from your manners.
7. This method took as long as three days to plant three hundred acres.
8. For a rifle team to become a success, many points must be accomplished.
9. The amount of money lost by both the strikers and the employers took a matter of years in order to regain them.
10. After intensive courses in hairdressing at the new college, everyone on our staff is trained to accentuate your beauty needs.

B. The sentences below contain equations with the verb *to be*. Identify subjects and complements. Then revise each sentence, changing subject or complement to make them work more logically together or using a more expressive verb than *to be*.

1. The source of my material is from two books.
2. A tragedy is when all the main characters die at the end.
3. The plans of a log cabin should be very compact and not too roomy.
4. College spirit is an experience long remembered after school is over.
5. In the play, the weavers' situation, which in broad terms is a people born

into a society where they must struggle to develop in all ways, is a basic problem of humanity.
6. Journalism is not a romantic life as some books play it up to be, and as some people believe; it is a hard job for anyone to undertake.
7. It can clearly be seen from the story that the desire to return Cassio to her husband's favor was because she honestly felt that it was best for him.
8. The nature of the adult illiterate has been one who has not had a chance to go to school and has never learned to read and to write.
9. The most outstanding of their rivalries were over a woman.
10. A follower and a leader are both qualities we must possess to enable us to achieve our goals.

C. Revise each of the following sentences by removing the expletive and recasting the sentence in normal order with a subject followed by a verb.

1. It is obvious that there should be more courses in fine arts taken by the average student.
2. There are more than a dozen cats waiting for the children to feed the birds.
3. There is no reason why Wayne should doubt his mother's word.
4. There was a tall white stallion standing all alone at the edge of the cliff.
5. It is in his book *The Diary of a Writer* that Dostoevsky describes how a mother hen defended her chickens from a brutal and sadistic boy.
6. If there is the desire to help, there are always lots of ways for parents to be saved money by the student.
7. It was when I was waiting in a registration line and I was talking with a graduate student that the realization came to me of how complicated a university is.
8. That was the time when there was an opportunity for me to buy my first colony of bees.
9. There were two chaperons in attendance at the dance, but still the uninvited guests soon outnumbered the invited ones.
10. It was because so many students had forgotten to register for the examination that there were new rules passed by the academic council.

D. Revise each of the sentences below by converting it to usual word order and using active verbs.

1. The corsage was worn by Wilma on her left shoulder.
2. The election was arranged by a group of dishonest party hacks so that the success of the reform movement was prevented.
3. Citizens of the United States were guaranteed freedom of speech by the First Amendment to the Constitution.
4. If the petition is signed by enough people, it will be considered by the assembly.
5. By using a spectroscope it is possible for many metals to be identified by a laboratory technician.

6. A very rigid censorship was imposed by the commanding officer on war news.
7. The ball was thrown accurately by the first baseman, but it was missed by the catcher, and the runner was waved home by the third-base coach.
8. Undeterred by the stories in the papers, a trip around the lake after midnight was contemplated by Jane and her roommate.
9. At the end of the passage our progress was arrested by a pile of huge boulders.
10. A small shop was opened on Fifth Avenue by two of my classmates where clothes could be designed by them to suit both the figure and the purse of the average office worker.

E. Rewrite the following passage to improve the predication. As the paragraph stands, several sentences rely upon SVC patterns in which the various parts cannot work together.

> Everyone knows that one of the worst places where the ecosystems are being disrupted is where the great whales are being systematically exterminated. Ocean-going refineries are the aspect of the fishing industry that some whalers are exterminating these wonderful mammals. Especially, whalers from Japan and Russia, even though those countries are supposed to be in civilized circumstances, with all the advantages that are modern educational systems. All this is what has been known for quite some time, but a recent discovery is the artistic abilities of some whales. The reason we know this is because a record has come out, *The Songs of the Humpback Whale* having been a revelation of what some sea life is capable. The artistic capabilities of the whales of this species is the variations they produce on musical sequences. They sing in what one reviewer of the record stated, perhaps because of the resonating bones in the whale's head, the music being electronic in character and it becomes almost stereo. One can only hope that the wide acceptance being accorded this record will be the occasion for renewed determination to put a stop to the environment that is our national and international heritage.

F. Mark every sentence in one of your essays in which you vary from usual word order. Then revise these sentences to the actor-action pattern and judge whether or not the change improves the essay.

G. Select a brief incident in the current news or something you recently witnessed. Tell it as a narrative, using your own words. Then make some comment upon the incident. For example, explain how it is beneficial or harmful, suggesting how such incidents can be prevented or encouraged in the future, or evaluate its importance.

When you have done so, classify your sentences by structure. You will probably find that in your narrative you have used mainly sentences and clauses having SVC patterns. You may find that in your second piece, an exposition based upon a narrative, either you have used more structures employing expletives and passives or you have been tempted to do so. Can you find good reason for using these expletives and passives? Change those you cannot defend, and notice the effect.

8

Combining Sentence Patterns: Coordination And Subordination

> *A sentence should read as if its author, had he held a plough instead of a pen, could have drawn a furrow deep and straight to the end.*
> HENRY DAVID THOREAU

Thoreau had worked with both plows and pens. He knew that drafting a sentence, like drawing a furrow, is harder than it may look. Most jobs are, because they take many skills and various tools and materials. Any lout could make a hole with a planting stick, very much as any child can invent a simple sentence like "Ruff has fleas." But handling a moldboard plow took some doing, as does drafting longer sentences so that they draw "deep and straight to the end." Two of the best devices are *coordination* and *subordination*.

These terms describe a fundamental purpose of writing—showing or creating relationships—and we have already discussed them as they relate to organizing ideas (see chapter 5). They apply also to ways of building sentences. In sentences, coordination expresses equality, that two or more elements—words or word groups—are equal to one another, have the same relationship to something else. Subordination indicates dependency, that one element supports another, is not equal to it.

The military provides an obvious analogy. Privates are subordinate to sergeants and coordinate with other privates. But just as people are not born privates or sergeants, ideas and words are not inherently coordinate or subordinate. A writer is creating and has more flexibility than a chief of staff in deciding which ranks will be established and what will go into each. A writer can have all privates or an elaborate combination of ranks.

To take a simple example, a writer commenting on someone's taste might say either "She likes pickles and ice cream" or "She likes pickles with ice cream." The first, where *pickles* and *ice cream* are coordinated, merely enumerates two items she likes to eat equally well, not necessarily at the same time. In the second, *with* signals subordination or dependency; she likes pickles, when served in combination with ice cream. Or compare these two sentences:

> He dropped to the ground, and the bomb exploded.
> After he dropped to the ground, the bomb exploded.
> After the bomb exploded, he dropped to the ground.

The first sentence indicates two actions happening simultaneously; they are equal. The second and third sentences establish a hierarchy, a sequential relationship in time—first one thing happened, then the next. Changing the element to be subordinated changes the meaning of the sentence. In sentences, as in the organization of a longer piece of writing, coordination and subordination are devices the writer can use to clarify relationships.

COORDINATING SENTENCES AND CLAUSES

As we indicated in chapter 5, SVC patterns combined in one sentence are conventionally called clauses; those that can stand as a single sentence are called independent. Independent clauses can be joined as coordinates, with different patterns varying the effect. Consider:

> His words leap across rivers and mountains. His thoughts are only six inches long.
> His words leap across rivers and mountains; his thoughts are only six inches long.
> His words leap across rivers and mountains, but his thoughts are only six inches long.

In the first version, the two ideas stand as independent sentences, although they are obviously related and are parallel in form. In the second version, the clauses are still independent—neither is subordinate to the other—but their interrelation is emphasized because they merge into one sentence, with a semicolon between them. In the third version, the function word *but* emphasizes the contrast between the ideas. E. B. White wrote the sentence this way.

Independent SVC clauses can be joined in three ways:

1. Putting the clauses in parallel form and using a semicolon to separate them:

> I have lived some thirty years on this planet; I have yet to hear the first syllable of valuable or even earnest advice from my seniors.

2. A variation of this pattern uses a conjunctive adverb (*however, nevertheless, moreover,* etc.) to signal coordination with a semicolon to separate:

> I have lived some thirty years on this planet; however, I have yet to hear the first syllable of valuable or even earnest advice from my seniors.

3. In a third pattern, a coordinating conjunction (*and, or, but, nor, for, so,* or *yet*) signals the coordination, and a comma separates the clauses:

> I have lived some thirty years on this planet, and I have yet to hear the first syllable of valuable or even earnest advice from my seniors.

Failure to provide adequate punctuation for these patterns suggests that the writer does not understand basic sentence structure and is a serious error—called a fused sentence or comma fault or comma splice (see chapter 17).

Unlike independent SVC clauses, clauses introduced by a function word (see chapter 9) like *before* or *if* or *until* become dependent, subordinate to an independent clause. But dependent clauses, like independent clauses, can be coordinated with one another, usually by using a coordinating conjunction. Observe:

> If you have any ideas about how we can improve our product or you know any ways of improving our service, I advise you to keep quiet about them.

Two dependent clauses connected by *or* are coordinate, and their working together is made clear by their parallel form and position.

COORDINATING LESSER SENTENCE ELEMENTS

A small child's talk is likely to move as a series of simple sentences: "I took my fish pole. I took Rover. I took my Daddy. I went fishing." Obviously the four sentences can be combined by coordination: "I took my fish pole and Rover and my Daddy and went fishing." This is still not a very mature remark, but it is more economical, avoiding the obvious repetition of *I* and *took*, and it relates simple ideas more directly.

Often ideas that could occupy a sentence or a clause may be reduced to a phrase or a word and coordinated. Consider the following:

> In the Indian Parliament a member may call his colleague a simian.
> In the Indian Parliament a member may not call his colleague a baboon.

The sentences are alike except for one item. The whole can be said with one sentence having a coordinate complement:

> In the Indian Parliament a member may call his colleague a simian, but not a baboon.

Most elements of a sentence can be used coordinately, and most sentences of any complexity have more than one sort of coordination. For instance, H. L. Mencken vented his disapproval of zoos as follows, although without italicizing his coordinate elements:

> The sort of man who likes to spend his time watching *a cage of monkeys chase one another*, or *a lion gnaw its tail*, or *a lizard catch flies*, is precisely the sort of man whose mental weakness should be *combated* at the public expense, not *fostered*.

PARALLELISM AND COORDINATION

Parallel structures reveal coordination. The writer puts coordinate items in like grammatical form, noncoordinate elements in some other form, and reinforces this parallel structure with word order and relationship words. Otherwise coordination may get confused, as a newspaper reporter demonstrated by writing the following:

> Among the items in the collection are the only known document bearing the signatures of Queen Elizabeth and Sir Walter Raleigh and a cigar-store Indian.

The reporter's copy may have included a comma after *Raleigh*, but even so the sentence seems to attribute more literacy to the statue than the writer probably intended. An easy way to revise sentences like this is to change the order of the items, putting the single coordinate element first.

> Among the items in the collection are a cigar-store Indian and the only known signatures of Queen Elizabeth and Sir Walter Raleigh.

The sentence is clear, although the collection seems unusual.

Parallelism can be more or less elaborate. When a zookeeper remarked that "We need good, strong cages to protect the animals from the public," he was using coordination very simply to join the words *good* and *strong*. The same device can knit together extremely complicated structures. For instance, in the sixteenth century, balanced and contrasted constructions became a fad, and when John Lyly wrote the following he was gaining a number of effects and also having fun with language:

> This young gallant, of more wit than wealth, and yet of more wealth than wisdom, seeing himself inferior to none in pleasant conceits, thought himself superior to all in honest conditions, insomuch that he deemed himself so apt to all things that he gave himself almost to nothing but practicing of those things commonly which are incident to these sharp wits, fine phrases, smooth quipping, merry taunting, using jesting without mean, and abusing mirth without measure.
>
> *Euphues*

The style is exaggerated, but the passage illustrates how intricately words, phrases, and clauses can be balanced against one another, with coordination kept clear by devices like the following:

1. *Give coordinate elements the same grammatical form.* The Mencken quotation uses grammatical parallelism:

$$\ldots \text{watching} \begin{cases} \text{a cage of monkeys chase one another} \\ \text{a lion gnaw its tail} \\ \text{a lizard catch flies} \end{cases}$$

The parallel grammatical structure of the three clauses emphasizes that they are coordinate, but consider the following sentence:

> Mary enrolled for painting, harmony, music appreciation, and to study art history.

Four items are put in a series, but the last is not parallel in form. Revision reinforces the coordination:

> Mary enrolled for painting, harmony, music appreciation, and art history.

2. *Use function words to signal coordination.* The following student sentence is clear partly because it repeats *in*.

> Bacon's "idols" dwell in the minds of men, but their temples are in London, in Moscow, and in Washington.

Compare the following sentence in which the parallelism is broken by inconsistent use of *the*.

> The only enemies of the sloth are the eagles, jaguars, and the large boas.

Either inserting *the* before the second element or dropping it altogether would restore the rhythm of the sentence and keep the coordinate items parallel:

> The only enemies of the sloth are eagles, jaguars, and large boas.

3. *Use word order to support coordination.* Signal words especially need to be placed carefully. Compare:

> You are either *late* or *early*.
> Either *you are late* or *I am early*.
> You are either *late* or *I am early*.

The first two sentences are clear because the signal words *either* and *or* appear just before the two expressions to be coordinated. The third is not clear because *either* is out of position. The following illustrates a similar danger:

> To be polite he first poured some of the wine into his glass so that he would get the cork and not the lady.

A revision changing the word order makes the modification clear:

> To be polite he first poured some of the wine into his glass so that he, and not the lady, would get the cork.

4. *Use coordinating structures only for items that can be logically coordinated.* Notice the following sentence: "The play was lively, witty, and the audience responsive though not very many of them." A diagram reveals that coordinated elements are not parallel:

> The play was { (1) lively / (2) witty / (3) the audience { (1) responsive / (2) not very many of them } }

Audience is not parallel with *lively* and *witty*, nor are the coordinated modifiers of *audience* parallel. The sentence seems to be coordinating elements that cannot logically be made parallel. The writer probably intended a pattern like the following:

(1) The play was { (1) lively
                    and
                   (2) witty }

and

(2) the audience was { (1) responsive
                       though
                       (2) small }

Or consider "New Orleans is exciting, surprising, and which I should like to visit again." *Exciting* and *surprising* are parallel in form and can be readily coordinated, but the final clause cannot easily be made parallel with them. The solution is to coordinate the two complements and also to coordinate the two clauses: "New Orleans is exciting and surprising, and I should like to visit it again."

Parallelism and Economy: Complete Patterns

Coordination, as examples above indicate, may promote economy, since parallel patterns are so well established that entire structures need not be repeated:

He knew the rules and (*he knew the*) regulations.

In a few minutes the stakes had been driven and the canvas (*had been*) spread on the ground.

He ran as fast as he could (*run*).

He had not learned how to read or (*how to*) write.

Usually such economies work only when the ideas to be carried over establish a form that will fit the second part of the parallel pattern. Consider, for example, the following sentence in which the reader is asked to supply part of the verb in one of two coordinated elements:

The liquor was seized and the kegs dumped into the sea.

The reader must supply a verb to precede *dumped*; the pattern of coordination suggests repetition of *was*, but *was* will not work after the plural *kegs*. Both verb forms must be supplied to make the parallel clear.

The liquor was seized and the kegs were dumped into the sea.

Or consider a similar example:

The water cask was nearly empty by noon and drained for evening rations.

Drained requires *was* preceding it, but the *was* of the first clause is a complete verb, not part of a verb like *was drained* and not parallel in structure. It won't carry over to be understood, and *was* needs to be repeated to make the coordinate elements parallel. Notice that *was* does carry over in a sentence like

> The water cask was filled in the morning and drained for evening rations.

In the following, a preposition is intended to carry over from one coordinate element to another.

> He was helpful and considerate of his friends.

If *friends* is intended to attach to *helpful* as well as to *considerate,* a second preposition is needed; *of* does not work after *helpful*.

> He was helpful to his friends and considerate of them.

Parallelism in Comparisons

Parallel patterns may express comparison, usually with function words like *than* or *as*. The following sentences illustrate standard economy:

> It was easier to take a cab *than it was easy to take* a bus.
> It was easier to take a cab *than to take* a bus.
> It was easier to take a cab *than* a bus.

Like other patterns of coordination, however, such constructions serve only when the elements to be compared are parallel:

> *My cousin* was older than *any other freshman.*
> It is easier *for a camel to go through the eye of a needle* than *for a rich man to enter into the kingdom of God.*

The items are in parallel form and comparable in meaning. But consider "His teeth were sharper than a tiger." *Teeth* and *tiger* are parallel in form, but their ideas cannot be compared. The sentence was presumably intended to compare teeth with teeth: "His teeth were sharper than a tiger's (*teeth*)." Such comparisons may be absurd—"His ears were longer than a jack rabbit"—but sometimes the illogicality of a comparison is not so apparent and a sentence may seem only vaguely confused. Consider:

> The battle against eating pumpkin seeds in school continues, as gum chewing does in most American schools.

The words coordinated are *battle* and *gum chewing,* but their ideas are not logically comparable. The writer may have intended to compare two battles:

> The battle against eating pumpkin seeds in school continues, as does the fight against gum chewing in most American schools.

Or the writer may have intended to compare the two activities:

> Eating pumpkin seeds in school continues, as gum chewing does in most American schools.

Consider another comparison in which coordinate elements are not parallel in form:

> During the war the value of the infantry was found to be on a par with the cavalry.

Value is coordinated with *cavalry,* but the intent obviously is to compare infantry and cavalry. A revision to make the coordinated elements parallel also clarifies the sentence:

> During the war the infantry was found to be as valuable as the cavalry.

Another colloquial pattern may be troublesome:

> That night our team was as good if not better than another team in the league.

To complete the parallel pattern, a connective is needed after *good. Than* is in the parallel position to be understood after *good,* but it doesn't fit there logically. Standard written English requires *as* after *good.*
    Another common colloquial pattern is usually inappropriate in writing: expressions like *so beautiful, most wonderful, biggest, finest, prettiest* used as vague expressions of enthusiasm.

> It was *such* a lovely party. He was the *nicest* man.

Logically such expressions start a comparison; and in standard writing the comparison should be completed or an adjective not implying comparison should be used.

> It was the loveliest party I had attended all year. He was the nicest man in the room.

Guide to Revision   Paral

FAULTY PARALLELISM

Revise to make coordinate elements parallel in structure.

ORIGINAL	REVISION
On the first day we visited the Metropolitan Museum, the Planetarium, and rode the ferry to Staten Island. [Museum, Planetarium, *and* rode *are not parallel in meaning, and should not appear in parallel form.*]	On the first day we visited the Metropolitan Museum and the Planetarium and rode the ferry to Staten Island. [*Insertion of* and *in place of the first comma breaks up the illogical series and makes the parallels clear.*]
Penicillin was found to cure most diseases more quickly, effectively, and less dangerously than did the sulfa drugs. [*The series is not a series as it stands. The sentence can be revised either to avoid the illogical series or to make it logical.*]	(1) Penicillin was found to cure most diseases more quickly and effectively and less dangerously than did the sulfa drugs. (2) Penicillin was found to cure most diseases more quickly, more effectively, and less dangerously than did the sulfa drugs.
The foreman insisted that his job was harder than a laborer. I knew her better than Mary. [*With parts of the comparison omitted, two meanings are possible.*]	(1) The foreman insisted that his job was harder than a laborer's. (1) I knew her better than Mary did. (2) I knew her better than I knew Mary.

ADEQUATE SUBORDINATION: MODIFICATION

With a few strokes of a crayon, a child can draw a stick figure, but the creation is no finished likeness. A portrait painter does more, makes an outline more accurately, adding details to distinguish the subject, and heightening some effects by subduing others. Similarly, a child can communicate with a simple sentence like "Willie eats bananas," but an adult might want a statement that would picture Willie's behavior, something more like this:

> Sometimes, when he is tired of his regular baby food, Willie eats ripe bananas crushed to a paste and mixed with a little milk.

The sentence has been developed by modification. Details have been added and most of them subordinated to the basic structure, "Willie eats bananas."

Sentences limited to the SVC elements are usually strong but may seem simplistic. The following passage makes little use of subordination.

> We are offered a penny for our thoughts. We consider what we have been thinking. Many things have been in our minds. From these many things we can select a few. The things we select do not compromise us too nakedly.

Even though the sentences are short and direct, the passage is not easy to understand. The reader gets no help in relating ideas, in seeing which depend on others. In the original the author used subordination to combine ideas:

> When we are offered a penny for our thoughts we always find that we have recently had so many things in mind that we can easily make a selection which will not compromise us too nakedly.
>
> James Harvey Robinson, *Mind in the Making*

The sentence is more complicated than the series of short sentences, but it is clearer.

Subordination and Economy

Subordination can sharpen prose, making it more economical by avoiding repetition and removing unnecessary words. Compare:

> Dramatics develops assurance. This is very valuable.
>
> Dramatics develops valuable assurance.

A sentence opening with a *this* that refers to the whole preceding idea is almost always a candidate for subordination. Strings of short sentences joined by *and* or *so* should also be checked for possible reduction of some elements to shorter subordinate form. For example:

> Joe likes to be the center of attention. So Joe joined the theatre club.
>
> Because he likes to be the center of attention, Joe joined the theatre club.

We searched for five hours. Then we found the child in an abandoned mine.
After searching for five hours, we found the child in an abandoned mine.

Usually both clarity and economy are best served when subordination reduces an item to the briefest form that makes sense. Compare the following:

Calling a spouse vile names is grounds for divorce, *and this is true if the names are put into language composed only of signs.*
Calling a spouse vile names *that are couched in the language of signs* is grounds for divorce.
Calling a spouse vile names *by using the language of signs* is grounds for divorce.
Calling a spouse vile names *in sign language* is grounds for divorce.

Notice what has happened to the idea of using signs for marital epithets. In the first sentence, this idea requires an independent clause and a rather complicated one. In the second sentence the idea has been reduced to the italicized dependent clause, in the third sentence to the italicized group of words introduced by *by*, and in the last sentence to the phrase "in sign language."

Selecting Items for Subordination

Deciding what to subordinate and in what patterns is one of the most complex jobs in writing. Compare the following, all of them descriptions of the same phenomena:

The girl in the green sweater	The green sweater on the girl
The girl wearing a green sweater	The girl's green sweater
The girl who wears a green sweater	The green sweater the girl is wearing

Two items, the girl and the green sweater, appear in all the expressions, with the physical relationship maintained; the sweater remains on the girl. In those on the left the sweater is grammatically subordinate to the girl; in the others the girl is subordinate to the sweater. That is, either the girl or the sweater can be selected as the object to be talked about and the other can be subordinated to it. The writer makes the choice, not because either item is necessarily more important, but because for immediate writing purposes he or she wants to relate the items in a certain way. In the following the subordination differs; so does the meaning:

The green sweater is ugly.   The green on the sweater is ugly.

Decisions about subordination affect both meaning and emphasis. Notice what can happen with varying treatment of the following three ideas.

> I was twelve years old. I got my first long pants. I took the girl next door to the movies.

Most obviously, perhaps, the first idea might be subordinated to the others as an indication of the time, with the last two ideas sharing equally the stress of the sentence:

> When I was twelve years old, I got my first long pants and took the girl next door to the movies.

A change in the subordinating word would vary both meaning and emphasis:

> Although I was only twelve years old, I got my first long pants and took the girl next door to the movies.

Centering attention on the second idea could produce a sentence like the following:

> Since I was now twelve years old and about to take the girl next door to the movies, I was allowed to buy my first long pants.

Or both the first two ideas might be subordinate:

> When I was twelve years old and in my first long pants, I took the girl next door to the movies.

The trip to the movies becomes the event that the writer wants primarily to talk about, and the acquisition of the pants declines.

Subordination should vary with the sentences that precede and follow. The last version above, for example, might be appropriate in a paragraph narrating a story about the friendship of a boy and girl. The context might suggest even wider variations in the pattern of subordination. Consider:

> When I had my first long pants and had taken the girl next door to the movies, I was twelve years old.

This unusual emphasis might be logical if the preceding sentence had read:

> The actual date of my twelfth birthday meant nothing to me.

A different preceding sentence might suggest the wisdom of a parallel pattern of subordination following it:

Guide to Revision **Sub**

INADEQUATE SUBORDINATION

Use subordination to improve an immature style, characterized by strings of short sentences or clauses joined by "and" or "so," by clumsy repetitions, or by excess use of "this" and "that" as subjects.

ORIGINAL

Louise was tired of listening to the concert and it was dark enough that her grandmother could not see her and so she slipped out into the lobby.
[The relationships between the three clauses are not accurately marked by linking them with *and* and *and so*.]

When Lord Byron was at Cambridge, he published *Hours of Idleness*. This was in 1807. The volume was Byron's first book of poems.
[Repetition of a subject or *this* as a subject may signal a need for subordination.]

Andrea stepped confidently into the hall. Joe pulled the rug from under her, when she fell down.
[A minor detail assumes major importance so that the subordination seems illogical or upside-down.]

REVISION

Since Louise was tired of listening to the concert, she slipped past her grandmother in the dark into the lobby.
[With ideas subordinated to a main subject-verb framework—she slipped—the sentence is clearer and more economical.]

In 1807, when Lord Byron was at Cambridge, he published his first book of poems, *Hours of Idleness*.
[The combination says everything in the original more clearly and more economically.]

(1) Andrea stepped confidently into the hall. When Joe pulled the rug from under her, she fell down.
(2) Andrea stepped confidently into the hall. Joe pulled the rug from under her, and she fell down.

At the age of eleven, I tore my knickers trying to catch a toad with which I hoped to frighten the girls at the Sunday School picnic. At twelve, I wore my first long pants to take the girl next door to the movies.

The second sentence fits the pattern of the first, draws the contrast between the events, and enforces the continuity.

Some sorts of details, however, are especially likely to profit from subordination. Consider:

> That night in a drafty hall at Red Lion Square, having escaped from an importunate hostess who wanted me to meet her niece, I heard a little greying old man, England's leading living novelist, Thomas Hardy, read Greek poetry with an understanding and love that bespoke a lifelong devotion to the classics.

The sorts of material subordinated here include the following: time (*that night*), place (*in a drafty hall at Red Lion Square*), incidental information (*having escaped . . .*), details of description (*little, greying, old*), identification (*England's leading living novelist, Thomas Hardy*). Such usually can be subordinated; they mention attendant circumstances, offer explanations, fill in minor bits, and keep attention focused on the main SVC pattern: *I* (subject), *heard* (verb), *an old man read poetry* (complement).

ADJECTIVE AND ADVERB

Modifiers are varied and behave variously. They differ in extent, from a single word to lengthy clauses. They differ in use; they can modify any of the major elements of the SVC pattern, along with other modifiers. They can appear at various positions in the sentence, and they have quirks peculiar to themselves, such as indicating degree. Many modify only one limited part of the sentence. Some of these, called *adjectives*, modify nouns. That is, they attach themselves to the sort of words that can serve as subjects, whether or not these nouns happen to be acting as subjects at the moment. Other terms, or sets of terms, called *adverbs*, can modify almost anything else in the sentence and may even seem to modify in all directions.

Adjectives are the simpler of the two. Many of them name qualities: *tough* courses, *tangerine* convertible, *bad* mess. But adjectives may suggest a variety of relationships, as in the following:

houseboat	boat that is a house
housecoat	coat to be worn in the house
house builder	one who builds houses
house paint	paint for a house

There are dozens more, like *house organ*, *housebound*, and *house arrest*. Such modifiers can save words; obviously, of the two columns above, the entries to the left are shorter. Adjectival modifiers may be more than one word, a phrase as in "The house *in the valley*," or a clause as in "The house *that Jack built.*"

Modifiers loosely called adverbs are a varied lot. Many adverbs attach themselves to verbs, and hence the name, *ad-verb,* meaning *to the verb.* They may also modify other parts of the sentence in patterns too complex to survey here, several parts of the sentence at once, or even the whole sentence. The opening modifiers in the following can be called sentence modifiers. Notice that they can be single words or groups of words.

> *Suddenly,* she broke through the thin ice.
> *While he hid behind the truck,* the kidnapper was reloading an automatic.

Many adverbs answer questions implied in such words as *how, when, where,* and *why.*

A few single-word modifiers can be used as either adjectives or adverbs, as in "It was a *hard* lesson and she worked *hard* at it"; the first modifies *lesson,* and the second modifies *worked.* Most single-word modifiers, however, are restricted. We can't say "The car was *redly,*" or "She swam *red."* *Dangerous* works only as an adjective; *always* or *too* only as an adverb. *Good* in standard English is an adjective, *well* an adverb:

> It was a *good* test, and he did *well* on it.

Good modifies *test; well* modifies *did.*

Modifiers ending in *-ly* are usually adverbs formed by adding the ending to an adjective: *dangerously, happily, slowly,* and so on. But a few adjectives end in *-ly—holy* or *leisurely,* for example—and don't have corresponding adjectives.

A modifier following a linking verb modifies the subject, which is a noun, and therefore an adjective form is standard:

> Her dress was red. The children seemed happy.

Difficulties develop, however, because some verbs are linking verbs only part of the time. In "He looked good," *looked* is considered a linking verb; *good* describes the subject. In "He looked well," it can be either, with a shift in meaning. If it is a linking verb, *well* is an adjective meaning "not ill," and it describes the subject. If it is not intended to be linking, *well* is an adverb modifying the verb *looked,* and the sentence says that he examined thoroughly, or was skilled at looking. We can say, "The wine tastes *good,"* with *good* an adjective modifying *wine,* and we can say, "The wine expert tastes well," if we want to compliment the taster's professional ability. But anybody who says "The wine expert tastes good" is guilty of either cannibalism or faulty usage.

Or compare: "He looked timid" and "He looked timidly." In the first, *looked* is a linking verb, linking the adjective *timid* to the subject. In the second sentence, *timidly* is an adverb, modifying the verb, describing

> ## Guide to Revision Adj, Adv
>
> # MISUSE OF ADJECTIVE OR ADVERB
>
> Use the adjective or adverb form the context requires.
>
> | ORIGINAL | REVISION |
> |---|---|
> | Jack can sure sing. [*Sure has developed a special meaning in this colloquial use.*] | Jack can surely sing. Jack can sing very well. [*More formal expressions do not translate the original exactly.*] |
> | When I called, they came quick. | When I called, they came quickly. |
> | The dog smelled badly. [*Adjectives rather than adverbs are required after linking verbs. Unless the writer intends a reflection against the dog's ability as a bloodhound, he needs the adjective.*] | The dog smelled bad. [*Since is could be substituted for the verb without making nonsense, smelled acts as a linking verb.*] |
> | She looked well in her new dress. [*This suggests that she either is skillful at looking or has recovered her health.*] | She looked good in her new dress. [*Good modifies she and produces the meaning probably intended.*] |

the manner in which *he* looked. Most native users of English will make such a distinction automatically. Those who do not can use a form of the verb *to be* as a rough test. If the modifier is an adjective, *to be* can replace the verb, as in *He was timid.* If the modifier is an adverb, *to be* cannot be substituted; we do not say *He was timidly.*

MODIFIERS AND WORD ORDER

Since modifiers are subordinate sentence elements, they support something else in the sentence. The reader needs to know what the modifiers support, what they modify. Word order provides the main clue. Thus the position of modifiers is crucial, especially since some occupy fixed positions and others are movable. Adjectives usually have fixed positions; one-word adjectives precede nouns, and longer adjectival sequences follow nouns:

> The *old* man *in the boat* grinned happily.
> I was the *first student* witness *that the board interviewed.*

There are a few variations. Appositive modifiers, which repeat in different words the expressions they modify, follow what they modify:

> The plainclothes police, *detectives,* took charge of the investigation.

Adjectives, usually more than one, may gain prominence in a position immediately after the noun they modify.

> The convertible, *red and shiny,* looked like a fire engine.

In this shifted position, modifiers are usually set off by commas, which mark the change from usual order. Sometimes, also, variations in order change meaning or emphasis. Compare:

> Our hearts were *light*.   *Light* were our hearts.
> They found the *deserted* village.   They found the village *deserted.*

Adverbs do not usually have fixed positions in sentence order. Phrasal and single-word modifiers of verbs, for instance, may appear in any of several positions, sometimes without much shift in meaning or emphasis. They may occur after the verb (He drove *slowly* down the street) or within complex verbs (She was *always* losing her gloves). They may precede the verb (I *soon* recovered). Some modifiers, especially those that indicate direction, regularly appear after the verb but either before or after an object (Take *back* what you said, but Take that *back*). Sometimes one position is obligatory, or almost so (Set the clock *ahead,* not Set *ahead* the clock).

A few limiting modifiers (like *only, nearly, very, just, almost, merely, ever, hardly, scarcely, quite*) are expected to modify whatever expressions immediately follow them, especially if they accompany other modifiers:

> They supplied *too* little *too* late.
> Very *quickly* we were *thoroughly* disgusted.

Compare the following:

> *Only* Virginia could hope to win the hundred dollars.
> Virginia could *only* hope to win the hundred dollars.
> Virginia could hope to win *only* the hundred dollars.

Or notice the position of *their* in the following:

> To understand the importance of the magazines, we investigated their sources of popularity.

The modifier should be in the standard fixed position before the word it modifies:

> To understand the importance of the magazines, we investigated the sources of their popularity.

Movable Modifiers in Fixed Positions

Since the same words or groups of words can be used as either fixed or movable modifiers, a reader must depend on word order to see how they apply and what they mean. From the sentence "The man *in the boat* was a tyrant," anyone understands automatically that "in the boat," being in the normal fixed position, is a modifier specifically locating the man. If the phrase is moved, the reader interprets it as a movable modifier that applies to the entire sentence, and the sentence takes on a different meaning: "*In the boat*, the man was a tyrant." The first sentence suggests that the man was a tyrant, presumably all the time. The second limits his tyranny to his time in the boat. As long as the sentence modifier is kept out of a fixed position, it may be moved, with changes in emphasis but no alteration of essential meaning. Observe the changes in meaning as the modifier moves in the following:

> *Playing in the park* the girl found a mushroom.
>
> The girl *playing in the park* found a mushroom.
>
> The girl found a mushroom *playing in the park*.

In the first sentence, "playing in the park" modifies the action of the entire sentence. In the second, however, the phrase identifies the girl. In the last, it has moved into the position of a fixed modifier of *mushroom* and suggests that mushrooms can flit about.

Negative sentences are especially troublesome if a modifier intended to apply generally is placed where it can apply to a specific word. Compare:

> Nobody was ever punished *because the camp was run so carelessly*.
>
> *Because the camp was run so carelessly*, nobody was ever punished.

With the clause at the end, the sentence is ambiguous; it can mean either what the second version says or that the managers of the camp were never punished for their careless administration.

Movable modifiers may be misplaced so that they apply with equal ease in more than one way. They "squint," seeming to look in two or more directions at once. This happens when an adverbial modifier follows a word that it would normally modify but precedes another word that it can modify. Consider "The person who lies frequently gets caught." *Frequently* can be taken to modify either what precedes it or what follows it. If the modifier is intended to modify the whole sentence, it should precede it: "Frequently, the person who lies gets caught." If it is intended to modify *lies*, then the sentence should be recast: "Anybody who lies frequently is likely to be caught."

Another sentence has a phrase placed so that it "squints," seems to look both forward and backward:

> She told me as soon as the dance was over she would marry me.

The sentence could have either of the following meanings:

> As soon as the dance was over, she told me she would marry me.
> She told me she would marry me right after the dance.

"Dangling" Modifiers

Sentence modifiers that do not themselves contain subjects attach readily to the subject or to the nearest noun. Compare:

> *Eating lunch on the lawn,* the children were amused by the speeding cars.
> *Eating lunch on the lawn,* the speeding cars amused the children.

The first is clear, but the second is ludicrous because the subject, *cars,* cannot logically supply the sense of a subject for the verbal, *eating.* Similarly, the modifier that opens the following sentence dangles:

> *Sitting on the bridge,* the huge steeple looked like part of a toy village.

The subject, *steeple,* seeming to govern *sitting,* perches the structure on the bridge. The sentence can be revised by using as a subject whatever was sitting on the bridge: "Sitting on the bridge, *we* could see . . ." The sentence can be revised, also, by providing the modifier with a subject of its own: "As *we* sat on the bridge, the huge steeple . . ." or by changing the modifier in some other way so that it does not rely on anything in the main clause: "From our position on the bridge, the huge steeple . . ."

Since introductory modifiers readily refer to the subject, confusion may result if the subject is postponed in favor of an expletive or if the sentence is passive (see chapter 7). Notice the following:

> *Finding new evidence,* there are details to be recorded by the secretary.
> *When finding new evidence,* details were recorded by the secretary.

The modifiers make sense only if the reader can tell who did the finding. Usually the name of the actor used as the subject of the sentence, in the position just after the modifier, supplies such information. In sentences like the above, in which the actor is not the subject, the modifiers dangle. Compare:

> *When the staff found new evidence,* the secretary recorded details.
> *When they found new evidence,* the staff dictated details to the secretary.

The revisions name the actor in the normal position in the actor-action-goal pattern.

Modifiers that do not attach to a subject, however, may be clear and idiomatic. For example, many modifiers are used independently so often that they are like function words (*owing to, concerning, regarding*). Also, many modifiers apply indefinitely to any person or idea: "Facing north, the mountain seems less forbidding," "Looking at the subject dispassionately, the conclusion seems clear." Or consider the following:

> *Talking with students,* the same questions arise time after time.

Since *talking* is so nearly complete in its meaning—like *fishing* or *swimming*—it does not attach to the subject *questions,* and the modification is clear.

Position of Conjunctive Adverbs

Modifiers that serve also as connectives are called conjunctive adverbs (see chapter 9). At the beginning of a clause, they modify the action of the entire clause. Placed within a clause, they throw stress on the words they follow. Preceding clauses or sentences usually indicate which sentence parts need emphasis and show where conjunctives are best placed:

> John was afraid to look at me; *however,* he was eager to look at Alice.
> John was afraid to look at me; he was eager, *however,* to look at Alice.

The position of *however* in the second sentence stresses *eager* and accents the contrast between *eager* and *afraid*. In the following, the position of *therefore* at the beginning of the second sentence gives it emphasis it does not deserve:

> He ate baseball, slept baseball, and dreamed baseball; and when he thought he thought baseball. Therefore, a mere football game could hardly make him blink an eye.

Consider a revision moving *therefore:*

> He ate baseball, slept baseball, and dreamed baseball; and when he thought he thought baseball. A mere football game, therefore, could hardly make him blink an eye.

The new position for *therefore* emphasizes the contrast between baseball and football that is the point of the sentence.

"Split" Constructions

Normally modifiers should not be allowed to split constructions by separating closely related sentence elements, particularly if the separating element is long or complicated. Sometimes separation is unavoidable or is desirable for special effects, but subject and verb, parts of the verb, verb and complement, parts of a verbal, or elements of a series should be separated only with caution:

> We may, if the weather clears, go to Birmingham.

Separation of parts of the verb *may go* might be desirable to put special emphasis on *may*, but usually the modifier, "if the weather clears," would appear at the beginning of the sentence. But consider the following in which long modifiers separate subject and verb:

> The *driver*, confused by the snow icing on his windshield wiper and the tires skidding on the ice and his wife yanking at his elbow, *yelled*.

Unless special emphasis is wanted, the unnecessary division of the basic pattern obscures meaning.
    Notable partly because it has become popularly celebrated as a usage "error," the split infinitive may obscure a structure. Usually a modifier does not work best between *to* and the remainder of an infinitive, where it may produce false emphasis:

> He promised to *firmly* hold our position.

The meaning is clear, and *firmly* would "squint" before *to*, but the sentence gains strength if *firmly* is moved:

> He promised to hold our position *firmly*.

On the other hand, a split infinitive may clarify modification.

> The sick man seemed to have *just* made an impatiently querulous answer.

Placed either before *to* or after *made*, the modifier *just* would change meaning, carrying something of the sense of *only*. Usually, however, the temptation to split an infinitive is a reliable signal that word order or sentence pattern should be changed.

Guide to Revision — Mod

MISPLACED OR DANGLING MODIFIER

Place modifiers in appropriate positions, where they do not cause ambiguity, or squint, dangle, or split elements.

ORIGINAL

She gave the book to her father that was bound in leather.
[*The final clause does not appear in the usual fixed position after* the book, *which it should modify, and seems rather to modify* father. *The word order can be changed (1, 2), or the sentence revised (3, 4). Usually misplaced modifiers are symptoms of wordiness; the cure is cutting and revising.*]

Having rotted in the damp cellar, my brother was unable to sell any of the potatoes.
[*The modifier applies automatically to the main action as it is expressed, to the subject-verb of the sentence. The result is the absurdly unsanitary state of the decomposing brother. The modifier should apply to an SVC pattern with* potatoes *as subject, but* potatoes *is not in the subject position.*]

He fired three shots at the lion with a smile of triumph on his face.
[*A sentence modifier at the end may fall into a fixed position.*]

REVISION

(1) She gave the book that was bound in leather to her father.
(2) She gave her father the book bound in leather.
(3) She gave the leather-bound book to her father.
(4) She gave her father the leather-bound book.

(1) Having rotted in the damp cellar, my brother's potatoes were unfit for sale.
[*Word order is changed so that the subject referred to by the modifier becomes the subject of the sentence.*]
(2) Since the potatoes had rotted in the damp cellar, my brother was unable to sell any of them.
[*The modifier is changed to a clause, which can include its subject,* potatoes.]

With a smile of triumph on his face, he fired three shots at the lion.
[*In this sentence the reader has no trouble locating the smile.*]

DEGREES OF MODIFICATION

Form changes in modifiers indicate three degrees of modification: positive, implying no comparison (*fast car, beautifully landscaped*); comparative, implying that one exceeds another (*a faster car, a more beautifully landscaped park*); and superlative, implying that a quality exceeds all others (*the fastest car in the race, the most beautiful mountain in Alaska*).

English shows degree in modifiers either with endings (*-er* or *-est*) or with function words (*more* and *most*).

Positive	Comparative	Superlative
red	redder	reddest
homely	homelier	homeliest
superficial	more superficial	most superficial
slow	slower	slowest
rapidly	more rapidly	most rapidly

One-syllable adjectives and a few adverbs are compared by attaching endings; longer adjectives and most adverbs are compared with *more* or *most*. Adjectives of two syllables are compared either way; a writer might say "He is stupider than an ox" but write "I never saw a more stupid boy."

Handling degree in modification involves usage problems:

1. A few modifiers retain irregular forms which can get confused: *good, better, best; well, better, best; bad, worse, worst; little, less, least; much, more, most; many, more, most.*

2. Using *more* or *most* plus *-er* or *-est* is now considered nonstandard, although it was once a device for emphasis. (*He was a happier person,* not *a more happier person*).

3. Some modifiers cannot be compared logically (*opposite, final, dead* in the sense of "deceased," *waterproof, entirely, previous, diametric,* for example). Strictly speaking, *fatal* cannot be thought of in degrees; a wounded person becomes dead or not dead. Colloquially, however, the function words indicating comparison (*more* and *most*) are often used to mean *more nearly* or *very,* and they are sometimes used with such words even in standard writing ("more dead than alive," "more perfect union"). Many such words are losing their traditional sense and assuming meanings that can be compared. *Unique* once meant "only" as in *his unique son,* but it has broadened in its meaning to "remarkable" or "unusual." Formal usage tends to resist these new meanings and to avoid comparison of modifiers like *complete* or *perfect.* Similarly, careful writers avoid loose use of words like *unique,* especially the comparative and superlative, along with compounds like "rather unique."

4. Formal practice also restricts use of superlative forms to compar-

isons among not fewer than three, although informal usage has never supported the distinction:

> Between the flatboat and the life raft, I should say that the raft offers *the better* (not *the best*) chance of shooting the rapids.

5. Extravagant superlatives trap a writer into making statements that cannot be substantiated, making the writing weaker than more soberly qualified prose. Consider:

> The Byington Parkway is the most modern highway in all the world.
>
> The costumes of the dancers were the most unique I had ever seen.

Guide to Revision   **Degree**

INAPPROPRIATE DEGREE OF MODIFIER

Revise to provide the degree of modification appropriate to the variety of English you are using.

ORIGINAL	REVISION
Stanley's singing was more better than his dancing.	Stanley's singing was better than his dancing.
She was the most outstanding scholar in the school. [Although outstanding *may mean no more than "excellent," it can seem redundant when compared.*]	She was the outstanding scholar in the school. [*Without* most, *the modifier is more economical and more forceful.*]
The Mount Rushmore Memorial represents Gutzon Borglum's most artistic achievement. [*A judgment of this sort can be no more than an opinion and is likely to impress the reader as an unreliable one.*]	(1) Some critics consider the Mount Rushmore Memorial Gutzon Borglum's most artistic work. (2) The Mount Rushmore Memorial is impressive in its mass and grand in its conception.

The superlative modifiers are not precise. Compare sentences that use more specific modifiers:

> The Byington Parkway utilizes many new techniques for highway construction.
>
> The costumes of the dancers were made of crepe paper and aluminum foil.

FOR STUDY AND WRITING

A. Combine the following groups of sentences into a single sentence using parallel structure.

1. Upon the chair hung a neatly folded suit. There was also a crumpled red tie there. A crushed gardenia was on the same chair.
2. Every person in the tournament knew bridge thoroughly. Each one was intelligent in playing. A firm determination to win was in every player.
3. Seated on the steps were a tan spaniel and brindle boxer. Angela, the Manx cat, was also there.
4. Good nurses possess a willingness to do more than their required tasks. They are also constantly alert to guess their patient's wishes.
5. A course of study in music may prepare a student for concert performances. It may also provide preparation for a career in teaching. And many students gain preparation for occasional recreational activity through their entire lives.
6. A nationalistic rather than a sectionalistic attitude developed in the West. This was partly because the West needed a national government to protect it from the Indians. It also looked toward the national government to provide aid in the development of transportation facilities. Furthermore, foreign affairs could be handled by a strong national government.
7. Without the mariner's compass, Columbus could not have discovered America. Neither could Vasco da Gama's trip to find a sea route to India have occurred. Magellan's sailing around the world would not have taken place without it, either.

B. Recast each of the following sentences so that items intended to be coordinate are parallel in form and meaning, or remove unwarranted parallel structures.

1. The typical hero wears light clothes as opposed to the "bad man" dressed in black.

2. Escalators should not be used by barefoot persons, pets, or for transporting strollers or wheelchairs.
3. Mark is a person of great integrity, vision, and has the rare ability to stimulate the best efforts of his associates.
4. Clare stated in her complaint that the defendant owned a large dog that walked the floor most of the night, held noisy midnight parties, and played a radio so that sleep was impossible until 1:30 in the morning.
5. She told her mother she wanted either a wedding in a church with flower girls, organ music, long trains, or a quick elopement to a justice of the peace.
6. I much prefer listening to concerts on the radio rather than to sit in the heat and discomfort of our auditorium.
7. His career, unlike most people who played a musical instrument, ended when he left school.
8. The job consisted mostly of planning and constructing roads, bridges, and various forms of surveying.
9. From the air the stream looked languid, twisted, and flowed on its course like some giant caterpillar en route to its cocoon.
10. He accused the senator of being a fool and too stupid to know the real issues.

C. Revise the following sentences to assure clarity in comparisons and other parallel structures.

1. When I looked into the cell I disliked Dandy Jack as much as the police officer.
2. The visitors found the cabin so beautiful, and Aubrey was such a handsome man.
3. There were great scientific advances, but precious little chance to use them until government regulations had been removed.
4. She looked as old or older than Methuselah.
5. After an hour of this conversation, I decided that I disliked Mary's cousin as much as Mary.
6. In *Othello* the structure is somewhat different from the other tragedies.
7. She liked Picasso better than any painter.
8. Because cars are so well built, drivers drive much faster than they can safely handle the car.
9. His arms dangled down longer than a baboon.
10. Geology, unlike most professionals, seems to have entered into a period of shrinkage in job opportunities.

D. Combine each of the following groups of sentences into a single sentence.

1. I am not a very good typist. This is because I have always typed with one finger. I have spent many hours at the typewriter, however.

2. Professor Nathan Keyfitz is from the University of Chicago. He used an algebraic formula. He devised it. He estimates 69 billion people have lived on the earth.
3. Crazy Horse was a great Oglala Sioux chief. He surrendered to government forces on May 6, 1877. Four months later he was killed when stabbed in the back by a guard at Fort Robinson.
4. Many flowers come out in the spring. They include violets, anemones, bloodroot, and trilliums. This is in the Middle West. These flowers appear about May. They cover the ground in woods and parks.
5. In 1864 Atlanta was one of the most important cities of the South. This was so for the reason that the Confederacy had developed it as an important railroad center. It was also developed as a manufacturing center. This was done in the belief that it was far from the center of military activity. It would therefore be safe.
6. I grew up in a small town. It was in the South. I have not visited this town for many years. To be exact, I have not been there for eight years. It is still, however, the place I think of as home.

E. The sentences below probably do not say what their writer intended. Revise them, paying particular attention to modification.

1. On approaching the village, the gold spire was the only evidence of civilization that we could see.
2. Although only pretending to shoot, the gun suddenly went off with a loud roar.
3. Having had no sleep for two nights, the dirty haystack actually seemed inviting.
4. Trying to climb in the window at night, the police caught the would-be burglars and immediately arrested them.
5. The nurse brought in Robert, Jr., to see his father in his bassinet.
6. No one is allowed to dump anything along this road except a city official.
7. He is asking the reader to adopt his point of view as well as the lady to whom the poem is addressed.
8. Joan decided that she would not marry him at the last possible moment.
9. We knew that the boat had been sunk because we had seen the battle.
10. When hardly more than a baby, a gang of older children threw me into the creek and told me to sink or swim.

F. Revise the following sentences by reducing italicized expressions to shorter modifiers, by making clauses into phrases or phrases into shorter phrases, or complex constructions into single words:

1. She specializes in answers *that are in the negative.*
2. He avoided tall girls *because of the fact that he was only five feet two in height.*
3. The doctor did not believe *in the factor of hereditary influences.*

4. Hybrids are formed by crossing two species *that are pure before they are crossed.*
5. *Smoking when a person is in bed* is prohibited.
6. The will, *which can never be conquered,* sustains the rebel.
7. *When breakfast had been finished,* the children got out their fishing tackle.
8. I was *the kind of child who was a blonde type.*

G. Use the facts given below for a brief composition. Subordinate as many of the details as the material warrants. Bring your version to class for comparison.

Alice Marriott wrote an article.
The article is called "Beowulf in South Dakota."
Alice Marriott is an ethnologist.
Alice Marriott studies American Indian tales.
The New Yorker published the article.
The New Yorker is a sophisticated magazine.
The author was collecting stories from an old Indian.
The Indian lived in South Dakota.
One day the old Indian was bored and restless.
The Indian looked as though he did not want to tell more stories.
The Indian asked a question.
The Indian wanted to know why the white people wanted his stories.
The Indian wanted to know if the white people had no stories of their own.
The author said she wanted to compare the stories of the Indians with the stories of the white people.
The old Indian became interested.
He acted pleased.
The Indian said that the author's idea was a good idea.
The Indian said he wanted the author to tell him one of the white people's stories.
The author retold the story of *Beowulf.*
The author used Indian terms and Indian concepts.
The author made Beowulf a great war chief.
Beowulf gathered the young men of the tribe around him.
Beowulf and the young men went on a war party.
Beowulf and the young men attacked the Witch of the Water and her son.
The Witch of the Water lived under a great stone in a rushing, dangerous river.
A great fight took place under the water.
There was blood welling up through the water.
The water was as red as the sun rising.

Beowulf killed the Witch of the Water and her son.
The Indian liked the story.
The author had to tell it over and over.
The Indian told it to his friends and the friends talked about it.
The Indians talked about Beowulf.
The Indians sounded like a seminar in literature.
The Indian did not tell any more stories that day.
The author had to go home and wait until the Indians recovered from *Beowulf*.
The old man told the author many stories.
The storytelling continued for weeks.
Another ethnologist was trying to get the old Indian to tell him stories.
Ethnologists have methods of working and standardized ethical practices.
An ethnologist who tries to use another ethnologist's information is unethical.
Two ethnologists are likely to confuse an informant.
A confused informant gives unsatisfactory evidence to both scientists.
The old Indian said he liked the author.
The author was the friend of the old Indian.
The Indian offered not to tell the other ethnologist Indian stories.
The author went back to her university.
The author heard that the other ethnologist wanted to question the old Indian.
Two or three years passed.
The author was reading a learned journal.
The author found an article signed by the other ethnologist.
The article was called "Occurrence of a Beowulf-like Myth among North American Indians."
The author wondered whether or not she should tell what she knew.

9

Coherence In Sentences: Function Words, Reference, Agreement

On the strength of one link in the cable,
dependeth the might of the chain.
RONALD ARTHUR HOPWOOD

In chapter 6 we discussed three kinds of signals that express English grammar: word order, inflection, and function words. Subsequent chapters have dealt mainly with the first of these, as word order regulates the basic patterns of the English sentence. But inflection, primarily the additions of endings to words, and function words are also important to the English sentence; they reinforce the links in the cable. Even experienced writers, while composing, make mistakes in reference and agreement. These need to be checked carefully during the revising and editing processes.

USING FUNCTION WORDS

In Modern English we can think of two sorts of words: those primarily carrying meaning, sometimes called content words; and those mainly signaling how words relate to one another. Of these, the meaning words are much more numerous, but the words that signal—function words or relationship words—do more of the work than may at first appear. In the following student sentence the function words have been italicized:

> *Although* the room contained many women *who would have* died unhesitatingly *for their* children, *when* a mouse appeared, courageous mothers *who had been* sitting *on* chairs found themselves standing *on the* tops *of* piano benches *or* clinging *to* strange men *for* protection.

Most of the italicized words have relatively little meaning, but try reading the sentence without them. *Although* relates the words before the first comma to the rest of the sentence and suggests that the clause it introduces contrasts with the main assertion. *The* warns us that we are concerned with a specific room. *Who* relates the following words to the rest of the sentence, especially to *women,* and implies that the idea involved in *women* will serve as the subject of a dependent clause. *Would have* has little meaning but specifies the form of the verb. *For* is best thought of as part of the verb, but it shows the relationship of *children* to the remainder of the sentence. To see how subtly function words blend into content words, try to find a definition that will fit both this *for* and the *for* toward the end of the sentence. *Their* has meaning as a possessive, but also recalls an antecedent, *women,* and points to the word after it, *children. When* warns that a dependent clause is coming and that the action in the clause determines the time of an event expressed elsewhere in the sentence. *A* introduces one particular mouse, but with the understanding that this mouse might as well have been any mouse. *On, of,* and *to,* like *for,* may be parts of verbs, but they also show how words like *chairs, tops,* and *piano benches* are related to other parts of the sentence. *Or* has a meaning, indicating a location in space. It joins *standing* and *clinging,* suggesting that the ideas expressed in the two words offer alternatives. And so on.

A single function word may be crucial to the entire meaning of a sentence. For example, we often recognize a question only because certain words signal questions:

> He spoke. *Who* spoke?

Or one function word can change the entire meaning of a sentence. Compare:

> *Because* I love you, I must leave you.
> *Although* I love you, I must leave you.

Since many function words have recently shifted uses within the language and are still shifting, they resist classification. Uses of *like* and *as,* for example, are currently changing. Function words are sometimes grouped as *determiners, auxiliaries, relatives, intensifiers, conjunctions,* and *prepositions,* but distinctions are not always sharp and often are not very helpful in the practical job of making sentences. Two of these groups, however, conjunctions and prepositions, warrant our attention.

CONJUNCTIONS AND CONJUNCTIVES

In general, conjunctions reinforce the two kinds of relationships discussed in chapter 8, coordination and subordination. As function words, they link parallel elements—coordinating conjunctions and conjunctive adverbs—or mark a passage as subordinate to some other part of the sentence—subordinating conjunctions. Notice the following:

> *Although* it was Sunday *and although* I knew I ought to get up for church, I turned over to take another nap.
>
> I jumped into the car without trouble, *but* Sharon slammed the door on her fingers.
>
> *If* that dog keeps up its yapping, it goes *or* I go.

And, or, and *but* join parallel clauses; they act as coordinating conjunctions. *Although* and *if* reduce their clauses to dependent status; they are subordinating conjunctions.

Coordinating Conjunctions

The few coordinating conjunctions (*and, but, for, or, nor, yet*) imply various but parallel relationships. *And* normally signals an addition; *but* emphasizes a contrast; *or* offers a choice. *For* can be thought of as either coordinating or subordinating. *So* is sometimes loosely treated as the equivalent of *and*, but careful writers use it for subordination, as an equivalent of *accordingly* or in such combinations as *so that*. Coordinating conjunctions may join parallel single words or longer sentence elements, including lengthy independent clauses. Sometimes they may introduce sentences:

> The wolf is today what he was when he was hunted by Nimrod. But, while men are born with many of the characteristics of wolves, man is a wolf domesticated, who both transmits the arts by which he has been partially tamed and improves upon them.
>
> R. H. Tawney, *Religion and the Rise of Capitalism*

Although the sentences could have been combined, the separation adds emphasis, placing *but* at the beginning of a new sentence. The device can be overworked. In general, it should be restricted to the following uses: (1) to give emphasis, as in the example above; (2) to break up a long sentence, if combining the parts would be awkward, but a more formal connective like *however* might seem ponderous; or (3) to establish a broad contrast, when the sentence beginning with *but* is to be balanced against two or more preceding sentences.

Correlative conjunctions (*either, or; neither, nor*) also join coordinate elements but work in pairs, with their position distinguishing which items are coordinate.

> They should *either* buy the house they have been renting *or* move to a different part of town.

Notice that each conjunction immediately precedes the verb it is coordinating. Moving *either* to the beginning of the sentence, for example, would make the coordination less clear.

Conjunctive Adverbs

Conjunctive adverbs (words like *however, moreover, nevertheless, then, hence, therefore, consequently, thus, furthermore*) connect parallel clauses, but at the same time modify elements within a clause. Observe the following:

> I wanted one of the then-fashionable slit skirts; however, I got Jinny's old plaid.
>
> She was in no mood to take advice. I was angry, however, and I told her what I thought of her leaving the party.

In both examples, *however* functions partly as a sentence modifier, modifying the subject-verb pattern in which it appears. It also links two clauses in the first example, and two sentences in the second. (For the position of conjunctive adverbs, see chapter 8.)

Subordinating Conjunctions

Subordinating conjunctions make clauses dependent. That is, they signal to the reader that a group of words built on the SVC pattern is not an independent unit, but part of a larger sentence. Thus words like *when, although, because, since, as, so that, though, if, unless, until, where, whether, while, after,* or *whereas* at the beginning of a clause mark the clause as a modifier, usually of the whole predication that follows or precedes it. Words like *that, how, what,* or *whoever* signal that clauses they introduce can function as nouns. Relative pronouns, *who, whom, whose, which,* and *that,* also function as subordinating conjunctions, introducing modifying clauses. Since subordinating conjunctions indicate the use of a clause and specify how it is related in meaning to its sentence, they should be chosen to reveal both functions. Compare, for example:

> *Although* she was his wife, she stayed at a hotel.
> *Because* she was his wife, she stayed at a hotel.

Before she was his wife, she stayed at a hotel.
Until she was his wife, she stayed at a hotel.
After she was his wife, she stayed at a hotel.
While she was his wife, she stayed at a hotel.
Whenever she was his wife, she stayed at a hotel.

Guide to Revision   Conj

MISUSE OF CONJUNCTION

Select conjunctions to define relationships accurately.

ORIGINAL

The sea was like glass, and that was the last calm day we had at the beach.
[*Probably, a contrast is intended.*]

You can play all sorts of games, and if you want to, you can spend the afternoon under a tree reading a book.
[*A choice seems intended.*]

While Father did not approve of alcoholic beverages, he always had some in the house for guests.
[While *is loosely used as an equivalent of* although *or* because. *Strictly used it means that one event takes place at the same time as another.*]

I can neither live with you or get along without you.
[Or *is not standard to correlate after* neither, *although it can be used after other negatives.*]

REVISION

The sea was like glass, but that was the last calm day we had at the beach.

You can play all sorts of games, or if you want to you can spend the afternoon under a tree reading a book.

Although Father did not approve of alcoholic beverages, he always had some in the house for guests.
[*The subordinate clause mentions a concession, and the concessive conjunction,* although, *has accordingly replaced* while.]

(1) I can neither live with you nor get along without you.
(2) I cannot live with you or get along without you.

It is not always easy to select the subordinating conjunction that will help readers see precisely the relationship you want to indicate. For example, *while*, which basically suggests a time relationship, is sometimes used loosely in other ways. In the following it is used as a coordinating conjunction:

> Arnold helped our score by winning the shot put, while he placed only a poor third in his favorite event, the discus throw.

With the usual meaning of *while*, the sentence says that he participated in both events at the same time. A coordinating conjunction like *but* would clarify. Or consider another use of *while*:

> While we never mentioned her illness, we were all aware of it.

Although would clearly be more precise.

Since also refers to time but has acquired other uses and sometimes can be ambiguous as in the following:

> Since my mother was only a little girl, she was not allowed to sit at the table.

The reader at first thinks that *since* refers to time rather than its probable meaning, which a more accurate conjunction would clarify:

> Because my mother was only a child, she was not allowed to sit at the table.

Relative Pronouns

Relative pronouns (*who, whom, which, that, whoever, whose*) function as pronouns, referring to a noun and standing for its meaning. But they also relate a clause to other parts of a sentence, working like subordinating conjunctions to introduce dependent clauses. In the sentence *He is the man who took the candy from the baby*, *who* introduces a clause and serves at its subject; it also refers to *man* as its antecedent. In *The book that he stole was a first edition*, *that* stands as a pronoun for *book*, but it also is an object in the clause it introduces. Questions in the usage of relative pronouns sometimes arise because of their multiple functions (see *that-which, whose,* and *who-whom* in the Glossary).

PREPOSITIONS

Unlike conjunctions, prepositions work only within the basic sentence, joining a noun or noun substitute to some part of a sentence. The preposition and the noun following it constitute a *prepositional phrase*. Choosing

> *Guide to Revision* **Prep**
>
> # MISUSE OF PREPOSITION
>
> *Choose prepositions that are idiomatic in standard English.*
>
> | ORIGINAL | REVISION |
> |---|---|
> | He is capable *about* almost any excess. | He is capable *of* almost any excess. |
> | He was interested and anxious *for* a change. | He was interested *in* and anxious *for* a change. |
> | I found the keys in back of the water pitcher. | I found the keys behind the water pitcher. |
> | He spoke in regards to the paving of the alleys. [When the construction is appropriate, the word is regard, *not* regards.] | (1) He spoke about paving the alleys. (2) He discussed paving the alleys. |

prepositions accurately is not always easy because convention, often arbitrary, may dictate which prepositions determine which meanings. British English requires the idiom "He lives in Oxford Street"; American English requires "He lives on Oxford Street." *Street* in England retains some of its medieval meaning and designates both the thoroughfare and the areas alongside it. Most users of the language cannot be expected to know such historical background. Accordingly, they must rely on a sense of idiom, of what is customary among users of the language, to decide whether to speak *to, with, for, of,* or *about* the devil. They must sense that they agree *with* a friend, *on* terms, *to* a proposal, and *about* someone's character.

Prepositions at the end of a sentence, long prohibited by an arbitrary rule, developed partly because words identical with prepositions become the second element in merged verbs like *get up* or *wake up* and partly from the etymology of the word *pre-position*. The rule has some validity, since final position may give a preposition unwarranted emphasis, but informally at least prepositions often end sentences. Compare "the man from whom he was running away" and "the man he was running away from." Winston Churchill condemned the proscription of the final preposition as "the sort of English up with which I will not put."

PRONOUN REFERENCE

Like conjunctions and prepositions, pronouns serve partly as function words to enforce coherence in the sentence. They carry meaning, repeating or echoing the sense of the words they stand for. But they also help continue thought through the sentence in patterns of reference. In the simplest pattern of reference, a single word—a pronoun like *he*, for example—refers to another word, a noun, which is called its *antecedent*. In the following sentences, antecedents are in italics.

> My *sister* said she had found the *book* that was missing from the shelves. (*She* refers to *sister* and *that* to *book*.)
>
> He believes that *everyone who attends the dean's teas receives special favors*, but this is not true. (*This* refers to the idea of the entire clause.)
>
> In his criticism of student government, the *speaker* said that students were naturally irresponsible. (*His* refers ahead to its antecedent, *speaker*.)

These sentences are clear, not only because customary word-order patterns are followed, but also because pronoun forms and meanings point a word toward its antecedent.

Patterns of Reference

Patterns can vary enough to make vague and inaccurate references a hazard for the writer. In general the following principles apply:

1. Subject as Antecedent The subject, as the most important noun or pronoun in a clause, and especially the subject of a main clause, tends to become an antecedent of a personal pronoun. Consider:

> Shakespeare was two months younger than Marlowe; *a record of his* baptism on April 26, 1564, was recorded.

Even though *his* could apply sensibly to either *Shakespeare* or *Marlowe*, and even though *Marlowe* is nearer *his* in the sentence, the reader knows that *Shakespeare*, the subject, is the antecedent of *his*.

2. Complement as Antecedent If the subject is obviously impossible as the antecedent of a personal pronoun, a complement tends to be the next choice.

> She took the rooster out of the sack and put a rock in *its* place.

Its cannot refer to the subject, but it does refer to *rooster*. Notice that while the meaning helps clarify reference, the order is essential here. We could change the chicken's fate by transposing *rock* and *rooster*.

3. Subordinate Word as Antecedent The less important the position of the word in a sentence, the greater is the difficulty of making the word an antecedent. Modifiers and other words in subordinate uses, however, may work as antecedents of pronouns in parallel structures.

> I visited the library and spent an hour looking through the book. I found nothing in *it*.

It refers to *book*; pronoun and antecedent have parallel uses and positions.

4. Immediately Preceding Noun as Antecedent A noun immediately before a relative pronoun tends to be its antecedent. Notice what happens when a relative pronoun is used in sentence 1 above:

> Shakespeare was two months younger than Marlowe, *whose* baptism in February, 1564, was recorded.

Although the personal pronoun *his* in the sentence above refers to the subject of the sentence, the relative pronoun *whose* refers to the noun nearest it, and the date has to be changed to keep the sentence accurate.

Deviations from these patterns usually cause awkward sentences. Consider the following:

> I should like to find out how authors were affected during the Depression and how it changed *their* styles of writing.

Even though *their* is widely separated from its antecedent, *authors*, it refers clearly to the word in the subject position. *Depression*, however, in a prepositional phrase, is not immediately recognized as the antecedent of *it*. If the sentence is revised to put antecedents and pronouns in parallel positions, the reference becomes clear:

> I should like to find out how the Depression affected authors, and how *it* changed their styles of writing.

Pronoun Forms and Reference

Form and meaning may determine pronoun reference, as in the following:

> John showed *his* sister *his* copy of the book that *she* had written.

Since *she* is feminine in form, it must refer to sister; the authorship is clear.

Notice, however, the difference if John had met his brother.

John showed *his* brother *his* copy of the book that *he* had written.

Because of meaning and order we could probably guess whose copy is involved, but we cannot guess who wrote the book. Revision to make John the writer might read

John showed the copy of the book he had written to his brother.

Making the brother the writer requires repetition:

John showed his brother his copy of his brother's book.

Indefinite Pronoun Reference

Pronouns, especially *this, that, it,* and *which,* may refer to a general idea rather than a specific antecedent:

I had thrown a loaf of bread at the Marquis, which hit him on the cheek, and *that* made me feel good.
Robert Graves, "Avocado Pears"

Which has a clear antecedent in *loaf of bread*, but no particular noun can be identified as the antecedent of *that*. But the meaning is clear; *that* refers to the entire action. This use of the pronoun, however, is subject to considerable abuse. Too often the construction disguises careless thinking; the pronoun is used to stand for an idea that the writer assumes the reader understands but has not been made clear to the reader. The indefinite use of pronouns may also be a symptom of inadequate subordination (see chapter 8). Consider:

Beret was constantly reminded of Norway and home and this made her nostalgic, which helped cause her insanity.

The meaning of *which* is implied in what precedes it, but indefinite reference muddies the sentence. The sense can be made clear by subordinating the material in the first clause and avoiding the indefinite references:

Constantly reminded of Norway and home, Beret developed nostalgia, which helped cause her insanity.

Sentences may begin with a dependent clause followed by a pronoun referring to a noun in the clause:

If this article makes a few people take democracy seriously, it will have served its purpose.

Guide to Revision   **Ref**

UNCLEAR PRONOUN REFERENCE

Revise to clarify reference of pronouns.

ORIGINAL	REVISION
Some critics have accused Chaucer of Frenchifying English, which has been disproved. [Which *has no certain antecedent.*]	Some critics have accused Chaucer of Frenchifying English, but the accusation has been disproved. [*No antecedent is necessary.*]
Charles lacked refinements, which annoyed her. [Which *seems to refer to* refinements.]	Charles's lack of refinements annoyed her. [*Revision to remove the indefinite reference clarifies.*]
The next morning he decided to fly to Phoenix, and this was where he made his fatal mistake. [*With the vague reference of* this, *several meanings are possible.*]	(1) The next morning he made his fatal mistake in deciding to fly to Phoenix. (2) The next morning he decided to fly to Phoenix, where he was to make his fatal mistake.
In Hemingway's book *For Whom the Bell Tolls*, he tells about an American teacher in the Spanish Civil War. [He *must refer to a person, but* Hemingway's *is not a person. It helps identify* book.]	In his book *For Whom the Bell Tolls*, Hemingway tells about an American teacher in the Spanish Civil War. [*With the pronoun in the dependent position and* Hemingway *as the subject, the reference of* his *is clear.*]
In the paper it says the weather will change. [*Colloquially* it *and* they *sometimes refer loosely to "people" or "society."*]	The paper says the weather will change. [*In standard prose* it *and* they *are avoided as indefinite pronouns.*]

It has a clear antecedent in *article,* with both antecedent and pronoun in the subject position. The construction has led to the colloquial popularity of a similar pattern in which the pronoun lacks even a vague antecedent:

> If there were some way to get all people to use the same dialect, it would be much simpler.

The general idea of the opening clause makes no sense as a subject for the main clause. Logical predication (see chapter 7) requires a subject:

> If there were some way to get all people to use the same dialect, communication would be much simpler.

WORD REFERENCE

Although pronouns exemplify reference most obviously, sentence coherence may depend on the accurate reference of other words (antecedents in the following are in italics):

> I *place* more faith in her judgment than you do. (*Do* repeats the idea of *place* and can be said to refer to it.)
>
> People in America believe *that everyone should share the good and the bad,* but this principle does not apply here. (*This principle* refers to the clause *that everyone should share the good and the bad; principle* is a plausible name for the idea of the clause.)
>
> He annoyed many people by his *smugness and intolerance,* attitudes developed from his early training. (*Attitudes* adequately restates its antecedent, *smugness and intolerance.*)

The accuracy of the reference depends partly on word order but more on meaning. Consider the last two sentences above as they originally appeared in student papers:

> Our country's democracy believes in everyone's sharing the good and the bad, and in this case the assumption would not hold true.
>
> He annoyed many people by being smug and intolerant, attitudes developed from his early training.

The first sentence is unclear in its predication, but the word *assumption* causes further trouble because there is no previous idea for it to refer to— no assumption has been expressed. In the second sentence, *attitudes* refers vaguely, because no attitudes have been precisely mentioned. *Smug* and *intolerant,* of course, describe attitudes, but do not name them. The reference would be clear to *smugness* and *intolerance,* which are attitudes.

Troublesome word reference can take various forms. Sometimes forgetfulness or a careless shift in thinking seems the only explanation.

> Of all the rules for students, I hated most being in by ten o'clock.

Being in is not a rule; the general term does not logically include the specific one. The easiest revision avoids the reference problem:

> I hated most the rule requiring students to be in by ten o'clock.

A modifier should refer logically to the word it seems to modify.

> She was appointed head dietician, vacated only the day before by a sudden resignation.

No doubt the position, not the dietician, was vacated. A revision might supply an expression for *vacated* to refer to:

> She was appointed head dietician, filling a position vacated only the day before through a sudden resignation.

Some words used as modifiers and determiners—words like *the, such, there, here, other, another, this, that, these, those*—may require antecedents:

> He offered to rewrite the examination, but *this* solution did not satisfy his instructor.
>
> After Wilfred had read the poem, the instructor announced that he would not allow *such* doggerel in his class.

This and *such* help identify *solution* and *doggerel* as words that restate and refer to other ideas in the sentence. In the following, however, the words do not refer clearly:

> He meant no harm by his pranks, but *this* result did not always come of his mischief. *Such* result came from one prank.

This and *such* only expose more sharply the inaccurate reference of the words they modify. The sentence was probably intended to mean something like the following:

> Although he intended no offense, his mischief was not always harmless, and one prank ended unhappily.

In the next sentence, *there* has no antecedent.

> I think that harbor dredging will be a very interesting subject. Since I have lived *there* for fifteen years, I am well acquainted with it.

Guide to Revision   WRef

UNCLEAR WORD REFERENCE

Revise to make words that refer to other expressions reflect the meaning of their antecedents accurately.

ORIGINAL	REVISION
The field of interior decorating holds vast opportunities for the people who want to apply themselves to the task. [A field *is not a task, and the faulty reference makes the sentence ambiguous.*]	(1) Interior decorating holds vast opportunities for people who want to apply themselves. (2) People who become interior decorators have vast opportunities. [*Here, as often, deletion is the cure.*]
Bowling Green, the name of my home town, is in the southern part of Kentucky. [Bowling Green *can be a name or a town, but only the town is in Kentucky.*]	Bowling Green, my home town, is in the southern part of Kentucky.
We saw a little adobe house and rode over. The man and his wife greeted us pleasantly. [The *suggests a previous mention.*]	We saw a little adobe house and rode over. A man and his wife greeted us pleasantly. [*With a the false reference disappears.*]

The writer needs to reveal where he has lived:

> I think that harbor dredging will be a very interesting subject, and I am well acquainted with it, since for fifteen years I have lived where I could observe an extensive dredging project.

AGREEMENT

No one would miss the meaning of "The boy walk (rather than *walks*) to school," but that *s* is required in standard written English. It is an example of one of the three signs of grammar we have discussed, inflection or the use of endings to reinforce grammatical relationships.

These endings are much less numerous in modern English than in earlier forms of the language and in many other modern languages, but the following inflections are standard:

1. *Pronoun Forms* Personal pronouns have different forms to distinguish different persons (*I, you, it*); to indicate number, whether they refer to one person or more than one (*I, we, he, they*); and to specify gender (*he, she, it*).

2. *Noun Endings* Nouns have endings, or sometimes internal form changes, to indicate whether they are singular or plural (*horse, horses*) or to show when they express possession (*his brother's book*).

3. *-s Verb Ending* Verbs add an *-s* to mark the third person singular form (*I walk* but *he walks, we swim* but *she swims*).

4. *Forms of* to be The verb *to be* has different forms to work with different persons (*I am* but *he is*) and to distinguish plural and singular (*she is* but *they are*).

Fitting these different forms together is called agreement in grammar. And standard English requires that two kinds of agreement be observed:

1. *Pronouns agree with their antecedents.* As described above, pronouns are devices for economy, for carrying on the sense of an antecedent without repeating it. But since pronouns have different forms, it is necessary to pick the form that is consistent with the antecedent. A feminine antecedent, for example *Alice* or *daughter*, would require a feminine form of the personal pronoun, *she* or *her*. To refer to *man*, the singular *he* would agree, but for *men* the plural *they* would be required.

2. *Verbs agree with their subjects.* Whenever the subject of a verb names a singular person or thing or idea (*the man, the book, the impossibility*), it requires the *-s* ending on the verb (*walks, belongs, seems*).

Users of English have little trouble with these agreement patterns most of the time, but sometimes it is hard to tell whether a subject or antecedent is singular or plural, and sometimes in a complicated sentence a writer can have trouble identifying an antecedent or subject.

Number of Subject or Antecedent

Broadly speaking, the intended meaning determines whether a subject or antecedent is to be considered singular or plural.

Two hours of his last twelve *were* gone.
Two hours *is* a long time.

In the first sentence *hours* is plural (like *they*) in sense, and the plural verb *were* agrees. In the second, in spite of its plural form, *two hours* specifies a single unit of time (like *it*) and takes the singular form *is*. Usually, however, form and meaning are the same, and a plural form used in a singular sense may seem imprecise. Consider:

> Late *hours was* responsible for his illness.

The sense of the subject is singular, but revising to avoid the differing forms produces a better sentence:

> Keeping late hours caused his illness.

Indefinite Pronouns

Indefinite pronouns, such as *everybody, anybody, everyone, each,* and *somebody,* are traditionally considered singular, specifying one of a group. They have been used so often, however, with a plural sense, to mean "all people," that colloquially they have long been considered plurals. Even in formal writing, for instance, *none* is singular or plural, depending on the sense intended. Compare:

> None of the children were on time.
> None of the children was hurt.

In the first, the writer wants to refer to the entire group—all the children were late. In the second, the writer indicates that not one child was hurt. But the writer could have made the first singular and the second plural to provide a different emphasis.
    A problem develops, however, with a word like *everybody* when the verb and a pronoun do not interpret it in the same way, as in the following:

> Everybody knows [singular] it is to their [plural] advantage to have a college education.

In formal English the use of *their* violates agreement, but alternatives are not easily available. As we point out in chapter 11, English has no neutral substitute for *their* except *his,* and *his* is now generally considered unsuitable because of its sexist implications. When we read the sentence, "A careless race car driver can lose his life," we tend to interpret *his* in its masculine sense, even though both men and women now drive race cars. The best solution is revision to avoid the problem, even though it may alter meaning slightly, as in the following:

> All people know it is to their advantage to have college educations.
> Everybody knows the advantage of having a college education.

Collective Nouns

In written American English, a collective noun is treated as singular unless the meaning clearly shows that the parts in the collection, not the collection as a whole, are being considered. Colloquially, however, plural verbs and pronouns are common even when the sense of the noun is not clearly plural (The staff *were* willing to work late). Certainly, in writing, the verb and any pronouns referring to the subject should agree:

> The company [*it*] considers John one of *its* [not *their*] best men.

The singular verb here marks the subject as singular, but consider:

> The committee [*they*] *differ* [not *differs*], some supporting the motion, some opposing it, and some calling it irrelevant.

Here the various members of the committee, not the committee as a unit, serve as subject. Making the subject *committee members* would clarify further.

Compound and Alternative Subjects

A compound subject usually is considered to be plural, even though its parts may be singular. We think of *corn* and *lettuce* as two things, as much a plural as *vegetables*. We would write "Corn and lettuce [*they*] *are* [not *is*] grown in the Midwest."

The intended meaning of a subject, however, usually determines whether it is considered singular or plural, and occasionally compound subjects join to form a noun expression whose sense is singular. Compare:

> *Ham and eggs are* among his most profitable products.
>
> *Ham and eggs is* a good dish.

The compound is plural in the first sentence, but in the second it names a single item on a menu.

Either, neither, or, and *nor* usually separate alternatives and do not combine elements as compounds. Colloquially, alternative subjects are often considered plural (Neither of them were afraid), but in writing, at least formal writing, alternative subjects govern verbs individually. If both alternates are singular, a singular verb or pronoun follows; if both are plural, verb and pronoun are plural:

> Virtue or honesty *is* [not *are*] its own reward.
>
> Neither Columbus nor Henry Hudson achieved *his* [not *their*] ambitions.

If one is singular and the other plural, usage varies. Some writers follow a rule that the verb or pronoun should agree with the item nearest it.

> Either the boys or their father is going to help.
> Either the dog or the chickens were doomed.

But most writers would avoid either sentence, especially the singular construction.

A clause or phrase used as a subject is considered singular and is followed by a singular verb.

> What you are looking for is in the closet.
> To know birth and death is to know life.

Obscured Subjects

In some constructions the subject with which a verb should agree may be hard to identify. For example, subject-verb-complement order is so well established in English that speakers may have trouble recognizing a subject that follows the verb and fail to make the verb agree with it. Colloquially, an introductory *there* or *it* may be taken for a singular subject and followed by a singular verb, even when the real subject is plural. In standard writing, however, the verb takes the number of its subject, even though the subject may follow it:

> There *were* [not *was*] only a few seats left.
> Behind the tree *were* [not *was*] two squirrels.

A similar problem arises when the subject and complement of a linking verb differ in number; is the subject the word following or the word preceding the verb? Usually the basic word-order pattern prevails, and the verb agrees with the word preceding it:

> Oranges were his main product.
> His main product was oranges.
> The answer to our problems is well-trained workers.
> Well-trained workers are the answer to our problems.

The last sentences seem awkward, especially because of the presence of plural *problems,* and probably should be revised to avoid the linking verb:

> To solve our problems, we need well-trained workers.

When a subject is modified, a writer may mistake the modifier for the subject, or part of it, and make the verb agree with the wrong word.

Colloquially, a subject modified by a phrase is sometimes thought of as a compound: "The captain with most of his crew were standing on deck." But in written English the subject would be identified without its modifier and the verb would agree with it:

>The captain with most of the crew *was* standing on deck.
>
>Jim, as well as his brothers, *plans* to study engineering.

Even when subject and verb are widely separated, they should agree.

>The employer of all sorts of people, highly trained scientists, unschooled laborers, callow youths, and hard-working stenographers, *has* [not *have*] wide understanding of human nature.

Employer is the subject, even though it is almost forgotten by the time the verb appears.

Agreement in Dependent Clauses

Within a dependent clause, a verb agrees with its subject in the clause. When that subject is a relative pronoun like *who*, it takes the number of its antecedent. The number of the verb in the clause, therefore, may reflect different meanings in different contexts. Compare:

>The court is concerned mainly with the group of delinquent children responsible for the vandalism. John is one of those children who *seems* unaffected by punishment.
>
>The courts have to deal with many different types of children. John is one of those children who *seem* unaffected by punishment.

In the first, the singular *seems* signals that *who* refers to *John.* The children have already been identified in the sentence, and John is the only one unaffected by punishment. In the second, *who* is made to refer to *children,* and all the children, not just John, seem unaffected. Usually no distinction in meaning is involved, and logic requires a plural verb.

>She is one of those people who always *complain* [not *complains*] about the weather.

Who takes its number from its plural antecedent *people.*

Agreement of Nouns That Refer

When one noun refers to another, it should agree with the antecedent in number. In this awkward sentence *an equal* refers to *women:*

Guide to Revision   Agr

FAULTY AGREEMENT

Revise to make verbs agree with their subjects in person and number or to make pronouns agree with their antecedents in person, number, and gender.

ORIGINAL

When everybody has expressed their opinion, the committee will decide.
[*Plural* their *is not consistent with singular* has.]

A family of Mexicans and one lone donkey was trooping down the road.
[Donkey *is singular, but the subject,* family *and* donkey, *is plural.*]

Either French dressing or mayonnaise go well with tomatoes.
[*The subject is singular,* dressing *or* mayonnaise, *not both.*]

There is two good reasons for protesting the decision.
[There, *although in the subject position, does not govern the verb.*]

My father was one of the many businessmen who was ruined by inflation.
[*The subject of* was ruined *is* who, *which almost certainly is intended to refer to* businessmen *and thus is plural.*]

Orrie, with his little sister, were squatting in the middle of the puppy pen.
[Orrie *is a singular subject, modified by* with his little sister.]

REVISION

When everybody has expressed an opinion, the committee will decide.
[*Eliminating the pronoun corrects the lack of agreement without risking the sexism of* his.]

A family of Mexicans and one lone donkey were trooping down the road.
[Were *agrees with* family *and* donkey.]

Either French dressing or mayonnaise goes well with tomatoes.
[*The singular* goes *has replaced the plural* go.]

There are two good reasons for protesting the decision.
[*Even though it follows the verb, the plural subject requires a plural verb.*]

My father was one of the many businessmen who were ruined by inflation.
[*The plural form* were *replaces the singular* was. *Only in an unusual context would* one *be the antecedent of* who.]

Orrie, with his little sister, was squatting in the middle of the puppy pen.
[*The singular* was *has replaced the plural* were.]

Women are treated as an equal when they work in the field.

Several women can scarcely be treated as one equal, and the sentence needs to be revised so that the noun agrees with its antecedent.

Women are treated as equals when they work in the field.
A woman is treated as an equal when she works in the field.

In the following, *dresses* is plural to agree with *robes:*

The men wear long robes that somewhat resemble *dresses* [not *a dress*].

FOR STUDY AND WRITING

A. In the following sentences select for each blank the appropriate present tense form of the verb in parentheses:

1. There _____ (be), after all is said and done and your life has mostly run away, only two rewards that make life worth living.
2. John was one of those lucky soldiers who _____ (seem) always to be where there is no battle.
3. A sales lot full of old cars, some with battered fenders and bashed grills, some badly needing paint, and some with broken glass and missing chrome, _____ (resemble) a portable junk yard.
4. In the United States, everyone who _____ (want) an education can have it.
5. Neither Darwin nor his critics today _____ (understand) the full implication of the theory of evolution.
6. Clarence is one of those men who never _____ (do) tomorrow what can be put off until next week.
7. Clark, with all his little brothers and sisters, _____ (be) trying to squeeze through the closing subway door.
8. Each of them, in spite of the most stubborn resistance to education, _____ (find) it impossible to escape learning something.
9. If either of you _____ (like) the sweater, you can have it.
10. If either Helen or Judy _____ (like) the sweater, I will give it up.

Coherence in Sentences: Function Words, Reference, Agreement 217

B. In the following sentences choose a pronoun to agree in number with the collective noun that is its antecedent:

1. The team took (its, their) positions about the field.
2. The Security Council will endeavor to reach (its, their) decision today.
3. The fraternity bowling team has just won (its, their) first victory.
4. If in a national park, (you, she, they) can find drinking water if (you, she, they) will ask a ranger.
5. The herd of wild burros follows (its, their) path up the canyon.
6. The club held (its, their) regular meeting Wednesday after school.
7. The Chamber of Commerce cast (its, their) votes for the new advertising campaign.
8. The convention of nurses kept busy brushing (its, their) respective teeth.

C. Revise the following sentences so that all pronouns or other reference words refer clearly to logical antecedents:

1. The only used trailers we found for sale had been lived in by families with children that had been all scratched up.
2. In the pterodactyl the hind legs were poorly developed, and thus we do not see any of them walking or crawling around on land.
3. If anything wrong has been done, I hope they put them in jail.
4. Television requires little mental activity, and in my opinion this is what we need.
5. Some of Cortez' horses were so outstanding in battle that it caused the Indians to consider them gods.
6. The chest had been her mother's, and she remembered the sorrow she had felt when she left for America.
7. Later several experimenters added more keys to the clarinet to give it range, and this is why its popularity increased.
8. In the first chapter of Susan Langer's book she talks about symbols.

D. If the italicized function word in each of the sentences below is faulty, choose a better form, or revise the sentence.

1. Mother always said that childhood is *when* you have the best time.
2. We spent our vacation in the Great Smokies, *and* we knew it would be cool there.
3. *While* I don't usually eat green onions, I sometimes do.
4. The reason I do not approve of federal aid for education is *because* we must protect our liberties.
5. He told me to move into the light *so as* he could watch the expression on my face.
6. I wrote a letter *in regards to* the advertisements for hair tonic.

7. Wilma liked to swim in the warm pool, *while* Joan preferred the invigorating water of the ocean.
8. *Being as* I have never learned to play bridge, I do not enjoy Mrs. Blackwell's parties.
9. *While* I do not like to complain about my guests, I do object to people who come in with their shoes dripping mud.
10. I had expected to love Venice, *and* when I got there I could not stand the smell of the canals.

E. Combine each of the pairs of clauses below into five different sentences, varying meanings or shades of meaning by varying conjunctions or conjunctive adverbs. You may change the order of the clauses and make necessary changes in forms of the words.

1. Mary asked me to go skating	I developed a headache
2. I slid down the drain pipe	I heard somebody scream upstairs
3. I have fast reaction time	I like sports
4. I have to ride the bus to school	I study the advertising on the car cards
5. The boat heeled over	He worked at the sails

F. Notice carefully the occurrence of *this* in the paragraph below, and revise so as to remove any vague reference.

Acetylene is usually only mildly poisonous and it is commonly available; this makes it a handy way of getting rid of vermin. It has other properties aside from being poisonous and convenient, and this is not always remembered. A garage owner recently provided an example of this. While he was driving to work, he became aware that a rat was chewing the cushion of the rear seat of his car, and hearing this, he stopped to kill the rat. This did not help much, because the rat scrambled under the back of the seat, which could not be removed although the seat could have been. Knowing this, the garage owner drove to his place of business, determined to poison or to smoke out the rat. This was sensible, and the garage owner got out his acetylene welding kit with a good fresh tank of gas, thinking this would kill the rat or get him out. It got him out. Shortly after the car was filled with gas, the garage owner saw his roof flying seventy-five feet into the air, this presumably being due to a short circuit in the automobile that had ignited the acetylene. Along with the roof went much of the owner's automobile, and parts of five others. This was not the only damage the owner saw around him. Six men had to be hospitalized because this was so unexpected that people stood still in the street staring while pieces of garage fell on them. The rat has not been seen since. Neither has the cushion. In spite of this, the garage owner is not taking out a patent on his rat exterminator.

10

Language and What to Know about It

> *Werodes wisa, wordhord onleac* [The leader of the warriors unlocked the word hoard]
> BEOWULF
>
> *If you can teach me a word, I will walk all the way to China to get it.*
> TURKISH PROVERB

A thousand years ago speakers of English had a revealing word for a vocabulary. They called it a word-hoard, a vocabulary bank, so to speak, and the lines above say that Beowulf unlocked his so that the words could come pouring out and be distributed among his hearers.

You may sometimes feel much the same way, that what you want to say is locked up in words and you need a key to unlock the treasure. In fact, no key exists—nothing as simple as a metal key, anyhow. But riches can be gotten out of a word bank. If we have no one key we do have a combination of them, some that will help immediately, some that work only through the months and years. This chapter introduces some of the long-term keys, ways of opening the word-hoard by learning more about language, what it is and how it works. It considers the history of language, particularly of the English language, and points out ways in which you can make language a more useful tool by knowing where words come from, how they change, and how they are related.

THE INDO-EUROPEAN FAMILY

The oldest ancestor of English we know is Indo-European. The word *know* is here being used in a limited way. We do not know this language in the sense that anybody has spoken it for thousands of years, or that it has survived in writing. Its speakers are long dead, and they could not write. We know about the language as we know there are—or at least have been— stars in the sky, because we see the light from them. This light may have been emitted from the stars years ago, but we know they must have been there or they could not have emitted the light. Similarly, we know there must have been a language, which we have named Indo-European; otherwise languages could not have descended from it.

The speakers of this tongue made up a large community, certainly as early as 3,000 B.C., in a temperate climate. They had words for wolves, bears, and pine trees, but no words for camels and palm trees. They did not have the words, because they did not know the objects that such words name. The evidence suggests they lived somewhere in east central Europe. They did not live near the sea; they had words for water standing and water running, but no words for the ocean. Their descendants acquired such words only after they had migrated. They had a tribal organization; they could hunt and fish, and they practiced some agriculture. They had domesticated animals—in fact, their learning to ride horses probably accounted for their migration.

We have reconstructed their language by going from the known to the unknown. We can describe their speech because we know something of how languages change, and because we have so many surviving bodies of speech that we can guess what the ancestor must have been like. Using such methods, working back from modern languages, and reasoning forward from a reconstructed prehistoric language, students have charted the great Indo-European language family about as it appears on p. 221.

The Indo-Europeans thrived and moved out in almost all directions. The chart shows that descendants of Indo-Europeans got as far southeast as India, where Sanskrit is the ancestor of modern Indic, as far south as Greece and Rome, whence Greek and Latin, north to the Arctic Circle, and as far west as the Atlantic Ocean. One group of these migrants from the Indo-European heartland, speaking a dialect of Indo-European that we call Proto-Germanic, moved west and north. One descendant of this tongue was Old English (also called Anglo-Saxon); it has close relatives in modern languages like Dutch, German, and the Scandinavian tongues. Languages as different as English, Persian, Latin, Lithuanian, and Celtic still carry signs

SIMPLIFIED CHART OF THE INDO-EUROPEAN LANGUAGE FAMILY

The chart emphasizes Western languages, especially those leading to English.

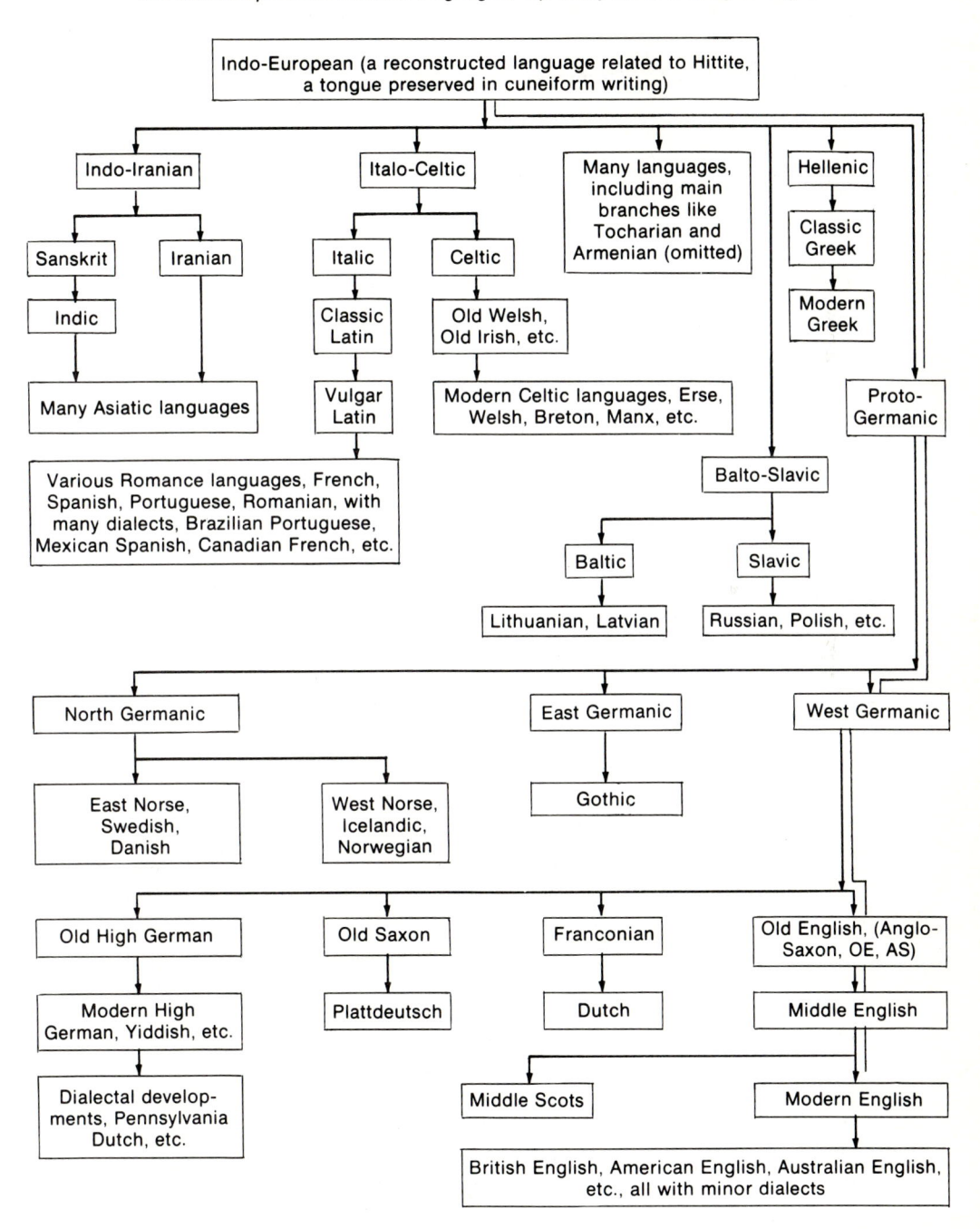

- **Indo-European** (a reconstructed language related to Hittite, a tongue preserved in cuneiform writing)
  - **Indo-Iranian**
    - Sanskrit
      - Indic
        - Many Asiatic languages
    - Iranian
  - **Italo-Celtic**
    - Italic
      - Classic Latin
        - Vulgar Latin
          - Various Romance languages, French, Spanish, Portuguese, Romanian, with many dialects, Brazilian Portuguese, Mexican Spanish, Canadian French, etc.
    - Celtic
      - Old Welsh, Old Irish, etc.
        - Modern Celtic languages, Erse, Welsh, Breton, Manx, etc.
  - Many languages, including main branches like Tocharian and Armenian (omitted)
    - Balto-Slavic
      - Baltic
        - Lithuanian, Latvian
      - Slavic
        - Russian, Polish, etc.
  - **Hellenic**
    - Classic Greek
      - Modern Greek
  - **Proto-Germanic**
    - **North Germanic**
      - East Norse, Swedish, Danish
      - West Norse, Icelandic, Norwegian
    - **East Germanic**
      - Gothic
    - **West Germanic**
      - Old High German
        - Modern High German, Yiddish, etc.
          - Dialectal developments, Pennsylvania Dutch, etc.
      - Old Saxon
        - Plattdeutsch
      - Franconian
        - Dutch
      - Old English, (Anglo-Saxon, OE, AS)
        - Middle English
          - Middle Scots
          - Modern English
            - British English, American English, Australian English, etc., all with minor dialects

of their common ancestry, such as words that are cognates, which had a common origin in Indo-European. In the following table, the common origin of a number of cognates is apparent:

English	Lithuanian	Celtic	Latin	Greek	Persian	Sanskrit
three	tri	tri	tres	treis	thri	tri
seven	septyni	secht	septem	hepta	hapta	sapta
me	manen	me	me	me	me	me
mother	moter	mathair	mater	meter	matar	matar
brother	brolis	brathair	frater	phrater	bratar	bhratar
night	naktis	nocht	noctis	nuktos		nakta

INDO-EUROPEAN BECOMES ENGLISH

What we call English was brought to the British Isles by Germanic-speaking peoples, mostly Angles and Saxons. Their conquest required two centuries or so, say roughly A.D. 450 to 650. The Germanic speakers had been preceded by several waves of Celtic speakers—that is, by other descendants from the Indo-Europeans, who had come by way of southern or west central Europe. The Germanic newcomers grabbed the readiest land, most of what is now England, pushing some Celts to the fringes, where they were somewhat protected by water or mountains. They and their languages survive in Scotland, Ireland, and Wales, and for a time persisted in places like Cornwall and the Isle of Man. Many Celts must have become slaves, servants, or serfs; but whatever happened to them, their new lords did not learn much of their language. Meanwhile, this was the main fact about the history of English until some fifteen hundred years ago: it was Indo-European as that language had grown and changed in one of its branches, Germanic. The Lord's Prayer in the language of the Anglo-Saxons looked like this:

> Fæder ure þu ðe eart on heofonum si þin nama gehalgod. Tobecume þin rice. Gewurðe þin willa on eorðan swa swa on heofonum. Urne gedæghwamlican hlaf syle us to dæg. And forgyf us ure gyltas swa swa we forgyfaþ urum gyltendum. And ne gelæd þu us on costnunge ac alys us of yfele. Soðlice.

BORROWING AND THE WORD-HOARD

The early history of English was largely a growth from within. When the Anglo-Saxons landed in England, they brought with them Indo-European as it had grown for a few thousand years in northern Europe, but not much else by way of language. They were not a sophisticated lot: They had encountered Roman soldiers and traders and had picked up a few terms. They must have overrun older peoples, probably including some seaside dwellers from whom they got words for sailing and seafoods. But of all the great Mediterranean cultures, from Egypt and Acadia to Athens, Rome, and Alexandria, they knew almost nothing. So when they set out across the North Sea they probably thought they were looking for better farm land, better fishing, and warmer weather. They did not know they were about to become one of the great linguistic borrowing peoples of all time.

For much of English history, cultural as well as linguistic, borrowing is the great basic fact. Some borrowing stemmed from conquest because, although conquest itself does not much spread language, it may lead to population shifts that do. During the time of King Alfred (d. 901?) some Danes and Norwegians overran parts of the British Isles. They were subdued, but they were too numerous to kill or drive out. They settled down and propagated both their vocabulary and their tow-headed offspring. Some of their terms can be spotted by a *k* in the modern spelling: *sky, skin, skirt, brisket*, or a hard *c*, *scare, scrape, ransack*. In 1066 Normans came, first the conquerors under William, then his horde of office-holders. They took over the government, the church, and education, and built great estates; accordingly, they introduced such words as *court, jury, judge, plaintiff, treason, rent, chaplain*. They brought with them the more gracious living of the Continent, as evidenced in *tailor, carpenter, mason*, and *chair*. An early lexicographer, Nathaniel Bailey, recorded a pat example. Farm work was done by the English natives, and farm animals were called by native names: *cow, bull, calf, hog, swine, sheep*. But when the meat of these beasts had been dressed (a French word) for the Norman seignoir's table it appeared with borrowed names: *beef, veal, pork, mutton*.

Much of this borrowing came about, furthermore, not from any conquests, but by peaceful exchange, mainly by import. The offshore islands, home of the unsophisticated Britons, were a backward part of the world, not made more civilized by the advent of somewhat barbaric Germanic tribesmen. Once channels of communication were opened with the Mediterranean lands to the south, culture flowed north. And with this flow came words, terms for physical objects like *jewels* and *jackets*, for skills and professions like *archery* and *medicine*, for studies like *arithmetic* and *chemistry*, for ideas like *quintessence* and *sovereignty*.

Inevitably, this flow followed the patterns of culture. Terms associated with Christianity started coming very early: *bishop, monk, mass, priest*. When chivalry developed in France and was imported into England, especially in the fourteenth and fifteenth centuries, it brought with it hundreds of terms for a knight's clothing, for his armor and weapons, for handling his horse, for his doings with his lord and his lady loves: *gorget, greave, caparison, seignior, gage*. With the revived interest in the classics during the Renaissance came learned and literary terms: *manuscript, rhetoric, epicurean-*

ism. Music, developing in Italy, brought Italian terms: *piano, piccolo, andante, concerto*. With gourmet cooking in France came terms for foods and cookery, even *gourmet* itself. Minor borrowings brought words from all over the world: *guru* from India, *sauna* from Finland, *teriyaki* from Japan, *cosmonaut* from Russia, *spoor* from Holland by way of Africa. This borrowing continued in the New World, of course, with *Tammany* and *chocolate* ultimately from Indian languages, *rodeo* and *hoosegow* from Mexican Spanish, and words from immigrants, like *kibitzer* from Yiddish and *Santa Claus* from German by way of Pennsylvania Dutch.

The great stream of borrowing combines the flow from both Classical and Romance languages. Some Greek words have been borrowed directly, especially by modern science: *psychosomatic, metacarpus*. Others were borrowed early from Greek into Latin, and thereafter found their way north, *ecclesiastic, phenomenon*. Terms came directly from Latin: *circus, maximum*. Anything that got into Latin, however it got there, was likely to descend into the Romance languages. Thus most English borrowings from Portuguese, Spanish, Italian, or French came ultimately from Latin; especially they came through French: *government, sergeant, sentimental*. This flood of words has been so copious that any dictionary you are likely to pick up will have as more than half its entries words from the Greek-Latin-French stream of borrowing.

Dialects and Migration

The word-hoard continued to grow as English speakers moved throughout the world and new dialects developed. British emigrants to what were then the colonies carried their words and their dialects with them. Thus Australian speech reflects London dialects. Canadian has been influenced by the Scots who migrated there. In the United States, the three basic dialects on the Atlantic seaboard reflect the different areas from which migrants came. New Englanders embarked from the South and Southeast of England. Early settlers in Virginia and the Carolinas came from Southern communities too, and thus Northern American English dialects and Southern dialects have much in common. Speakers from the Midlands dominated settlement in New Jersey and Pennsylvania, so that their dialects contrast with those to the north and south. Thus a word like *dear* is likely to be pronounced without a final r-sound in Connecticut and Georgia, but not in Philadelphia. All these dialects moved west, getting somewhat jumbled as their speakers mingled. But dialects die slowly, and dialectal differences hundreds of years old can still be identified on the Pacific coast. In the San Francisco area, at least two sorts of dialects persist, remnants of Northern speech that arrived by sea from Boston and New York and Midland speech that came overland from Pennsylvania to the Middle West, and eventually over the mountains by wagon train.

Effects of Growth and Change

The results of these growing pains of English—dialectal and otherwise—permeate modern English. Some of them help make English an uncommonly rich medium, but some, by their seeming inconsistency, plague the modern writer. Take spelling. Spellings as different as *pearl, girl,* and *curl*—not to mention *Merle*, which has a different history—now rhyme in American English, although they have spellings that reflect different backgrounds. *Meat* and *meet* are spelled differently because they were once pronounced differently, as were *made* and *maid*, and *to, too,* and *two.* Many words, including *enough, though,* and *borough*, end with a *gh* that either has no sound at all or the improbable sound of *f*. The explanation is that Old English had a hackle sound, now lost, that was for a time spelled *gh*.

The centuries, also, made great changes in vocabulary. Some words died out, many that were no longer needed, but a few that were useful and still would be if we could get them back. One was an impersonal pronoun, *man* (but not our modern word *man*), the equivalent of *anybody, everybody, somebody, people, a person.* We have no such general-purpose word any more, and have to use *they,* or *one,* or something else unhandy or awkward—including the passive.

Mainly, the years have brought us a great wealth of new uses for old words. Almost any common word would serve as an example, but take *home.* It came from an Indo-European root meaning *to rest, lie down,* and it kept this limited meaning in Old English. It was not much used, but it appears in the Lindisfarne Gospels in a sentence that can be modernized, "In my father's house are many homes," many places to rest. It has since become one of the most powerful words in the language—*Be it ever so humble there is no place like home.* It became a verb: A missile can *home* in on its target. The same word became an adjective, as in *homing pigeon, homing instinct,* and an adverb: *go home.* It found a place in dozens of compounds for ideas the Anglo-Saxons had not much needed: *home plate, homework, home brew, homestead, home office, homeroom,* and *home economics,* along with many they could have used but did not: *homely, homemade, homebody,* and *hometown.*

Meanwhile, changes were moving through grammar. Indo-European, the ancestor of both Old English and Latin, had a highly inflected grammar, using many grammatical endings. Much of this inflectional system was preserved in Latin, and much of it was still used in the ancestor of Old English; but most of it has vanished from Modern English.

That is, English once relied on a highly inflectional grammar, with many endings and changes in form. A few of these changes have survived, in the difference between *girl* and *girls, they do* and *he does.* But mainly, Modern English relies on what is called a distributive or analytic grammar, in which word order and relationship words take over much of the grammar formerly handled by changes in word form. This change began in Proto-

Germanic, the form of English that stands between Indo-European and Old English, and the change is probably still going on. Part of this shift affected the verb system. Indo-European had verbs like those that have survived in *sing, sang, sung* and *write, wrote, written*, but English has not made such verbs for more than a thousand years. Instead, a more simplified system became standard, as in *study, studied* and in *discover, discovered*.

The two systems got mixed up. When the progenitors of English started west from the Indo-European homeland, they were embarking on a whole series of new experiences. They encountered the sea; they became Christians; they were swept over by Roman and later Continental cultures. For all this they needed new verbs, and the new verbs were all built on the simplified pattern using only one ending, *-d, -t,* or *-ed*. This became the fashionable way to speak, and many of the old verbs were changed to the new way. An old sequence like *gieldan, geald, guldon, golden* became *yield, yielded,* but as late as a few hundred years ago Shakespeare could make a character say, *He holp the heavens to rain,* the new form *helped* having not yet entirely replaced the older forms like *hulpon* and *holpen*. But all this happened irregularly. Changes were faster in some dialects than in others, and they changed variously among various speakers. When *bring* lost a few of its forms, some people kept the old past participal *brought,* but others preserved *brang* or *brung,* or the new form *bringed,* which never caught on.

In short, most of what is commonly called "bad grammar" is variation in usage and stems from old forms that became unfashionable or new forms that never quite made it. Historically, *brang, brung,* and *bringed* are as good as most accepted verb forms, but they were unlucky. Forms now frowned on thrived in dialects that became unfashionable. Linguistically, there is nothing wrong with them, but they have become social outcasts, the victims of dialectal variation and the whims of fashion.

BUILDING A VOCABULARY

The more words we know and the more uses of these words we can distinguish, the more choices we have as writers. And the more we can understand the working of words, the better we can use them. Vocabulary is both of these, recognizing words and having a feeling for them. We now have to ask how knowing something of the history and nature of the English language can help build vocabulary.

Much building of word-hoards is unconscious. We all have a wealth of vocabulary because we have, in effect, inherited it, and it has continued to grow without our conscious help. Babies start learning vocabulary shortly after birth, and they acquire the language to which they were born, quite literally as a birthright. They start, unconsciously, with a hearing vocabulary, including terms that are moved into a speaking vocabulary, and eventually into reading and writing vocabularies. The shapes of words, especially, are learned in these ways, but uses are learned unconsciously, also.

Native children learn sequences like "the ice-cream cone"; they never need be told that "cone cream ice the" is wrong. Such acquisition is probably the best language learning; certainly it is the fastest and easiest.

Few human beings, however, could ever become fluent in a language if they commanded only unconsciously learned linguistic data, which are limited in quantity and to a degree in character. Thus the more language people need, the more they must learn consciously.

First, we might notice that almost everyone has at least four basic vocabularies. The first is a relatively small number of words that we may call the *speaking vocabulary*, composed of words that come readily to the speaker's tongue. Some speakers may use only a few hundred words in this way; even a moderately articulate person uses only a few thousand. Literate people have a second vocabulary, a *writing vocabulary*, which includes the words in the speaking vocabulary, plus other words that they can call up. A good writer may employ a vocabulary of ten thousand, twenty-five thousand, perhaps fifty thousand words. Less fluent people may suffer from a writing vocabulary little larger than their speaking vocabularies. Literate persons have also a *reading vocabulary*, including words they would not use in conversation or in writing but would know when they see them written. For most people the reading vocabulary is much larger than either the speaking or writing vocabulary. The fourth vocabulary, the largest of all, we may refer to as the *acquaintance vocabulary*. It includes the other three, but it includes, also, words that the owner has seen or heard before but whose meaning can only be guessed from context. Vocabularies of this sort can be very large.

This distinction among four vocabularies has practical use for a writer, since a writing vocabulary is almost certainly smaller than the reading and acquaintance vocabularies. To increase a store of words for writing you have only to move terms from the larger vocabularies into the writing vocabulary, a much easier job than learning a word from scratch. Often, recognizing the historical relations of a word will be enough to make the transformation. Consider words like *pedestal, pedestrian* as an adjective, and *pedicure*. Most literate Americans would recognize these words but might not use them much in writing. They depend on the root *ped-*. But this root is the equivalent of English *foot*; it is the old Indo-European **ped-*. The asterisk designates a reconstructed form. It remained almost unchanged when it came down through Latin but became *foot* as it descended straight into Modern English. Thus a pedestal is a base on which something rests, as though on a foot. *Pedestrian* refers to a person going on foot. *Pedicure* means care of the feet. Seeing the relationship of such words to the common word *foot* should help move them toward the writing vocabulary.

Most English words have come to us in one of two ways: They have descended from Indo-European straight into English, as what we have called native words, like *foot, head,* and *eat*; or they are words borrowed through the Greek-Latin-Romance stream, words like *rhetoric* and *psychosomatic*. The words of the first sort are so short and common that every adult knows most of them. Only the borrowed words give trouble; they tend to be longer and less used. Fortunately, most of the borrowed words are related to a native word, as *pedestal* is related to *foot*, since the Classical and Romance languages came from Indo-European, too. A writer has only to see this relationship and the strange, borrowed word will seem more like one of the family.

The difficulty, of course, is that *pedestal* does not look or sound much like *foot*. Sounds have changed in the various lines of descent from Indo-European, and spellings roughly reflect these changes. Explaining most of these vagaries is too complex for this book. The study is called etymology, and every serious writer will want to go into it. It is fascinating, and will help a writer build a vocabulary.

Prefixes and Suffixes

Speakers of English stick terms together to make new terms. We stuck *rail* and *road* together to name a new means of transportation, and then we stuck *air* and *plane* together to name another means. More recently we have made *jetway* and *spaceship*.

The Indo-Europeans relied on the same device, known as compounding. Some terms were used so much in this way that they developed a special sort of life as terms that could attach themselves to many words. That is, they could serve as affixes, either prefixes (before) or suffixes (after) the original word, bits like *un-*, *retro-*, and *-ible*. The habit of attaching affixes descended into many of the offspring of Indo-European, including English and the languages it has borrowed from, and English has picked up affixes from various sources. Thus *un-* and *in-* in modern English are both versions of the same term, *un-* from English and *in-* from Latin, both from a root meaning what *no* and *not* mean. Thus we have *unknown* and *unreal* and at the same time *indecent, inhospitable, immature,* and *irresponsible,* with all the prefixes meaning "not." The last two illustrate another tendency that sounds may alter adjacent sounds as language changes. To see how this works, you have only to pronounce *in-mature* and *in-responsible*. Here the sound of *n* blended into the following sound and disappeared from the spelling.

The use of affixes is still highly active in contemporary English, constantly producing new words, some of them short-lived. The fad of a few years ago for attaching *-wise* to almost anything—"It will be cold weatherwise"—has almost disappeared. The popular slang suffix *-ville* in *dullsville, splitsville, togethernessville,* has pretty much run its course. The Old English *-estre,* an ending designating a feminine agent, became *-ster* and was generalized to produce words like *gangster, oldster,* or more recently *pollster*. Borrowed suffixes are equally flexible. The verb-forming *-ize,* which came from a Greek word meaning "to make," is currently attached to almost anything: *tenderize* is to make tender, *finalize* to make final. The last is still provoking controversies over usage, perhaps because of its popularity among bureaucrats. *Hamburger* means somebody or something that comes from Hamburg, Germany, but the origin faded in American English as *-burger* became a commercial suffix in *fishburger* or *cheeseburger* or a name for almost any sandwich. Words like *cafeteria, auditorium,* and *panorama* have by analogy produced suffixes for an almost endless stream of creations: *washateria, snackateria, lubritorium, tireatorium, bowlerama, seafoodorama.* Most of these are not likely to be established in the language.

Native English affixes are so common that everyone knows them: *-able, by-, -ful, off-, out-, -less, with-,* and many others. And many borrowed affixes are equally common, related to common English terms, either affixes or words. Following are samples from one initial letter:

> *ab*—related to *of, off,* meaning away from; can be *a-, am-, ap-, at-,* etc., as in *absolve, abstain, apology.*
>
> *ad*—related to *at,* meaning to or toward; can be *ac-, af-, ag-,* etc., as in *advice, attack, affect.*
>
> *anti*—related to *end,* and the rare English prefix *and,* as in *an(d)swer,* to swear (talk) back; meaning against, as in *antiwar;* the same root accounts for *ante-,* meaning before, in the sense that the past can be contrasted to the present, as in *anteroom, antecedent.*

There are hundreds more, with or without English relatives. Some are related to English words, not affixes, such as Greek *mega-* as in *megaton, megalogopolis, megabucks. Mega* is the Greek form of the term that is *much* in English and has essentially the same meaning. You will do well to be alert to the power of these little syllables as building blocks for words and clues for increasing vocabulary.

Suggestions for Vocabulary Building

Following are practical suggestions for building your vocabulary:

1. *Shift words into speaking and writing vocabularies.* Since reading and acquaintance vocabularies are relatively large, you can build your word bank by consciously using terms from these when you speak and write.

2. *Learn words by groups.* Many English words can be related to words in other languages through a common root in an ancestor language. Starting with a native word and adding loan words, you can work with the group as a family and may learn a dozen words more easily than you could learn one word otherwise.

3. *Work with prefixes and suffixes.* By learning the significance of some of the basic affixes in the language, you can increase your recognition vocabulary almost at once. Since affixes are used widely in word formation, each one you learn has the potential of adding many new words.

4. *When you learn a word, learn enough about it to make it your own.* The

history of a word is not only interesting in itself; it also is an excellent aid to memory and a clue to how the word may be used.

5. *Learn words you will use.* You may be able to amaze your friends if you know the meaning of *ento-ectad* (it means from inside out), but words completely strange are hard to learn and easy to forget. Learn more about words you have encountered and are likely to encounter again, or need in your own writing and speaking. Move words from your acquaintance vocabulary to your working vocabularies, from your reading vocabulary to your writing and speaking vocabularies.

6. *Once you learn a word, use it.* Do something deliberately to keep your new words; find work for them. Introduce them into conversation, or into your next essay.

WHAT DICTIONARIES ARE FOR

The best single tool for both vocabulary building and word choice is a dictionary. Regrettably, dictionaries are not so helpful as they might be, because most users do not know what they are good for. This is something of a paradox. Probably nowhere in the world have dictionaries been so extensively purchased, so widely admired, and so persistently consulted as they are in the United States. Most Americans assume they know what a wordbook can do, and they consult "the dictionary" with a faith that is touching if not entirely justified. Often they try to use a dictionary for what it is not and for what it was never intended to be. Accordingly, they fail to get from it what they might.

More than two centuries ago, Dr. Samuel Johnson found out, to his embarrassment, what a dictionary can and cannot do. While planning and editing his *Dictionary of the English Language* (1755), he tried to obtain subscriptions by promising that with it he would purify the language and fix it in this newfound purity. During the years he spent editing the volume, he realized that language always changes, that nobody can purify it, nobody can fix it, and nobody can determine what it will become. Most of his contemporaries thought that language should be and could be purified and fixed; many people still believe this. But the fact is that nobody, not an emperor, a gangster, a grammarian, a president, a lexicographer, or anybody else, can successfully determine language. At best, lexicographers can hope to describe it, and even that description will be inadequate and will not last. The language will go right on shifting even before the dictionary can be printed and adopted. Language use changes while the dictionary lies open before the expectant user.

Thus lexicographers do not tell people how to use language. They do not prescribe speech; they collect it. They read and listen and record what they find. They try to discover how the language is used, in written and oral form; and if communication through computers ever becomes suitable enough so that we can call computer signs a language, lexicographers will need to ask how it is used in computer form. They recognize that language can be employed more or less formally, more or less traditionally, and that it is shot through with the forces of dialect and usage. They study the collected evidence as part of the history of a language, and in the light of modern linguistics. They try to analyze the results and to describe them, partly in written words, partly in conventionalized symbols, and they assemble all this information in usable form. The result is what we call a dictionary.

What do these procedures mean for the user of the dictionary? Obviously they mean that whoever consults the book should try to use it as it was meant to be used, as a tool for understanding the language, whether wishing to interpret an abstruse piece of writing, or wanting to say something more precisely.

HOW A DICTIONARY IS MADE

A modern dictionary rests upon citations of specific uses of words. Such citations are collected by the million, and in the great scholarly dictionaries, a portion of them are reprinted. This reprinting can become expensive and cumbersome. The *Oxford English Dictionary* endeavored to print citations for all uses of all words in the language, but the job became so huge that the completed dictionary fills more than a dozen large volumes, and the editors had to cut it off arbitrarily. A wordbook that must be convenient cannot reprint many citations.

Citations of actual uses of words, however, are behind the definitions in modern dictionaries. One recently published desk dictionary, for example, gives the following as one use of the word *scalp*: "[*Colloq.*] to buy and sell in order to make small, quick profits." The entry also includes a symbol indicating that the use is an Americanism. The editor who prepared that definition would probably have begun by reviewing earlier dictionaries, and these would have included the scholarly *Dictionary of American English* (1944). Some reader for that dictionary had noticed the following in *Harper's Magazine* for 1886:

> [The scalper buys] any quantity of grain that may be offered, sells it at an advance of 1/8th cent per bushel, thus scalps the market.

The dictionary reprinted this passage, along with further instances of the same use of *scalp* in 1897 and 1902. Accordingly, that dictionary defined "to scalp the market" as "to buy and sell grain or stocks, taking small profits quickly as the market fluctuates." The editors labeled the words *Colloq.*, presumably thereby responding to the indications in all three citations that the word was normally confined to the speech of a limited group and was rare in writing.

This sequence of events suggests how lexicographers work. They were relying upon the known verified occurrences of a word. None of them presumed to go outside this evidence and make any expression of personal convictions. They wanted to discover the meaning and the social standing of a use. They did not need to consider spelling and pronunciation because those matters were handled elsewhere, but if they had suspected that *scalp* is pronounced differently as a term in finance than as a term in anatomy, they would have pursued the same technique. They would have tried to learn how the word was spoken by those who used it. Lexicographers sift the evidence and marshall it into a reference work, using conventional symbols for economy and endeavoring to write in a style at once factual, clear, and concise.

WHAT A DICTIONARY IS GOOD FOR

A modern desk dictionary should provide at least the following:

1. *An Entry—a Word, Phrase, Abbreviation, Combining Element, or the Like* Dictionaries vary in their selection of entries, partly because it is not easy to determine what should be considered a word. Is *fast* one word because of its spelling, or four words because it can be any of at least four parts of speech? The *Century* has seven entries for *fast*; some dictionaries have one. Is *fasting* a separate word, or a form of *fast*? Furthermore, all dictionaries can print only a selection from the million or so possible entries.

The entry also indicates spelling. When two or more standard spellings of a word exist, the entry includes them (*traveler, traveller; catalog, catalogue*), or it provides cross references for variations like the British *gaol* and the American *jail*. The order in which two spellings are listed does not necessarily mean that one is "preferred" to the other, only that the editors find both spellings in common reputable use. To print, they had to put one of the two ahead of the other.

2. *Pronunciation* Usually just after the entry word, the entered term is transcribed into some system of phonetic symbols, often summarized at the bottom of alternate pages and explained in an introduction. No desk dictionary can record all common pronunciations; *orange* is said to have a dozen pronunciations, and *charivaree* can be pronounced with two, three, or four syllables. As with spelling, when more than one pronunciation is offered, the order of presentation does not indicate a preference, only that all the variations recorded are in standard use.

3. *Grammatical Information* After the pronunciation usually appears a symbol like *n.* for noun or *v.t.* for verb, transitive, indicating the common uses of the word. These recognize what is sometimes called "privilege of occurrence," the suitability of the word to work as adjective or noun or some other part of speech. The designation does not necessarily restrict possible conversion of the word to other uses.

4. *Etymology* All but elementary dictionaries include some etymology, a history of the word, usually in square brackets after the grammatical designation, and usually after only one of related entries.

5. *Usage* Many dictionaries provide usage labels, like *slang*, *obs.*, *U.S. dial.* as an indication of the situations in which a word is commonly appropriate. Often the label applies to only one definition of a word. *Scalp*, for instance, may be labeled colloquial or slang in a sense like "scalp the market" but would carry no label as a name for the covering of the skull.

6. *Definitions* Most words have several meanings; some like *get*, have dozens. Defining these uses, setting limits to them, and describing the impact of the word within its limits becomes the most difficult job for the lexicographer and, usually, the service most useful to users of the dictionary. In many dictionaries different meanings are designated by numbers and letters.

7. *Synonyms* For some entries, the last section is a list of synonyms (and possibly antonyms) discriminated from one another. There are also specialized synonym books: dictionaries of synonyms, thesauruses intended to suggest a synonym to a writer trying to think of a precise word, and even wordbooks with a desk dictionary and thesaurus printed in parallel columns so that a user can go readily from one to the other.

FOR STUDY AND WRITING

A. Look up each word below in the dictionary and record its etymology.

1. alphabet
2. ballot
3. Bible
4. cabbage
5. calendar
6. constable
7. dinner
8. fiddle
9. fowl
10. stranger
11. jelly
12. kennel
13. language
14. magazine
15. television
16. tooth
17. undulant
18. paper
19. umpire
20. cuisine

B. Many English words come from Latin. Sometimes the Latin word has changed little or not at all; for instance, Latin *circus*, a circular place and then a celebration held in a circular place, has become English *circus*. Some Latin words, by slight changes or by combining with other words or affixes, have given us many words. For each of the following Latin words, try to find at least ten descendants in English that make some use of the parent word: *dicere (dictus), mittere (missus), pendere, currere (cursus), stabilis (stabulum, stare), facere (factus), liber*.

C. The following words were created by compounding either in Old English or in a language from which the compound was borrowed. Look up each word in the dictionary and write the words from which it was formed.

1. delicatessen
2. nostril
3. democracy
4. window
5. garlic
6. barn
7. landscape
8. pajamas
9. hussy
10. municipal

D. Following are pairs of words, similar in meaning, one of each pair originating in Old English and one in French. Remembering that Norman French was the official and court language in England during the period after 1066, although English persisted among the common people, decide which word in each pair is a native English word rather than a borrowing from French. Check your answers in a dictionary.

1. help, assistance
2. beef, cow
3. begin, commence
4. corpulent, fat
5. judgment, doom
6. deer, venison
7. king, sovereign
8. work, labor
9. wretched, miserable
10. buy, purchase

E. These words were created through some process other than compounding or adding affixes. Look up each word and describe its origin: *kodak, bus, grovel, smog, cockroach, laser*.

F. Look at several samples of your own writing. What kinds of words do you seem to prefer? Does this change depending on the type of writing you are doing? For example, is your vocabulary different in writing a letter to a friend and writing a laboratory report for class? Can you see any uses of borrowed—or specialized—language in your vocabulary? What kinds of vocabulary do you think you should incorporate into your writing?

11

Word Choice: Usage

> *Broadly speaking the short words are best, and the old words,*
> *when short, are best of all.*
> WINSTON CHURCHILL

> *I like the exact word, and clarity of statement, and here and there*
> *a touch of good grammar for picturesqueness.*
> MARK TWAIN

In the above quotation, Churchill was reacting against the notion that using ponderous, stuffy words makes a writer sound learned and elegant. And during World War II, when rallying the free world to resist Hitler's armies, he relied, in his most admired speech, on old and short Anglo-Saxon words.

> We shall not flag or fail. We shall fight in France, we shall fight on the seas and oceans, we shall fight with growing confidence and growing strength in the air, we shall defend our island, whatever the cost may be, we shall fight on the beaches, we shall fight on the landing grounds, we shall fight in the streets, we shall fight in the hills; we shall never surrender.

But when Churchill wrote with a different purpose for a different audience, he used a different vocabulary.

> Emigration to the New World presented itself as an escape from a sinful generation. There they [the Pilgrim Fathers] might gain a livelihood unhampered by Dutch guilds, and practice their creed unharrassed by English clerics.
>
> *A History of the English Speaking Peoples*

The writing is crisp, and Churchill prefers a solid old word like *sinful* to the more recent *corrupt* or *decadent*, but many of the words are neither old nor short. Finding the exact word often requires a vocabulary beyond the old and the short, and both the native words and the borrowed words in English have important uses.

NATIVE WORDS AND BORROWED WORDS

Modern English words are of two sorts: homey, powerful words, mostly one or two syllables, or specialized, precise words, mostly longer. The first kind, the words that Churchill professed to like best, are mostly native words, and for good reason. When the Norman French took over what is now England in 1066, they killed many of the educated speakers of English, but the farmers and other laborers went right on living and talking much as they had. They talked English, and thus they preserved the core of the language. The grammatical words are all native words, like *the, she, is, who, and, by, that.* The family words are mostly native: *father, sister, man, wife.* The words needed for physical word tend to be native: *walk, run, plow, pull, land, lit,* and *work* itself. The names of things everybody experiences all the time, *sun, moon, day, rain, cold,* and *dirt,* tend either to be native or to have come from the Danes and Norwegians. Words for things we cannot live without tend to be native: *love, hate, eat, water,* and *sleep.*

    The Normans imported their own educated people, who brought their educated terms with them, French and Latin terms. The Normans also promoted more borrowing by opening channels of trade, bringing floods of new goods and new ways of living, which required new words. The readiest way to get them was to borrow them. Most borrowed words came into English to fill a specific need. Thus they include many specific words, with limited uses but precise meanings, the kind of words that are indispensable for scientific, technical, professional, and learned communication. The old, native words tend to give power to the language; the new, borrowed words provide precision and accuracy. Writers need both, and they need to know how to choose the best ones for their immediate purpose.

ACCURATE WORD CHOICE

Clear communication also requires accurate word choice. Inaccuracies may be simple blunders. A writer may not be sure of the difference between

Word Choice: Usage   237

Guide to Revision — W

INACCURATE WORD CHOICE

Revise to make diction more accurate or more precise.

ORIGINAL	REVISION
Rosemary and Al got different answers. [*The meaning is uncertain. Did Rosemary and Al differ from each other? Did their later answers differ from their earlier answers? Did they differ from those obtained by other students?*]	(1) Rosemary and Al got inconsistent answers. (2) Rosemary and Al got varying answers. (3) Rosemary and Al got answers that differed from those in the manual. [*The sentence may need to be recast.*]
The capture of the ridge had seemed an inhuman feat. [*The writer has apparently confused words similar in form but not in meaning.*]	Capturing the ridge had seemed impossible. [*The writer probably meant to say that the feat seemed humanly impossible, or superhuman.*]
He told them that the difference in size was just an optical allusion.	He told them that the difference in size was just an optical illusion.

affect and *effect* and may confuse a sentence by mixing them up. A student who writes about the abominable snowman as the *abdominal snowman* provides unintended humor. Or a writer may fail to think carefully. The following appeared in a nationally syndicated column: "Near Rochford, England, water gushes with such force that it operates a watermill within 60 yards of its source." If the mill is only six inches from the source it is still within sixty yards. The author may have meant "more than sixty yards from" not "within sixty yards of." Both constant attention and an understanding of how meaning works are necessary for precise diction.

For convenience we might use the word *meaning* to suggest the power of words to do things to and for people, although strictly speaking no word has meaning as a physical object can have length. The bars of metal in the Bureau of Standards, which determine our inches and feet, keep the same length at a given temperature, no matter who measures them, so long as the measuring is accurately done, but no words are kept at a controlled temperature in the Bureau of Standards. Words exist only in people's minds, and all minds are different. No word has a "meaning" that it inevitably calls up in everyone, without variations.

On the other hand, communication is impossible without some agreements about meaning. Mrs. Malaprop, a character in Sheridan's *The Rivals*, made herself famous and added the word *malapropism* to the language by misusing words she did not understand. When she complimented herself on a "nice derangement of epitaphs" and said that someone was "headstrong as an allegory on the banks of the Nile," she certainly did not mean what her listeners understood by *derangement, epitaphs,* or *allegory.* Mrs. Malaprop could indulge her whims if she wished; words have no mystical connection with a particular "meaning." But communication is possible because at any time in history, by common agreement, people associate particular words with some thoughts and not with others. Writers who are ignorant of the agreements or pay little attention to them, who do not choose words with precision, risk inaccurate communication.

HOW WORDS MEAN

People can agree about meaning because words relate to things in the real world and are, relatively speaking, common and enduring. But accurate choice of words is difficult because words are related to things through various human minds. A word is a symbol a human being uses to reveal an idea about something.

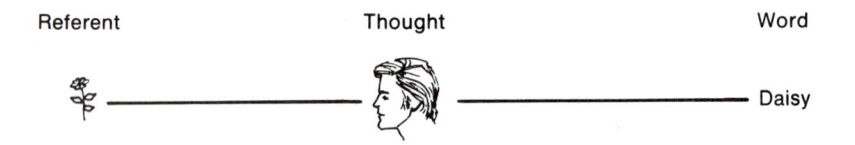

Referent — Thought — Word — Daisy

A writer or speaker can use *daisy* as a symbol to express a thought about a referent, a particular flower growing in a meadow. Speakers of English, by general agreement, use this symbol when they think of this particular kind of flower. The symbol would not work if the writer were thinking of a four-footed animal that brays or of a carved representation of George Washington. Neither would it work for writing in French or German. Conversely, any users of the language, readers or listeners, could interpret this symbol similarly.

Word   Thought   Referent

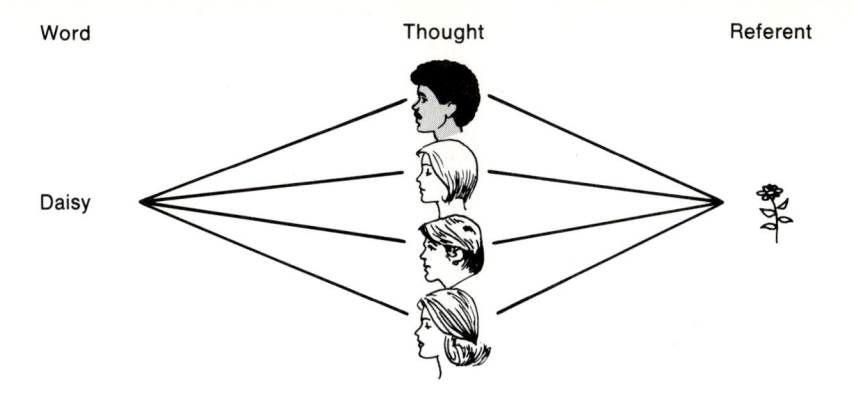

Daisy

Furthermore, a writer may have various thoughts about a referent growing in a meadow and may choose any one of a number of words quite different from *daisy*, as in the following illustration:

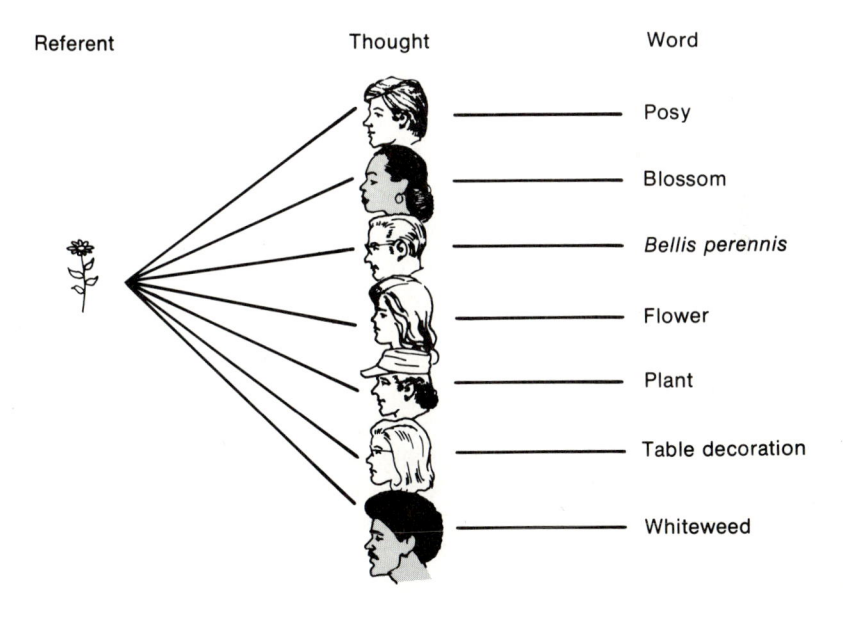

Referent   Thought   Word

Posy

Blossom

Bellis perennis

Flower

Plant

Table decoration

Whiteweed

Each of these words—like many others—has the same referent, but each conveys a slightly different thought about the referent. *Plant* indicates that the writer is distinguishing the referent less precisely than does *flower*; *posy* suggests something about the background and attitude of the person; *bellis perennis* is the scientific name of the flower; *whiteweed* and *table decoration* indicate special attitudes toward the referent.

Words in Their Contexts

Words affect and are affected by the words they accompany. The writer needs to choose words with care, selecting so that in both denotation and connotation they are appropriate in their contexts. The denotation of a word is its literal or basic or dictionary meaning. But a word also has a connotation, the suggestions that accompany the basic meaning because of the ways in which the word is customarily used. The denotation of the word *pig*, for example, is clear, a synonym for *hog* or *swine*. But the word has many connotations, associations beyond the central meaning—dirt, greed, gluttony. As early as 1848 it was a derogatory name for a police officer. In other contexts it could connote the cuteness of "this little pig went to market."

Or notice the variations in the meaning of the word *love* in the following sentences:

>My *love* is like a red, red rose.
>
>The *love* of money is the root of all evil.
>
>Greater *love* hath no man than this, that a man lay down his life for his friends.
>
>Friendship is *Love* without his wings.
>
>God is *love*.
>
>They fell in *love* at first sight.

The word *love* appears in each sentence, but the connotations and even the denotations differ. The context, the company the word keeps, reveals its meaning.

The writer must choose words with their contexts in mind. The lists of discriminative synonyms in dictionaries suggest how words fit different contexts (look up, for example, *joke*, *wit*, or *wise*). Even synonyms cannot be changed at random; for example, dictionaries list *exonerate* as a synonym for *clear*. Substituting *exonerate* would sharpen meaning in a sentence like "The attorney hoped to clear the ex-convict," but it would not serve in a sentence like "Tom cleared the dishes from the table" or "The pole-vaulter could not clear twelve feet."

Abstract and Concrete Words

Almost anyone could sketch the referent for *daisy*, and the resulting picture may also serve for of the word *flower*, but a picture of the referent behind the "full" meaning of the word *flower* would be impossible to draw. It would have to include not only daisies but also irises and begonias, the blossoms on thistles, the bloom stage in a field of corn, in fact everything in the writer's experience that made up the idea implied by the word. Or consider drawing a picture of the referent behind the word *beauty*. Thousands of bits from the writer's experience would be necessary, and a picture would become virtually impossible.

Obviously *flower* is more general than *daisy,* and *beauty* is more general than *flower. Beauty* can also be said to be *abstract,* whereas *daisy* is *concrete.* Roughly, we can say that abstract words refer to generalities or to ideas, and that concrete words refer to things or objects. Concrete words stand for a thought about a referent that can be pictured or specified; abstract words go back to referents so complex or general that they cannot be visualized. These statements require at least two qualifications. First, *abstract* and *concrete* are relative terms, like *general* and *specific* (see chapter 3). Compare the following:

> There was *something* on the table.
>
> There was a *creature* on the table.
>
> There was a *tarantula* on the table.

Creature is more concrete than *something, tarantula* more concrete than *creature.* The ideas become more specific; the words become more concrete and increase in exactness and suggestiveness as they do so. Second, just as the general develops out of the specific, abstract expressions grow from more concrete ones. *Color* stands for a thought that would be hard to express if we had only more concrete terms like *red, yellow, blue, green.*

Both abstract and concrete terms are necessary for communication, but abstractions have a way of broadening so far that they become meaningless blankets to cover everything in the vicinity of the writer's idea. Consider the following as a wordy way of saying "The question is basic":

> The question in this regard is directly related to the basic circumstances of the situation.

Or consider the following sentence proposed by George Orwell to illustrate how some writers might translate a passage of the Bible:

> Objective consideration of contemporary phenomena compels the conclusion that success or failure in competitive activities exhibits no tendency to be commensurate with innate capacity, but that a considerable element of the unpredictable must invariably be taken into account.

Although the sentence exaggerates deliberately, it suggests how abstractions can obscure ideas. This is the passage from Ecclesiastes that Orwell has "translated":

> I returned, and saw under the sun, that the race is not to the swift, nor the battle to the strong, neither yet bread to the wise, nor yet riches to men of understanding, nor yet favour to men of skill; but time and chance happeneth to them all.

Instead of one general statement, the original uses five specific examples; instead of abstractions like *consideration, phenomena, conclusion, success,* and *failure,* the original uses more concrete words like *race, battle, bread,* and *riches.* In short, writing becomes more vivid or objective as specific details appear in concrete terms or when the longer borrowed words—like *consideration* and *phenomena*—are replaced by strong native ones—like *battle* and *bread.*

Denotation and Connotation: Slanting

Roughly speaking, the idea a word sparks about a referent is its denotation, what is sometimes called its "dictionary meaning." *Flower* and *table decoration,* therefore, have different denotations; but *flower* and *posy* have a common denotation. Still, no botanist today would write that "the begonia bears monecius posies"; a botanist would feel that *posy* is unsuited to scientific description. On the other hand, one might wish to suggest that some wallpaper was old-fashioned by saying, "It was cluttered with pink posies." That is, each of these words can do something more than point to a particular thought. This power of a word to make emotional and interpretive suggestions is the word's *connotation.* It is part of the meaning of a word.

Connotation is always individual. To a garden lover, the word *flower* may suggest hours of pleasure in the sunshine, a sense of pervading joy. To someone else, it may suggest bad taste as reflected in plastic decorations in a cheap restaurant, or if one has been ill from mimosa, it may even suggest nausea. But even though connotation is personal, most people share much of the connotative power of a word, for most of us have somewhat similar heritages. The word *home* connotes something different for each of us, but most people share feelings about the word, and would distinguish them from other feelings associated with *house* or *hotel.* Thus, to a degree, the emotional qualities of words can be used to communicate, and the connotative power of words is so great that most good writers make conscious use of it.

In general, connotations emphasize characteristics of a referent or attitudes toward it. *Statesman* and *politician* may describe the same man or woman, have the same referent.

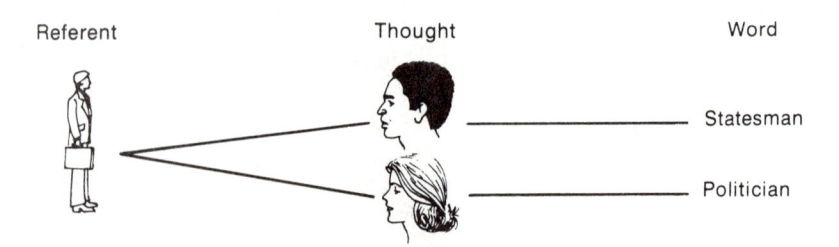

Referent	Thought	Word
		Statesman
		Politician

But the thoughts called up differ. The two words stimulate contrasting emotions so that *statesman* emphasizes wisdom, dignity, vision, and integrity, whereas *politician,* especially in recent American use, may suggest intrigue, time-serving, and self-interest. Accordingly, whether we like it or not, connotation colors meaning, and many writers use it deliberately, whether to persuade, move, or trick the reader.

Concern about propaganda has alerted our society to the emotional impact of words, especially as used in politics or advertising. Compare the following descriptions of the same incident:

> Senator A ranted interminably this afternoon in a bigoted attack on the new save-the-schools budget.
> Senator A delivered a full and detailed address this afternoon in a spirited criticism of the governor's give-away budget.

In their emotional content, the words in the first sentence are clearly "slanted" or "loaded" against the senator; words in the second seek to move the reader to approve the speech. To suggest that "emotional" words should not be used is absurd, but you should be aware of their limitations and their weaknesses. From neither of the statements above does the reader know what Senator A did. The connotations of the words outweigh their denotations. Many similar words in English, especially words like *freedom, communist, radical, liberal, fascist, relevant, militant, minorities, women's rights,* or *civil liberties,* have developed such varied connotations that they can be used only with care and skill to avoid distortion. Furthermore, misleading use of the emotional power of words is as false as any other kind of verbal lie because the connotations of a word are part of it. The writer who intentionally distorts the truth by choosing "loaded" or "slanted" words should be challenged on the basis of integrity rather than on language skill.

Euphemism and Doublespeak

Connotation also plays a role in euphemism and doublespeak. Euphemism, the use of "softer" or "more pleasant" expressions to avoid referring directly to something regarded as socially taboo or improper, may be grounded in superstition about the power of words, but it develops in most languages. In many cultures, for instance, speaking directly of death has been taboo. Modern English has a variety of substitutions for *die: to pass away, pass on,* or *be no longer with us.* Anything associated with death may get similar treatment; *undertaker* may be disguised as *mortician* or *funeral director* and *cemetery* as *memorial park. Inebriated* or *tipsy* for *drunk, mentally disturbed* or *unbalanced* for *insane,* and *sanitary engineer* for *garbage collector* are other examples.

As linguistic politeness, euphemism is probably harmless—though sometimes silly—but the increasing political enthusiasm for "doublespeak" suggests alarming ways of misusing the power of words. George Orwell's

1984 dramatizes the danger. The new language, newspeak, manages to distort moral values, to create a favorable attitude toward war, for instance, by calling it *peace*. Current distortions have not gone so far, but some current facts approach Orwell's fiction. Many of the examples are attempts to sell war: bombing becomes *air support;* a retreat is *strategic withdrawal;* destroying a village is *pacification;* the military phrase *protective reaction strike* is obscure enough to cover anything from a raid to an invasion, recently softened to *incursion*. Other examples affect almost all sorts of public information—in attempts to protect the status quo or muster support for a point of view. Slums or ghettos are the *inner city;* persons are not fired or dismissed, they are *terminated* or sometimes *deselected;* government bureaus have been instructed not to speak of poverty, but to use *low income* instead.

In part, of course, the central question is ethical—whether or not to use language to obscure and to lie. It is also a practical writing problem, since a vague vocabulary tends to spread. You need to be wary of terms that have sprouted like weeds and become faddish, and remain either downright deceptive or at best vaguely abstract. In a sentence like "They decided to evaluate the situation at all levels," *situation* is vague and *levels* even less precise. Other catchall phrases may replace such terms with little change in meaning—and no improvement in communication: *in all phases* or *on all facets* or *from all aspects*. Such verbiage may be called *jargon,* especially when used needlessly. *In an intoxicated condition* is neither clearer nor fancier than *intoxicated* or even *drunk; of an unpredictable nature* has no advantage over *unpredictable; He studied in the area (or field) of philosophy* says no more than *he studied philosophy*. Terms to look on with suspicion include *angle, area, aspect, breakdown, circumstances, deal, claim* (verb), *picture, point, facet, factor, setup, situation, phase, basic, regard* (noun), *fundamental, force, rate* (verb), *hassle, worthwhile, unique, outstanding, viable, put over, put across, point in time, overall, life style, system, state of the art, type, input, utilize, feedback, phenomena, interface.*

FIGURATIVE LANGUAGE: METAPHOR

Connotations can be used as well as abused. Emotional meaning can make writing more precise, more interesting, more intense, especially in figurative language, in such devices as metaphor. Metaphor, or comparison in language, is more than embellishment; it is part of language itself. We use metaphors constantly in conversation (*He ran like crazy; he is a little devil*). Words develop through metaphors; we speak of the *hands* of the clock, the *foot* of the bed, the *head* of the household, the *legs* of a chair. Sails *belly,* and crowds *thunder* applause as the *shell shoots* across the *line*. We no longer think of the italicized words as figures of speech, but they developed as metaphors, and words are developing in this manner constantly. Metaphor, then, is a device by which connotations of words provide precise and vivid meanings. Consider the following relatively elaborate comparison from *Romeo and Juliet:*

> This bud of love, by summer's ripening breath,
> May prove a beauteous flower when next we meet.

The metaphor is complex, but essentially it uses the word *flower* to express the referent usually denoted by *love.*

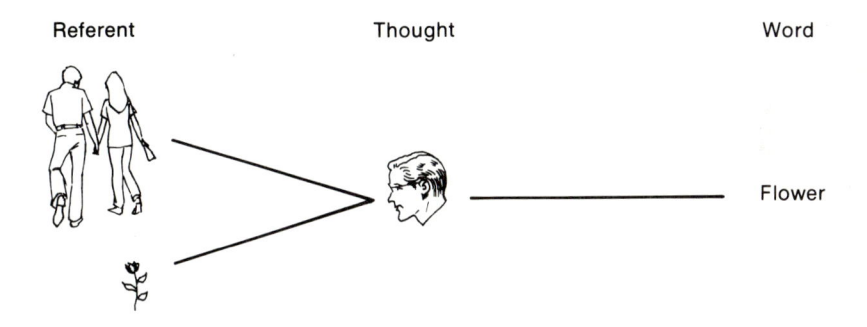

    Referent   Thought   Word

                                                                                     Flower

By using the word *flower* rather than the word *love,* Shakespeare emphasizes parts of both the connotational and denotational meanings of love. He makes us think of the "flowerlike" qualities of love, its ability to grow, its beauty, its relation with time. The metaphor, in its context, allows the writer to exploit the emotional meanings of the words.

Like any powerful tool, figurative language can hurt the unwary user. The publisher of a supposedly artistic magazine solicited subscriptions by declaring:

> A creative person who has no political crystallization, not merely cuts the production end of his work, but loses a vital gut that is part of the social continuum.

Doubtless the promotor thought this was being both profound and witty, but it sold few subscriptions. Possibly prospective readers were not attracted to this picture of the artist, chopping off his production end while disembowelling himself and undergoing crystallization. Most mixed figures are not so laughable, but many words in common use are old figures of speech, and may retain enough of their figurative flavor to trouble a perceptive reader. A mixed metaphor lurks even in an overworked phrase like *the leading factor.* Mathematically, factors are the numbers that, when multiplied, make a product, but if the factors of 6 are 2 and 3, how can either of them be the leader?

ECONOMY IN DICTION

English works best when used efficiently. People in dreadful need use few words. "Help!" "Fire!" "Murder!" say more than "I am in need of assistance," "There is a conflagration," and "A person is being illegally dispatched." Of course complicated ideas and fine distinctions require elaborate treatment. They cannot be considered in few words, but the fewer the better, so long as the expression is adequate. Good writing results from a wealth of ideas and an economy of words, not from a desert of ideas and a flood of vocabulary. Most writers, especially beginning writers, should throw words out. Following are some suggestions for economy in writing:

1. Cutting Deadwood Good writers resolutely cut out the words doing no work. Notice that if the italicized words are omitted, the following sentences are clearer and sharper:

> *It happened that* she was elected *to the position of* secretary *and this was* [of] the oldest club *that existed* in the city.
>
> Although he had always considered his sister *to be of the* awkward *type,* he found her *to be* a good dancer.

One common variety of deadwood is caused by doubling—using two words or phrases when one would convey the meaning more sharply:

> The climb up the mountain was *long* and *grueling.*
>
> Because *accurate* and *reliable* information is *necessary* and *essential* to the company's success, we must *try* and *begin* the new accounting system immediately.

One of each italicized pair could be omitted.

2. Direct Expressions Often shorter, more direct routes to meaning can be discovered. Notice, for example, the substitutions suggested in brackets for the italicized words in the following sentences:

> Meg's tears *had the effect of making* [made] Gordon regret *the accusation that he made hastily* [his hasty accusation].
>
> *By the time the end of the month rolled around* [By the end of the month] *it seemed to us a certainty* [we knew] that our first business venture would *be a success* [succeed].
>
> The committee will *take up consideration of* [consider] the issue.

Some of the problems above are caused by nominalization, substituting more wordy noun constructions for direct and concise verbs—for example, *have a discussion* for *discuss*, *hold a meeting* for *meet*, *reach a decision* for *decide*. Another abuse of nominalization is stringing together several nouns or noun phrases until the meaning becomes obscure.

> The committee will make a *data processing interface system decision* based on the new *input information*.
>
> The committee will use the new information to select the interface system for data processing.

3. *Economy in Modifiers* The more the modifiers pile up in a sentence, the less impact each one will have. Often cutting modifiers is desirable to increase the significance of those that remain. Words like *very, really, surely, actually, merely, simply, great*, and *real* are especially likely to accumulate, often doing more to obscure than to clarify. Consider whether the modifiers italicized in the following sentence should be omitted.

> As I crept *hesitantly* out of the *dark*, dingy, *grimy* hotel and felt the *blazing*, withering sun on my back I was *very* sure I did not *really* want to *actually* spend a month in the city.

Often the effect of modifiers can be embodied in telling nouns or verbs. *Liar*, for most purposes, says everything in "a person given by nature or habit to disseminating untruths"; *charge* or *accuse* says more than "lodge a protest against."

Brief writing is not necessarily good writing. Expression in a complicated world must usually be detailed, and details require words, many of them. Even publishers, who have to pay printing bills, often advise authors to "write it out," but granted that the writer uses space enough to express himself, the fewer words the better. Notice the following:

> Spring comes to the land with pale, green shoots and swelling buds; it brings to the sea a great increase in the number of simple, one-celled plants of microscopic size, the diatoms. Perhaps the currents bring down to the mackerel some awareness of the flourishing vegetation of the upper waters, of the rich pasturage for hordes of crustaceans that browse in the diatom meadows and in their turn fill the waters with clouds of their goblin-headed young. Soon fishes of many kinds will be moving through the spring sea, to feed on the teeming life of the surface and to bring forth their own young.
>
> Rachel L. Carson, *Under the Sea Wind*

This is good writing, not because it is brief, but because it is economical. Carson is saying something more than that the mackerel, after hibernating off the continental shelf, mysteriously wake up every spring. She is fitting the annual migration of the mackerel into the impelling cycle of the seasons. Explanation requires detail, and details require words. In the last line, for instance, "teeming life" could be reduced to *life,* but the account would suffer. Note how much is implied in a passage like "hordes of crustaceans that browse in the diatom meadows." Word economy is not sparing words; it is putting them to work.

    Not all writing needs to be or should be as artful as Carson's, but the principle of getting clear, direct meaning in tight, economical prose is

---

Guide to Revision   *Wordy*

WORDINESS

Revise for economy, eliminating redundancy and repetition.

WORDY	CONCISE
Although the story is in the supernatural class, Hawthorne manages to put over his point and show the effects on a person when he is confronted with the fact that everyone contains a certain amount of evil in his physical make-up.	Hawthorne uses the supernatural to suggest that evil appears in everyone. [*The original version was cluttered; with the verbiage cleared away, the writer can make the sentence direct and precise.*]
The abnormal condition within Hamlet's mind is a governing factor that is the foremost force in molding his character traits.	The turmoil in Hamlet's mind altered his character. [*This may not be true, but it suggests what the writer meant to say.*]
But if you get right down to the facts in the case at this point in time, we cannot reorient this tract of real estate, nor can we determine what disposition is fated to be made in the future of this acreage fresh from God's hand, and last but not least we cannot render a decision as to whether or not this section of the earth's surface is to be employed for purposes other than divine.	But in a larger sense, we cannot dedicate—we cannot consecrate—we cannot hallow this ground. Abraham Lincoln, Gettysburg Address [*The first version is an obvious parody of Lincoln's famous sentence, but it illustrates how useless words obscure rather than clarify.*]

important for any communication. Consider, for example, the following memo:

> It has come to our attention that the toaster recently purchased by you may have been one of a small group inadvertently shipped from the factory with a minor defect in one of its parts. This defect can cause a malfunction in the mechanism of the toaster which could result in excessive heating. If you will return the toaster at your earliest convenience . . .

In direct prose, the memo says:

> The toaster you bought is defective and will burn the toast.

DIRECTION IN MEANING

Words may have meanings that will make sense in only one "direction." We can say "Jewels have an attraction for Irene" or "Jewels attract Irene," but *attraction* will not work in the opposite direction. Barring the unlikely meaning that Irene somehow draws jewels to her, we cannot say "Irene has an attraction for jewels." The following sentence illustrates the same problem:

> The Elizabethan audience had a great fascination for wars and duels.

An audience could fascinate, but it could not fascinate a duel. Compare:

> Wars and duels fascinated the Elizabethan audience.

Consider another sentence:

> An enemy of the prairie dog never manages to approach the "town" unawares.

The writer is probably thinking of the fact that the citizens of the "town" will not be unaware, but in the sentence the word turns in another direction to modify *enemy* and convey an unintended meaning. Compare:

> No enemy of the prairie dog can approach the "town" undetected.

The following sentence shifts direction in another way:

> I have a very inadequate feeling when I think of writing about this book.

An "inadequate feeling" is probably possible, but probably not what was intended here. The writer probably meant to say:

> I feel inadequate when I think of writing about this book.

TRITE EXPRESSIONS: CLICHÉS

Many expressions in English cannot stand popularity. Idioms, of course, and standard expressions appear over and over without losing their effectiveness, but slang or other attempts at cleverness or vividness emerge after overuse with as little vigor as any other stale joke. Metaphors which do not enter the language as new words often become trite. The writer who first referred to a wife as a *ball and chain* may have been amusing on the comic-strip level; the thousandth person who imitated him was not amusing on any level. Expressions which have been so tarnished by time that their charm, and often even their meaning, is gone are called trite or hackneyed expressions or clichés. Trite expressions are dangerous partly because they paralyze the mind. Orwell called them "prefab phrases," and as ready-made channels for thought they invite the writer to cease thinking. An editorial writer commented in a discussion of academic freedom in a university:

> Any teacher who disagrees with his dean's academic views is not playing on the team and should turn in his suit.

Guide to Revision   **Trite**

TRITE EXPRESSIONS: CLICHÉS

Revise to eliminate trite, hackneyed expressions.

ORIGINAL	REVISION
When war first reared its ugly head, John Q. Public took it in his stride and played ball.	Faced with war, we did what had to be done.
In our day and age, in this great country of ours, progress has taken place by leaps and bounds.	America has progressed.

The "team" metaphor was worn out long ago, but the writer fell into the set pattern easily. The convenience of the trite expression led to an argument by false analogy.

DIALECT, USAGE, AND CORRECTNESS

While sketching the growth of English we noticed regional dialects—a Brooklynite does not talk like a Texan. But language varies by cultural levels also and among economic and professional groups. The resulting social dialects may give writers more help—and do them more damage—than do the regional variations.

In *Huckleberry Finn* Mark Twain makes Huck say, "When we was passing by the kitchen I fell over a root and made a noise. We scrouched down and laid still." This sounds like a frontier boy who has been taught more with razor strops than with textbooks. For another speaker, using another voice, Twain might have chosen *were* instead of *was* and *lay* instead of *laid*. He chose on the basis of usage, weighing who customarily uses a term and how a reader might react to it. Twain also chose the dialectal term *scrouches*; for another speaker he might have picked *crouched* or *scrootched*.

Dialect was formerly understood as one of the characters in George Eliot's *Adam Bede* conceived it:

> They're cur'ous talkers i' this country, sir; the gentry's hard work to hunderstand 'em. I was brought up among the gentry, sir, an' got the turn o' their tongue when I was a bye. Why, what do you think the folks about here say for 'heven't you?'—the gentry, you know, says 'heven't you'—well, the people about here says 'hanna yey.' It's what they call the 'dileck' as is spoke hereabout, sir. That's what I've heard Squire Donnithorne say many a time; 'it's the dileck,' says he.

That is, to George Eliot's speaker a "dileck" was English "as is spoke hereabout." But we recognize that the speaker also used a dialect and we can conclude further that Squire Donnithorne spoke a dialect, although neither he nor the man proud of having been "brought up among the gentry" would have called it that. They probably thought of a dialect as something to be ashamed of. It is not; everybody speaks a dialect, or several dialects, inevitably. In fact, languages cannot be used except through dialects. We all speak as we do because of the circumstances to which we were born, how and where we lived, what we have done and whom we have known, and somewhat because of what we have or have not done to police our language use. From a linguistic point of view, one dialect is as good as another; if a dialect did not serve the needs of some people, it could not exist. No doubt a herdsman's "hanna yey" served him as well as the squire's "heven't you," considering the life each of them lived. Of course dialects are not equally useful; they are not equally fashionable, equally suited to all times and places. Presumably the squire could have passed as a gentleman and a substantial person wherever he might go, whereas the herdsman with his "hanna yey" would have been branded at once as unschooled. Thus people born to an unfashionable dialect may wish to cultivate a more fashionable manner of speech.

Varieties of Usage

Variations in language habits, in usage, can be classified in many ways, most of them overlapping; the following are some of the most notable:

1. Regional Dialects The term *dialect* is used to describe any kind of subdivision—any discernible variant—of a language, but it is especially associated with particular usages common to a region or area. Thus, in America we may speak loosely of a southern dialect or a New England dialect.

2. Cultural Levels Differences in usage related to social and cultural relationships may be obvious but complex and hard to specify—for example, the distinction between the language of the educated and the uneducated. Thus, "she don't know English" might be called uneducated, "she doesn't know English" educated. A similar widely used classification distinguishes standard from nonstandard English. Standard English is the language used by educated people, the language that commands respect and esteem, that provides social and professional status. Nonstandard is in social disrepute, like bad table manners; *ain't* and *them guys* are labeled nonstandard. Other kinds of cultural distinctions may be specialized—the cant of criminals or hobos, the slang of musicians, the shoptalk of psychiatrists. Social attitudes also prompt people to label some expressions—not very consistently—as obscene or affected or in poor taste.

3. Functional Varieties Probably more important, though less likely to stimulate popular controversy, are variations in usage to suit different purposes and different kinds of situations. That is, varieties may be distinguished within standard English. No one of these is "better" than the others, but one may be more appropriate. For example, contractions (*won't, aren't*) are certainly standard English; they are appropriate in speech and some informal writing but not in formal writing. Three functional varieties are commonly distinguished, although they are only approximations. Formal English has the advantage of wide currency and permanent value; it is used in serious books, official statements, and in some periodicals, including scholarly and scientific journals. Informal English is more popular, more familiar, employing some devices generally associated with speech, common in newspapers, most magazines, and many books directed to a wide public. Colloquial English is the language of speech, of familiar conversation, but it may also appear in personal letters or other writing intended to be conversational in tone.

Usage and "Correctness"

Faced with the prospect of alternatives in language, usually reasonable people may react violently. They may either lament the seeming chaos and urge that some authority should set us right or refuse to recognize the reality of variations and aggressively defend their own attitudes on the prepositional purity of *like* or the evils of the split infinitive. In reality, of course, arguments about what is "correct" are usually futile. Variations in language are facts; they exist, whether we like them or not. They exist because users of a language change it, adapting it to fit their changing and increasing needs. Immutable standards of "correctness," therefore, even though they might be convenient, are impractical.

It does not follow that usage makes no difference, that anything goes. Usage makes a great deal of difference, but decisions on usage, unfortunately, require more than discovering a rule and following it. Selection among varying usages, like any rhetorical selection, requires anticipating results. Facts about usage—the company an expression usually keeps, the attitudes various kinds of people have toward it, the emotional reactions it is likely to arouse—are part of the information on which writers and speakers act. You decide to say "I did it" rather than "I done it" because the expressions have different associations, and you choose the one that will have the effect you want. You can anticipate the effects of each and choose accordingly. You would have more trouble deciding to say "Two and two is four" or "Two and two are four." Both versions are common; usage is divided. You can only use your best judgment. But the more you know about language, the more appropriate your choices are likely to be.

Writers and speakers, of course, do not consciously choose among all the alternatives each time they utter a sentence. They write and speak by habit. The practical problem for most students is to develop facility in standard English, especially in the sort of standard English appropriate for formal or some informal writing. This kind of English does not come naturally to everybody, but it is necessary for the serious business of the world. Any student hoping to exert influence on affairs must command it. You need to use standard English, not because other people use it or because someone has made a rule—any more than a carpenter cuts a board with a saw because other carpenters do or because someone has made a rule about saws. A carpenter uses a saw because it works better than a bread knife. Good counsel in identifying standard usage will be found in the better dictionaries and in numerous books on usage.

Sexism and Usage

In the past twenty years, English usage, obviously influenced by the feminist movement, has become conscious of the male orientation of the language and of the fact that various kinds of words and phrases express sexual bias. Editors have generally adopted policies designed to avoid any sexist use of the language, especially the use of stereotypes and of *he* as a neutral pronoun.

Stereotypes in writing are often subtle and hard to detect. For example, a reporter might write, "The reception was attended by Dr. John Jones, a prominent local physician, and his attractive brunette wife, Mary." The sentence not only puts the wife in a subordinate position; it also distinguishes her only for her physical characteristics. The reverse seldom appears: "The reception was attended by Dr. Mary Jones, a prominent local physician, and her muscular blond husband, John."

Many stereotypes and other words that today have sexist overtones have developed because the word *man* is used in a double sense: to refer to people in general (*"All men are created equal"*) or to refer to male beings (*"Adam was a man"*). The double use is so much a part of tradition and literature that changing it is difficult. But modern styles are attempting to avoid generic terms like *chairman* and *freshman* and *Congressman*, even though substitutions are difficult. In business, stereotypes exist because many positions were once restricted to men. For *businessman, fireman, policeman, salesman,* or *craftsman,* modern editing would substitute *executive, fire fighter, police officer, salesperson,* or *artisan.* Usually it is possible, with no weakening of the writing, to avoid at least the most obvious of the words carrying sexual bias.

Probably the most difficult problems involve use of the pronoun *he.* The English language has no pronoun to refer to a person of unknown sex except *he,* which has played a double role for centuries as both masculine and neutral. When we say "The writer sharpens his pencil," we are using *his* to mean a person, somebody, not necessarily a male. But *he* tends to jump out of its sexless role. Recent research shows that when the generic *he* is used, people often think it refers to men. In a sentence such as "A doctor always sends his bills promptly," it's hard to escape the suggestion that doctors are male. And in "We will hire the most qualified person regardless of his sex," *his* is awkward at best.

Current editorial policy, then, is to recast any sentence that uses *he* to refer to a person of unknown sex, and the alternatives are not always easy. Using *he or she* or *s/he* is one alternative, but it is clumsy and wordy. Shifting to plural or avoiding the pronoun altogether is more satisfactory when it is possible.

The following is objectionable because the pronoun clearly becomes masculine rather than neutral:

A good lawyer will be sure that he informs his clients of their rights.

Revision removes the suggestion that the lawyer must be male and also is more direct:

A good lawyer will be sure to inform clients of their rights.

The following implies that all children are male:

> The typical child does his homework right after school.

Shifting to the plural works here:

> Most children do their homework right after school.

The following encourages a different stereotype, that all teachers are female:

> A teacher should always know her subject.

The plural will also work to change this sentence:

> Teachers should always know their subject.

Guide to Revision — Usage

INAPPROPRIATE USAGE

Revise to make usage appropriate, relying on standard nonsexist usage except for special effects. For particular locutions see the Glossary, Appendix A.

ORIGINAL	REVISION
Lizzie was so tired that she *couldn't hardly* get ready for bed.	Lizzie was so tired that she *could hardly* get ready for bed.
The children's clothes were *laying* in a disordered heap on the bed.	The children's clothes were *lying* in a disordered heap on the bed.
The Senator had *drug in* the new argument only for its emotional effect.	The Senator had introduced the new argument only for its emotional effect.
A writer should always check *his* manuscript for spelling errors.	Writers should always check *their* manuscripts for spelling errors.

FOR STUDY AND WRITING

A. Anthony Burgess's fantasy *A Clockwork Orange* is told in the words of a character who uses a "nadsat" (teenage) vocabulary of the future. Read independently, most of the words would be nonsense to a reader of English, but many meanings can be guessed from context. A number of the words in the following passage from the opening of the novel have been listed below. Consider each word in its context, and then guess at a meaning for the word.

> There was me, that is Alex, and my three droogs, that is Pete, Georgie, and Dim, Dim being really dim, and we sat in the Korova Milkbar making up our rassoodocks what to do with the evening, a flip dark chill winter bastard though dry. The Korova Milkbar was a milk-plus mesto, and you may, O my brothers, have forgotten what these mestos were like, things changing so skorry these days and everybody very quick to forget, newspapers not being read much neither. Well, what they sold there was milk plus something else. They had no licence for selling liquor, but there was no law yet against prodding some of the new veshches which they used to put into the old moloko, so you could peet it with vellocet or synthemesc or drencrom or one or two other veshches which would give you a nice quiet horrorshow fifteen minutes admiring Bog And All His Holy Angels and Saints in your left shoe with lights bursting all over your mozg. Or you could peet milk with knives in it, as we used to say, and this would sharpen you up and make you ready for a bit of dirty twenty-to-one, and that was what we were peeting this evening I'm starting off the story with.

1. droogs
2. rassoodocks
3. mesto
4. skorry
5. veshches
6. moloko
7. peet
8. vellocet
9. horrowshow
10. mozg

B. In the following sentences, one word or set of words is italicized. It means approximately what a word in its context should, but there is a more exact word. By thinking of words you know, or by using lists of synonyms in a thesaurus or a dictionary, revise the sentences, using a more exact word.

1. She *signed up* for the magazine.
2. After the wreck, divers worked for weeks in the sunken ships trying to *save* some of the cargo.

Word Choice: Usage   257

3. Several army officers had been involved in the complicated political *planning* that led to the revolt.
4. The next speaker *turned down* completely all the traditional principles of the party.
5. He promised that he would never *change* from the course he had set when he entered the ministry.
6. Gold, since it can be hammered to the thinnest gold leaf, is obviously a *soft* metal.
7. The new hotel was a *big* structure, dwarfing all the buildings near it.
8. We must now face the *hard* task of clearing the city of the mud and debris left by the flood.
9. They tried to *get* money from the old shopkeeper by threatening to kidnap his grandson.
10. Since nobody else knew how to operate the machinery, the old engineer was *important* to the directors of the project.

C. Each of the sentences below is followed by words that can be synonyms for the italicized words in the sentence. Discuss the differences caused by changing the words.

1. Her mother *pressed* her to stop using drugs. *(exhorted, urged, commanded, begged, importuned, stimulated, influenced, provoked)*
2. The general was not willing to pay the *price* of victory. *(value, charge, cost, expense, worth)*
3. Sharon felt no *fear* as she faced the microphone. *(dismay, alarm, horror, anxiety, dread)*
4. The president did not have enough *power* to enforce the rules. *(potency, puissance, strength, energy, force)*
5. His *pride* would not allow him to dress as the other members in the club did. *(vanity, haughtiness, superciliousness, egotism, vainglory)*
6. *Examination* of the evidence showed that the jury had been wrong. *(Inquiry, Inquisition, Scrutiny, Investigation, Review)*
7. The judge had no *sympathy* for lawbreakers. *(pity, commiseration, condolence, tenderness, agreement)*
8. His devices were so *transparent* that nobody was deceived. *(translucent, lucid, diaphanous, limpid, luminous)*
9. The entire *company* joined in the song. *(group, throng, assemblage, flock, circle, audience, congregation, sorority)*
10. Many members of the audience were *moved* to tears. *(incited, prompted, impelled, instigated, actuated)*

D. Substitute fresher, more expressive terms for the trite expressions in the sentences below. You may find that you must use more revealing words than those in the original, since trite expressions can become nearly meaningless.

258 Word Choice: Usage

1. It appears like the Washington moguls believe this VIP is incapable of fending for himself lest he misses the boat entirely. Hence we get this ostentatious parade of potentates who hope to literally boost their nominee into office by finagling us native sons of the west into swallowing their platform—hook, line, and sinker—which would for fair kill the goose that laid the golden egg.
2. Crime never pays and true Americanism requires that we stamp it out, each and every time a crime wave raises its ugly head in this great and glorious land of ours.
3. The last examination had put me out like a light, and accordingly, although I was down in the dumps—it was blue Monday for me—I decided to burn the midnight oil.
4. He took the unwelcome news like a man. He became sober as a judge, but I knew he was true as steel, all wool and a yard wide, and that he would snap out of it.
5. He was tall, dark, and handsome, with lean flanks and piercing eyes, always smelling faintly of good English tobacco and well-oiled leather, every inch a man's man.

E. The passages below are wordy, many of them because they contain jargon or redundancies. Rewrite them in good English. Some sentences may mean almost nothing, for blanket terms characteristically fill space with words, not with meaning. If a sentence has no discoverable meaning, write a sentence which says what you imagine the writer may have intended to say.

1. With so many unemployeds out of a job, depressed conditions of a recession are certainly inevitable.
2. It was pretty surely certain that we would lose the initial opener.
3. The person in search of worthwhile science fiction material can find the basic circumstances at every facet of modern literature.
4. Formerly in the olden days there was no free popular education available to all without charge.
5. Adley's design was the most unique among all those submitted.
6. Although this may not be the overall case, it does include the majority of advertisements, and the factors in the movement are to the extreme.
7. In this day and age the problem of drinking intoxicating beverages has had a much freer scope in recent years than was the case at an earlier period in time.
8. The big day rolled around, but Hamlet, who had the inclination for abruptness of action, curbed his burning desires, and therefore slowness of action resulted.
9. The way this story was written made it seem to make me feel that it could really have actually happened to me.
10. In spite of all the illegal crimes he had committed, the leader of the gang went entirely scot-free.

F. The following sentences contain sexist language. Revise in accordance with current conventions.

1. If a student is to be successful, he must first assess his abilities, then pursue a course of studies which reflects his strongest qualities.
2. The dinner was attended by many local civic leaders and their wives.
3. A new computer programmer will soon realize that to be promoted in this company, he has to spend hours away from home and his nights out of town.
4. A nurse must be able to retain her composure even under the most trying situations.
5. Today's businessman has to deal with a wide range of individuals—from his corporate chairman of the board to the girls in the office who do his typing and the cleaning ladies who work after hours. Often this causes him stress, and in many cases he takes this stress home to the little woman and kids.

G. Create your own figurative language by completing this pattern: (*general word*) is like (*specific word*) because . . .

General words	Specific words
Happiness	a winding road
Writing	a shiny red wagon
School	brown scuffed shoes
Freedom	a gusty day

Example: Happiness is like a gusty day because you never know what new surprise will blow into your life.

You can make endless analogies like this by randomly listing words and then working on comparisons. Try expanding one of these analogies into a paragraph or an essay.

12

Style

> *The style of an author should be the image of his mind, but the choice and command of language is the fruit of exercise.*
> EDWARD GIBBON

    Style is interesting and important to talk about, but difficult to define, for *style* has a variety of meanings. Whether we are talking about a way of living, of dressing, or of writing, the meaning of *style* differs. But *style* usually refers to what makes something distinctive or individual. We talk about the style of Elizabethan writers or black humorists, about a formal style or an episodic style. Critics commonly characterize the style of an individual author, relying often on metaphorical descriptions like *urbane* or *sophisticated* or *turgid* or *stilted* or *fluid*. These are never very precise, but they illustrate that style does refer broadly to the overall impression that a piece of writing makes and that cultivating a good style is a continuing concern of writers.

    Actually, then, we have been talking about style throughout this book, often without using the term. The decisions, conscious and unconscious, made during the writing process—the planning, developing, and revising of a composition—all determine style. The choice of tone and point of view, the command of paragraphs and sentences, the handling of individual words, all contribute to a writer's style. When E. B. White describes "The World of Tomorrow" by noting the "artificial carnations," a "glass bird," a "terra-cotta zebra," and the "chrome steel lamp . . . in a glass pit hermetically sealed," we feel from his selection of details and his choice of words the cold artificiality of the world he is imagining. As White's writing illustrates, style combines the writer's unique characteristics as an individual and the specific manner adopted for a piece of writing. It is both art and artifice, inherent ability and learned response.

Writers have been talking about style, almost since the study of rhetoric began, providing a variety of definitions and an abundance of advice. For our purposes here, however, consider Edward Gibbon's comment: "The style of an author should be the image of his mind, but the choice and command of language is the fruit of exercise." That is, although style may reflect a writer's mind, a writer can through study and practice, through "choice and command of the language," make this a better image.

In this chapter we look at some of the distinguishing marks of style, characteristics that can be observed and that account for differences between styles. Second, we provide a few suggestions on ways of developing, as the "fruit of exercise," an appropriate and effective style.

CHARACTERISTICS OF STYLE

Although stylistic differences are often hard to describe in anything but general terms, it is often possible to isolate and observe some of the characteristics of a piece of writing that make it distinctive. Consider, for example, the following two passages, obviously different in their styles:

> A. The barrel of the mortar is mounted at the same elevation and in the same direction if two or more projectiles are to follow the same path through the air. Some of the conditions which affect the elevation and direction of the barrel are play in the mechanism of the mount, degree of accuracy of the sight, settling of the base plate while the first few rounds are being fired, and the accuracy with which the gunner lays and re-lays the mortar. The gunner can minimize errors caused by these factors by accurately laying the mortar between each round, by choosing a level, firm spot for the base plate, and by requiring the loader to load the piece without applying any pressure on the barrel of the mortar. Correct maintenance and care of the mount and sight reduce to a minimum the introduction of mechanical play or inaccuracy.
>
> Department of the Army, *ROTC Manual*

> B. They were going at his request to look at a section of his trench. Orderly Room had ordered him to make arrangements for machine-gun performances there. He couldn't. It didn't exist. Nothing existed. He supposed that to have been the new Austrian gun. New probably, but why

Austrian? The Austrians did not usually interest themselves much in high explosive. This one, whatever it was, threw something that buried itself and then blew up half the universe with astonishingly little noise and commotion; just lifted up, like a hippopotamus. He, Gibbs, had hardly noticed anything as you would have if it had been, say, a mine. When they came and told him that a mine had gone off there he would not believe them. . . . But you could see for yourself that it looked exactly as if a mine had been chucking things about. A small mine. But still a mine. . . .

Ford Madox Ford, *Parade's End*

The passages differ in purpose and in subject matter, and accordingly differences in rhetorical selection produce differences in style. We notice that A sounds more formal and relies more heavily on borrowed words—*elevated, mechanism, minimize*. B, on the other hand, has a brisk, informal tone, in part because of the colloquial diction—*blew up, chucking things about*. Obviously, then, much of what we discussed in Chapter 11 regarding word choice also concerns style. For example, a person who writes "I was matriculated at my alma mater in 1988" is adopting a more formal style than the writer who chooses "I entered college in 1988."

The passages differ also in their sentence patterns. Even though the two passages have almost the same length, the second has more than three times as many sentences, three of them incomplete, several of them very short. The passages differ, also, in the linguistic units they employ, even in the grammatical units, as the following summary suggests:

1. Passage A contains 42 nouns and no pronouns; B contains 21 nouns and 20 pronouns.
2. Passage A has 4 active verbs, 2 passive verbs, and 2 uses of *to be*; B has 19 active verbs, no passives, and 1 use of *to be*.
3. Passage A has 23 prepositions; B has 7.
4. Passage A has 2 subordinate clauses; B has 6, even though its sentences are much shorter.

Such comparisons could be multiplied, without producing conclusive results. Attempts to construct grammatical profiles is the business of specialists and not our concern here. But this kind of analysis has practical implications. It demonstrates once again that writers can control their style. The limited comparisons here, for instance, suggest that writers are likely to produce prose more like that of A than B if they rely on nouns rather than active verbs, if they multiply prepositional phrases.

SENTENCE LENGTH AND VARIETY

The most obvious difference among sentences is that some are longer or shorter than others, and sentence length has a good deal to do with the stylistic effect of any piece of prose. Notice the variety in sentence length in two paragraphs from Ernest Hemingway's *A Moveable Feast*, recounting a meeting with writer F. Scott Fitzgerald and his wife Zelda. Zelda was nearing a nervous breakdown, but the men, unaware of her illness, assumed she was just drinking too much and behaving badly.

> Zelda had a very bad hangover. They had been up on Montmartre the night before and had quarreled because Scott did not want to get drunk. He had decided, he told me, to work hard and not to drink and Zelda was treating him as though he were a kill-joy or a spoilsport. Those were the two words she used to him and there was recrimination and Zelda would say, "I did not. I did no such thing. It's not true, Scott." Later she would seem to recall something and would laugh happily.

Here many of the sentences are short; even the longer sentences are mainly built up from brief patterns strung together. The writing is choppy, intentionally so. The most staccato passage is that quoted from Zelda, and the style of the whole is appropriate as a reflection of the conversation behind the scene; the sentence structures contribute something to the meaning of the passage.

That Hemingway did not always write this way is clear from his immediately preceding paragraph:

> Scott Fitzgerald invited us to have lunch with his wife Zelda and his little daughter at the furnished flat they had rented at 14 rue Tilsitt. I cannot remember much about the flat except that it was gloomy and airless and that there was nothing in it that seemed to belong to them except Scott's first books bound in light blue leather with the titles in gold. Scott also showed us a large ledger with all of the stories he had published listed in it year after year with the prices he had received for them and also the amounts received for any motion picture sales, and the sales and royalties of his books. They were all noted as carefully as the log of a ship and Scott showed them to both of us with impersonal pride as though he were the curator of a museum. Scott was nervous and hospitable and he showed us his accounts of his earnings as though they had been the view. There was no view.

The sentences are longer, with more coordination, more modifiers, more detail. Only the last is short—four words—and it is short for a purpose, to close the paragraph with a sudden, dramatic, ironic turn.

Neither short sentences nor long sentences are good in themselves, and most skilled writers use both sorts. Sentence length depends on what is being said to whom and why, and usually the length takes care of itself. But sentence length does affect style, and writers sometimes can improve a style by considering whether the length of their sentences provides the kind of emphasis they want.

SOUND AND RHYTHM IN SENTENCES

Most modern prose is intended primarily for silent reading, but sound patterns echo even in silent reading, and a sense of underlying intonation or rhythm is part of total effect. Alliteration, for example, the repetition of initial sounds, as in "flight of fancy," may bind a phrase together but may also pall with overuse. An unexpected rhyme may hinder understanding. An old mathematics text surprises the reader with a sentence ending in an unintended jingle: "and yet no force, however great, can stretch a cord, however fine, into a horizontal line that shall be absolutely straight." Some writers even avoid combinations of sounds that are hard to pronounce. Certainly the rhythm of prose, the pattern of accents in the sentences, is part of stylistic effect.

John F. Kennedy, addressing the Canadian Parliament, probably did not analyze the rhythms in the following carefully, but he certainly knew what he was doing:

> Geography has made us neighbors. History has made us friends. Economics has made us partners. And necessity has made us allies. Those whom nature hath so joined together, let no man put asunder.

Two sorts of rhythm dominate here. The first four sentences are short, blunt, and parallel. Ordinarily so skillful a writer as Kennedy would never use four childishly simple sentences one after the other, but here he had a purpose. He wanted those four salient facts to strike his hearers like blows, and probably he wanted the rhythm to become just a bit monotonous before he changed it. When he did change the pattern the effect was dramatic, partly because the final sentence echoes the marriage ceremony, as though he were the officiating priest solemnizing the sacrament joining two great nations.

The next day Kennedy said essentially the same thing again, but he said it in another way and with other rhythms:

> In the effort to build a continent of economic growth and solidarity, in an effort to build a hemisphere of freedom and hope, in an effort to build an Atlantic community of strength and unity of purpose, and in an effort to build a world of lasting peace and justice, Canada and the United States must be found, and I am certain will be found, standing where they have always stood, together.

This sentence resembles the earlier passage. The four parallel clauses beginning with *in* suggest the four staccato sentences, but here, instead of establishing something, the rhythm suggests that the speaker is building up to something. He is; the final word, *together,* climaxes and clinches the whole.

CUMULATIVE AND PERIODIC SENTENCES

Style also depends on the general type of sentence structure the writer prefers. The basic SVC sentence serves many needs—to greet friends, to get food, to ask directions. As we have seen, however, subtle thinking and sophisticated communication require longer sentences, developed through devices like coordination and subordination. Inevitably the parts of these more complex sentences must be organized, and two organizational patterns are natural: (1) The SVC pattern can be completed at once, with various modifying and coordinated elements following it; or (2) some elements of the basic pattern can be withheld while modifying elements build up until the final word closes at once the SVC and the sentence. Compare the following:

> Tolerance, good temper, and sympathy are no longer enough in a world which is rent by religious and racial persecution, in a world where ignorance rules, and science, who ought to have ruled, plays the subservient pimp.

> In a world which is rent by religious and racial persecution, in a world where ignorance rules, and science, who ought to have ruled, plays the subservient pimp, tolerance, good temper, and sympathy are no longer enough.

The first version, with subordinate material appended to an initial SVC, exemplifies what may be called a *cumulative sentence*; E. M. Forster wrote the sentence this way. The second version, changed so that modifiers appear first and the SVC is postponed for a final climax, exemplifies the *periodic sentence*.

For a language like English, relying heavily on word order, the cumulative sentence may provide the natural emphasis—making a statement and then appending qualifications. Such sentences grew naturally in English; the author of *Beowulf* used them, as did Chaucer and other early writers. The periodic sentence, also, has a long tradition in English, fostered by the school rhetoric founded on Classic Latin and Greek. Both types of sentence—the cumulative sentence, apparently native, and the periodic sentence, carefully cultivated—have uses in modern writing.

The Periodic Sentence

Since Latin and Greek seldom used word order or position for grammar, classical speakers could place words anywhere they pleased for emphasis. Accordingly, orators devised what were called "colors of rhetoric," cultivating figurative language and elaborate displays of word patterns. These patterns, including balance, contrast, climax, and the tricolon, fitted readily into the periodic sentence. English and American orators have imitated such sentences. Notice the following from Lincoln's Gettysburg Address: "But, in a larger sense, we cannot dedicate—we cannot consecrate—we cannot hallow this ground." With a tricolon, three parallel elements—"cannot dedicate, cannot consecrate, cannot hallow"—the sentence builds to a climax from human dedication to divine hallowing, climaxing sense and structure at once. The next sentence is balanced as well as essentially periodic, as the following suggests:

The world will { little note / (nor) / long remember } what we say here

(but)

it can never forget   what they did here.

The oration comes to a crashing conclusion with a period that builds through a tricolon and a tricolon within a tricolon:

    that we here highly resolve
       that these dead shall not have died in vain
       that this nation, under God, shall have a new birth of freedom
         (and)
       that government { of the people / by the people / for the people } shall not perish from the earth.

Most modern writers do not compose orations, particularly not orations modeled on the classics, but notice the following from Macaulay's review of Boswell's biography of Samuel Johnson:

> Everything about him, his coat, his wig, his figure, his face, his scrofula, his St. Vitus's dance, his rolling walk, his blinking eye, the outward signs which clearly marked his approbation of his dinner, his insatiable appetite for fish sauce and veal pie with plums, his inextinguishable thirst for tea, his trick of touching the posts as he walked, his mysterious practice of treasuring up scraps of orange peel, his morning slumbers, his midnight disputations, his contortions, his mutterings, his gruntings, his puffings, his vigorous, acute, and ready eloquence, his sarcastic wit, his vehemence, his insolence, his fits of tempestuous rage, his queer inmates, old Mr. Levitt and blind Mrs. Williams, the cat Hodge and the negro Frank, all are as familiar to us as the objects by which we have been surrounded from childhood.

Macaulay's audience liked such sentences, and they do assort numerous details into a neat order, but most modern prose is more relaxed. Restrained use of parallelism continues, however, and good modern writers find use for the periodic structure, as in the following description of the birth of an Americanism:

> When head, wings, and claws were added by Gilbert Stuart, the celebrated painter, the result was by a stroke of genius called a *gerrymander*.
>
> Thomas Pyles, *Words and Ways of American English*

The Cumulative Sentence

Modern prose writers rely most on cumulative patterns, in which the main SVC sequence is completed early, and details are added, primarily as modifiers. Cumulative structures are especially common in fiction, as in the following William Faulkner sentence:

> She went out of sight up the road: swollen, slow, deliberate, unhurried and tireless as augmenting afternoon.
>
> *Light in August*

The first two words complete the main pattern and modifiers complete the cumulative sentence. Or notice a longer sentence with the same general pattern:

> He took all his pain and what was left of his strength and his long gone pride and he put it against the fish's agony and the fish came over onto his side and swam gently on his side, his bill almost touching the planking of the skiff and started to pass the boat, long, deep, wide, silver and barred with purple and interminable in the water.
>
> Ernest Hemingway, *The Old Man and the Sea*

This sentence carries with it a great weight of detail, but it does so with ease and with no sense of strain. Instead of building to a climax the sentence moves like waves, instinct with life, and with crests and valleys. Sentences like these, because they can move in varied rhythms, team well together.

Similar structures serve, also, for modern nonfictional prose. The following describes a teen-age delinquent on trial for having participated in the gang murder of a helpless old man:

> It was not hard to see evil in Jack Koslow, the oldest defendent. So manifest was his sickness of soul that he could have posed as one of the tormenting demons that populate Hieronymus Bosch's vision of hell. His skin had been described as "sallow," but that gave no hint of its dead green-whiteness, in eerie and surprising conjunction with thick hair that was dark red and wholly without shine, receding from his forehead in a high crest. His features were delicately ugly; a long thin curved nose with a sharply articulated ridge; a thin, downturned, and usually derisive mouth, lips colorless, the upper extending slightly above the lower; weak but bony chin; a white, undeveloped neck. His eyes were strangest of all.

They were dark brown and seemed pupilless, and their look was hooded as if by a transparent extra lid. When Koslow walked in and out each day manacled to his guard, you could see how tall and thin he was, and how his narrow head hung forward from his body like a condor's.

Marya Mannes, *But Will It Sell?*

The fourth sentence, beginning "His features were delicately ugly," may profitably be compared with the sentence above from Macaulay describing Johnson. Macaulay's conclusion that the details "are as familiar to us" as objects of our childhood, does not make the characteristics of Johnson more vivid or more impressive. It seems contrived to fill out the periodic pattern, an elaborate way to get the list presented. Mannes, in her cumulative sentence, presents details as if she were sitting in the courtroom recording as she observed. The details themselves produce the effect, with a climax in the "white, undeveloped neck."

STYLE AND PARODY

The style of a piece of prose results in part from rhetorical choices, in part from what a writer brings to the writing. The qualities that make prose individual appear when a writer has something to say and selects one way of saying something rather than others. Any sort of choice or invention that becomes habitual marks the writer's style, gives it a particular flavor. Such choices involve almost every subject treated in this book, and in others. A leaning toward the long unfamiliar word rather than the shorter common word would mark a style, as would a fondness for one sentence pattern or one type of organization. An individual style may reflect the writer's ability to create, a readiness to seize upon ideas and develop them in a unique way.

Parodies provide ready clues to some of the distinguishing characteristics of a style, since parodies are verbal caricatures that criticize a style by exaggerating, even to absurdity, some of its qualities. Of the following paragraphs, the first is an example of a distinctive, though not necessarily distinguished, modern style, and the second is a critical parody of it:

. . . They rushed down the street together, digging everything in the early way they had, which later became so much sadder and perceptive and blank. But then they danced down the streets like dingle-dodies, and I shambled after as I've been doing all my life after people who interest me, because the only people for me are the mad ones, the ones who are mad to live, mad to talk, mad to be saved, desirous of everything at the same time, the ones who never yawn or say a commonplace thing, but burn, burn, burn like fabulous yellow roman candles exploding like spiders across the stars and in the middle you see the blue centerlight pop and everybody goes "awww." What did they call such young people in Goethe's Germany? Wanting dearly to learn how to write like Carlo, the first thing you know. Dean was attacking him with a great amorous soul such as only a con-man can have. "Now, Carlo, let *me* speak—here's what I'm saying . . ." I didn't see them for about two weeks, during which time they cemented their relationship to fiendish allday-allnight-talk proportions.

Jack Kerouac, *On the Road*

I was just thinking around in my sad backyard, looking at those little drab careless starshape clumps of crabgrass and beautiful chunks of some old bicycle crying out without words of the American Noon and half a newspaper with an ad about a lotion for people with dry skins and dry souls, when my mother opened our frantic banging screendoor and shouted, "Gogi Himmelman's here." She might have shouted the Archangel Gabriel was here, or Captain Easy or Baron Charlus in Proust's great book: Gogi Himmelman of the tattered old greenasgrass knickers and wild teeth and the vastiest, most vortical, most insatiable wonderfilled eyes I have ever known. "Let's go, Lee," he sang out, and I could see he looked sadder than ever, his nose rubbed raw by a cheap handkerchief and a dreary Bandaid unravelling off his thumb. "I know the WAY!" That was Gogi's inimitable unintellectual method of putting it that he was on fire with the esoteric paradoxical mood. I said, "I'm going, Mom," and she said "O.K.," and when I looked back at her hesitant in the pearly mystical United-Stateshome light I felt absolutely sad, thinking of all the times she had vacuumed the same carpets.

John Updike, *On the Sidewalk*

This style does not follow the advice of Samuel Butler that a style should "attract as little attention as possible." The tricks are so obtrusive that parody is relatively easy. But the parody reveals, by what it selects to ridicule, the bent of Kerouac's style.

The parody focuses on the subject matter, the preoccupation of the original with "madness" for life or a "great amorous soul." At the same time it makes fun of the tone, exaggerating the enthusiasm of the discussion and the triviality of what is discussed. The absurdity of the "beautiful chunks of some old bicycle crying out without words of the American Noon" suggests that the details of the original do not justify Kerouac's frenzied manner. Likewise, the parody points to habits of language that characterize the author's style. It picks up Kerouac's tendency to sprinkle adjectives, to pile up modifiers in a long string after the main pattern, to fancy racy and unusual diction, and to seed his prose with self-conscious images and pretentious but vague literary allusions.

Here is another pair, a passage from a novel and a parody:

Sight of the old gilt clock had made Arthur Winner think of his father—indeed, the room was full of such mementos. A little-disturbed museum, its collection, informal and unassuming, preserved, evidences of that many-sided mind, of the grasp and scope of interests, of perceptions so unobtrusive as to be nearly private, of quiet amusements and quiet enjoyments. Seeking Arthur Winner Senior's monument, you could look around you. You could ask yourself, for example, how many lawyers—or, to give the point proper force, how many small-town lawyers, born and brought up in a fairly-to-be-called rural county seat like Brocton—would, fifty or more years ago, have had the interest—let alone, the taste, the eye—to pick over, unaffected by then current ideas of what was fine or beautiful, of what was rare or valuable, the then next thing to junk—the secondhand, the old-fashioned, the discarded—and select, exchanging a few dollars for them, exactly the items that the antique trade (at that time hardly born) was going to look on as prizes half a century later. Would you guess one in a thousand, or one in ten thousand?

James Gould Cozzens, *By Love Possessed*

Author Winner sat serenely contemplating his novel. His legs, not ill-formed for his years, yet concealing the faint cyanic marbling of incipient varicosity under grey socks of the finest lisle, were crossed. He was settled in the fine, solidly-built, cannily (yet never parsimoniously, never niggardly) bargained-for chair that had been his father's, a chair that Author Winner himself was only beginning to think that, in the fullness of time, hope he reasonably might that he would be able (be possessed of the breadth and the depth) to fill. Hitching up the trousers that had been made for his father (tailored from a fabric woven to endure, with a hundred and sixty threads to the inch), he felt a twinge of the sciatica that had been his father's and had come down to him through the jeans. Author Winner was grateful for any resemblance; his father had been a man of unusual qualities; loyal, helpful, friendly, courteous, kind, obedient, cheerful, thrifty, brave, clean and reverent; in the simplest of terms: a man of *dharma*.

Felicia Lamport, "James Gould Cozzens by Henry James Cozened"

The parody ridicules a sentence pattern, exemplified in the next to last sequence of the original and the second and third of the parody, in which ideas are qualified and then the qualifiers qualified, with essentials of the main pattern postponed until the very end. The parody implies that details of the original are trivial—the number of threads to the inch in Author Winner's trousers—and makes fun of pretentious diction, "the faint cyanic marbling of incipient varicosity." Even the "unusual qualities" that Author Winner admires are those attributed to Boy Scouts.

FITTING STYLE TO THE OCCASION

One style will not fit all occasions. Just as we would not wear jeans to a formal dance or formal attire to a picnic—unless we wanted to create an unusual effect—we wouldn't put a quick letter to a friend and a formal recommendation to the dean in the same style. A writer is not limited to a single style but always considers the occasion and the audience for a piece of writing. The following are examples of some obvious variations in style.

1. *Objective*   A telephone directory or a compilation of statutes reveals little of the opinions or prejudices of its writers, but it has a style. It is objective and impartial, setting forth facts in a straightforward manner. Scientific works, histories, newspaper accounts, factual magazine articles, business letters, or informative bulletins are likely to be primarily objective in style. This opening of a news story reports facts objectively.

> Videoconferencing—the use of audio-visual equipment to connect people thousands of miles apart—is becoming an important communication and training tool for business. Video telecasts with two-way audio hookups allow participants not only to see and hear speakers but also to take part in discussions on microphones or by picking up telephones.

2. *Formal*   Serious writing frequently, though not always, promotes a formal author-reader relationship, dictated more by literary tradition than by the habits of speech. Consider the following selection from Emerson's essay "Self-Reliance":

> Trust thyself: every heart vibrates to that iron string. Accept the place the divine providence has found for you, the society of your contemporaries, the connection of events. Great men have always done so, and confided themselves childlike to the genius of their age, betraying their perception that the absolutely trustworthy was seated at their heart, working through their hands, predominating in all their being.

Formal expression appears in the vocabulary, in the patterned, balanced rhythm of the sentences, in the elevated manner. The style suits Emerson's occasion and purposes. Documents concerning affairs of state or scholarly treatises might be expressed in this style. But a similar style would be laughable in a student theme pleading for softer seats in the gymnasium.

3. *Informal*   Much modern writing is intimate and genial. Cleveland Amory begins a column this way:

> You hear a lot these days about speed-readers. But we can tell you from experience that nowadays the problem isn't really speed-reading at all—it's speed-stopping. The fact is there is so much published today, the art of knowing when to stop reading not only can increase your literary life but also can, literally, save it.

The purpose is serious, but Amory sounds as though he is a friend with his feet on the coffee table, telling about a good idea he's just had. He assumes a personal attitude to the reader (addressed as "you"). He uses common everyday diction, and his sentences move quickly.

4. *Emphatic, Enthusiastic*   Especially in fiction, writers may heighten style and overstate for emphasis. Observe an emotional scene in Charles Dickens' *Bleak House*:

> I saw before me, lying on the step, the mother of the dead child. She lay there, with one arm creeping round a bar of the iron gate, and seeming to embrace it. She lay there, who had so lately spoken to my mother. She lay there, a distressed, a sheltered, senseless creature.

The repetition of "She lay there" and the charged language of the "distressed . . . senseless creature" who appears to embrace the cold iron gate emphasize the emotion behind the passage. The context may justify the patterned, figurative style, although out of context the passage sounds inflated. Such a style conveys emotion, but it rings false if not justified.

5. Understated   A quite different style appears in Norman Mailer's account of a death in *The Naked and the Dead*:

> Abruptly he heard the mortars again, and then right after it a machine gun firing nearby. A couple of grenades exploded with the loud empty sound that paper bags make when they burst. He thought for an instant, "There's some soldiers after them Japs with the mortar." Then he heard the terrible siren of the mortar shell coming down on him. He pirouetted in a little circle, and threw himself to the ground. Perhaps he felt the explosion before a piece of shrapnel tore his brain in half.

In contrast to Dickens, Mailer treats a death with almost exaggerated restraint, points to facts rather than describing emotions. The unadorned, direct diction and the short, mostly simple sentences create a quiet, controlled style. Many modern writers use understatement, letting the facts convey the desired emotion.

6. Ironic   Compare the following passage from *The Pickwick Papers* with the passage from *Bleak House* quoted above:

> Rising rage and extreme bewilderment had swelled the noble breast of Mr. Pickwick, almost to the bursting of his waistcoat, during the delivery of the above defiance. He stood transfixed to the spot, gazing on vacancy. The closing of the door recalled him to himself. He rushed forward with fury in his looks, and fire in his eye.

The passages by Dickens differ. In *Bleak House* the style is dramatic and tense. In *The Pickwick Papers* the scene shows a humorous character reacting to a belligerent little doctor who has just said, "I would have pulled your nose, sir." The incident is dramatic but not tragic, and the tone is ironic. That is, the reader understands from the context not to interpret the words literally—that the breast of Mr. Pickwick is more "noble" in size than in courage, that the "fury" in Mr. Pickwick's looks or the "fire in his eye" is more ludicrous than frightening. Irony may vary from this sort of tolerably subtle whimsy to bitter sarcasm. It may be the tone of a sentence like a young woman's "Aren't you afraid we'll be early?" to a date who has kept her waiting in the dormitory hall until the play is half over. It may be the tone of an entire essay like Swift's famous "Modest Proposal," suggesting that if Irish children are to be starved they had as well be butchered. Writing may be ironic whenever a statement in its context suggests a sense different from—often opposite to—its literal meaning.

DEVELOPING A STYLE: READING

Perhaps the best-known comment on style is Buffon's "The style is the man himself." Insofar as this is true, one obvious way to improve style is to improve oneself, and one of the best ways to do that is to read. Reading also is one of the best ways to develop style by studying techniques and increasing the possibilities for rhetorical choices. The creators of English prose have habitually steeped themselves in the work of their predecessors—from the cadences of the Bible and the versatility of Shakespeare to the terser rhythms of modern writers.

An author good enough to be worth imitating may be the best writing teacher. Robert Louis Stevenson describes how he "played the sedulous ape"; that is, he imitated writer after writer, deliberately, until he had mastered their ways. "That," Stevenson concludes, "is the way to learn to write. . . . Before he can tell what cadences he truly prefers, the student should have tried all that are possible; before he can choose and preserve a fitting key of words, he should long have practiced the literary scales." Stevenson goes on, "Perhaps I hear someone cry out: But this is not the way to be original! It is not; nor is there any way but to be born so." Stevenson's method may not work for everybody, but reading and observing, noticing how skillful writers gain their effects, can improve a writing style.

DEVELOPING A NATURAL STYLE

Imitation can help a writer, but it also has risks. Mimicking what seems clever or unusual in a popular writer, for example, is not likely to make a style seem original. Neither will attempts to reproduce the superficial characteristics of an unusual style—to omit periods or capital letters, to write in incomplete sentences, to affect nonstandard diction. Originality and a natural style are more than novelty and trickery. For a student writer, then, the most practical advice is to work on developing a style that expresses the writer's individuality and originality, that is honest and sincere.

Many beginning writers are afraid to be themselves on the page, afraid they will not sound like some imaginary model of what college writing should be. For instance, the student in the following paragraph adopted an unnatural style, apparently assuming that it was elevated or literary.

> In this paper I will attempt to discuss my belief that the position of one in a family setting is a key factor in the development not only of one's personality type but also of the development of one's behavior patterns.

Compare this with the more direct style of another student writing on the same topic.

> I came from a rather large family. I am the youngest of nine—seven boys and two girls—and I think my position as the youngest has greatly influenced me.

With a natural style, the writer can write specifically and sound authentic and honest.

A major requisite for a natural style is interest in the topic and enough information about it to justify confidence. The student who wrote the following was writing naturally and confidently about what she calls "My Spanish Love Affair."

> Foreign languages have always fascinated me. I don't know why. There was no special motivation for me during my growing-up years. My first and only exposure to a foreign language was anything but inspirational—a high school Latin class. Besides being a bore, that class literally gave me nightmares. I would wake up in a sweat, convinced that today was the big test, and I didn't have the words memorized. After that experience, my fascination went into long hibernation. Truthfully, I thought my interest had died completely. But eventually a series of events occurred in my life that not only awakened my sleeping interest, but got it to the point of fascination and then beyond. The beginning came when I decided to return to college. In the end, I would be bilingual.
>
> Jeanne Verdeyen

The passage sounds natural and honest. The language is conversational, and the relatively simple and direct sentence structures are appropriate for a paper addressed to her classmates. The writer can look at herself objectively, sometimes with humor, although she is serious about the subject. The reader encounters a real person on the page. More than three centuries ago, philosopher Blaise Pascal wrote: "When we encounter a natural style, we are astonished and delighted; for we expected to see an author, and we find a man." Or a woman, in this instance.

FOR STUDY
AND WRITING

A. Robbins Burling, in an essay on how rewriting helped him, gives advice to teachers for ways students can learn to rewrite and increase their stylistic techniques. Here is one of them:

> Offer various sentences to students and challenge them to rewrite them in as many ways as possible. Start, for instance, with a quaint example such as "These are the times that try men's souls." See if you can elicit, "These times try men's souls," "Souls are tried by times like these," "Times like these try men's souls," "In times like these, men's souls are tried," "It is times like these when the trying of men's souls takes place," etc. Hold a discussion on the pros and cons of various versions, but do not pretend, let alone insist, that one form is inherently better than all the others.

Here are additional conventional sentences. Rewrite each of them in at least five ways and be prepared for such a discussion as Burling suggests.

1. Now is the time for all good men to come to the aid of the party.
2. The quick, brown fox jumps over the lazy dog.
3. Write as the common people do, but think as the wise men do.
4. Satan finds work for idle hands to do.
5. Some circumstantial evidence is very convincing, as when one finds a trout in milk.

B. Much rewriting should extend beyond sentences, and some of the best revision results from combining sentences, by subordinating a sentence, or part of it, to another sentence. For example, Burling's sentence might become part of the following: "Times like these, although they may try men's souls, offer the ambitious young person opportunities that might never appear in more settled periods." Now take one of the sentences you rewrote in Exercise A and try to use all or part of it as a subordinate part of a more elaborate sentence. Using the suggestion above, produce at least five sentences.

C. Another way to develop style is imitation. Below is a short excerpt from Truman Capote's "Miriam" and a student imitation of the passage. The student chose a different subject, but observed Capote's original sentence patterns. You can do the same with any piece of fiction or nonfiction you are reading.

> It was while waiting at the corner of Third Avenue that she saw the man: an old man, bowlegged and stooped under an armload of bulging pack-

ages; he wore a shabby brown coat and a checkered cap. Suddenly she realized they were exchanging a smile: there was nothing friendly about this smile, it was merely two cold flickers of recognition. But she was certain she had never seen him before.

Truman Capote

It was while waiting at the corner of Lake Street that he saw the girl: a call girl, long-legged and beautiful under the awning of the X-rated book store; she wore a short red dress and black high heels. Suddenly he realized they were exchanging a smile: there was something friendly about this smile: it was more than two flickers of recognition. He was certain he had seen her somewhere before.

Kathy Hartman

D. The following sentences have been converted from cumulative to periodic patterns. Rewrite each as a cumulative sentence.

1. Considering the nature and necessity of foul language, a difficult theme and one seldom treated with detachment, I propose to make a short enquiry.
2. Not as people mainly, but as machines, with their bodies, the mass of human beings serve the state.
3. In that evolutionary choice made long ago in some misty past—but not so remote that it can't be reached with the long arm of the mind—by some unknown forerunner of *Homo sapiens,* the roots of heterosexuality are buried.
4. The appropriate view, that the failure of the Western democracies during this catastrophic half of the twentieth century is due to the failings of the democratic peoples, is the view we must take.
5. A part of the psyche which can be negatively distinguished from a personal unconscious by the fact that it does not, like the latter, owe its existence to personal experience and consequently is not a personal acquisition is the collective unconscious.

Or take one of the following statements and add a number of cumulative details, qualities, or comparisons to flesh out the statement. Use the Hemingway sentence as an example for your writing.

> The gypsy was walking out toward the bull again,
>   walking heel-and-toe,   *detail*
>   insultingly,   *quality*
>   like a ball-room dancer,   *comparison*
>   the red shafts of the banderillos   *detail*
>   twitching with his walk.

1. A strange odor filled the air.
2. The pony stood trembling beside the fence.
3. They counted the money.

E. As the sense for sentence patterns has become stronger in English, writing has become more economical. The following, from chapter 2 of Exodus in the King James Bible, recounts the birth and some incidents in the early life of Moses. To follow the action, one should recall that by order of Pharaoh all male Hebrew children were to be killed. The writing represents good English prose of about three hundred fifty years ago. Retell the story as best you can in modern English. Then compare the versions, noticing where you have been able to be briefer and terser than the original by omitting parts of constructions that the authors of the King James Bible thought essential.

1. And there went a man of the house of Levi, and took to wife a daughter of Levi.
2. And the woman conceived, and bore a son: and when she saw him that he was a goodly child, she hid him three months.
3. And when she could not longer hide him, she took for him an ark of bulrushes, and daubed it with slime and with pitch, and put the child therein; and she laid it in the flags by the river's brink.
4. And his sister stood afar off, to wit what would be done to him.
5. And the daughter of Pharaoh came down to wash herself at the river; and her maidens walked along by the river's side; and when she saw the ark among the flags, she sent her maid to fetch it.
6. And when she had opened it, she saw the child: and, behold, the babe wept. And she had compassion on him, and said, This is one of the Hebrews' children.
7. Then said his sister to Pharaoh's daughter, Shall I go and call thee a nurse of the Hebrew women, that she may nurse the child for thee?
8. And Pharaoh's daughter said to her, Go. And the maid went and called the child's mother.
9. And Pharaoh's daughter said unto her, Take this child away, and nurse it for me, and I will give thee thy wages. And the woman took the child, and nursed it.
10. And the child grew, and she brought him unto Pharaoh's daughter, and he became her son. And she called his name Moses: and she said, Because I drew him out of the water.

F. In *Tough, Sweet & Stuffy*, Walker Gibson offers what he calls "a kind of Style Machine, of a pre-Model T order." Gibson points out that his machine will "not discriminate between good and bad writing," and is "full of bugs"; but it is designed to help identify characteristics of different sorts of prose. It consists of a series of questions, to be answered by classifying and counting. The following questions are a simplification of the Style Machine.

Choose any two samples of writing and answer each question. Then discuss any differences in the styles of the two revealed by your examination. What conclusions can you draw based on your analysis?

1. How many words in each passage have more than two syllables?
2. How many words in each passage are verbs?

3. How many of these verbs are forms of *to be,* used as finite verbs?
4. How many of these verbs are passives?
5. How many of the words in each passage are nouns?
6. How many of the words in each passage are pronouns?
7. How many of the words in each passage are adjectives?
8. How many main or independent clauses in each passage have a subject-verb or subject-verb-object pattern?
9. How many main or independent clauses in each passage have a linking verb or a passive form?

G. Do a similar analysis based on a recent piece of your own formal writing. Then compare this to the writing you do in your journal. What does this reveal to you? Are there any changes in your style that you should work on?

13

Argument, Persuasion, Reasoned Writing

> "To begin with," said the Cat, "a dog's not mad. You grant that?"
> "I suppose so," said Alice.
> "Well, then," the Cat went on, "you see a dog growls when it's angry, and wags its tail when it's pleased. Now I growl when I'm pleased, and wag my tail when I'm angry. Therefore, I'm mad."
> LEWIS CARROLL,
> *Alice's Adventures in Wonderland*

Alice is not persuaded by the logic of the Cheshire cat. "I call it purring, not growling," she says—a question of definition. She might also have questioned the Cat's use of evidence and the logic of his conclusion. The questions she would have been raising are basic to some of the most important kinds of writing, from early times to the present—writing that attempts to influence decisions or to persuade.

Argument and persuasion are types of discourse that have long influenced world events. Classical rhetoricians called rhetoric "the art of persuasion" and identified three appeals—rational, emotional, and ethical—on which persuasion is based. Much contemporary prose—formal arguments in a court of law, political campaign speeches, newspaper editorials, or advertisements for skin lotion—fall into this category. Each is intended to make a reader or listener agree with an opinion or accept a point of view.

THE APPEALS

Argument and persuasion are intimately related to exposition. In exposition we assemble details—facts, illustrations, analogies, descriptions, anecdotes. And we may do the same in argumentation. The difference is in the purpose of the writing. The purpose of exposition is to offer information in order to explain or clarify. The purpose of argument and persuasion is to take a position and defend it, using rational, emotional, or ethical appeals.

The Rational Appeal relies on logic, reason, and common sense. The writer assembles evidence, facts, statistics, and statements from authorities to make a case.

The Emotional Appeal capitalizes on the emotions and feelings of the audience. The writer may appeal to the audience's sense of fair play or to their fears and prejudices.

The Ethical Appeal exploits the reliability of the writer, the trustworthiness, which results from an established reputation or from the voice created on the page.

But there is also a difference between argument and persuasion, based on both the purpose and the origin of the writing. Argument has as its purpose the discovery of truth through application of reason. Its origin is doubt or uncertainty, the result of conflict. And it can achieve its purpose only through appeals to logic and reason. For example, after a lengthy investigation, a city engineer might argue that a special type of sewage treatment plant would be the most efficient and cost-effective means of cleaning a polluted river flowing through the town.

Persuasion, on the other hand, has as its purpose assent or agreement, acceptance of the position of the persuader. It develops from a position already adopted by the writer, not from a conflict. And its end can be achieved in more than one way, by appealing not only to reason but also to emotion. A preacher urging a congregation to repent for their sins or to donate to the annual flood relief fund would be an example. And in both of these instances the ethical appeal, of the city engineer or the preacher, would influence the success of their presentations.

PERSUASION AND ETHICS

In all kinds of writing, of course, ethics—the motives, the honesty, the reliability of the writer—is involved. In persuasion, however, ethical questions are especially pertinent because of the ready availability of means for deception. Ezra Pound commented cynically that rhetoric is "the art of dressing up some unimportant matter so as to fool the audience for the time being." Centuries ago Plato attacked the Sophists in Athens on the same grounds—that they were using rhetorical skills in persuasion without regard to the purposes for which the skills were being used, that they were being unethical.

Questions of ethics still exist. Is a political candidate justified in appealing to an audience by attempting to arouse racial prejudices? Should an advertiser attempt to persuade readers of the virtues of a shaving lotion by implying that it will make young men irresistible to the opposite sex? Is national security a sufficient reason for exaggerating enemy atrocities to exploit the patriotism of an audience? Are hidden appeals to the subconscious of the television viewer ethical?

These are not easy questions, but they are pertinent to any discussion of persuasion. The discussions in this chapter take for granted the integrity of the writer, assume that the writer wants to make a reader change an opinion, not by deception but by creating understanding.

THE BASIS OF ARGUMENT
AND PERSUASION: THE PROPOSITION

An argumentative or persuasive essay rests on a proposition, which may take either of two forms: It may assert that something is true, or it may say that something should be done. It also may state either of these negatively, that something is not true or that it should not be done. A proposition of the first kind might be:

> Socialized medicine would (or would not) improve health care for senior citizens.

Or it might make a more specific assertion:

> Socialized medicine would (or would not) lower the quality of health care by removing incentives for physicians.

A proposition of the second kind might deal with the same subject:

> The government of the United States should (or should not) establish a system of socialized medicine.

Either type of statement may become the basis for an argument, but there are restrictions on the kinds of propositions that are arguable.

1. Conflict and uncertainty must be present. You can't argue profitably about facts or tastes. A statement, "Health care costs in the United States increased ten times between 1960 and 1980," is not an arguable proposition; it simply requires verification, not argument. You don't argue about the amount of money in a purse; you count it.

"Sugar-free cola doesn't taste as good as the real thing" can't produce a useful argument. Arguing about a matter of mere taste can lead nowhere. Phrased differently as an assertion, the proposition would be arguable: "Sugar-free cola is a health hazard."

A truism, "Electing more honest public officials would give us a more honest government" or "When people are out of work, unemployment exists," obviously provides no basis for argument.

2. Clarity and specificity in the proposition are essential. A proposition to be argued, like any thesis statement, makes a commitment; and the clearer the commitment, the easier it is to verify and substantiate. In general, propositions of the first kind, assertions, are easier to support than appeals for action. For example, "The United States should adopt socialized medicine because it is democratic" could be argued. But producing a convincing paper would not be easy. It would require defining the complexity of *democratic*, and it would also require accepting the dubious logic that being democratic is adequate reason for any kind of action. A more specific proposition of the first kind would be more easily defensible: for example, "Socialized medicine would allow equal health benefits for people at all economic levels."

STRATEGIES FOR ARGUMENT AND PERSUASION

The strategies for argument and persuasion are essentially the same, and in general they follow the patterns for development discussed in chapter 3. That is, the proposition makes a commitment, and the response to the commitment is supporting evidence or illustrations. A number of strategies, however, have special importance for argument and persuasion. Definition clarifies a proposition. A description of the background of the case, establishment of common ground, or refutation are common devices for building an argument. The strength of an argument rests on evidence supporting the proposition, on the writer's use of induction. Reasoning, or deduction, is essential to persuasion.

Definition

Definition affects writing in at least two ways. It can be used for development, as in chapter 3, and it is a basic device for argument and persuasion, where effectiveness often depends on a clear understanding of terms. In another of Alice's adventures in Wonderland, Humpty Dumpty avoids the problems of definition that weaken the argument of the Cheshire Cat. *Glory* he defines as "there's a nice knockdown argument for you." Alice objects, but Humpty insists that when he uses a word it means "Just what I choose it to mean—neither more nor less." Humpty departs rather more than desirable from the established meaning for his definition, but his approach illustrates how definition can help a writer avoid misunderstanding by defining terms.

In writing, a definition does not always need to be scientifically precise, but it does need to help the reader see how key terms are being used. Notice the following, which seems at first glance to be a definition:

> In the true sense of the word, a conservative is the person who really keeps our society from disaster. We should honor the conservative as the preserver of our traditions, not vilify him as a foe to progress.

This opening sentence introduces the term on which the argument of the paper turns, but it does not specify what is meant by *conservative.* Compare a revision:

> If we consider a conservative as the person who is reluctant to change until convinced that the new is better than the old, we can see that the conservative keeps our society from disaster.

Even though it is brief, this definition clarifies the entire argument. Sometimes, however, more extended definitions or definitions of another sort may be required. Following are descriptions of some of the most useful routes to definition, using as examples various well-known definitions of man, with the word *man* used in the generic sense to refer to both men and women.

1. *Classification and Differentiation* The classical Aristotelian definition identifies within a class—a gong is a metal disk that produces a loud sonorous tone when struck with a mallet. It puts the object into a class, metal disks, and then differentiates it from other disks by specifying that it makes a sonorous sound when struck. Such definitions are much used in dictionaries and in science, where they have the virtue of brevity and, within limits, of precision, but formal definition can be less accurate than it might seem. Diogenes is said to have criticized the definition of man as a "two-legged animal without feathers" by bringing in a plucked chicken and saying "This is Plato's man." The definition was revised by adding "with broad flat nails." In effect, Diogenes had shown that differentiation can be tricky, and formal definitions may not be very revealing, even when classification is correct and the differentiation adequate.

2. *Description* Physical qualities such as size, shape, color, weight, height, length, or degree, can define by describing. The following mostly uses descriptive details:

> Man is the highest type of animal existing or known to have existed, but differs from other animals more in his extraordinary mental de-

velopment than in anatomical structure. . . . The main structural characters distinguishing man are: his completely erect posture and gait, from which follow the modification of the feet for walking, . . . the size and perfect opposability of the thumb; the scarcity of hair on most parts of the body; the distinctness of the chin; the comparative uniform size and even arrangement of the teeth; and most of all the enormous development of the brain, especially of the cerebrum, and the smooth rounded skull and high facial angle.

Webster's New International Dictionary, 2d ed.

3. Examples, Instances Examples may clarify a definition. "Nouns are words like *horse, typewriter, disease,* and *happiness*" gives a clearer working notion of what a noun is than do more elaborate discussions. The following develops a metaphoric definition of man with significant details to show what is meant by calling man a thinking reed:

> Man is but a reed, the most feeble thing in nature, but he is a thinking reed. The entire universe need not arm itself to crush him. A vapor, a drop of water suffices to kill him. But if the universe were to crush him man would still be more noble than that which killed him, because he knows that he dies, and the advantage which the universe has over him: the universe knows nothing of this.

Blaise Pascal, *Thoughts*

4. Content Objects, and even difficult concepts, may be defined in part by noticing what they are made of. The following is presumably anonymous:

> A man weighing 150 pounds approximately contains 3,500 cubic feet of gas, oxygen, hydrogen and nitrogen in his constitution, which at 70 cents per 1,000 cubic feet would be worth $2.45 for illuminating purposes. He also contains the necessary fats to make a 15-pound candle, and thus, with his 3,500 cubic feet of gases, he possesses great illuminating possibilities. His system contains 22 pounds and 10 ounces of carbon, or enough to make 780 dozen, or 9,360 lead pencils. There are about 50 grains of iron in his blood and the rest of the body would supply enough to make one spike large enough to hold his weight. A healthy man contains 54 ounces of phosphorus. This deadly poison would make 800,000 matches or enough poison to kill 150 persons.

5. Origin Many objects, and even principles and beliefs, can be described by noting their origin and growth, or the process can be reversed, deducing an origin by an eventual development. The two may work together, as in the following:

> Since fossil evidence for man's ancestry is fragmentary and unsatisfactory, we can only try to deduce the form from which he evolved by

studying what he is. Most of the living primates are tree-dwellers, and there can be little doubt that our own ancestors were so at one time. The structure of the human arm and shoulders bears mute witness to a long-lost habit of swinging from branch to branch . . .

Ralph Linton, *The Study of Man*

6. Comparison   Analogies and figures of speech may serve as the basis of extended definitions. They are usually not appropriate in restrictive definition, but they may promote clarity, charm, and insight, and they combine well with other approaches.

> Man is a rope stretching from the animal to the superman—a rope over an abyss.
> F. W. Nietzsche
>
> Man is a god in ruins.
> R. W. Emerson
>
> The world is a pot and man is a spoon in it.
> Old Proverb
>
> Man is not a circle with a single centre; he is an ellipse with two foci. Facts are one, ideas are the other.
> Victor Hugo

7. Contrast   Within limits the writer can tell what something is by demonstrating what it is not.

> Man is neither an angel nor a brute, and the very attempt to raise him to the level of the former sinks him to that of the latter.
> Blaise Pascal, *Thoughts*

8. Interpretation   A description can be combined with an interpretation; the result is not likely to be objective, but it may gain effects denied to strictly objective writing.

> What a piece of work is a man! how noble in reason! how infinite in faculty! in form and moving how express and admirable! in action how like an angel! in apprehension how like a god! the beauty of the world! the paragon of animals! And yet, to me, what is this quintessence of dust?
> William Shakespeare, *Hamlet*

Background or History of the Case

Like a definition, a discussion of the background or history of a topic is a means to clarify an argument. It gives the reader a perspective from which to view the problem and to understand the evidence presented. A student arguing that all athletes using steroids should be banned from competition might point out that steroids were introduced in athletics during the 1972

Olympics and then describe how their use has spread. The city engineer writing a proposal for a new sewage plant might start with a history of the present plant and its problems or with a study of other proposals that have been tried, and failed, in the past.

Common Ground

If two points of view are totally opposed and irreconcilable, persuasion is not likely to occur. It is, therefore, usually sensible for the writer to seek some ground of agreement as a point of departure. For example, supporters of a mayoral candidate charged with spreading false rumors, could probably be brought into agreement with an opening statement like:

> The goal of any election campaign in America is to provide voters with the most accurate and most complete information about the candidates and to elect the best-qualified officials.

Refutation

Another way to establish credibility and acceptance of an argument is to show the opposing view. Often, the writer will take the strongest evidence against a proposition and demonstrate why it is irrelevant or wrong. The student writing about steroids would probably want to acknowledge that steroids do have medical benefits for the elderly and for some young children. The writer urging the adoption of socialized medicine might want to cite facts and statistics to counter arguments that this would increase health care costs in America.

The following student paper illustrates some of the basic strategies for argument and persuasion.

Athletic Injustice

In the world of sports today, many great athletes are being done a tremendous injustice. Professional athletes in one sport are being banned from amateur competition in other unrelated sports in the Olympic Games. These players are being unjustly penalized because they make their livings as athletes.

The Olympics is without a doubt the greatest competition in the world for amateur athletes, and the countries represented take great pride in the successes of their athletes. The United States is no exception, yet many of our greatest athletes are not allowed to participate because they are professionals in other sports. For example, many professional football players are also standouts in track and field, but because of the rules governing competition in amateur track and field, they are barred from competing. One man who exemplifies this is Renaldo Nehemiah. Nehemiah is the world record holder in the 110-meter hurdles, and very probably the greatest ever in that event. Several years ago, however, he became a professional football player and was subsequently barred from competing in amateur track, thus losing the gold medal that was virtually guaranteed him in the 1984 Olympics. All this because he chose to make football his career.

Many people, I'm sure, could fallaciously justify this ruling against Nehemiah by saying he is a professional athlete and therefore cannot compete as an amateur. If the rulings were consistent, this might be a valid argument. But throughout the world of sports, except for the Olympics, professionals are allowed to compete as amateurs. An example is the famous professional football player John Brodie. While quarterbacking for a professional team, he twice competed in the United States Amateur golf championship. He was considered one of the top amateur golfers in the United States, despite being a professional athlete.

The problem seems to revolve around the U.S. Track and Field Association and the U.S. Olympic Committee, since they are the groups that have made the questionable judgments. In fact, they have contradicted themselves, in a manner of speaking. In the case of Jim Thorpe, the star of the 1912 Olympics, who won two gold medals (decathlon and pentathlon), the Olympic Committee took away his medals and recognition because he had played baseball for a small salary prior to the games. Then recently they returned his awards to his family, saying they had made a mistake. If they can reinstate Thorpe as gold medalist, how can they justify keeping professionals like Renaldo Nehemiah from competing?

It is time to change these views. Amateurism and professionalism are outdated concepts which do not recognize the tremendous cost of training and participating in sports. The person who makes his living as an athlete in one sport should not be penalized when it comes to participating in other unrelated amateur activities. With the rules of the U.S. Olympic Committee, the country as a whole as well as the athletes are suffering. It makes one wonder if the "best" is really the "best," or if there is someone better out there who is being suppressed by outdated regulations.

The paper illustrates how various strategies can be employed to complete an argument. The first paragraph presents a workable proposition. The second establishes some common ground for the writer's position and those who might oppose it, and then it presents evidence, with a specific example, to clarify the problem. The third paragraph opens with a refutation, supported with another specific example. The fourth paragraph adds information on the background of the problem with another specific example to cast doubt on the fairness of the current rules. And the final paragraph concludes, requesting a change in the rules.

INDUCTION:
GENERALIZATION AND EVIDENCE

The most common pattern for argument—in fact, for the development of almost any kind of writing—involves induction, the process of reasoning that produces generalizations and provides evidence to support them. We use this two-way process all the time. For example, a student crossing the campus notices a "no parking" sign blocking her vision of the fountain in front of the library. Mildly annoyed, she looks for similar intrusions and finds another traffic sign partly covering two azalea bushes. Alerted, she observes more signs, garbage cans beside the entrances to two buildings, and beside the university greenhouse an unpainted storage bin with hoses hanging out of it. She makes a tentative generalization that the appearance of the campus is being spoiled by the carelessness of the building and grounds department. She decides to write a letter to the campus newspaper. By induction she has moved from observing a number of instances to a generalization that will serve as a main idea for writing. She then reverses the process, using induction in the second way, to supply instances as evidence to support and illustrate her generalization. She probably needs to look for additional evidence to develop her letter. Furthermore, part of the generalization is a hypothesis, that the building and grounds department is responsible for the signs and cans. She needs to verify the causal relationship she has assumed.

Evidence: Fact and Opinion

Two sorts of evidence are available both to produce and to support generalizations, fact and opinion. Compare the following sets of statements:

>*Opinion:* Martha is a bad girl.
>*Fact:* Martha took two pieces of candy without asking.
>
>*Opinion:* Snidehart is a murderer.
>*Fact:* Two witnesses saw Snidehart with a gun in his hand a few minutes after the cashier was shot.
>
>*Opinion:* College football is on the way out.
>*Fact:* In many major universities, football costs are increasing faster than gate receipts.

Facts report what has happened or what exists. They result from observation or measurement; they can be tested or verified. Opinions may be generalizations resulting from extensive observation by an expert, but they may also be hearsay or prejudice. Either facts or opinions may be useful to support a proposition in an argumentative essay, but both need to be tested.

Facts have advantages as evidence because they are subject to verification. But they need to be verified, and accurate evaluation of alleged facts can be difficult. Statistics of all sorts, for example, can be misleading, especially if an interpretation is masquerading as a fact. An essay supporting a political position is vulnerable if the figures on government spending can be questioned. Or testimony by an observer is fact only if the competence of the observer is certain. In general, however, factual evidence is the most effective support in an argument.

Opinions are deceptively easy to come by. We hear them all around us; and often, especially if we think uncritically, we accept them because other people do. And when we need to put words on paper, opinions and judgments often occur to us first. But opinions have the disadvantage of stopping rather than advancing discussion. Confronted by a statement such as "Your plan is stupid," a writer can only agree or say "It is not"—neither of which produces much understanding. But opinions can be useful as evidence in an argument if they represent genuine authority or expertness. The citing of authority can be an effective way of supporting a proposition, if the credentials of the authority are unquestioned or can be established.

Using Inductive Reasoning

Whether evidence is fact or opinion, it becomes part of the inductive reasoning process in an argument. And a writer needs to examine that process whenever it is used, considering both the validity of any generalization and the adequacy of evidence to support it. The following are pertinent questions.

1. Is the generalization too hasty, based on hearsay or prejudice rather than evidence? Human beings readily jump to conclusions. A mother, quite innocently, indulges in what is known as wishful thinking to select only a small part of the evidence and to conclude that her child has been grossly wronged by a teacher. Reporters from newspapers of rival political parties, perhaps not innocently, make different generalizations by selecting only part of the facts in their report of a mass meeting. Such generalizations, reflecting prejudice and hope rather than evidence, may be useless for serious writing because they cannot be supported.

2. Is the evidence adequate? A generalization that all cows are black and white, made by a city boy after his first visit to a farm specializing in Holstein-Frisian cattle, is not reliable; it is based on too few instances. A visitor's "firsthand account" of the attitude of the Chinese toward the United States, based on a two-day guided tour of Beijing, is not trustworthy; the evidence is inadequate. Especially dangerous, because they may be attractive, are single experiences of an author.

3. Is the evidence relevant? A writer who uses statistics about football gate receipts as evidence that football builds character is not convincing; the evidence is not relevant to the generalization. It might be pertinent to some other proposition—that football helps finance college athletic programs, for instance. Testimony of a large number of students that examinations should be abolished is not evidence for the proposition that examinations are not fair tests of knowledge.

Various kinds of emotional appeals are usually irrelevant as evidence. Name-calling is one. Slipping in a clever—but irrelevant—comment or slogan is another. The number of ingredients in a headache tablet is not necessarily relevant to the efficacy of the medication. Neither the absence nor the presence of suds guarantees that a soap cleanses well. Suntanned blondes in swimsuits do not establish the virtues of cigars, beer, or automobiles. Juries are cautioned to avoid such irrelevancies as the diction of the defense attorney or the dress worn by the defendant.

4. *Is the evidence typical?* Poll takers and statisticians have developed techniques of sampling as one application of inductive reasoning, making the leap to a generalization on the basis of selected typical instances. The method is useful, but it is hazardous, unreliable if the cases selected are not typical. A poll of its subscribers conducted by a business magazine is not likely to provide reliable evidence on the attitudes of Americans toward taxing corporations. Consider the following:

> Required physical education courses tend to improve study habits and to raise grade point averages for college students. A poll of physical education majors at State College reveals that more than 90 percent testified that they studied better and made better grades while they were taking the required physical education courses.

5. *Does the evidence show cause or only coincidence?* A person dealing with causes may be tempted to generalize quickly or to admit as evidence material that is not properly evidence at all. We play with a toad on Monday and discover a wart on our finger on Friday. We find a horseshoe at ten o'clock, throw it over our left shoulder at 10:02, and find a $10 bill at noon. If we conclude that playing with the toad caused the wart or that finding the horseshoe was responsible for our good luck, we are making the error known as the *post hoc ergo propter hoc* fallacy, "after this therefore because of this." The following passage illustrates the fallacy as it often appears in writing.

> Governor Jones was elected two years ago. Since that time constant examples of corruption and subversion in government have been unearthed. It is time we got rid of the man responsible for this kind of corrupt government.

Although there is no evidence of causation, the coincidence is cited as evidence of cause. Sequence in time does not provide evidence for causation; establishing a causal relation requires direct evidence that one event led to the other.

6. *Is statistical evidence complete and pertinent?* Statistics can be useful evidence, but incomplete or unanalyzed statistics can lead to false conclusions. A campus newspaper once reported, quite accurately, that during the year, 50 percent of the women in one college of the university had married their instructors. People were outraged until it was revealed that the college was the college of engineering, and the total number of women students for the year was two. Consider the following:

> Statistics show that everyone in the office is making enough money to live comfortably. The average salary, computed on certified figures for last year, was a little more than $31,000 per year per employee.

At first glance the statistics may seem to apply to the generalization. But it is possible that only two salaries, those of executives at $68,500 each are as high as the average and that some are very low.

7. *Is the evidence up to date, unprejudiced, and from a competent witness?* The Battle of Gettysburg does not necessarily provide evidence for current military strategy. A biography commissioned by a political party for its major candidate is suspect as evidence. If a nine-year-old reports that a neighbor is a witch, the evidence must be discounted. A baseball fan in the right-field bleachers probably has less reliable information about the last pitch than the umpire.

8. *Is the evidence more than an illustrative analogy?* Analogy is useful for development and even definition, but it is usually not valid as evidence, at least not as proof. A writer trying to explain the breeds of horses to city children might wish to say that just as racing automobiles have light wheels and chassis, and trucks have very heavy running gear, racing horses are relatively light and draft horses very heavy. This is an analogy. But a horse is not a machine, and an automobile is not an organism. The writer cannot prove anything about a horse by evidence from an automobile but may be able to promote understanding of the structure of the horse by noting similarities. Consider the following use of analogy:

> Modern corporate business executives, in their use of ingenuity, are like the Indians of western Canada. Needing light during their foggy winters, they discovered a new use for the candlefish, which had long been a staple of their diets. This fish is so fat when it swims inland to spawn in the spring that the Indian has only to stick a rush into the fish's back and light it. The fish will then burn like a candle. It is evident, therefore, that modern business owes its success to the ability of Americans to take advantage of their natural resources.

The comparison of the ingenuity of the executives with that of the Indians is an interesting analogy, but it does not justify the conclusion of the final sentence.

DEDUCTION

Like induction, deduction is essentially common sense. Induction moves toward a generalization, a premise. We observe that cat A and cat B and cat C and dozens of other cats have tails, and we conclude that all cats have tails. Deduction moves in the other direction. We start with a premise such as all cats have tails, and we conclude that Tabby, a cat we have only heard about, has a tail. Manx cats and amputations suggest some of the hazards of both inductive and deductive logic.

In practice, logical thinking progresses by chain reaction, with induction and deduction working together. A lawyer building a case to prove that Elbridge Dangerfield is guilty of murder uses inductive reasoning. She observes that the victim was shot through the heart. Dangerfield was found in the victim's room just after the shooting with a smoking revolver in his hand; the bullet taken from the victim's body was fired from the gun Dangerfield was holding. The victim had been blackmailing Dangerfield. Thus the lawyer reaches the generalization that Dangerfield is probably guilty of murder. She has reasoned inductively, but an insurance agent sitting in the courtroom as the jury announces its verdict uses deduction to conclude that Elbridge Dangerfield is a bad insurance risk. His reasoning could be formalized as follows, in a series of patterns known as *syllogisms*:

Major Premise: Anyone judged guilty of murder may be executed.
Minor Premise: Elbridge Dangerfield has been judged guilty of murder.
Conclusion: Elbridge Dangerfield may be executed.
Major Premise: Any man who may be executed is a bad insurance risk.
Minor Premise: Elbridge Dangerfield may be executed.
Conclusion: Elbridge Dangerfield is a bad insurance risk.

The insurance agent has seen the relationship among the generalizations and has been able to reach a valid conclusion.

The Syllogism

The insurance agent's thinking has been put into a pattern of formal logic that is mainly artificial but is useful for testing the validity of any deduction. A syllogism breaks a pattern of thought into three statements—a major premise, a minor premise, and a conclusion—linked by a common element called the *middle term*. Oversimplified, the syllogism and deduction are like an algebraic formula: If a equals b and b equals c, then a equals c. The common or middle term is b.

We can think of deduction as a way of relating groups of classes. The statement "Daisy, since she is a cow, is a ruminant" involves three elements, or terms, which might be represented by three circles, representing classes of different sizes.

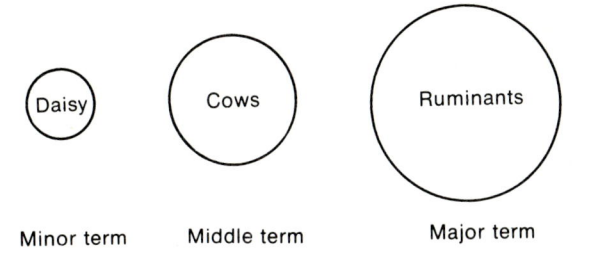

Daisy	Cows	Ruminants
Minor term	Middle term	Major term

The minor term indicates the small class, the major term the large class, and the middle term the class somewhere between the other two in size. When the statement about the terms is put into its logical steps, it reads:

Major Premise: All cows are ruminants.
Minor Premise: Daisy is a cow.
Conclusion: Daisy is a ruminant.

The statements say something about how the terms are related or, if we think of the terms as circles, about which term includes the others. By the authority of the major premise, the middle circle can go into the larger one; but the minor premise puts the small circle into the middle one. Necessarily, the small circle must also be included in the large one:

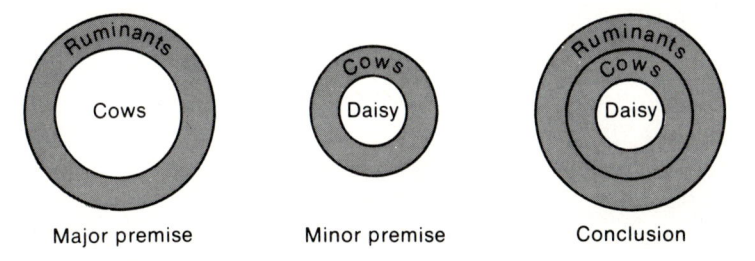

Ruminants / Cows	Cows / Daisy	Ruminants / Cows / Daisy
Major premise	Minor premise	Conclusion

Clearly Daisy belongs in the class of ruminants. The conclusion is *valid* because it follows logically from the premises stated. It is *true* if the premises are true.

Deduction and Writing: The Enthymeme

If writing followed formal patterns like those devoted above to Daisy's eating habits, it would be both cumbersome and dull. In practice, deductive arguments are both shortened and telescoped. A deductive statement appears not as a full syllogism, but as what classical rhetoricians called an *enthymeme*. This is a logical statement that includes a conclusion and one premise but omits one of the premises that would appear in a syllogism, usually because it can be assumed. Furthermore, the enthymeme is more flexible than the formal syllogism because it may work from premises that are probably, not necessarily, universally true. The syllogism about Daisy produces a true conclusion because the main premise, that all cows are ruminants, has been established as true. But writing is usually concerned with more complex, less obvious arguments.

An enthymeme like the following is more likely to be useful in writing:

> The price of beef will go up. We had a dry winter on the cattle ranges.

This can be called an enthymeme both because the major premise behind the argument is assumed but not stated and because the assumption is not universally true. It can, however, be analyzed into the syllogisms behind it:

Major Premise:	A dry winter produces less food for grazing.
Minor Premise:	This was a dry winter.
Conclusion:	There will be less food for grazing this year.
Major Premise:	When there is less food for grazing, to raise cattle costs more.
Minor Premise:	There will be less food for grazing this year.
Conclusion:	It will cost more to raise cattle this year.
Major Premise:	When it costs more to raise cattle, beef prices go up.
Minor Premise:	It will cost more to raise cattle this year.
Conclusion:	Beef prices will go up.

When the enthymeme is stretched out into the series of syllogisms it implies, it lacks the certainty of a conclusion like "Daisy is a ruminant." Exceptions to any of the premises can be imagined; a depression may drive beef prices down in spite of feed shortages. But the premises have enough probability to make the enthymeme useful in a discussion.

Using Deductive Arguments

Argumentative writing makes extensive use of the enthymeme, which puts logic into concentrated form, and may be deceptive. It may, for example, be based on an untenable premise, a generalization from insufficient data. Or it may imply flawed reasoning that can be revealed by expressing the enthymeme as a syllogism. That is, the conclusion may not follow from the premises, and the statement may be a *non sequitur,* Latin for "It does not follow." The following are suggestions for avoiding logical fallacies.

1. *Testing Assumptions* Logical arguments are likely to be expressed in enthymemes in which some of the premises are assumed, not directly expressed. A writer needs to identify the assumptions behind statements to be sure that they are defensible. An editorial writer argues: "Police records prove that the youth center on Western Avenue is encouraging juvenile delinquency; it should be closed." The writer is assuming that any institution that encourages juvenile delinquency is bad and should be closed. Probably most people will accept this assumption and therefore the argument.

A travel agent writes: "The sight-seeing tour into the mountains should begin before 2:00 p.m. so that it can be completed before dark." Nobody is likely to disagree with the assumption that sight-seeing is better in daylight than in darkness.

But consider another statement: "Government welfare programs should be discontinued at once, because laziness should not be encouraged." When the assumptions behind this statement are pulled out they are not so readily acceptable: that people on welfare are there because they are lazy, or that welfare programs encourage laziness. Or, consider another: "That violin is more than a hundred years old and must be valuable." The assumption that anything more than a hundred years old is valuable cannot support an argument. Bad violins were made a hundred years ago as well as five years ago. Since an assumption is unexpressed, a writer can readily be tricked into relying on an untenable major premise. Consider:

> A liberal arts course is a waste of time because it does not train students for a profession.

The assumed premise is that any course that does not train students for a profession is a waste of time. Although some readers might accept this premise, it is not a supportable generalization.

2. *Including Steps in the Argument* Although writing would probably sound childish if it included every step in every deduction, writing can be obscure if it omits too much. Even though an argument may be clear in a writer's mind, it may be confusing to a reader if major steps are omitted. Consider:

> Apparently the *Titanic* had been built very well, for the crew did not know the lifeboat assignments.

The sentence is absurd; no one would accept the ignorance of the crew as a reason for believing that the ship was well built. But the writer probably did have something like the following in mind:

> Everyone on the ship considered the *Titanic* to be so well built that she was unsinkable. Members of the crew were so confident of the ship's safety that they had not even learned their lifeboat assignments.

With all the steps included, a logical connection can be established between the soundness of the ship and the ignorance of the crew.

3. Distributing the Middle Term Playing with syllogisms and logical fallacies can get complicated, but analysis of the middle term may provide a check on reasoning. The middle term, the common element in a deductive sequence, is the key to many an argument. In the simple syllogism above identifying Daisy, the middle term, *cow,* is the common element to which both the other terms can be related. And a deductive argument is not valid unless this middle term is "distributed" at least once.

To be distributed, a term must include or exclude all members of its class: "all cows" or "no cows." In "All cows are ruminants," *cows* is distributed, made by *all* to embrace an entire class. Similarly, in the following syllogism, *cows* is distributed as "no cows": "No cows read books; this student is reading a book; this student is no cow." We can draw a conclusion about a single member of a class because we have said something about all members of the class.

Similarly the following syllogism is valid, though not necessarily true.

> *Major Premise:* All communists read Karl Marx.
> *Minor Premise:* Ivan is a communist.
> *Conclusion:* Ivan reads Karl Marx.

The middle term is *communist,* and it is distributed in the first statement. Or *reads Karl Marx* could be used as the middle term and distributed.

> *Major Premise:* Anyone who reads Karl Marx is a communist.
> *Minor Premise:* Ivan reads Karl Marx.
> *Conclusion:* Ivan is a communist.

With the middle term, *reads Karl Marx,* distributed, the syllogism is valid though untrue because the major premise is untrue. But the following, with the middle term not distributed, is not valid.

> *Major Premise:* All communists read Karl Marx.
> *Minor Premise:* Ivan reads Karl Marx.
> *Conclusion:* Ivan is a communist.

One term is distributed as "all communists," but it is not the middle term. The middle term is *reads Karl Marx,* and it is not distributed. Although arguments like the above are often accepted—especially when there are emotional reasons for liking the conclusion—they are no more valid than the following:

> *Major Premise:* All chickens have feathers.
> *Minor Premise:* This canary has feathers.
> *Conclusion:* This canary is a chicken.

4. *Stabilizing the Middle Term* The middle term must not only be distributed, it must have the same meaning in all premises. In the syllogism about Daisy, the middle term *cow* clearly refers to a class of animals, and the argument is valid. A century or so ago, however, the word could refer to another sort of object, which one traveler defined as follows: "A cow is a kind of floating raft peculiar to the Western rivers of America, being composed of immense pine trees tied together, and upon which a log cabin is erected." Obviously, this object was not a ruminant, and if one confuses the two kinds of cows, the result is nonsense. With the navigating cow, as against the ruminating one, a syllogism might read as follows:

> *Major Premise:* All cows have log cabins on them.
> *Minor Premise:* Daisy is a cow.
> *Conclusion:* Daisy has a log cabin on her.

Cow is distributed, but refers to quite different things in the two premises. It has become what is sometimes called a "sliding middle term."

Confusion of terms like these is not likely: even rafters, who were not notable for their conscious skill with syllogisms, would hardly have started a comment using *cow* to designate a raft and then have proceeded to use *cow* to name a ruminating animal. But not all words are so readily distinguished. Consider the following:

> *Major Premise:* All acts that threaten the American way of life are treasonable.
> *Minor Premise:* The new bill on civil rights threatens the American way of life.
> *Conclusion:* The new bill on civil rights is treasonable.

The syllogism seems technically valid. But the common element, "threatens the American way of life," shifts meaning in the context of the two premises. In the major premise it is vague, but likely to be accepted as referring to something generally agreed to be threatening. In the second premise, however, the context makes the meaning of the middle term shift, so that "threatens the American way of life" suggests a clearly prejudiced view of what is threatening. With the middle term undefined, the logic is faulty. When Mark Twain said, "It is easy to give up smoking. I have done it thousands of times," he was making a similar shift in the meaning of the middle term, "to give up." The result is humorous but not logical.

5. *Avoiding Circular Argument*   Sometimes what pretends to be a logical argument merely repeats an initial assumption, leading the reader in a circle. Such writing does not advance an argument or add information to support a conclusion. Consider the following:

> *The Bellelli Family* by Degas is a remarkable psychological group portrait. The portrait shows the master's sense of composition and color, but its enduring charm grows from its revelation of family relationships. The psychology of the family makes it truly a group painting, not just a depiction of a collection of people on one canvas.

The passage starts with a generalization about the picture, but only restates this judgment in different terms. The following revision suggests how the initial premise could be developed logically with relevant evidence.

> *The Bellelli Family* by Degas is a remarkable psychological group portrait. With relaxed poses and naturalistic lighting the artist has centered attention upon the two children, who in turn center upon the mother. The image of the father breaks patterns of both composition and color, and the artist seems to be saying that this father, like so many others, has his interests elsewhere.

FOR STUDY AND WRITING

A. Below are the opening paragraphs of The Declaration of Independence and Martin Luther King's "I Have A Dream." Compare the type of appeals being used in each. Then determine the audience and purpose of each. What relationship do audience and purpose have to the appeals each writer has chosen?

> When, in the course of human events, it becomes necessary for one people to dissolve the political bonds which have connected them with another, and to assume among the powers of the earth the separate and

equal station to which the laws of nature and of nature's God entitle them, a decent respect to the opinions of mankind requires that they should declare the causes which impel them to the separation.

We hold these truths to be self-evident: that all men are created equal; that they are endowed by their creator with certain inalienable rights; that among these are life, liberty, and the pursuit of happiness . . .

Five score years ago, a great American, in whose symbolic shadow we stand, signed the Emancipation Proclamation. This momentous decree came as a great beacon light of hope to millions of Negro slaves who had been seared in the flames of withering injustice. It came as a joyous daybreak to end the long night of captivity.

But one hundred years later, we must face the tragic fact that the Negro is still not free. One hundred years later, the life of the Negro is still sadly crippled by the manacles of segregation and the chains of discrimination. One hundred years later, the Negro lives on a lonely island of poverty in the midst of a vast ocean of material prosperity. One hundred years later, the Negro is still languished in the corners of American society and finds himself an exile in his own land. So we have come here today to dramatize an appalling condition.

B. Advertisements are forms of persuasion. The texts below have been reprinted from two ads for telephones. Is there a difference in the appeals in each? Can you tell who may be the intended audience? Discuss which advertisement you find most effective.

1. To test the sound quality of our new fiber optic line, we literally dropped a pin in Chicago and actually heard it over the phone in Dallas. A distance of 799 miles.

    That's the magic of US Sprint™ fiber optics. Pure sound quality. None of the typical hiss, static or other annoyances you've been forced to accept when you call long distance over the older lines of AT&T.

    And independent tests showed that 3 out of 5 business people preferred the superior sound quality of US Sprint's fiber optic lines over AT&T. On the very first call.

    That's why we're building what will be the first 100% fiber optic long distance company across America. So start saving now by calling US Sprint today. Where fiber optics give you phone calls so clear and quiet you can actually hear a pin drop.

2. If you've been disappointed by a cheap phone, you're not alone.

    But maybe it's because the companies making them don't know what people expect in a phone. Like crystal clear sound. A good design. Construction solid enough to take a little rough handling.

    The very things that people who grew up with AT&T phones take for granted.

    Over a century ago, AT&T began making reliable phones that stood the test of time. We're still doing it. So if something's not up to our standards, we know it won't be up to yours.

    You get what you pay for.

C. Below are listed some propositions for argumentative or persuasive papers. Read them and estimate how long a paper would need to be to adequately discuss each. Revise any that you think are too broad or that are indefensible.

1. Euthansia is a complex problem.
2. Euthansia is a personal issue that can only be decided through cooperative discussion of the family members and medical staff.
3. All students at the university should be required to take two years of foreign language.
4. The new bond issue is a stupid idea.
5. The bond issue to widen River Avenue has serious disadvantages for residents of the area.
6. The 1960s were an era of great changes in all facets of music.
7. The Beatles were responsible for ushering in a new age in popular music.
8. The Beatles are the best musical group in the last thirty years.
9. Free speech is essential to democracy.
10. Free speech has been jeopardized by recent book bannings in several states.

D. The passages given below contain generalizations that are illustrated or supported by evidence. Comment on the reliability of each generalization, indicating whether it is merely illustrated or is supported by evidence. Point out especially instances of inadequate or unreliable evidence, of misused analogies, or of faulty causation.

1. The enclosed manuscript contains about 22,000 words. In order to arrive at this figure I counted the words on ten typical pages, computed from this total the average number of words per page, and multiplied this average by the number of pages.
2. Some people think there is nothing to spiritualism, but they have never seen any of the proofs. I was convinced last year when a friend of mine told me what he had actually seen. He had been to a meeting where a woman went into a trance, and then pretty soon people all over the room started trying to talk with spirits out of the other world. It couldn't have been faked, because the spirits knew the people they were talking to and could remember things that happened a long time ago. And a couple of the spirits even materialized and floated around the room. They didn't look much like real people, of course, because they were spirits, but you could see them so plainly there was no doubt about them.
3. The Japanese people are completely in accord with American democratic principles. This is the conclusion of Mr. J who has just returned after spending a week in Tokyo visiting his son who has been in Japan for some time as the American representative of a large corporation. Mr. J reports that in spite of his handicap in not knowing the Japanese language he was able to collect many favorable opinions about this country in his conversations.

4. Clearly Mr. B cannot be guilty of using his business offices to disguise the headquarters of a worldwide syndicate distributing illegal drugs. Two of his business partners testify without reservation to his honesty and good character.
5. The Roman Empire collapsed when Rome became too prosperous. We should be sure to avoid too much prosperity for the United States.
6. During the past month living costs in America have risen .4 percent. This figure is based on statistics compiled by governmental bureaus through sampling prices of selected commodities and on rents in important areas throughout the United States. It does not take any account of changes in federal or state taxes.

E. Discuss the logical truth and validity of the reasoning in the following passages:

1. Students, like all young people with active minds, are easily susceptible to any idea like communism, which seems to hold out hope for the impractical idealist. It is easy to see why our colleges should be shot through with communism.
2. People who are poor lack ambition; if they did not lack ambition they would not be poor.
3. The editorial in the last student newspaper says that only a student can understand the need for a better intramural program on the campus. Well, I am a student, and I certainly think that the program we now have is all anyone could ask for. The editorial writer should be more logical.
4. The money was taken between eleven o'clock and noon from the desk in this room. Nobody has left the room since eleven o'clock. One of the persons present in the room must have taken the money. John was in the room. Obviously, he took the money.
5. All governments, for reasons of security, must deceive the public from time to time. This bulletin issued by the government therefore must be false.
6. Houses with shallow foundations should be avoided at all costs; but since this house has an unusually deep, reinforced foundation, you can have no reason for rejecting it.

F. Each of the statements below assumes a major premise that is not stated. Supply the assumption behind each statement.

1. She must be intelligent if she is on the honor roll.
2. All high school students should have courses in driver education; careful driving is something they should know about.
3. The people next door go to church regularly; they will want to make a contribution to the Red Cross.
4. He cannot be expected to be in sympathy with American ideas of democracy; he was born in Europe.
5. It should be a good dress; it cost more than any dress in the store.

6. You could tell she was a gossip because she criticized some of the most important civic leaders in town.
7. General B is certain to make a good university president; look how successful he was during the war.
8. Socialists really support the American system of government, for they believe in government by the people.
9. It is ridiculous to suppose that we can ever get rid of anything that has existed in our society as long as nationalism has.
10. Many television serials are bad for children as they deal with wild and improbable adventures.

G. Free write or brainstorm for ten minutes about an issue that is important to you or a proposal for change that you would like to see take place. As you look at your writing, do you see any ideas for an argument or persuasive paper?

14

Discussion, Examinations, Impromptu Writing, Business Letters, The Résumé

A man may write at any time, if he will set himself doggedly to it.
SAMUEL JOHNSON

In an examination those who do not wish to know ask questions of those who cannot tell.
SIR WALTER RALEIGH

The principles we have been considering apply variously to poems and plays as well as to technical reports and newspaper editorials. For students they apply immediately to course work and other activities, where they must explain what they know—participate in discussions, answer examination questions, write letters and impromptu essays, discuss a poem or a film, or report the results of a library investigation. All such types of writing develop most readily through combinations of the general and the specific. Even a brief comment in class is more convincing if it states a proposition clearly and supports this generalization with specific evidence, if it points toward a main topic or toward an instructor's question.

DISCUSSION

Discussion can be thought of as cooperative communication, in which two or more people work together. It differs from a speech or an essay because more than one person takes part and a speaker may respond to a commitment somebody else has made. Commonly it progresses as a sequence of questions and answers.

Questions help keep talk going, but some kinds of questions are more helpful than others. A question requiring only a brief, factual answer— "What does DNA stand for?"—may allow an instructor to check a student's preparation or a student to get a bit of information. But it may end rather than stimulate a discussion. Another sort of question may enlarge the subject—"Why do biologists get so excited about DNA?" Essentially the same question, drafted more sharply, might pin the topic down— "Does knowing about DNA make test-tube babies possible?" Questions that are temptingly attractive may elicit pleasant bits of information, but they may also turn aside a discussion that might otherwise get somewhere—"Wasn't the discovery of DNA more serendipity than science?" Many discussions are not intended to bring out new information, but to give various individuals a chance to register their opinions. A promoter wants to build a shopping center in a congested district; some of the neighbors welcome the project, but others do not. Frank talking may promote a compromise that everybody can live with. Thus as society becomes more complicated and knowledge more specialized, discussion takes over an ever-increasing part of human communication.

Most people have not much studied the practical art of discussion. They may not have learned a courteous restraint that will allow others a chance to speak. They are even less likely to have studied the drafting of questions, so that they can ask for just what they want without rambling. Some may ask questions in an attempt to show off. Similarly, some may not have learned to control answers, to address a question directly. Especially they may not have learned to welcome answers they do not like. Of course questions and answers can be deliberately perverted. Anybody can pose an irrelevant question, hoping to change the subject. An unscrupulous lawyer may ask, "Isn't it true that you have frequently been seen leaving a massage parlor?" hoping the jury will remember the question after they have forgotten the witness's outraged denial. Fortunately for the student, however, most class discussions are intended to seek or reveal truth, not to obscure it.

Television interviews, like those conducted on "Meet the Press," illustrate how questions and comments can be skillfully handled. Television commentator Barbara Walters is said to compose over 150 questions before beginning an interview. Anthony Quinn, a widely experienced American actor, was asked how he would distinguish between American and British dramatic interpreters. He replied that he thought that Shakespeare had phrased the distinction in the line "To be, or not to be, that is the question." He then went on to explain. The best British actors, he said, like John Gielgud and Lawrence Olivier, were the product of exacting training. They had learned to act, to project character and emotion without entirely participating in either. Their training and their art had led them not to try "to be" the person in whose role they were cast, but to create the impression of this person by using the techniques they had learned. On the other hand, he pointed out, no such rigorous training for actors exists in America, and hence an American actor does try to be the person he portrays. Quinn illustrated from his own experience. He had been cast in the part of Quasimodo in *The Hunchback of Notre Dame,* and had tried so hard to comprehend what being a monster would be like that his face and body had become contorted. Doctors had to labor with him to get him back to his normal self.

Quinn's answer shaped itself into the pattern of a standard expository paragraph. Playing on the well-known line from Shakespeare, he opened with a topic sentence that committed him to explain the special meaning he was giving *to be*. He thus provided a basis for organizing his comment in two parts. He first discussed British acting, showing how British-trained actors do not try "to be." He then turned to American actors, explaining why they do try "to be" and illustrating with a striking example from his experience. Quinn had undoubtedly thought often before about the topic. Students in a class discussion are likely to be neither as experienced in extemporaneous speaking as Quinn nor as lucky in getting a question they have already thought about. But they can work toward the kind of organized and developed comment Quinn produced.

THE EXAMINATION PAPER

The question-answer procedure becomes more formal in the examination, which is intended not as an exchange of ideas but as an opportunity to reveal the knowledge students have acquired and their understanding of its significance. There is some justification in the complaint about examinations that "They don't want to know what you know, but what you don't know." But generally, examinations are thought of positively, and the student's best approach is to use them this way.

Oral examinations have some advantages because they proceed much like discussions, but for undergraduates written examinations are most common. They take many forms. Most types, even the various short-answer ones, are designed to do more than test memory. Statements to be marked *true* or *false*, multiple-choice questions, or questions with blanks to be filled all require the student to handle ideas in the ways this book has been suggesting. Questions that allow some kind of free response—ranging from those that ask for a one-sentence definition to those that specify a topic for an extended essay—challenge students most directly to display their writing ability.

Preparing for Examinations

Like any other kind of writing, an answer to an examination question works best after some prewriting, some preparation. For an examination paper, furthermore, prewriting gains added importance because the answer is impromptu and the writer works under pressure, with little chance to rewrite. In one sense this preparation occurs over the entire period of the course, and a few frantic hours of black coffee and borrowed notes will not substitute for eight weeks of attention. Nevertheless systematic review, planning for writing, can help.

Education is not merely learning facts; history is not knowing dates, and literature is not associating works with their authors. Knowledge of facts is not the end of a course of study, but it is usually a necessary preliminary to the more important ends. Thinking and understanding are thinking and understanding about something, and certain facts are essential. A good examination question is not likely to request only a recitation of facts, but an adequate answer will need facts to support and develop it. The difference between a C or D answer and an A answer may reflect the amount of information you can supply to bolster your arguments. More particularly, a good answer requires plenty of precisely chosen detail, but to select just the right details, you must have a variety to choose from.

Merely reading a textbook or a set of notes over and over, hoping to remember enough from the exposure to get by, is not an efficient way of learning. You are much more likely to remember if you think of facts in groups, as they relate to subjects. Reviewing the history of psychology, and noticing how Freud's theories about sex shocked people, you may want to recall anything else you know about similar prejudices. If you have read any of Hardy's novels, you may have heard what a furor Hardy's treatment of sex stirred among late Victorians. If you have read about the outrage visited on Stravinsky's *The Rites of Spring*, each of the three outbursts is likely to become more real; and should you need dates, one set will serve roughly for all three events. Or if you are reviewing a physics course, you can remember formulas better if you group those relating to electricity and think of them as meaning something, not just as numbers or letters.

A review ought to be just that—a second view—and anybody should be able to see more the second time through the material. If you find in reviewing for an examination that you are only recalling what you once knew and are getting no new insights, you can reasonably charge yourself with reviewing too superficially. One good technique is to try to anticipate the questions you will be asked—not by psychoanalyzing the instructor or by collecting guesses from other students, but by trying to pick out the important topics that have been considered in the course and going over what can be said about them. For any course many specific questions are possible, but the number of general subjects likely to be stressed is limited. In a course in history you can anticipate questions that ask you to analyze causes, to trace the development of an institution like the Supreme Court or the British Parliament, or to evaluate the influence of religion or of revolutionary writing during a particular period in history. Very often lecture notes, the textbook, and exercises or questions in a textbook suggest ways of organizing ideas and information.

The anecdote concerning Anthony Quinn, related above, suggests a good technique for review. You should ask yourself the best questions you can think of and draft oral answers. You should start with a carefully thought out topic sentence and develop it with concrete evidence. If you find you do not have the evidence, you know what to review. This device will tend both to direct your study and help to fix key material where it will be readily at hand—and you may even find that you have use in an examination for the paragraph you have already composed in your mind.

Analyzing Questions

A few practical considerations are worth mentioning because under the pressures of time they may be forgotten. The most obvious is to check directions carefully—to observe any specifications on the form the answer is to take, such as a limitation on length; to note whether any choice among questions is allowed; to be aware of all the parts of a question. Usually you will do well to scan the entire examination before writing anything and to allot time for answering each question, allowing a few minutes after finishing for checking.

Equally obvious advice is to read the question carefully. Short-answer questions depend primarily on careful reading, seeing all the implications of a true-false question or weighing carefully the relative accuracy of multiple-choice alternatives, of which more than one may come near to the best answer. For questions requiring essay answers, careful reading is the first step in planning an answer.

The main point of a question should be the target for the main idea of the answer. Particularly when there are limits on time, you should start an answer by directing it precisely as the question prescribes, paying attention to key words and also qualifications in the question. If a question reads "What were the political reactions to Lincoln's Emancipation Proclamation of 1863?" the answer should not ignore the qualification in the word *political*. A survey of events leading to the proclamation, a discussion of the effects of the proclamation on slaves in the South, or speculation about Lincoln's humanitarian motives would not be relevant. An answer should also be developed with strict attention to the differences between introductory words like *how, why, what,* and *when* and phrases like "the reasons for," "the purposes of," and "the effects of." If a question reads "Why did the movement for racial equality become especially prominent in the 1960s?" an answer is not adequate if it becomes a plea for tolerance or a set of examples to show that inequalities still exist. When the question is not phrased as a question, the verb that carries the main predication of the sentence needs particular attention. Verbs like the following appear regularly in questions phrased as directions, and the success of an answer may depend on interpreting their meaning: *explain, discuss, comment on, describe, narrate, construct, reconstruct, trace, defend, analyze, outline, compare, contrast, develop, argue, justify, illustrate, cite evidence for, list, name, review, define, identify, clarify.* Following are samples of different types of questions and suggestions about how they might be analyzed:

1. Describe the procedures required for amending the Constitution of the United States.

The question is precise, requiring only an organized presentation of information. A good answer might begin with a summary statement: "The Constitution of the United States provides for amendments through a process of action by the Congress and ratification by the various states." It might then be organized in two parts, the first listing in chronological order the steps required for taking an amendment through the Congress and the second outlining the procedures and requirements for ratification by the states.

2. Did the New Deal of the 1930s effect any changes in the fundamental structure of American government?

A question of this sort might technically be answered with a simple *yes* or *no*, but obviously its appearance in an essay examination implies that the answer should not only express an opinion but also justify it. Often, as in this case, there is no right or wrong answer. Here the answer turns on an interpretation of "fundamental structure." A *yes* answer would need to describe the specific changes that occurred as a result of New Deal policies, indicating the sense in which the writer considers the changes fundamental. A *no* answer might discuss various New Deal policies and argue that they had no lasting effect on the structure of the government. And a *yes-no* answer might also work, showing the kinds of changes the New Deal policies made and explaining the senses in which the changes were and were not "fundamental."

3. Discuss George Orwell's *1984* as a comment on the importance of freedom of speech.

The question restricts the answer to a single aspect of the satire in Orwell's novel, but it suggests an answer that generalizes about the criticism in the book and then illustrates with detail. The answer might begin with a statement like "Orwell's *1984* emphasizes the importance of freedom of speech by presenting its absence as one of the major instruments of tyranny in his imaginary totalitarian world." The answer could then describe in detail some of the ways free speech is restricted in the novel—the development of newspeak, the uses of censorship to mold opinion, and the ultimate loss of the ability to think independently because of the curtailment of free expression.

4. Compare and contrast attitudes toward war in Heller's *Catch-22* with those in Hemingway's *A Farewell to Arms*.

The question requires comparison and thus suggests an answer divided into two parts. One writer might discuss attitudes toward war in one novel and then the other; another might prefer a division on the basis of points of difference or similarity, with the attitudes in each novel discussed for each topic. A generalization might open the discussion and provide a basis for unifying it—for example, "Although they describe two different wars, *Catch-22* and *A Farewell to Arms* both look at war realistically. But whereas Hemingway's novel implies an underlying respect for war, Heller's satirical approach suggests something nearer tolerant contempt." Then the student could describe illustrative passages from each novel.

5. The character Fortinbras is sometimes omitted in productions of *Hamlet*. Does his omission in any way weaken the play? Discuss any importance he may have in the presentation of central themes of the play.

This longer question requires pulling together a number of bits of information and some interpretations of the play. The question provides a focus and a limitation—on the character of Fortinbras. It also requires some consideration of basic themes of the play and of the character of Hamlet. The answer, again, might begin with a generalization—for example, "Fortinbras serves as a foil to Hamlet, a representation of what Hamlet is not but might have been. He therefore helps to define Hamlet's character and to develop themes of the play." The answer could proceed by illustrating different parts of this generalization—citing scenes or incidents in which Fortinbras presents a contrast to Hamlet and then supporting the contention that this contrast contributes to characterization and to expression of themes. A question of this sort is usually intended to give students a chance to show that they can do original thinking and can organize thoughts.

6. "Without aid from Europe the colonists would never have been successful in the American Revolution." Discuss this statement.

Questions written around a quotation are usually intended to stimulate speculation or even disputation. There may be no "right" answer. A student might consider arguments both to support and to contradict the statement, describing as precisely as possible what aid the colonists received from Europe, explaining how that aid affected their cause, and suggesting what might have occurred had there been no such assistance. A question of this sort has inevitably been chosen with care; the student should read it with unusual attention.

WRITING EXAMINATIONS AND IMPROMPTU ESSAYS

Many examination questions differ from the samples above, but all such questions are exercises in impromptu writing. All impromptu compositions, whether examination answers or in-class essays, present special problems. They must be written in a limited time, usually with not much leisure for thinking about the specific question or topic, and without much time for revision or rewriting. Under such pressure, you may spend too many minutes developing a relatively minor point, one not central to the main question or topic, leaving insufficient time for the main subject. You may be tempted to pick the first familiar-sounding words in a question and start writing. A student, writing an examination on American history and crammed with information about the Revolutionary War, may face the question "How significantly did the American Tories affect the progress of the Revolutionary War?" Noticing hastily that the question involves the war, which has been discussed at length in class, the student launches into a chronological account of campaigns and strategies. Later the same student is surprised to find that the answer has been given a low grade—it was not directed to the point of the question.

Even for impromptu writing, a few minutes spent in preliminary planning are not wasted. If the topic for an impromptu essay is announced in advance, a student can prepare a rough outline and think about usable illustrations. For unannounced questions or topics, rough notes for a plan jotted in the margin or on scratch paper may speed and improve the writing. Since impromptu writing does not allow time for elaborate planning or complex organization, working from a thesis statement (see chapter 1) and illustrating it specifically usually works best. And one practical help for framing a topic statement for an essay answer is to begin—at least in thinking about the answer—with a statement using the exact words of the question. An answer to the question "What were the major characteristics of Surrealist art?" might begin "The major characteristics of Surrealist art were . . ." As in most writing, the development that follows the statement of the main idea works best when it includes specific illustrations and examples. In timed examinations the student should reserve time enough to correct spelling and punctuation errors and to make minor revisions.

Following is an example of a successful student essay answer in a timed examination:

The Question The fifteenth- and sixteenth-century voyages of exploration produced lasting changes in the policies and social structure of Western Europe. Would you say that these voyages tended to hasten or delay the growth of national states? Explain.

The Answer

Opening answers question directly; then outlines topics to be considered	The exploration of the fifteenth and sixteenth centuries hastened the growth of national status. The reasons have to do with danger, wealth and trade, and national pride.
Begins treating topics in order of opening paragraph	One of the prime ingredients for the beginning of national states was a common danger from the outside. Because countries went to war

	over the right to control certain colonies and trade routes, they had to unite within in order to fight off an aggressor.
Transition to second topic	Other forms of competition between one country and another contributed to the growth of national states. Competition for land and wealth was fierce. The resources of the new land, such as
Specifics to illustrate	coffee, spices, and minerals, were considered valuable. Each country was eager to gain land because the products of the land meant more wealth,
Statement to show relevance of topic	as when Cortez conquered the Aztecs. A unified country could best succeed in the form of competition.
Further explanation of relevance of discussion of trade to development of nationalism	These resources made available by the discoveries increased the power of mercantilism. With the opening of new trade routes, the northern and western European states were able to break the Venetian-Arab trade monopoly with the Indies. The colonization led to a system involving a state-controlled market between the colony and the mother country. This permitted the nations of Europe to become economically separate units, with no common market existing between them—a situation that fostered nationalism.
Further explanation of relevance of discussion of trade to development of nationalism	These resources made available by the discoveries increased the power of mercantilism. With the opening of new trade routes, the northern and western European states were able to break the Venetian-Arab trade monopoly with the Indies. The colonization led to a system involving a state-controlled market between the colony and the mother country. This permitted the nations of Europe to become economically separate units, with no common market existing between them—a situation that fostered nationalism.
Example to illustrate further	It is interesting to note that Italy, which did very little exploration, took longer to become a unified nation than did the other countries of Europe.
Third topic	Another feature in producing national states was the national pride these voyages tended to produce. The voyages were financed by governments. New discoveries were associated with the sponsoring governments and added to their prestige and to the spirit of nationalism within the countries.

LETTER FORM AND CONVENTIONS

Letters, especially business letters, are currently less conventionalized in diction than they once were. In style, they are now straightforward and pointed, avoiding once-fashionable stock phrases such as "Yours of the fifth instant received," or "Anticipating a reply at your earliest convenience, I remain . . ." Conventions in form, however, are still standard and are referred to as semiblock and block style. Observing them is economical and likely to improve reception of your letter.

1. *Typing* Business letters should be typewritten whenever possible, single-spaced unless very short, and without obvious corrections. If handwritten, they should be neat and legible.

2. *Return Address and Date* In the semiblock style, the writer's address should appear in the upper right-hand corner of the page, with the date of writing below it. In the block style, the return address and date are flush with the left-hand margin. Both styles have a single-spaced return address and a double space before the date.

On stationery with a printed address, only the date is required. Names of streets and states are usually spelled out, although abbreviations like *St.* and *Ave.* are becoming more common.

3. *Inside Address* The name and address to which the letter is directed appears, usually in three or more lines, on the left, spaced below the return address and single-spaced.

4. *Salutation* The salutation, followed by a colon, includes the title of the addressee: *Dear Mr. Morrison: Dear Professor Connor: Dear Ms. Howard:* When the letter is addressed to a company or institution, with no name available, *Dear Sir or Madam:* is the very formal salutation. Less formal is the greeting *Ladies and Gentlemen:* or *Dear Addressee:*. Some writers prefer to omit the salutation if they cannot address a person.

5. *Body* Business letters may be typed in block style, with no indention for paragraphs, but with double spacing between them. The older style, indenting each paragraph five spaces, is still common.

6. *Complimentary Close* In semiblock style, the close is centered under the return address. In block style, it begins at the left-hand margin. Standard closings, followed by a comma, include: *Respectfully yours* (formal and usually in a letter to a superior), *Very truly yours* or *Yours very truly* (formal), *Sincerely yours* or *Yours sincerely* (less formal and standard for most purposes), *Cordially yours* (familiar).

7. Signature The letter should be signed below the complimentary close, with the name of the sender also typed for identification.

The following sample letter illustrates the semiblock style:

```
                                    920 West Eleventh Street
                                    Ames, Iowa  50010

                                    March 14, 1988

Professor David Jennings
Department of English
South Carolina
Columbia, South Carolina  29208

Dear Professor Jennings:

I should be grateful if you would write a
letter of recommendation for me and send it to
the University of Iowa, where I am applying to
the law school.

I was a student in your courses, History of
the Language and Applied Linguistics, in the
fall of 1982 and received my degree in 1984
with a minor in English.  At that time we
discussed my taking some graduate work in
literature, but I decided to teach.

Since then I have been teaching high school in
Ames.  The experience has been rewarding, but I
have decided to apply to law school.  I should
appreciate anything you could write about me
and my course work while I was your student.

I enclose a form supplied by the law school and
an addressed envelope.  Thank you for your help.

                                    Sincerely yours,

                                    George Walker
                                    George Walker
```

This letter illustrates block style:

```
721 Greensboro Avenue
Rock Island, Illinois  61201

October 15, 1988

William James, Director of Sales
Meredith Manufacturing Company
1595 Sheridan Road
Wilmette, Illinois  60091

Dear Mr. James:

Would you kindly send me information regarding
your new telephone system, Model C-100?

I recently attended the Tele-Convention in
Chicago and watched a demonstration of this new
system. I was impressed by its efficiency and
am now interested in installing this model in
my home office.

I appreciate your attention to this request.

Very truly yours,

Anna Armstrong
Anna Armstrong
```

You probably will write many different types of business letters—letters requesting a service as did Mr. Montgomery or information as did Ms. Armstrong, letters complaining of inadequate service or demanding reparation, letters of application for a summer job or a full-time position. In all cases, the easiest format to follow, as demonstrated in the two sample letters above, is based on a three-part structure. Like a short essay, this structure proceeds from the general to specifics and uses concrete and precise diction.

1. *Opening Paragraph* Make a general statement (like a thesis) expressing the purpose of your letter.

> I am writing to request a refund of the $20.00 I was overbilled when I stayed at the Valencia Hotel on June 15, 1987.

2. *Middle Paragraph* List any specifics, qualifying circumstances, or special details that reinforce and clarify the general statement of paragraph one.

> I arrived at the hotel at 4:00 p.m. and the front desk clerk informed me that I did not have a reservation. Fortunately, I had my reservation confirmation, #870-15A. He apologized and assigned me a room. Last week I received your bill and found I had been overcharged by $20.00, based on my original reservation.

3. *Closing Paragraph* Restate the purpose, if necessary, and end positively.

> To expedite my refund, I have enclosed a copy of my original reservation and my bill. I look forward to your prompt reply.

LETTER OF APPLICATION

The purpose of a letter of application is to present your qualifications for a position. You are convincing a prospective employer that you are the right person for a specific job. Follow the format above. Begin by clearly identifying the position you are applying for. In the next short paragraph or two, mention why you feel you are suited for the position—your education, a special skill, even an outside hobby—and why you are interested in working for the particular company or organization. Close on a positive note and ask for an interview.

Once you have drafted your letter, revise as needed, checking carefully for grammatical, mechanical, and spelling errors. You want your letter to be as professional as possible. Remember, too, that while a résumé may remain the same for several applications, your letter should be tailored to the particular job and organization. Following is an example of a letter of application:

```
935 Orangedale Road
Rosemont, New Jersey  08903

April 16, 1988

Mr. Kevin Holland
Caughlin Park District
Caughlin, New Jersey  08102

Dear Mr. Holland:

I am applying for the position of coordinator
of the new arts education program at Caughlin
Park District.  I understand that the position
begins in the fall of 1988.

I expect to be graduated this June from
Rosemont College and have always been
interested in children and their artistic
development.  As you will see from my résumé, I
majored in art and minored in elementary
education.  I had extensive experience in these
fields--both inside and outside the classroom.

In fact, for the last three years, I have been
assistant director at the College's summer
program for school children; this year I will
be full-time director.  Not only, then, do I
have experience with children's education, I
understand administration and can be counted on
to create a challenging, well-structured
program.

I believe strongly in the new arts education
program at Caughlin Park and would like to work
with your organization.  I am available for an
interview and will call to request an
appointment.

Sincerely yours,

Vonnie McFarland
Vonnie McFarland
```

THE RÉSUMÉ

The résumé is a formal statement that lists your personal data, education, work experience, military experience if applicable, and unusual honors, awards, or interests. It should list references by name, title, address, and phone number, or contain a note, "Reference supplied on request." In preparing a résumé, try to limit yourself to one or two pages, so that an employer can review your qualifications quickly. Revise and edit your résumé carefully for a professional appearance. An example of a résumé follows:

RENE ROSENBERG
700 East Peckham Lane, #209
Lake Forest, Illinois 60045

Education

1981-84   Mary College, Bismarck, North Dakota.
               B.A. in English/Communication.

1979-1981   Bismarck Junior College, Bismarck, North Dakota.
               Majored in Political Science.

1975-1979   New Salem High School, New Salem, North Dakota.
               Graduated June 1979; second in a class of 61.

Experience

June 1984   Editor, *Alumnae News*, Lake Forest College, Lake
to present   Forest, Illinois.
               Duties: Responsible for editing monthly
               magazine for graduates of the college. Also
               planned layouts, budget, production,
               scheduling, and distributing of magazines.
               Managed a staff of four. Increased circulation
               from 4,000 to 7,500 per month.

September   Gift Accounting Assistant, Mary College,
1982   Bismarck, North Dakota.
to December   Duties: Typing gift receipts, maintaining
1984   files, preparing bank deposits, composing and
               typing correspondence, maintaining campaign fund
               records.

June 1979   Mark-up Clerk Automated, U.S. Postal Service,
to September   Bismarck, North Dakota.
1982   Duties: Preparing mail for computer
               processing, entering data into computer,
               labeling, casing, sorting, and boxing mail.

December   Secretary, Montana-Dakota Utilities, 400 North
1977 to   Fourth Street, Bismarck, North Dakota.
June 1979   Duties: Creating and maintaining files for
               legislative bills from four states, routing
               copies of bills to proper departments,
               composing correspondence, organizing manuals
               for company's board of directors.

<u>Awards</u>
<u>and</u>
<u>Affiliations</u>   Cum laude graduate, Mary College.
First place, Creative Fiction, Mary College,
    1983
Member, National French Fraternity.
Member, AAUW.

<u>References</u>
Mellissa Oaks, Admissions and Records
Lake Forest College
Lake Forest, Illinois   60045

Leonard Winston
Department of English
Mary College
Bismarck, North Dakota   58501

Rosalie Hall, Coordinator
Alumnae Relations
Lake Forest College
Lake Forest, Illinois   60045

FOR STUDY
AND WRITING

A. Take a few minutes and list the qualities of a good discussion leader. Then do the same, listing the responsibilities of a person involved in a discussion. Other than in a classroom, where would these qualities apply?

B. Frame three questions you might be asked in an exam for a course you are taking. Then write an answer to one of them.

C. Following are a number of possible questions that might appear in essay examinations on various subjects. You will probably not have information to produce full answers to most of them, but for each write a comment, indicating what the question requires of an answer, what type of development you would expect, and what kinds of information a good answer would require.

1. What is the doctrine of laissez faire in economics?
2. Compare attitudes toward life expressed in Browning's "Rabbi Ben Ezra" and FitzGerald's translation of *The Rubáiyat of Omar Khayyám.*
3. What evidence is there that racial differences do not affect intelligence?
4. Describe one difference between the basic philosophical principles of Plato and Aristotle.
5. Outline the procedures for extracting the square root of a number.
6. In what ways does Shakespeare's *The Tempest* conform to the classical dramatic unities?
7. What are the most important characteristics of a sonata?
8. Can the principles of Mendel's law be applied to heredity in human beings?
9. How did attitudes of the national government of the United States during the period following the Civil War retard the development of the South?
10. Is there any evidence that television programs have an influence on the behavior of children under six years of age?
11. According to the advocates of the system, what are the advantages of using the International Teaching Alphabet in the teaching of reading?
12. Describe innovations in composition that appeared in paintings of the Italian Renaissance.
13. What is the relation of the sentence "Good fences make good neighbors" to the main theme of Robert Frost's poem "Mending Wall"?
14. In what respects could Arthur Miller's play *The Price* be said to fit Aristotle's analysis of tragedy?
15. How important was federal legislation to the progress of the Civil Rights movement in the 1960s?

D. In an examination in American history, one question stated: "Discuss the major advantages held by the North on the eve of the Civil War." Four representative answers appear below. Read each, noting the strengths and weaknesses of the answer. Try to assign the grade such an answer would receive.

1. Good resources like money, etc. Manufacturing and commerce were centered in Northern cities instead of south. This gave north quite an advantage, (It seems to me that this question is unfair since the material was never covered in class.)

2. The North possessed the following advantages:
    1. It had a larger population on which to draw (22,000,000 as against 9,000,000).
    2. It held a commercial and financial advantage (foreign commerce and banking capital).
    3. It had almost a complete monopoly on production of war materials (iron, steel, etc).

3. To the student of American history nothing is more interesting than our own Civil War, or—as the Southerners like to call it—the War between the States. This was a war that had been brewing for a long while, all the way back to the Missouri Compromise, or, if one wanted to be really precise, all the way back to 1619 when the first slave was imported to Virginia. This is a long time. In spite of the attempts of many honest people to resolve the differences. War came, and with it great change. The Four Horsemen (death, famine, etc.) really rode rough-shod. On the eve of this war both sides held certain advantages but we are particularly interested in the advantages of the North. The North was a more populous area. The result was that many people lived in the North, and thus the North had a greater population upon which to draw. Besides this, it had almost all the steel and iron mills in the country in cities like Pittsburgh, etc. This meant that the North could have the "mostest" even if it didn't get there "fustest."

4. On the eve of the Civil War the North held at least three major advantages. In the first place, it had a larger population to draw on for army service. In 1860 there were roughly 22,000,000 in the North whereas there were only 9,000,000 in the South. The difference was even greater than these figures would indicate because more than one-third of the South's nine million were slaves. In the second place, the North held certain important commercial and financial advantages. For example, it controlled most of the foreign commerce, since trade had centered in ports north of the Potomac River. Even foreign goods destined for the South had poured through Northern warehouses. Finally, the North had an almost complete monopoly on the production of war materials. Not only were almost all the iron, steel, textile, and munition factories in Northern possession, but almost all of the technicians and skilled laborers were also there.

E. Write a letter to your school or local newspaper, complaining about some problem you would like to see corrected. Be sure to proofread carefully before submitting it.

F. Prepare your résumé and write a letter of application for a position that interests you.

15

Writing About Literature

> There is more treasure in books than in all the pirates' loot on Treasure Island . . . and best of all, you can enjoy these riches every day of your life.
> WALT DISNEY
>
> When you reread a classic you do not see more in the book than you did before, you see more in you than was there before.
> CLIFTON FADIMAN

Writing and reading interact, and accordingly, the study of composition usually includes some attention to literature, which provides ready illustrations of rhetorical principles. A sonnet shows how form and organization can work; a good poem illustrates precision and economy in diction; a short story or novel may demonstrate the value of direct sentence patterns. Thus writing about literature has double value for a study of writing; it encourages analysis of the kinds of techniques you are learning, and it provides manageable subject matter. People like to talk about the books they have read or the films they have seen. And people learn about themselves and about life by thinking about what they have read.

At first, writing a paper about literature may seem a formidable assignment—after all, most serious literary criticism depends on wide reading and extended study. And facing innumerable possibilities, some writers miss all their opportunities by turning to one of two extremes—attempting so little that their papers are insignificant or attempting so much that they cannot begin to write.

For example, in a class assigned to write an analysis of the play *Othello*, a student may go to the first extreme and only summarize or paraphrase:

> *Othello* is a very interesting play. In the beginning two men who do not like Othello, Iago and Roderigo, are talking, and Iago says that he is unhappy because he has not got a promotion. Then they go to Brabantio's house and wake him up to tell him that his daughter has run away with Othello. Brabantio goes out looking for Othello, finds him, and accuses him of bewitching his daughter . . .

The writer has outlined what happened but has not analyzed events or characters, has not asked *why* or *how* the play works. A good summary of the plot of a story or of a scene or a paraphrase of a poem may become part of a paper. It may also be a useful exercise in preparing a paper. But the paper that does nothing but retell a story adds no new insights for a reader. People are interested in reading about literature because comparing their experience with that of others may give them new understanding or fuller appreciation.

At the other extreme, a student might attempt a project so ambitious that the writer would have to depend on broad generalizations and the opinions of other critics. Assume that this student decides to write an essay entitled "The Significance of *Othello* in the Development of Tragedy." Such a paper would require knowledge of many tragedies, but the student has read only a few. Reading a book about tragedy would help some, but not much. Quotations from the book would not ring true, because they are far from the writer's own view and experience. This kind of paper may sound like a parody of literary criticism, echoing phrases and lacking substance. At worst, such a paper becomes pretentious, tending to assert critical clichés, that Shakespeare was "a master of the art of depicting characters" or that "*Othello* reveals deep insight into human nature."

As a student, you have had many experiences and can respond critically to literature, relying on what you already understand. When reading, the rhetorical stance is reversed. You become the reader, not the writer, of a work and react to the ideas, the characters, the images presented, gauging them against what you know about life. Papers about literature can be made to grow like any other piece of expository writing, if you choose a central idea you are familiar with and develop it with information from the story or poem or play being considered. Using this approach, a third student writing about *Othello* might decide that jealousy had indeed destroyed many relationships and pursue this idea, demonstrating how Iago manipulates Othello or why Othello is such easy prey for Iago's schemes.

This chapter will propose a way to write about literature without being trivial or pretending to wide knowledge. Following are some approaches that may produce ideas for writing about literature. Obviously not all possibilities are treated, and the topics are not mutually exclusive. They are offered as ways of focusing or unifying discussion, not as ways of limiting it. Thus a paper centering on the themes of a story may well include analysis of the characters as they embody these themes. A paper on characterization may include discussion of imagery as it distinguishes characters.

MEANING: THEME

Although Archibald MacLeish in "Ars Poetica" says that "A poem should not mean/But be," most works of literature have meaning, and a paper may explain what or how they mean. At its simplest such a paper is explication, telling what words and sentences say and imply. A Shakespeare sonnet, for example, might warrant a line-by-line interpretation. Discussion of a ballad like "Edward" or "Lord Randal" might reveal the story that is implied by the poem but not directly told:

> "Lord Randal" does not tell a story, does not use the methods of narrative, but a story is obviously behind it. Lord Randal is poisoned and about to die. We are not told how or why or by whom he was poisoned, but when he tells his mother that he had his dinner with his true-love and that she gave him "eels boiled in broth," we make an obvious connection. We are not told anything about the mother's feelings for his true-love, but the mother's quick suspicion makes us sure that the two were not totally compatible. The poem progresses with a series of hints about the narrative it implies . . .

This explanation of one version of the ballad is only part of a longer discussion, but treatment of imagery and the emotional force of the poem are unified by this explanation. Sometimes a discussion of meaning requires examining the background of a story or poem. A paper on Stephen Crane's *Red Badge of Courage* might explain scenes of the novel by providing information about military tactics during the Civil War. Or it might illuminate the scene in which the hero's arm is amputated by describing surgical techniques of the period. An explanation of George Meredith's sonnet "Lucifer in Starlight" might include the information presupposed by the poem about the myth of Lucifer, the archangel who rebelled against God and was thrown out of heaven. On the basis of such background the paper could explain how Meredith's poem develops the myth.

A discussion of meaning in a literary work may expand to treat its themes. The theme is not just a general subject—charity, or integrity, or war. It is what the work says or suggests about that subject, that charity may be a disguise for hypocrisy or that war is humiliating to those who participate in it. A theme may be directly stated, with the story clearly devoted to illustrating it, or it may be implied. A work may have no obviously expressible theme, or it may have several. Usually it is complex enough so that a single sentence expresses it only inadequately. A student writer may wish to expand a theme, expound it, or apply it to society.

Reading, obviously, should not become a hunt for a message or a moral. A story or poem does not necessarily attempt any high-sounding observations about life. But almost any literary work tends to extend its implications, to stretch the reader's vision. Nathaniel Hawthorne's *Scarlet Letter* tells about the lives of three characters, but inevitably the dilemma of a Hester Prynne or an Arthur Dimmesdale suggests similar problems for all of us and stimulates us to think about issues beyond the covers of the book. The novel makes a number of comments on human behavior: that a guilty conscience can destroy a human being, that rigid and arbitrary codes of behavior can do more harm than good, that Puritanism was partly based on hypocrisy, that hate can destroy as surely as guilt. These are not necessarily *the* themes of the novel, but they represent the kind of thematic statement that might serve as the central idea for a paper on the novel. A student might use a statement like one of these as the main idea and then discuss various aspects of the novel—characterization, point of view, setting, or handling of dialogue—as they illustrate or clarify this concept.

A paper on themes in Andrew Marvell's poem "To His Coy Mistress" might begin thus:

> Marvell's "To His Coy Mistress" is most obviously a plea for seduction, like many other poems of its time, expanding the theme that, since life is short, one should live for the moment. The dramatic speaker develops logical arguments to convince the lady that her coyness is a crime, to urge "Now let us sport us while we may."
>
> In the first section of the poem he describes with amusing exaggeration the leisurely course their love might take if they had "world enough, and time." He would spend a hundred years praising her eyes, "Two hundred to adore each breast: But thirty thousand to the rest." In the second section . . .
>
> As the poem develops, however, broader implications of the theme emerge, and the poet seems to be exploiting the fairly conventional argument to make observations on time and its effects on life. The first section speculates about a kind of timeless state, extending both before and after the present—he would love "ten years before the Flood." In the second section he returns to reality, hearing "Time's wingèd chariot" and seeing "deserts of vast eternity" ahead. And then in the third section . . .

The paper could be filled out with details from the poem supporting further the observations about themes.

VOICE:
POINT OF VIEW AND TONE

Especially for creative writing, the voice—the author's tone and point of view (see chapter 2)—may stimulate a critical paper. In Browning's "My Last Duchess" the Duke of Ferrara is arranging the details of his next marriage, while analyzing the shortcomings of his most recent duchess—whom he presumably had murdered. A study focusing on the voice in the poem might move in any of several directions. It might imply a generalization like "Browning's 'My Last Duchess' develops dramatic irony because the reader interprets the words of the speaker in more than their literal sense." The paper could give examples from the poem illustrating how the duke unintentionally reveals his own pettiness. Or the paper might open with a statement like "Told from any other point of view Browning's 'My Last Duchess' would have turned out to be a quite different poem." The essay could weigh the effect if the poem had been told by an omniscient observer, by the emissary whom the duke is trying to overawe, by the prospective new duchess, or by one of the servants.

Analysis of fiction readily focuses on point of view and tone. Eudora Welty's short story "Petrified Man" begins as follows:

> "Reach in my purse and git me a cigarette without no powder in it if you kin, Mrs. Fletcher, honey," said Leota to her ten o'clock shampoo-and-set customer. "I don't like no perfumed cigarettes."

A critical paper on the Welty story might show how the immediate impression made by a character colors the reader's interest and sympathy. Similarly, in discussing Joseph Conrad's *Lord Jim,* a student might show how the novelist, by using a first-person narrator as a passing acquaintance, can report events and delineate characters with the objectivity of an omniscient observer, while preserving the intimacy of a personal account.

CHARACTERIZATION

Since literature is usually about people, a discussion of characters or of characterization provides one ready way to organize a critical paper. An author can reveal characters in several ways, depending on the medium. In a novel or story, characters can be described directly, sometimes with details about experience, sometimes with a view of how the character's mind works. In a script for a play or film, such direct description is limited to stage directions, but the dramatist has the advantage of an actor who becomes the character. A director can, in fact, establish broad outlines of characterization by the character's appearance—most obvious in conventions like the moustache of the melodrama villain or the white hat of the hero in the Western movie. Usually a character is revealed through words and actions. Browning, in "My Last Duchess," never describes the Duke of Ferrara, but the duke reveals his arrogance and pride and cruelty through his choice of words; he resents that the duchess ranked his "gift of a nine-hundred-years-old name / With anybody's gift," and he points out carefully that he chooses "never to stoop." In Flannery O'Connor's "Revelation," Mrs. Turpin's hypocrisy is apparent in most of her actions—her treatment of Mary Grace and of the black women who work on her farm. The author can also present characters by recording how others react to them or what they say about them. Readers interpret these reactions in the light of their understanding of all the characters. When Polonius reports that Hamlet is mad for love, readers weigh this pronouncement against what they already know about both Hamlet and Polonius—especially the evidence that Polonius is a pompous fool.

Most frequently such studies analyze characters as they appear in the literary work. A paper on James Thurber's "The Secret Life of Walter Mitty" might begin as follows, starting with three sentences expressing a thesis:

> Viewed from one direction, Walter Mitty, the main character of Thurber's short story, is only comic, an object for derision, an almost pathetic slave to self-deception. From another direction, he is a common man's hero, ascending into a world of heroism and aspiration, while combating the forces of suburban conventionality represented by his wife. The juxtaposition of the two views makes the story an example of genuine humor, in which an element of seriousness lies just beneath the surface of the fun.
>
> The comedy in the story grows partly from the incongruity between the henpecked Mitty in the car and the television hero of the Mitty fantasies. In real life Mitty doesn't need his gloves, but puts them on and expresses his individuality only by taking them off when his wife has left. He protests that he doesn't need overshoes, but he buys them. In his daydreams he is Dr. Mitty, the authority on streptothricosis, or Captain Mitty waiting to get that ammunition dump.
>
> But while we laugh at Mitty's attitudes, we are also on his side, pleased at his triumph over his wife . . .

The sketch could go on developing its second point with illustrations from the story and building further the analysis of Mitty's character.

This type of study presents some hazard because it may tempt the writer to confuse a literary character with a real person. Forgetting that the character exists only as a created fiction, the writer may wander into endless speculation about matters neither mentioned nor implied in the work and therefore not susceptible to supported presentation—whether Walter Mitty divorced his wife two years after the end of the story, what kind of prenatal influences might have hardened Lady Macbeth. A commonplace expression of praise in student papers—that "the characters are true to life"—is applicable only figuratively. Literature interprets life and illumines life, but literature is not life.

CONFLICT AND PLOT

In fiction and drama, the characters are usually involved in conflicts, and the sequence of these conflicts constitutes the plot. A play or a novel may include several conflicts, often of different sorts—between two characters or groups of characters, between a character and forces of the environment, or between ideas or motives or pressures within a character. *Hamlet* develops a series of complex conflicts, including those between Hamlet and the king, Hamlet and his mother, Hamlet and Laertes, Hamlet and the tradition of revenge, and within Hamlet's mind between his feeling of obligation to follow the ghost's command and his reluctance to act. Analysis of all the conflicts and interlinking plots in a novel like *War and Peace* would require an extended essay.

A paper on William Faulkner's story "Spotted Horses" might focus on the point of view, on the results of having the story narrated by the sewing-machine salesman who observes the events, or on the character of Flem Snopes, who is behind the sale of the wild horses. A writer might also focus on conflicts of the story, as did one student who began a criticism as follows:

> Faulkner's "Spotted Horses" describes a series of conflicts between characters—between Flem Snopes and Henry Armstid, between Flem and Mrs. Armstid, between the Armstids and the Texas man—but the central conflict is between Flem and the entire community, which he manages to cheat and dominate. Although the story is primarily humorous, its development of this central conflict makes an ironic comment on the power of unprincipled shrewdness to exploit ignorance and misdirected pride.
>
> Flem Snopes is clever and extremely skillful at anticipating the reactions of his fellow townsmen. He sponsors the sale of mustangs . . .

The analysis characterizes Flem and others and describes the way in which Flem wins his advantage, but it gains unity by keeping attention on what the writer selects as the central conflict.

FORM AND TECHNIQUE

Topics can grow from examination of the way a literary work is constructed, from the way the writer uses conventions. A paper may concentrate on the use of setting or atmosphere:

> In "The Fall of the House of Usher" Poe uses the setting, the bleak, decaying Usher mansion, almost as a character. The crumbling walls of the house seem as alive as the disintegrating psyche of Roderick Usher that they symbolize.

Or a discussion of a play may center on the way a dramatist handles the necessary exposition:

> In the first scene of *Hedda Gabler* Ibsen gives the audience all the information it needs about the past lives of the characters through Miss Tesman's visit and her conversation with her son and Berta, the maid.

The paper could develop through specific examples of the kinds of information that emerge in these opening conversations.

Poetry, especially, since it depends heavily on convention and techniques, may be discussed in terms of its prosody—its rhythm, meter, rhyme, and other sound patterns.

The sound patterns of a poem can become intriguing. A discussion of Browning's "My Last Duchess" might consider the way in which the poet handles iambic pentameter couplets, making such frequent use of run-on lines and rhythmic variations that the reader may be unaware that the poem is rhymed. A line-by-line analysis of versification in a Dickinson poem can be informative, marking accents and considering the effects of regularity of rhythm or variations from regularity. For any poem that follows a set pattern the writer may wish to show how the poem fits its form, to describe the rhyme scheme and meter, to show how the ideas are distributed in the various parts of the pattern.

A discussion of a play or film may center on the staging or direction. An essay on a television drama might expose its reliance on stock devices, the car chase through crowded city streets or the detective's pursuit of a criminal through the endless corridors of an empty warehouse. Or it might praise the skillful use of the camera to emphasize details of the plot. A paper on a Shakespeare play might consider the advantages and disadvantages of a bare stage, of modern or period costuming, of stylized or natural acting. A paper might focus on the effects of the conventionalized staging for Thornton Wilder's *Our Town*. It might notice the music that complements the action of the play or the kinds of sound effects—the rain in W. Somerset Maugham's *Rain* or the drums in Eugene O'Neill's *Emperor Jones*.

STYLE ANALYSIS

Often an interesting critical paper can go even further in examining details of the form and technique of a work, looking at particular characteristics of its style. For example, a paper might comment on the differences between the prose of Ernest Hemingway and William Faulkner by looking at details of their sentence structure. One approach would be to list the verbs in several paragraphs from each novelist and then to consider whether the choice of verbs affects the impression of the prose.

Another approach would be to collect data on the relative number of cumulative and periodic sentences used by a writer. Or information on how sentences begin can prove interesting; how many begin with the subject and how many have modifiers preceding the subject. Collecting data on how frequently the author uses passive sentences or sentences with expletives can often explain part of the effect of the prose.

Consideration of diction is often revealing. Does the author tend to use more borrowed words than native words? Are there many technical words? Is the diction formal or colloquial? Does the author use contractions? Such studies can be especially interesting in fiction that reveals character through diction. What are the characteristics of Huckleberry Finn's diction that help a reader understand his character?

Even detailed grammatical analysis can provide interesting insights into a writer's prose. Noting the adjectives or active verbs compared with the number of forms of *to be* can tell something about how a passage works. It can also tell why we like a certain prose style, as the student writer of the following discovered:

> Reading the prose of D. H. Lawrence, one is impressed by the vividness and power of his language. Each scene described takes on color, form, and life. This vitality results from a variety of poetic techniques—the use of the simile, the present participial form of verbs, and descriptive adjectives.

The student continues, recording specific instances of these stylistic characteristics of Lawrence's prose, drawing conclusions about his style.

A good stylistic analysis has the advantage of being objective and specific, and it often leads to further critical discussion.

FIGURATIVE LANGUAGE AND LITERATURE

Metaphors and other figures of speech can provide attractive approaches to literature, especially since figurative language can make both meaning and emotion more precise. A number of modern studies isolate images in Shakespeare's plays and reveal how the images reinforce themes—for example, how the characterization of Macbeth is sharpened by recurring metaphors picturing him in clothes too large for him. An analysis of a poem may explain metaphors and trace the connections between them. A paper on one seventeenth-century poem might begin:

> Robert Herrick's "Corinna's Going A-Maying" develops an ironic contrast that grows from the poet's use of metaphor. In a kind of cheerful blasphemy Herrick couches his plea for the seduction of the lady in terms of religious ceremony.
>
> In the first stanza the birds have said matins and "sung their thankful hymns," and the poem urges Corinna out to celebrate May Day because "'tis sin, / Nay, profanation, to keep in."

The paper could continue tracing the religious metaphors in the poem.

Related to figurative language is the use of devices like allegory and symbolism. Allegory, in fact, is sometimes called extended metaphor. In the most obvious type of allegory, abstractions like Knowledge or Good Fellowship become characters in the work. Allegories may be highly complex, as in Edmund Spenser's *Faery Queene*, with characters representing more than one idea and perhaps also various historical figures, with enough uncertainties that readers and critics still argue about their identifications.

We have already observed that language is symbolic, that words are symbols for thoughts. In literature, symbolism involves not only the use of words as symbols but also the use of objects, persons, actions, or phenomena in such ways that they have significance beyond themselves. In Sylvia Plath's *The Bell Jar*, the jar, which is used in science to create a vacuum, becomes symbolic of the confinement and suffocation that is one of the themes of the novel. In Hawthorne's *The Scarlet Letter*, the *A* that Hester Prynne wears on her breast becomes a central symbol with many levels of meaning. In one sense the letter serves as a sign, as a one-to-one equivalent standing almost literally for Hester's sin, adultery. As the novel progresses, however, the letter makes broader and more complex suggestions as a symbol of Hester's feelings of guilt and also of the newfound strength of character that grows from Hester's suffering and courage. When Hester removes the letter, the reader can sense her feelings of lightness and release. When she embroiders the letter, the reader recognizes her growing pride and self-reliance. Thus Hawthorne's symbol becomes more varied and subtle as the book progresses, but even so his use of the device is relatively simple compared with the symbolic complexity found in the novels of James Joyce and Virginia Woolf and in the poems of William Butler Yeats and Dylan Thomas.

In drama, symbols are often physical objects or actions on the stage or screen. In *Hedda Gabler*, Thea's hair becomes symbolic of the relationship between Hedda and Thea, not only of Hedda's envy of Thea but also of her feelings of guilt about her. We learn in the play how Hedda, whose hair is "not particularly abundant," has pulled Thea's hair and once threatened to burn it. In the play Hedda strokes Thea's hair in one central scene in which she is envious of Thea, and then strokes her hair again at the very end of the play as she goes off to her death. Films are especially suited to the use of visual symbols because the camera can readily emphasize or even exaggerate them. A paper discussing a film might focus on a central symbol:

> In Orson Welles's *Citizen Kane* the rosebud symbol contributes both to suspense in the plot and to the characterization of Kane.
> The picture of the rosebud is introduced. . . .

The paper could trace the uses of the symbol in the film, elaborating the meanings of the symbol as they suggest Kane's yearning for a contentment he cannot identify but can associate through the symbolic rosebud with the innocence of childhood.

COMPARISON AND CONTRAST

Any of the topics suggested above might be varied by using it in a comparison—between two characters or between two treatments of a similar theme, or between two methods of handling the exposition in a play. Comparisons generally work best if they are limited to particular aspects of pieces of writing. A paper comparing a novel or play with a film based on it, for example, is likely to succeed if it can focus on a central basis for the comparison. A paper might develop the following:

> The film version of Shakespeare's *Henry V* has advantages over the play on the legitimate stage because of the wide range of the camera.

The paper could cite instances—battle scenes, cavalry, cannon firing—in which the film gets effects impossible on a stage.

A student explaining a preference for *Death of a Salesman* over *The Glass Menagerie* focuses on technique, the manner of presentation, in making the following case:

> *The Glass Menagerie* and *Death of a Salesman* share a common theme, that of man's ability to trap himself in a world of dreams; yet they treat this subject in quite different manners. The narrator of *Menagerie* releases his thoughts abruptly, directly to the audience, and the feelings of the other characters are displayed in a stage legend. The characters in *Death of a Salesman* reveal their feelings to the audience through dialogue and actions, making this the more realistic and universal play.

Comparison may be useful in describing a character; a scholar, observing that Romeo has been called "an early study for Hamlet," remarks that the statement is "true enough to be misleading," and continues as follows:

> The many ideas that go to make up Hamlet will have seeded themselves from time to time in Shakespeare's imagination, sprouting a little, their full fruition delayed till the dominant idea ripened. We can find traits of Hamlet in Romeo, in Richard II, in Jaques, in less likely habitations. But Romeo is not a younger Hamlet in love, though Hamlet in love may seem a disillusioned Romeo. The very likeness, moreover, is largely superficial,

is a common likeness to many young men, who take life desperately seriously, some with reason, some without. The study of him is not plain sailing. If Hamlet's melancholy is of the soul, Romeo's was something of a pose; and there is Shakespeare's own present convention to account for, of word-spinning and thought-spinning, in which he cast much of the play, through which he broke more and more while he wrote it; there are, besides, the abundant remains of Brooke's Romeus.

Harley Granville-Barker, *Prefaces to Shakespeare*

This passage clarifies the writer's interpretation of Romeo by contrasting him with Hamlet.

Possible topics are almost infinite. Especially if the writer has some background in literature or can undertake some study of literary questions, dozens of other ways of discussing literature become available. A paper may relate a work to a literary type or genre—*Hamlet* or Arthur Miller's *Death of a Salesman* as tragedies, Joseph Heller's *Catch-22* as satire. A paper may consider relations between a work and the society or culture it reflects—the depression and John Steinbeck's *Grapes of Wrath,* James Baldwin's *Go Tell It on the Mountain* or Mark Twain's *Huckleberry Finn* as discussions of poverty and segregation in the United States, Edith Wharton's *House of Mirth* as an expression of feminist concerns. A paper may consider various ways in which a work is part of literary history—for example, how Alexander Pope's *Rape of the Lock* relates to eighteenth-century ideas of the epic, how Milton's "Lycidas" expresses the pastoral tradition, how F. Scott Fitzgerald's *This Side of Paradise* exemplifies the apprenticeship novel. For papers of this sort, however, as well as for those based exclusively on the work itself, the writer needs to focus attention on a central idea and then support this idea and other generalizations with specific details and quotations from the text.

A PERSONAL RESPONSE TO LITERATURE

The devices above all focus on literature as a work of art and suggest discussion of literature within its conventions of character, plot, setting, and language. There is, however, another kind of paper about literature that you may be assigned. This is the personal-response paper. Whenever we read, we react on the basis of our experience and knowledge. We may read Kurt Vonnegut's *Slaughterhouse-Five* and understand our feelings about the absurdity of war more clearly. We may read Kate Chopin's *The Awakening* and recognize the cause of many unhappy marriages. One student said that when she read Salinger's *Catcher in the Rye* at age fifteen, she laughed all the way through it; when she read it again at age sixteen, she cried. The story had not changed, but the student had; her experiences had changed and she reacted differently.

Writing a personal-response paper means reading a work and then paralleling it to your own feelings or beliefs or experiences. In such a paper, you are no longer critically objective; you become involved in the story. In a sense, you recreate the work and write about its meaning to your life. Such a paper can be revealing and rewarding, as one student found out when asked to write a response to Alice Walker's *The Color Purple*. She became angry, embarrassed, and finally compelled by the story, which resembled her own youth. She wrote a personal response, directing it to Alice Walker; an excerpt follows:

> Sofie became Mama Liz, big boned, dark complexioned, mammoth breasted, and as stubborn as the day was long, but oh what a heart. She was full of compassion and empathy for all who encountered her. It's the wonderful memories like those that made the reading of your book painful. Celie and Sofie's language was so familiar to me that in spite of the pain, I settled into the good memories the dialogues conjured.

The paper continues to note these parallels, the "good memories" evoked by her reading. The focus is on the student, what the work meant to her.

RESEARCH FOR WRITING ON LITERATURE

Much serious writing, except what grows from personal experience—and even some of that—requires something resembling research, and writing about literature is no exception. Some study, although intended to lead eventually to enlarged critical understanding, is occupied almost exclusively with research. *Moby Dick* becomes more exciting if the reader knows something about whales, and obviously, Herman Melville knew things about whales that he would not have learned in any forecastle or in a whale boat. Even for a study of the White Whale as symbol, a critic would want to canvass what Melville knew about whales and where he got his information. Melville was extremely productive in the decade before 1852 but published little during the next forty years. A writer interested only in the literary quality of Melville's work will still want to know why the creative artist produced so erratically. Was he ill? Was he too busy earning a living? Was he depressed by the reception of his books? Had he run out of ideas? Some reading in Melville's biography, in his letters, and in the reviews of the day might provide answers. Even if a writer wants to say only that Melville's poetry has been ignored at the expense of his prose, the wise writer will do well to check to see whether this is one of the clichés in Melville criticism or whether it is something approaching a discovery.

A student may wish to clarify the subject matter of a work, turning to literary history or to conventional reference works to do so. Even questions like the influence of Old Norse on the writings of Emerson permit somewhat objective investigation. What references are there in Emerson's published works, in his letters and journals, in recorded conversations with friends? Which languages could he read? What translations were available to him? Which books did Emerson have in his library, and what volumes did he borrow? Whom did he meet when he went to England? Research may also reveal the influence or the reputation of a work. How many copies of *Wuthering Heights* have been printed? Into what languages has it been translated? How was the book reviewed on its appearance? What have critics had to say about it more recently? Such questions can be approached as research projects, and even when introduced into a paper having critical purposes they permit focusing on an appropriately limited topic.

Thus research in literature is much like research in other areas. The materials differ with the subject, but approaches and methods are similar, whether the subject is a political party or a poem. The principles, to be discussed in chapter 16, still apply.

MECHANICS FOR WRITING ABOUT LITERATURE

When referring to authors, usually full names are given for a first reference, and last names are used subsequently. Emily Dickinson becomes Dickinson after the first use, not Emily or Ms. Dickinson; Shakespeare does not become William or Will. In references to writers, sexist language should be avoided; Anne Sexton is a poet, not a poetess.

Tense forms and conventions need special attention in writing about literature.

Present forms are used in describing the content of literature or film:

In the novel, Fitzgerald *describes* suburban life in the 1920s.

"John Brown's Body" *is* an attempt to write an American epic.

In the first act, Macbeth *becomes* thane of Cawdor.

When you write about a work of literature, you are assuming that it exists and that what the characters do or think occurs in the present or continues to occur. You may have read it in the past, but you are talking about the work as it exists, not about your reading of it. For events in the work, you use present forms. Macbeth murders, not murdered, Duncan, because you are thinking of the play, not of your reading of the play.

On the other hand, you do look back at events connected with the creation of the work or its publication or performance. For such events, you use past forms:

Milton's *Paradise Lost* was published in 1667.

Shakespeare wrote *Macbeth* in the early seventeenth century.

Notice the variety of verb forms that may be required in one paper to keep the time and point of view consistent.

1. Shakespeare *was* thirty-eight years old when the first edition of *Hamlet* appeared in London.
2. He *had earned* a reputation as one of the leading dramatists of his day.
3. *Hamlet has been discussed* and *criticized* more than any of the other plays.
4. It *is* a favorite on the modern stage.
5. In the play, Hamlet *is faced* with a decision.
6. Ironically the only course consistent with Hamlet's character and satisfactory to the audience *leads* to disaster.

For standard handling of titles of works, see chapter 18. For conventions with quoted material, see chapter 17.

FOR STUDY AND WRITING

A. Read the poem below several times and make notes in response to the numbered questions.

> I'm nobody! Who are you?
> Are you nobody, too?
> Then there's a pair of us—don't tell!
> They'd banish us, you know.
> How dreary to be somebody!
> How public, like a frog
> To tell your name the livelong day
> To an admiring bog!
>
> Emily Dickinson

1. Who seems to be speaking in the poem?
2. To whom does the poem seem to be speaking?
3. What is the poem about?

4. Did you like anything in the poem, or anything about it?
5. What do the words "how public" tell about the poet or the poem?
6. What is the effect of the last two words in the poem?

Based on your notes, write a paragraph in which you bring together the most important things you have to say about the poem.

B. In this selection from *Macbeth*, Lady Macbeth is berating her husband because, having proposed to murder the king, he now prefers not to. Based on this short bit of dialogue, write a brief character sketch of Lady Macbeth.

> LADY MACBETH
> Was the hope drunk
> Wherein you dress'd yourself? and hath it slept since?
> And wakes it now, to look so green and pale
> At what it did so freely? From this time
> Such I account thy love. Art thou afeard
> To be the same in thine own act and valour
> As thou art in desire? Wouldst thou have that
> Which thou esteem'st the ornament of life,
> And live a coward in thine own esteem,
> Letting "I dare not" wait upon "I would,"
> Like the poor cat i' the adage?
>
> MACBETH
> Prithee, peace:
> I dare do all that may become a man;
> Who dares do more is none.
>
> LADY MACBETH
> What beast was't, then,
> That made you break this enterprise to me?
> When you durst do it, then you were a man;
> And, to be more than what you were, you would
> Be so much more the man.

C. Read the opening paragraph of John Steinbeck's "The Chrysanthemums" and analyze the language used to describe the setting—the Salinas Valley of central California. From the description, what kind of world is Steinbeck creating and what might be the central themes or concerns of the story?

> The high grey-flannel fog of winter closed off the Salinas Valley from the sky and from all the rest of the world. On every side it sat like a lid on the mountains and made of the great valley a closed pot. On the broad, level land floor the gang plows bit deep and left the black earth shining like metal where the shares had cut. On the foothill ranches across the Salinas River, the yellow stubble fields seemed to be bathed in pale cold sunshine, but there was no sunshine in the valley now in December. The thick willow scrub along the river flamed with sharp and positive yellow leaves.

D. The novel *The Great Gatsby* is narrated through the point of view of one character, Nick Carroway. We meet Nick on the first page of the novel. From what he says here, can you tell what effect his point of view will have on the story?

> In my younger and more vulnerable years my father gave me some advice that I've been turning over in my mind ever since.
> "Whenever you feel like criticizing anyone," he told me, "just remember that all the people in this world haven't had the advantages that you've had."
> He didn't say any more, but we've always been unusually communicative in a reserved way, and I understood that he meant a great deal more than that. In consequence, I'm inclined to reserve all judgments, a habit that has opened up many curious natures to me and also made me the victim of not a few veteran bores.

E. Read a recent novel, preferably one so recent that you have seen no reviews of it. Check back through the present chapter, refreshing your memory about the various sorts of literary studies. Select five approaches that would be suitable for the novel you have read, and write a thesis sentence for each. Then select one of these approaches and write a brief critique of five hundred to a thousand words.

F. Read a book that has become the basis of a film, a TV series, or something using a medium other than print. Compare the two in one specific way. Here are some questions you might want to ask yourself: Did one version produce effects the other did not, and why? Did one do more justice to the main idea than did the other? Did one make use of stereotypes more than did the other? Which presented the more interesting characters? Did you get something by experiencing two versions that you might not have had from either alone?

G. Write a personal response to a book that had a special significance in your life. This can be a book from childhood, adolescence, or even later, but try to recall what it was that touched or moved you when you were reading, and how this affected your life.

16

The Investigative Paper

> *Nothing's so hard but search will find it out.*
> ROBERT HERRICK
>
> *Humane scholarship . . . moves and must move within two worlds at once—the world of scientific method and the world, in whatever degree, of creative art.*
> JOHN LIVINGSTON LOWES

The modern world, perhaps particularly the modern American world, relies upon objective information. Theoretically nothing can be known objectively; most information must filter through human brains, and we are notoriously inexact. But a complex society requires reliable information, and if information cannot be totally reliable, we need to make it as reliable as we can. Fortunately, with the proper tools and techniques, we have learned to observe and report with a high degree of objectivity. Still, the use of language and of the mind in connection with investigative study warrants special attention.

Research writing, however, is not basically different from the types of writing we have been discussing. The process is the same—continuing prewriting, writing, and revising. And you may have already done research for a paper—read articles in a magazine before writing about solar energy or talked to a relative in an advertising agency before writing about subliminal messages in commercials. The first step, of course, is to settle on a subject.

CHOOSING AND LIMITING A SUBJECT

Sometimes an instructor assigns a specific research topic, and you need only begin. But often an instructor provides a general subject that you must limit into a workable project. And sometimes no subject is assigned, and you must discover a general subject and limit it. However a research paper is assigned, your topic should have these four qualifications: (1) It should be within the range of your capabilities; (2) it should be suitable for objective treatment; (3) it should not require material unavailable in your library or other sources; and (4) it should be restricted enough to permit detailed work. A study of an American Indian language would work only if you had adequate linguistic knowledge. "Why I believe in the Republican Party" would work only if it focused on collecting objective evidence, but it would still be very broad. "President Reagan's Fiscal Policies from 1980 through 1986" would be more workable. Most college libraries have more than enough material for most subjects, but if you have limited resources, you should choose a topic that is suited to them. In particular, you should narrow your topic enough so that you can investigate it in detail.

As we discussed in chapter 1, you can limit a subject by analysis in many ways—in time and space, by selecting results or causes, by classifying trends, streams of influence, processes, groups, or types. You can also restrict your subject and focus your thinking by establishing a purpose and tentative thesis for the paper and identifying the audience you want to address (see chapters 1 and 2). For example, one student, wanting to write about the Indians of the American West, realized that this topic was too broad. He tried limiting it in several ways:

General topic: Indians of the American West.

Limited by time/space: The survival of the Indians of the Great Basin after the Civil War.

Limited by causes: An analysis of the clash between the American settlers of the westward movement and the Indians of the Great Basin.

Limited by purpose: The clash of cultures that existed in the Great Basin between 1860 and 1900 eventually destroyed the native Americans of the area and paved the way for the westward movement.

> *Limited by thesis:* Although the westward movement was responsible for significant economic growth in America, the price paid by the native Americans of the Great Basin was devastating.

Another student, an education major, chose a different general topic and considered various ways of limiting it:

> *General topic:* Early childhood education.
>
> *Limited by time/space:* Recent improvements in child care facilities for preschool children, aged three to five.
>
> *Limited by type:* Discussion of the major types of childcare facilities available today for preschool children.
>
> *Limited by purpose:* An argument that preschools which uphold four specific sets of criteria are beneficial to the child.
>
> *Limited by thesis:* Preschool, a necessity for most couples today, can be a rewarding experience for the child if the school meets these four criteria.

Further restriction of a topic may continue even into the final draft of a paper. You may not realize the breadth of a subject until you compile a working bibliography and start reading. And you may, as you write, be able to focus your ideas more sharply. But without preliminary restriction of a subject you cannot even start intelligently.

USING SOURCES

For most research papers you will need to look at materials gathered by others, in libraries, laboratories, public offices, or other depositories. You might, for example, project a paper on some aspect of military training. You could draw from your own experience, recalling incidents from a high school ROTC course, from military service, or from conversations with friends. You might question the value of military training in a college program and get a start by interviewing military officers and ROTC instructors at your college.

THE INTERVIEW

The interview is often overlooked in doing research. But most authorities are glad to discuss their field of interest with others, if the interviewer appears sincere and behaves professionally. If you are at a college or university, you are surrounded by authorities. Professionals outside a campus are also excellent resources and can be helpful at all stages of the research process. The student writing about Great Basin Indians, for instance, bogged down in the middle of his project and was directed to an anthropology professor; the student writing about preschool education interviewed the director of a large preschool and a first-grade teacher after completing most of her reading. Another student, interested in dentistry, was unsure how to begin. During an interview with a local dentist, she learned about forensic dentistry—the use of dental charts and impressions to establish identities in courts of law.

  In arranging for an interview, professional courtesy is required. Phone ahead, introduce yourself and your project, ask for an appointment, and appear promptly, prepared with a series of specific questions. Take notes on the interview and be sure to list it on the Works Cited page. If you wish to record the interview, ask permission. After the interview, a follow-up letter of thanks is appropriate.

THE LIBRARY: THE CARD CATALOG

A library can supplement experience, and the key to using it is the card catalog, which tells you what books the library has and how any book is classified and how you can find it. Formerly most libraries arranged books according to the Dewey Decimal System; most college libraries have now replaced this with the Library of Congress System. To use the library you need not know the system; you need only know the alphabet.

  The card catalog is a file of cards, at least two for each book or set of books and often also for files of periodicals, pamphlets, microcards or microfilms, and other items. The cards are arranged alphabetically by author, title, and subject. The following illustrates an author card:

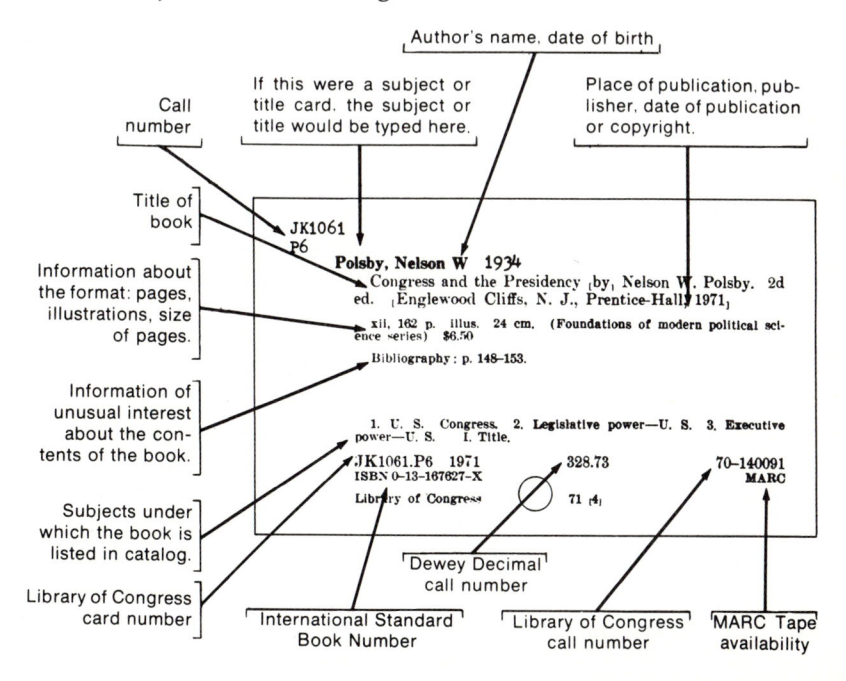

If you want to locate the book described on this card and know the name of the author, you look in the catalog in the alphabetical spot for Polsby. Then you use the call number to lead you to the proper shelf for the book, if the library operates on an open-shelf plan. Or you can copy the call number and hand it to an attendant, if the library uses a messenger system. If you know the title but not the author, you can find the title card, alphabetized under *Congress,* and again get the call number. If you know only that you are interested generally in legislative power, you can look under *Legislative power—U.S.* as a subject to find Polsby's book as well as others. When you are unsure about how a subject might be listed, consult the *Library of Congress Subject Heading.* There you will find a complete list of all subject headings used by the Library of Congress System and cross-references to related topics.

COMPUTER SEARCHES

Usually the *Library of Congress Subject Heading* and the card catalog are reliable ways to start research. But today many libraries have facilities for university-wide computer searches, which—like the card catalog—index books in the main and branch libraries. Other libraries can provide computerized periodical searches. Some of these are specialized by discipline, such as *Business Index;* some are more general—for example, *InfoTrac Database*—and index popular magazines and periodicals by subject, as does *Reader's Guide* which is discussed below.

With such indexes, students, working at terminals, can locate a subject heading, such as *Soldiers—Equipment and Supplies,* and access periodical information on their topic. The following is a sample of a print-out summarizing material in one article:

SOLDIERS
—EQUIPMENT AND SUPPLIES

Combat couture under fire; soldiers make heavy going of their new look in fatigues. (new battle dress uniform) il Time.v123-Jan 9 '84 p24(1) 21C0135

Additionally, these computers will print-out lists of all articles found, by subject. If your library offers computer searches, you should learn to use them, for they will simplify your work. Since, however, computers usually index only current periodicals, you may often need to consult the more traditional printed indexes.

PERIODICAL AND NEWSPAPER INDEXES

The individual pieces in newspapers, magazines, anthologies, and other collections cannot usually be located through the card catalog. The names of books and periodicals will appear there, but the items within them must mostly be sought through other means, especially through periodical indexes. The more popular are "cumulated"; that is, they are re-edited and republished to keep them up to date. For instance, *The Readers' Guide to Periodical Literature,* which indexes relatively popular magazines, appears every month. Monthly issues are cumulated every three months and then combined into an annual issue. Similarly there are two-year, three-year, and five-year cumulations, by which time the book has become so large that the cumulation begins all over again. In this way, the user need not thumb through the numbers for each month. No index can include any large portion of the periodicals available. You should check the list of titles treated in each index, which will usually appear in the front matter.

To conserve space, most indexes—both computerized and printed—are skeletonized. Since styles vary from index to index, the entry should be expanded when the note is taken, using the table of abbreviations supplied. An entry in the *Reader's Guide* looks like this:

```
It's time to admit our cars are too big. B.
    Yates. il Car & Dr 20:9 F '75
```

Each volume of the *Guide* has two tables in the front, one telling how to expand titles, the other giving a list of abbreviations. Using these tables, you might take this reference as follows:

> Yates, B. "It's Time to Admit Our Cars Are Too Big." *Car and Driver* 20 (Feb. 1975): 9.

Here you have most of the information expanded; when you write you can adapt it to any style you are using. This article, like the one in the computer print-out, is illustrated, as indicated by the symbol *il*, but you need not record this fact unless you expect to use it. The author's name has probably been abridged, too; the author might be Barbara Yates, or Burton F. Yates. Details like these can be checked when you use the article.

The only surviving general periodical index is *Reader's Guide to Periodical Literature* 1900–. It succeeds *Poole's Index to Periodical Literature,* 1802–1907, and should never be ignored, since important articles, even on technical subjects, may appear in popular journals. Such subjects, too, may appear in newspapers, some of which are also indexed—for example, the *Wall Street Journal* (since 1957), *The New York Times* (since 1913), and the London *Times* (since 1907). These popular sources, however, usually should be supplemented with specialized indexes.

SPECIALIZED INDEXES

All fields have such specialized indexes; usually a list in the front of each volume identifies the journals indexed. For some subjects, especially in the sciences, these indexes may be called abstracts—for example, *Chemical Ab-*

stracts, 1907—or they may appear as a special issue of a periodical. Following are some of the most useful specialized indexes, not all of them cumulated:

Annual Bibliography of the Modern Humanities Research Association, 1920-

Applied Science and Technology Index, 1958-, formerly *Industrial Arts Index*, 1913-58

Art Index, 1929-

Biological and Agricultural Index, 1964-, formerly *Agricultural Index*, 1916-64

Book Review Digest, 1905-

Business Periodicals Index, 1958-

Education Index, 1929-

Engineering Index, 1884-

Essay and General Literature Index, 1900-

Humanities Index, 1974-, formerly *Social Sciences and Humanities Index*, 1965-73, and *International Index*, 1907-65

Public Affairs Information Service, 1915-

Social Sciences Index, 1974-

For additional indexes see Eugene P. Sheehy, *Guide to Reference Books*, 9th edition, 1976.

REFERENCE BOOKS

Books that tell you something about almost anything have many uses. They may give you quick answers to simple questions or may give you a fast start on more complex questions and even provide an elementary bibliography. But they are usually superficial and readily out of date. They should never be taken as the final word.

Such books are so numerous and are proliferating so rapidly that only a few can be mentioned here. Reference to Sheehy, mentioned above, can help. The following are some of the major categories:

General Encyclopedias

Academic American Encyclopedia, 1984, 21 vols.

Collier's Encyclopedia, 1976, 24 vols.

Encyclopedia Americana, international ed., 1977, 30 vols.

Encyclopaedia Brittanica, 15th ed., 1979, 30 vols.

Specialized Encyclopedias and Handbooks

Almost all fields have encyclopedias—religion, philosophy, computer processing, architecture, and astronomy, to name a few. The following are a few examples:

>   *Encyclopedia of Military History*, rev. ed., 1977, 15 vols.
>   *New Catholic Encyclopedia*, 1967.
>   *McGraw Hill Encyclopedia of Science and Technology*, 1977, 15 vols.
>   *The New Grove Dictionary of Music and Musicians*, 1980, 20 vols.

Often more useful are handbooks, many of them annual, like *Handbook of Chemistry and Physics*, 1913–. They are numerous, but some of the most handy are the Oxford companion series: *Oxford Companion to American History*, 1966, . . . *to American Literature*, 1983, . . . *to Classical Literature*, 1966, . . . *to English Literature*, 1985, . . . *to the Theatre*, 1983.

Dictionaries of quotations have wide use. The following are examples:

>   *Dictionary of Quotations*, ed. Bergen Evans, 1968.
>   *Familiar Quotations*, ed. John Bartlett, 15th ed., 1981.
>   *The Oxford Dictionary of Quotations*, 3d ed., 1979.

Atlases, including the following, are storehouses of more than geographical information.

>   *Commercial Atlas and Market Guide*, Rand McNally, 1981.
>   *The International Atlas*, Rand McNally, 1974.
>   *National Geographic Atlas of the World*, 5th ed., 1986.
>   *The National Atlas of the United States*, 1970.

In addition to specialized yearbooks like *Yearbook of the United Nations*, 1947, generalized yearbooks can provide handy factual information.

>   *Facts on File*, 1940–.
>   *Guinness Book of World Records*, 1980.
>   *The New York Times Encyclopedic Almanac*, 1967–.
>   *Statesman's Yearbook*, 1864–.
>   *Statistical Abstract of the United States*, 1868–.
>   *The World Almanac and Book of Facts*, 1968–.

Collections of brief biographies include the following:

American Men of Science, 1979.

Current Biography, 1940–.

Dictionary of American Biography (called *DAB*), 1927–80, 16 vols. and index.

Dictionary of National Biography (called *DNB*), 1882–1953, 22 vols. British biographies.

International Who's Who, 1935–.

The National Cyclopedia of American Biography, 1898–.

Twentieth Century Authors, 1942–.

Webster's Biographical Dictionary, 1976.

Who's Who in America, 1899–.

BULLETINS AND PAMPHLETS

Bulletins, pamphlets, and other irregular issues vary, and libraries handle them variously. The Bureau of American Ethnology issues *Bulletins*, which may run to hundreds of pages of original research not elsewhere available. In a university having an active anthropology department, such bulletins may be cataloged like books. In city libraries they are likely not to be. On the other hand, a brochure describing the beauties of a lake resort may be almost worthless. Such fugitive pieces may be filed under a local topic, but not cataloged. Some specialized indexes, such as the *Biological and Agricultural Index* mentioned above, include bulletins and pamphlets. The voluminous publications of the federal government are variously indexed through a series commonly known by its binder's title, United States *Document Catalogue*. A researcher can legitimately ask the document librarian for help with it.

THE WORKING BIBLIOGRAPHY

Early in any investigation, you need to prepare a trial or working bibliography. This supplies information useful in restricting a subject and records data that will be needed later for citations and a list of works cited.

The working bibliography includes all the books, articles, pamphlets, and other documents that you can locate through the conventional sources—library catalogs, periodical indexes, checklists, and bibliographies printed in standard reference tools. As you work with your subject, you will add items to this bibliography—for example, works cited in books in which you are doing preliminary reading.

Let us assume that you have decided to write about building roads. You begin generally, looking up *roads, transportation,* and *road building* in several encyclopedias. You find that modern methods of building roads have developed in the last two centuries. You then look up social histories, like Traill's *Social England,* and books on transportation. In some of these you find extensive bibliographies and bibliographical footnotes, and you make cards for these. On one of them you note that when Josiah Wedgwood's dishes became popular in Europe, Wedgwood built private roads, because the public roads were so bad he had to pack his dishes on muleback, and when packs slipped off mules, that was the end of the dishes. You become interested and try to find out about Wedgwood and his ware. In the *Dictionary of National Biography* you find biographies of Wedgwood and bibliographical suggestions for further investigation. You locate an elaborate series of British local histories, called the *Victoria County Histories,* and surmise that the county history for Wedgwood's shire will tell you something about the roads of the area and probably refer to more detailed studies that will include Wedgwood's roads. By now you are well on your way to seeing how ornamental fine china contributed to the revolution in road building. From now on you have only to use reference works intelligently and faithfully.

Source Cards

As soon as you begin locating items that may be pertinent to your subject, you should start compiling source cards. You should work systematically, to avoid both errors and the need to repeat your work. The following are generally accepted procedures:

> Record items on uniform small cards or slips of paper; three-by-five-inch cards are customary.
>
> Record only one item on each card, so that the cards can be readily rearranged and irrelevant works can be removed from the list.
>
> Keep cards for irrelevant items, noting on them that they have been checked; this precaution will prevent wasting time checking the same item more than once.
>
> Record the information in accordance with the style described below.

A library card and the source card that results from it look like this:

```
┌─────────────────────────────────────────────────────────────┐
│  PE                                                         │
│  1133                                                       │
│  K85    Kurath, Hans, 1891—                                 │
│  1964         A phonology and prosody of modern English. Ann Arbor, │
│           University of Michigan Press [1964]               │
│               158 p. 24 cm.                                 │
│                                                             │
│                                                             │
│           1. English language–Phonology.   2. English language–Versification. │
│         I. Title.                                           │
│                                               hm 10/69      │
│       PE1133.K85   1964                                64–13467 │
│                                  ◯       421.5              │
│       Library of Congress                   [3]             │
└─────────────────────────────────────────────────────────────┘
```

┌───┐
│ *Kurath, Hans. A Phonology*   │
│ *and Prosody of Modern England.*   │
│ *Ann Arbor, MI: Univ. of*   │
│ *Michigan Press, 1964.*   │
│   │
│ *A careful study of Am.*   │
│ *pronunciation and dialects*   │
│ *Some history — mostly*   PE   │
│ *Atlantic seaboard.*   1133   │
│   K85   │
│   1964   │
└───┘

    The name of the author is reversed, as it was on the catalog card, so that the card can be filed for ready reference. The whole card should be checked, but especially the author's name. Printing it in block capitals may save misreading. If you mistake *Kurath* for *Kuralt* or *Kaplan,* you may cause yourself endless trouble. The title is underlined to avoid confusing it with anything else, and all the details of publication are taken so as to identify the particular edition. For your convenience, you should include the call number in case you need to check the item later and some indication of how the book relates to your topic. This may have to be added after you consult the book itself.

    A source card for a periodical or newspaper article resembles that for a book. The following is an example of an entry in *Reader's Guide to Periodical Literature* and a card based on it.

It's time to admit our cars are too big. B.
Yates. il Car & Dr 20:9 F '75

> Yates, B. "It's Time to Admit
> Our Cars are Too Big." Car
> and Driver 20 (Feb. 1975):9
>
> Illustrated — little fact

The last name of the author has been put first for filing. This index does not include first names of authors, but in a research paper the author's full name should be given as it appears on the work itself. When you examine the article, check it against the card, and add the full name or any other necessary information. The title of the article is enclosed in quotation marks and the name of the periodical underlined. If the title is abbreviated in the index, expand it on the card. Using the style on the source card that is to be used later on the Works Cited page will save time.

TAKING AND PRESERVING NOTES

Taking notes can be a bother. But needing a piece of information or a reference and finding you forgot to make a note—or that you have no notion where you put it, or that the note is too sketchy to be any good—can be a bigger bother. A writer trying to be objective and accurate needs notes, a system for taking them, and determination to make the system work.

The wrong way to take notes is to write them consecutively in a notebook. There they become a jumble, following the order of the book from which they were taken—usually not the order needed. There they are unidentified. They cannot be classified, particularly if written on both sides of note paper. As a result, the writer knows only that the notes are somewhere and has to hunt for them. Most research workers find that cards or uniform slips provide the most practical means of taking and preserving notes; they permit the most flexible system, and in the end are the most economical. Begin by getting cards or slips; usually three-by-five source cards prove to be too small. Four-by-six note cards will serve many purposes, but some writers prefer half-sheets of paper. If slips are used, the paper should be heavy enough to be handled easily, and slips should be cut uniformly so that they can be filed. Basic rules for taking notes are:

1. *Adopt a system and follow it.* You must doggedly resist the temptation just "to jot this one down in my notebook" or "to remember this until I get some note cards."
2. *Copy notes directly onto cards.* Copying from a notebook onto cards wastes time and encourages error.
3. *Identify the source of the information, including the page number, on the card.* Any note must be precisely identified. If you are using a working bibliography, you can abbreviate the reference to the author's last name, a short title or a number to identify the source, and a page reference. If a quotation runs over to a second page, the location of the page break should be indicated.
4. *Enclose verbatim quotations within quotation marks.* Knowing when to quote verbatim and when to summarize is never easy. In general you may want word-for-word accounts for material very well phrased; material central to the discussion; and controversial matter, especially if you expect to oppose it. Any direct quotation—even a two- or three-word phrase—must be enclosed in quotation marks on the card to avoid plagiarism later. If the quotation is not marked on the card, you may unintentionally write it into your paper as your own work.
5. *Write only one piece of information on a card.* If a card contains only a single piece of information, it can be classified by subject. This will help later in organizing the paper.
6. *Classify notes with key words on the nature or use of the material taken.* When the note is complete, it should be filed according to subject. For this purpose, you should adopt a number of words under which material can be filed. These words may be headings of your outline.
7. *Avoid taking unnecessary notes.* Some material important for a general understanding of the subject will soon become so familiar that you will not need to collect further notes on it. It is well to read generally on a subject before starting to take notes and to skim through a book before taking notes on it.
8. *If in doubt, take the note.* Taking the right evidence, just enough material and no more, is hardly possible. It is better to record too much rather than too little.
9. *Take concrete, specific, exact material.* Occasionally generalities are useful, but usually the more specific the notes, the better. Facts, figures, dates, statistics, verbatim quotations, or factual digests are useful. Researchers often collect too much general material and not enough concrete, objective material.

10. *On the whole, avoid long quotations.* When long quotations are necessary, a reproduction may save time and errors. Libraries provide machines for inexpensive copying.
11. *Be accurate and neat.* Type or write legibly; take special pains with titles, figures, the spelling of names, or with any material in which blunders cannot be caught by context.
12. *Double-check every note card.* If the final paper contains misquotations, misspellings, or mispunctuation in copied material, the reader may distrust the whole paper.

The following card is an example of a note for a paper on the importance of clothing and supplies in the Revolutionary War. Clothing and supplies, of course, are subjects of all the cards and need not be entered on any of them. One important subtopic, however, is the importance of uniforms. Thus *uniforms* becomes the first key word to identify the note. *American* subdivides the cards concerning uniforms, and *from France* further identifies this note.

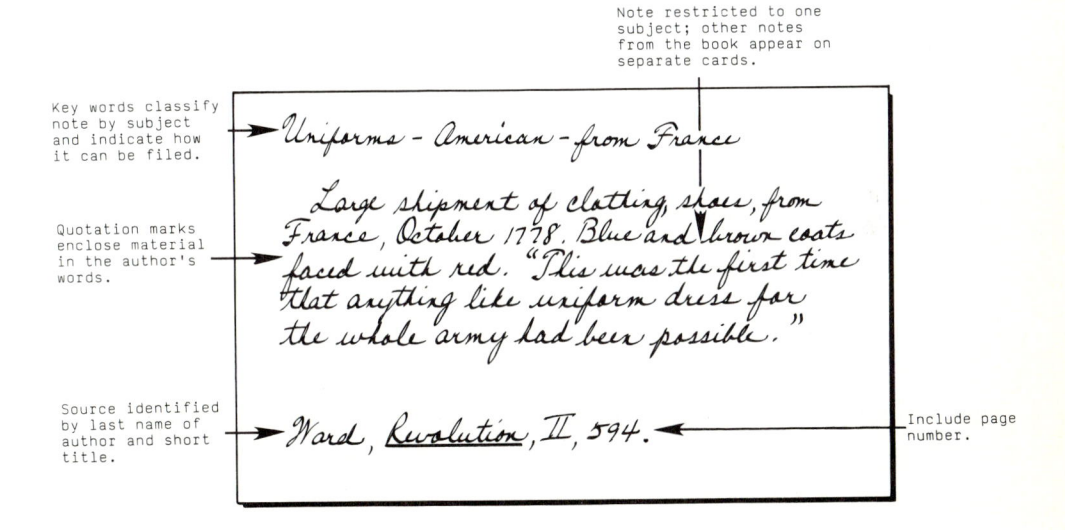

```
Note restricted to one
subject; other notes
from the book appear on
separate cards.

Key words classify
note by subject                Uniforms — American — from France
and indicate how
it can be filed.
                               Large shipment of clothing, shoes, from
Quotation marks                France, October 1778. Blue and brown coats
enclose material               faced with red. "This was the first time
in the author's                that anything like uniform dress for
words.                         the whole army had been possible."

Source identified
by last name of                Ward, Revolution, II, 594.               Include page
author and short                                                         number.
title.
```

Direct Quotation, Paraphrase, and Summary in Notes

Taking notes means deciding what to record and how to phrase it. Should you copy a passage verbatim, paraphrase it, summarize it, or skip it? Copying a passage verbatim is taking a direct quote, using the author's own words and phrases. With the availability of copying machines in most libraries, it is sometimes efficient to include an entire page, attaching it to your note card for filing. If material is omitted from a direct quotation, use an ellipsis (. . .); if an editorial comment is needed for clarity, enclose it in square brackets ([ ]). A paraphrase expresses the idea of a passage in your own words and style and often incorporates direct quotes identified by quotation marks. A summary is a much shorter version of the original, in which you focus on the central idea.

For a paper on Mark twain's humor, consider the note cards a writer might make on the following passage from *Roughing It*.

> He [Hyde] said it was pretty well known that for some years he had been farming (or ranching, as the more customary term is) in Washoe District, and making a successful thing of it, and furthermore it was known that his ranch was situated just in the edge of the valley, and that Tom Morgan owned a ranch immediately above it on the mountainside. And now the trouble was, that one of those hated and dreaded landslides had come and slid Morgan's ranch, fences, cabins, cattle, barns, and everything down on top of *his* ranch and exactly covered up every single vestige of his property, to a depth of about thirty-eight feet. Morgan was in possession and refused to vacate the premises—said he was occupying his own cabin and not interfering with anybody else's—and said the cabin was standing on the same dirt and same ranch it had always stood on, and he would like to see anybody make him vacate.
>
> "And when I reminded him," said Hyde, weeping, "that it was on top of my ranch and that he was trespassing, he had the infernal meanness to ask me why I didn't stay on my ranch and hold possession when I see him a-comin'! Why didn't I *stay* on it, the blathering lunatic—by George, when I heard that racket and looked up that hill it was just like the whole world was a-rippin' and a-tearin' down that mountainside—splinters and cordwood, thunder and lightning, hail and snow, odds and ends of haystacks, and awful clouds of dust! Trees going end over end in the air, rocks as big as a house jumping 'bout a thousand feet high and busting into ten million pieces, cattle turned inside out and a-coming head on with their tails hanging out between their teeth!—and in the midst of all that wrack and destruction sot that cussed Morgan on his gatepost a-wondering why I didn't *stay and hold possession!* Laws bless me, I just took one glimpse, General, and lit out'n the country in three jumps exactly."
>
> Mark Twain, *Roughing It*

Direct Quotation   The writer believes the exact words of the author are essential to the paper:

> Exaggeration, examples
>
> "slid Morgan's ranch, fences, cabins, cattle, barns, and everything down on top of *his* [emphasis T's] ranch and exactly covered up every single vestige of his property, to a depth of about thirty-eight feet." 150
> " . . . it was just like the whole world was a-rippin' and a-tearin' down that mountainside—splinters and cordwood, thunder and lightning, hail and snow, odds and ends of haystacks . . . rocks as big as a house jumping 'bout a thousand feet high and busting into ten million pieces, cattle turned inside out and a-coming head on with their tails hanging out between their teeth!" 151
>
> *Roughing*

Paraphrase The writer wants to keep the sense of the original and to approximate its length and tone. The following is a paraphrase of the first two sentences of the Twain piece.

> Background of Hyde/Morgan problem
>
> Most people knew that Hyde had been a farmer, or a rancher, in the Washoe District for quite a while, that he was successful, and that his ranch was located in a valley below Morgan's, which was on a hillside. Their problem all began with a landslide that came and dumped all of Morgan's ranch on top of Hyde's, until there was not a trace of Hyde's left. 150
>
> *Roughing*

Paraphrase and Direct Quotation Combined A longer paraphrase, combined with direct quotes, might be more useful. It preserves the sense of humor of the original and provides specific illustrations to be used later in the paper.

> The Hyde/Morgan Dispute
>
> T. makes rancher named Hyde tell how in a landslide "Morgan's ranch, fences, cabins, cattle, barns, and everything" slid down and "exactly covered up every single vestige of his property, to a depth of about thirty-eight feet." Morgan refused to vacate, saying cabin "was standing on the same dirt and the same ranch it had always stood on," and asked Hyde why he had left when he "see him a-comin'." 150 What Hyde had seen was "just like the whole world was a-rippin' and a-tearin' down that mountainside," bringing with it "odds and ends of haystacks . . . trees going end over end in the air, rocks as big as a house jumping 'bout a thousand feet high and busting into ten million pieces, cattle turned inside out and a-coming head on with their tails hanging out between their teeth!" In the face of this, Hyde "lit out'n the country in three jumps exactly." 151
>
> *Roughing*

Summary   If the writer anticipates only a brief mention of the passage, perhaps as an example of humor in Twain's writing, a notecard like the following would be sufficient:

> Humor: Tall Tales in Twain
>
> T. makes a rancher called Hyde give very funny account of how another ranch landed on top of his. Good picture of way landslide came down mountain, using exaggeration and wild details. 150–51
>
> *Roughing*

AVOIDING PLAGIARISM

In discussing research, it is hard to avoid the topic of plagiarism. Plagiarism is the academic and literary equivalent of robbery, taking somebody else's property. If you copy somebody's test answers, take an essay from a magazine and pass it off as your own, lift a well-phrased sentence or two and include them without crediting the author or using quotation marks, or even pass off somebody's good ideas as examples of your own genius, you are guilty of intellectual thievery. If you are caught you should expect punishment or contempt or both.

This is not a book about ethics, and we have no sermons to urge the moral reform of anyone determined to cheat—except to observe that plagiarism is usually detected and may lead to appropriate punishment. We want mainly to help students avoid unintentional plagiarism, to be sure that they understand what intellectual honesty requires. Plagiarism out of ignorance may be less reprehensible than willful attempts at deception, but its results are the same. And it is small comfort to be condemned for carelessness and stupidity rather than dishonesty. Making distinctions is not always easy. Following are some ways honest writers can be as honest as they mean to be.

Using the Ideas of Others

Very properly, we all learn from the past and adapt the work of others to our own uses. But adapting is different from adopting. Using is different from copying.

The difference is in intent and in the handling of the adapted material. Assume that you are assigned to write on new youth movements in religion. You find an essay in a digest journal on the Jesus movement in London, divided into four main parts with subheads. You read it hastily, accepting what is said. Then you write your own paper, using the organization of the essay with the same four parts, making the same introduction by paraphrasing a story told by the author of the article. You add a brief conclusion asserting that the four points you have made seem to you the most important things to be said about the movement. You then turn in the paper as your own work, maybe even believing that it is. Actually the typing and a good deal of shortening are your only contributions. You have appropriated somebody else's property and tried to profit from it, acting as a kind of literary fence. On the other hand, if you decide you would like to learn about the Jesus movement in London, read a series of articles about it, take notes, think about your evidence and develop your own interpretation, and then write your paper using the material to develop your own ideas, you are using sources legitimately. You are creating, not copying.

Plagiarism and Paraphrase

Students are more commonly careless than corrupt, but carelessness can result in plagiarism. A frequent cause of unintentional plagiarism is the mistaken idea that a few surface changes make the use of another's material legitimate. If you change a word or two, shift order, omit sections, and appropriate a passage, you have only distorted the original. You are still guilty of pilfering what remains. Compare the following passage and an excerpt from a paper that made use of it:

> The life of all great mystics consists of the same steps. We must accept their experiences as described by them. Only those who themselves have led the life of prayer are capable of understanding its peculiarities. The search for God is, indeed, an entirely personal undertaking. By the exercise of the normal activities of his consciousness, man may endeavor to reach an invisible reality both immanent in and transcending the material world. Thus, he throws himself into the most audacious adventure that one can dare. He may be looked upon as a hero, or a lunatic. But nobody should ask whether mystical experience is true or false, whether it is auto-suggestion, hallucination, or a journey of the soul beyond the dimensions of our world and its union with a higher reality. One must be content with having an operational concept of such an experience. Mysticism is splendidly generous. It brings to man the fulfillment of his highest desires. Inner strength, spiritual light, divine love, ineffable peace. Religious intuition is as real as esthetic inspiration. Through the contemplation of super-human beauty, mystics and poets may reach the ultimate truth.
>
> Alexis Carrel, Man the Unknown

The following appeared, without credit or quotation marks, in a paper on the same subject:

> All the great mystics go through the same steps, and we have to accept their experiences. For those people who have lived a life of prayer, the search for God is an undertaking that is personal and that lets him be above the everyday world around us. Mysticism is the greatest adventure that one can dare, and although a mystic may be called a hero or a lunatic, he is concerned with a higher reality. Mystics are splendidly generous people, and religious intuition is as real as esthetic inspiration.

This writer is guilty on two counts: first of appropriating another's work without credit, and second—having misunderstood Carrel's passage—of writing nonsense. The first sentence picks up key words from the original, but distorts the first two sentences enough to make the meaning obscure. Similarly the last sentence takes two passages from the original, but misunderstands "mysticism is splendidly generous" and produces "mystics are splendidly generous people." Instead of working mechanically from the words of the passage, trying to disguise any pilfering, the writer should have read carefully and tried to understand. Once the idea can be paraphrased in the writer's own words, any passage quoted verbatim can be credited to Carrel with careful use of quotation marks.

Plagiarism and Note-Taking

Another cause of unintentional plagiarism is careless note-taking. The writer forgets to record the source on a note card and fails to use quotation marks for phrases lifted from the original. Consider the following fairly detailed note from the Carrel passage:

> Only those who have themselves led the life of prayer, that is, the mystics, are capable of understanding its peculiarities, because the search for God

> must inevitably be a personal undertaking. One should not ask whether mystical experience results from auto-suggestion, hallucination, or a journey of the soul beyond worldly dimensions in its unions with higher reality. Mysticism, being splendidly generous, brings its fullfillment in inner strength, spiritual light, divine love, and ineffable peace, and mystics may share with poets the ultimate truth.

This note has the virtue of accuracy, but almost inevitably it would betray the writer into dishonesty. A few days after the note had been taken the writer would have forgotten how much of it was actually taken from Carrel and might easily use quoted portions without crediting the source.

The following note would at least avoid the dangers of plagiarism:

> Carrel says that the activities of mystics, although they may strike more worldly people as strange, or even as insane, have their justification in that mystics, like poets, "may reach the ultimate truth." The mystic "throws himself into the most audacious adventure that one can dare"; mysticism is "splendidly generous," and the mystic's end is to "reach an invisible reality both immanent in and transcending the material world," and thus to cultivate "inner strength, spiritual light, divine love, and ineffable peace." 119

Differences between this note and the one above suggest the following minimal rules as insurance against plagiarism:

1. Try to understand a passage as a whole before paraphrasing any of it.
2. State in your own words anything you summarize, and be careful not to let your wording be colored by the original.
3. When you can provide no adequate summary of your own, or when the wording of the original is so good that you wish to preserve it, scrupulously surround it with quotation marks.
4. Always record the page number of your source so that it can be acknowledged in a citation. Remember that a citation alone is not enough to identify a direct quotation. Even a short passage in the words of the original must be enclosed in quotation marks.

WRITING AND REVISING THE PAPER

Once you have finished your research and assembled your information, you are ready to write. Organize your material and outline the paper, reviewing chapter 5 for help. The first attempts may be sketchy, but through rewriting and revising, the investigative paper will take shape.

And in this paper, revision assumes special importance. For one thing, you are working with material that needs to be consistently and logically presented. Your readers are following you into uncharted territory, so your arguments and ideas must be presented precisely. Here are some questions to ask yourself as you revise:

1. Does my introduction make clear what the paper is about? Have I given the reader sufficient information or background? Have I explained the problem clearly, defined any terms that may be unfamiliar or new? Is the point of the paper, the thesis, clearly stated?
2. Have I arranged the information clearly? Does the argument follow logically? Do I provide transitions or even summaries when material is long or involved? Have I provided sufficient supporting evidence? Have I incorporated source material—quoted and unquoted—correctly and documented accurately?
3. Is my conclusion clear and forceful? Have I satisfied all the questions or controversies raised in my paper? Are my conclusions based on solid research?
4. Have I maintained a consistent and appropriate style throughout the paper?

Most of these questions are pertinent to the revision of any paper. Two considerations, however, are especially related to research writing: the style of an investigative paper and conventional documentation. Both should be checked during the revision and editing phases of writing. Additionally consult proper manuscript form, chapter 18, conventions regarding quotations, chapter 17, and title references, chapter 18.

STYLE IN THE INVESTIGATIVE PAPER

The style of a research paper should be objective and relatively impartial. If you have opinions to express, you should label them clearly. Research writing mainly employs the third person, although convention now allows the use of the first person. This practice avoids excessive use of the passive voice, especially when you need to describe your research—for instance, how you set up equipment or collected data. But a research paper should be couched in objective terms.

The reader of any difficult or controversial paper always wants to know whether the author is right, whether the evidence is sound. But writers cannot always be sure; they do not always have adequate evidence. Thus, in research writing you should make clear what you know certainly and how. You should alert the reader to the uncertainty in qualified assertions, those you have made because the evidence is good, although inconclusive. Finally, you should identify any observations that are guesses that you have made just because they are your best guesses. Part of the secret of a good objective style grows from learning to keep the reader informed, unobtrusively, of the writer's own evaluation of the evidence.

Another problem bothers almost every research worker: What should you do when the authorities disagree? They do disagree. Most important problems cannot be settled certainly and finally, and even for minor questions the evidence is often contradictory. If you find no reason for preferring one of the disagreeing sources, you can present the evidence on all sides and cite all authorities. If you think one argument is better than the others, you can present it and then cite opposing evidence in the text or in an endnote. Even if you are sure that one side is right, you should cite opposing opinions.

Evaluating evidence and dealing with inconsistencies are parts of the same problem for the researcher. In the following excerpt from a study of compulsive gamblers, Tim Stronach acknowledges these inconsistencies and evaluates them for the reader:

> Nancy Ashton in *Gamblers: Disturbed or Healthy?* divides all the known research on the subject into three categories. The first category sees all "gambling as pathology." The second category views "gambling as normal or healthy." In the third category, the gambler and gambling activity are defined in terms of "personality trait orientation" (54).
>
> Older bodies of research tend to fall under the first category; that is, all forms of gambling were seen as pathological. Freud saw "gambling as a substitute for masturbation, which also involves the hands and leads to both excitement and guilt" (Ashton 55). These older views were often biased. A puritanical attitude that viewed any and all forms of gambling as evil had natural tendencies to moralize and see participants as guilty.

INCORPORATING RESEARCH IN THE PAPER

The research data you use in your paper lend authority and credibility to your discussion. These should be incorporated as naturally as possible into your text, often by a direct reference to the author and title of the material or by an introductory remark:

> As Thomas Mann points out in "Psychoanalysis, the Lived Myth and Fiction," . . .
>
> Dr. Max Sugar notes in *Adolescent Parenthood* that . . .
>
> Other critics have said . . .
>
> It is generally agreed that . . .

Often a summary or a paraphrase is all that is necessary to support your position. Information can be placed in a specific sentence within a paragraph or in a summary paragraph:

... than the schools without programs. The next year, all schools in the district had a sex education program, and there was a 50 percent decline in venereal rates in the year following the programs (Dickman 36). In Los Angeles County ...

Not surprisingly, modern research into the adolescent and adult lives of compulsive gamblers has shown that their gambling activity started early. Most gambled as youths and most were initiated to this gambling activity through exposure to relatives who gambled. Interestingly, it has also been found that among compulsive gamblers men outnumber women four to one (Wellborn 75).

Direct quotations are especially effective in research writing. They should be used whenever the original author's words make the point more strongly than your summary or paraphrase, when the weight of authority is important to your argument, or when several key words or phrases reinforce your point. Sometimes a quoted word, phrase, or sentence is preferable to copying a lengthy passage.

> One hundred percent of all violent prison inmates surveyed and 64 percent of all juvenile delinquents were found to have been subjected to "extreme corporal punishment" (Falk 119).

> A profile image of a compulsive in a recent *Psychology Today* article lends support to this theory. Charlie K "consistently failed to win the attention and affection of his father" (53).

> As Robert Penn Warren writes, "Faulkner's images of violence ... are ... not of the South but of the soul" (11).

Longer quotes, usually four or more lines, are indented ten spaces and double spaced. Quotation marks are not used, unless recording conversation or another quotation within the quotation.

> An example of Twain's exaggeration appears in *Roughing It*:
>> Morgan's ranch, fences, cabins, cattle, barns, and everything [slid] down on top of *his* [Twain's emphasis] ranch and exactly covered up every single vestige of his property, to a depth of about thirty-eight feet. (150)

> In commenting on James Joyce's use of myth in *Ulysses*, T.S. Eliot states:
>> In using myth, in manipulating a continuous parallel between contemporaneity and antiquity, Mr. Joyce is pursuing a method which others must pursue after him.... It is ... a way of controlling, or ordering, of giving a shape and a significance to the immense panorama of futility and anarchy which is contemporary history. (483)

Here we see three conventional uses of punctuation with quoted material:

1. Ellipsis—three dots to indicate any material omitted from the original quote; a fourth dot represents the period if the omitted material is at the end of the sentence.
2. Brackets—to indicate an authorial inclusion and to clarify a quotation.
3. Colon—to introduce long formal quotes. Short, informal comments use only a comma (Benjamin Franklin said, "Early to bed, early to rise.").

Lines in poetry or drama are usually treated as long quotes and set off as above.

> Eugene O'Neill took the title of his play, *Ah, Wilderness*, from "The Rubáiyát of Omar Khayyám":
>
> A Book of Verses underneath the Bough,
> A Jug of Wine a Loaf of Bread—and Thou
> Beside me singing in the Wilderness—
> Oh, Wilderness were Paradise enow!

If this quotation is incorporated in the text, however, divisions between the individual lines are indicated by slashes; original capitalization and punctuation are maintained:

> Eugene O'Neill took the title of his play, *Ah, Wilderness*, from "The Rubáiyát of Omar Khayyám": "A Book of Verses underneath the Bough,/A Jug of Wine, a Loaf of Bread—and Thou/Beside me singing in the Wilderness—/Oh, Wilderness were Paradise enow!"

DOCUMENTATION

As we see in the excerpt above, research writing involves documentation; that is, the researched information used in the paper is supported by reference to sources, which appear in parenthetical citations within the paper. The citations refer a reader to the list of Works Cited at the end of the paper, a complete list of all works used in preparing the paper.

You may be familiar with the footnote form formerly recommended for research in the humanities by the Modern Language Association (MLA). In 1984 MLA's *Handbook for Writers of Research Papers* recommended a new form of documentation, the parenthetical citation. This form is called author-page system and is a simplified way to indicate sources. Most social sciences use the author-date system described in the *Publication Manual of* the *American Psychological Association* (1983). Sciences require a number system described in the *CBE Style Manual,* published by the Council of Biology Editors (1983).

In this book we have adopted the MLA style. For papers written for courses outside the humanities, you should check with your instructor on documentation style. The form, however, is not as important as the principles of accurate reference. Once you understand these, it is easy to adapt to a preferred style. Regardless of style, all documentation has the same purpose: to identify a source precisely and to assist the reader who wants to check it in more detail or use it to find further information.

Parenthetical Citation

In the text of your paper, you must cite any direct quote, paraphrase, or summary of another's ideas. These citations should be placed close to the material being documented, sometimes at the end of the sentence in which they appear and before the final period of the sentence:

" . . . not of the South but of the soul" (11).

With long indented quotations, the citation note follows the final period of the quote:

. . . which is contemporary history. (483)

You do not need to document facts that are considered common knowledge or could be easily referenced, like the date of Shakespeare's birth or that Leonardo da Vinci painted the Mona Lisa.

In writing in-text citations with the author-page system, common sense is the guide. You are giving the citation to your reader as a courtesy, so knowing how much and what kind of information to include is best tested by asking yourself whether your reader can quickly turn to your page of Works Cited and find complete information on the source. For example, the following contains an author-page citation:

Interestingly, it has also been found that among compulsive gamblers men outnumber women four to one (Wellborn 75).

The citation tells the reader that full information on the writer's authority can be found on page 75 of a book or article by Wellborn listed on the page of Works Cited. If the writer had included the name of the author in the sentence, the citation would not repeat it:

Interestingly, Wellborn has found that among compulsive gamblers men outnumber women four to one (75).

If the writer had used more than one work by Wellborn for the paper, it would be necessary to include a short title for the specific work cited:

> Interestingly, Wellborn has found that among compulsive gamblers men outnumber women four to one ("Gambling" 75).

The most common citations appear in the following examples:

A Work by One Author

> Statistics indicate that there is no discernible difference in the murder rates between states which have capital punishment and those that do not (Shapiro 35).

A Work by Two or Three Authors

> This physical abuse is known as corporal punishment and is permitted by our courts in every state but New Jersey (Commager and Wise 174).

A Work by More Than Three Authors

> As early as 1690 more than twenty thousand Englishmen had established homes in the new world (Perkins et al. 4).

The work was compiled by four authors, but it can be identified by the name that appears first on the title page. *Et al.* means "and others."

A Work by a Corporate Author

> Still others may feel that since there are 880,000 unwanted adolescent pregnancies a year in the United States (Planned Parenthood 37), teenagers obviously know too much already.

A Work with No Author Mentioned

> The Justices issued individual opinions citing the "arbitrary" and "freakish" way in which the death penalty had sometimes been imposed ("Courts and Law" 284).

Since no author is given, the title is used.

An Author Quoted in Another Source:

> Salvation is found only in the physical, by "sublimating the actual to the apocryphal," Faulkner once said (qtd. in Meriwether and Millgate 255).

Note the abbreviation *qtd. in* for a statement from another source. It is always best to go to the primary source, but it is not always possible.

Two or More Works by Different Authors in the Same Citation

Several critics charge that the novelist never paints a happy picture, but always sees the world in "one stage or another of decline" (Warren 11, Reed 2).

To avoid cumbersome citation notes, this sentence could be written:

Warren and Reed charge that the novelist never paints a happy picture, but always sees the world in "one stage or another of decline" (11,2).

WORKS OF LITERATURE

1. If a single piece of fiction or nonfiction is the single source for a paper, only the page number need be in the citation. The following is from a paper on George Orwell's *1984*:

"Newspeak was the official language of Oceania and had been devised to meet the ideological needs of Insoc, or English Socialism" (246).

If, however, several sources by the same author are being used, for example Orwell's *1984* and "Politics and the English Language," a short reference to the title should appear in the citation to avoid confusion. "Politics and the English Language" could become PEL for purposes of citation.

2. When quoting from poetry, drama, or the Bible, page numbers are not appropriate, and lines, acts, and scenes, or references to books and verses should be used. For a poem, references are to lines:

Eliot's Prufrock is aware of his inability to act decisively. [I] "Am an attendant lord, one that will do / To swell a progress, start a scene or two." (112–113).

A quotation from a play, for example *Julius Caesar*, can be cited by a reference to act, scene, and line with a period after each (*Cae*.3.1.47. If the play is identified in the text, no reference to the title is necessary. Citations for long poems, such as the *Iliad*, can refer to parts and lines (*Il*.5.33). References to the Bible cite book, chapter, and verse (John 3:16).

Some instructors may prefer the more traditional use of Roman numerals in literary references. In that case, the reference to *Julius Caesar* would read (*Caesar* III.i.47); the reference to the *Iliad* would be (*Iliad* V.33).

ENDNOTES

Endnotes should not be confused with footnotes, which have been replaced by parenthetical citations. Endnotes have a special function in research writing; they can be used for material that would not fit in the text of the paper or that would be disruptive. An endnote, for example, might present controversial matter or opposing views that you wish to acknowledge but not discuss. It might consist of details or statistics that would interrupt the progress of the discussion. Or it might offer information—although peripheral to the subject—that you think a reader would be interested in pursuing.

Endnotes are indicated by consecutive superscript numbers—small, slightly raised numbers—that appear in the text and also at the beginning of the endnote. The reference is treated as a citation, and the source should be listed among the works cited. Endnotes are written as short paragraphs with the first word indented and each entry double-spaced. Usually they are collected at the end of the paper; occasionally they may be located at the bottom of the page that refers to them.

An example of an endnote page from a paper on William Faulkner's *Light in August* is on page 366.

WORKS CITED

A list of all works consulted, including all those cited in the paper, is appended to a documented paper in the section on Works Cited. Usually, unless a note page intervenes, the page (or pages) of Works Cited receives the next consecutive page number after the text. The entries are listed in alphabetical order to provide easy reference—by last names of authors, by the name of the agency if a government bureau or other group issues a work, and by the first word of the title after *a* or *the* if there is no author. When more than one work by the same author is listed, the works are usually arranged in alphabetical order, with the author's name replaced after the first entry with three hyphens:

Faulkner, William. *Light in August.* New York: Modern Library, 1968.
---. *Sanctuary.* New York: Vintage, 1958.

A long list of works cited may include one list for books and another for periodicals, or it may reveal subdivisions of a paper or chapters of a book.

The list of Works Cited is compiled from the cards of the working bibliography, supplemented by additional titles collected during the research process. In typing, the first line of the entry begins at the margin and the next lines are indented. Each entry is double-spaced.

As a general rule, each entry contains three kinds of information, separated by periods.

1. Author's full name, last name first, with a notation to designate an editor or translator.

Notes

[1] Although it is common to pair *Sanctuary* and *Light in August*, I have chosen to concentrate on *Light in August*, not because *Sanctuary* does not demonstrate many of Faulkner's major themes, but because it presents only a one-sided view of life. I agree with Brylowski, who says, "Only in *Sanctuary* did Faulkner fail to offer the optimistic counterpoint to his negative vision of life" (98).

[2] The labelling of the first and last chapters (or Lena) as a framing device is a simple solution to a more complex problem within the novel. Many critics find that there is no solution. Howe says there is a "structural incoherence" in the novel (153), Reed that there is a "lack of schematic unity" (141).

[3] Slatoff notes that what upsets Joe is not his repressive Protestant society, but the unpredictable and illogical women in his life (182). However, Slatoff does not realize that these two problems are actually variations of the same self-hatred.

2. Title of the work, including volume or edition numbers.
3. Publication information. For books, the standard form is publication city: publisher, year. Sometimes the state needs to be listed to identify the city. San Francisco does not need identification by state, but Belmont, CA, does. Use postal abbreviations for states.

For periodicals the form varies, but still requires the three types of information separated by periods.

1. Author's full name.
2. Title of the individual article, essay, or entry cited.
3. Publication information. This includes the title of the journal or magazine or collection from which the article was taken, the date of publication, a volume or edition number if available, and page numbers locating the article.

SAMPLE ENTRIES

The style in the following sample entries is recommended by the Modern Language Association and detailed in the *MLA Style Sheet*. Because this is only a simplified list, the *Style Sheet* should be consulted for additional information.

Books

One Author

Sugar, Max, M.D. *Adolescent Parenthood.* New York: Spectrum, 1984.

Two or Three Authors

Gonzalez, Roseann Duenas, Mary Carmen E. Cruz, and Ann Berger Thomas. *Copy, Combine, and Compose.* Belmont, CA: Wadsworth, 1983.

More Than Three Authors

Perkins, George, et al. *The American Tradition in Literature.* 6th ed. New York: Random, 1985.

Corporate Author, Agency, or Group

President's Commission on Higher Education. *Higher Education for American Democracy.* Washington, D.C.: GPO, 1947.

Work in More Than One Volume

Sandburg, Carl. *Abraham Lincoln: The War Years.* 4 vols. New York: Harcourt, 1939.

Reprint of an Older Edition

Lewis, C[live] S. *The Allegory of Love: A Study of Medieval Tradition.* 1936. New York: Galaxy-Oxford UP, 1958.

Work with Editors

Bradbury, Malcolm and Howard Termperley, eds. *Introduction to American Studies.* London: Longman, 1984.

Edition with an Author and Editor

Chaucer, Geoffrey. *The Works of Geoffrey Chaucer.* Ed. F. N. Robinson. 2d ed. Boston: Houghton, 1957.

Translation

Solzhenitsyn, Alexander I. *Gulag Archipelago.* Trans. Thomas F. Whitner. New York: Harper, 1974.

Book in a Series

Wallerstein, Ruth. *Richard Crashaw: A Study in Style and Poetic Development.* Univ. of Wisconsin Studies in Lang. and Lit. No. 37. Madison: U of Wisconsin Press, 1935.

Chapter from a Book

Ryser, Fred A. Jr. "Marshbirds." *Birds of the Great Basin: A Natural History.* Reno, NV: U of Nev. Press, 1985.

Work in a Collection

Dewey, John. "Does Human Nature Change?" in *Confrontations: Readings for Composition.* Ed. James K. Bowen. Glenview, IL: Scott-Foresman, 1969.

Periodicals

Daily Newspaper

Hoppe, Arthur. "Nobody Comes Clean." *San Francisco Chronicle* 23 Dec. 1986: 31.

Daily Newspaper with Section Numbers or Special Editions

Kerr, Walter. "Two That Try to Break the Rules—and Fail." *New York Times* 27 Dec. 1970, sec 2: 1.

Weekly Periodical

Alpert, Hollis. "But Who Wrote the Movie?" *Saturday Review* 26 Dec. 1970: 9.

Monthly Periodical

Green, Johnny. "The Gambling Trap." *Psychology Today* Sept. 1982: 50–55.

Journal with Consecutive Pagination

Faigley, Lester. "Competing Theories of Process: A Critique and a Proposal." *College English* 48 (1986): 527–42.

Journal with Separated Pagination

McCloskey, Donald N. "The Literary Character of Economics." *Daedelus* 113.3 (1984): 97–1119.

A Review

Petrocelli, William R. "What You Should Do Until the Lawyer Comes." Rev. of *Everybody's Guide to the Law* by Melvin Belli and Allen P. Wilkinson. *San Francisco Chronicle* 6 Jan. 1987: 40.

Editorial

Pfaff, William. "The Failed Vietnam Revolution." *San Francisco Chronicle* 23 Dec. 1986: 30.

Unsigned Article

Many newspaper and magazine articles are unsigned. For these, the bibliographic form is the same as illustrated above, but the title becomes the first element of the entry.

"Hope for Victims of Another Addiction." *Futurist* Oct. 1981: 26.

Reference Works

"Capital Punishment." *World Book Encyclopedia*. 1962 ed.

"Courts and Laws." *The 1973 World Book Year Book*. 1973 ed.

Page numbers are not necessary, because the topics are arranged alphabetically.

Signed Article in an Encyclopedia

Sapir, Edward. "Language." *Encyclopaedia of the Social Sciences.* 1933 ed.

Pamphlets and Bulletins

Washoe County School District Sex Education Advisory Committee Report. 20 July 1981.

Nonprint Sources

Eugene B. Fleischer's *A Style Manual of Citing Microform and Nonprint Media* illustrates many forms that you may need. A few of the more common are in the following examples:

Lecture, Speech, Address

Odell, Lee. Keynote Speech. Opening Sess. Convention on College Composition and Communication. New Orleans, 19 Mar. 1986.

Motion Picture

Star Trek I: The Movie. Dir. Gene Roddenberry. Paramount Pictures, 1980.

Television Program

A Christmas Carol. CBS, Chicago 23 Dec. 1986.

Play

The Man Who Came to Dinner. Dir. David Hettich. Reno Little Theatre, Reno, NV. 6 Dec. 1986.

Performance

San Francisco Ballet: "Nutcracker." Opera House, 20 Dec. 1986.

Interview

Sampson, Ross G. Personal Interview. 17 June 1985.

A SAMPLE PAPER

Following is the final draft of a student paper on gambling, including end notes and the list of Works Cited. The paper illustrates the conventions described above as well as some of the strategies for presenting information—for example, asking directly in the introduction the questions to be investigated and using the various techniques of exposition to organize the paper.

Brother Can You Spare a Dime:

A Study of Compulsive Gamblers

Tim Stronach

English 102, Section 3

Mr. Webb

May 9, 1987

Brother Can You Spare a Dime: A Study
of Compulsive Gamblers
Tim Stronach

Wanted--Compulsive Gamblers. Experience helpful, but not required. All applicants must be willing to work long hours, lose large amounts of money, and borrow or steal to finance their ventures. People suffering from a low self-image in search of a strong identity are especially desirable. Contact your nearest casino, bookie, or betting parlor for further information.

If an Atlantic City casino ran an advertisement similar to the paragraph above in the Sunday paper for a year, it would probably get no response. Still, Gamblers Anonymous estimates that between six and nine million compulsive gamblers exist in the United States today (Commission 151). How does an occasional gambler become compulsive? Why are some people who gamble more likely than others to become pathological gamblers? What attracts them?

Nancy Ashton in <u>Gamblers: Disturbed or Healthy?</u> divides all the known research on the subject into three categories. The first category sees all "gambling as pathology." The second category views "gambling as normal or healthy." In the third category, the gambler and gambling activity are defined in terms of "personality trait orientation" (54).

Older research tends to fit in the first category; that is, all forms of gambling were seen as pathological. Freud, who first wrote on the subject, tied all gambling to the Oedipus complex. He viewed gambling as "infantile" and saw gambling as a substitute for masturbation, which also involves the hands and leads to both excitement and guilt (Ashton 54). Bergler's popularized view characterized gamblers as having "an unconscious wish to lose" in order to punish themselves for latent aggressions they felt as children (Ashton 55). These older views were often biased. A puritanical attitude that viewed any and all forms of gambling as evil had natural tendencies to moralize and judge all participants guilty.

The older researchers in category one tended to form negative hypotheses which lumped all gamblers together. Those in the second category assert that gambling may be considered "normal" or "pathological" depending on the personality and behavior of the gambler in question. The third group, with the "personality trait orientation," seeks to classify together only those gamblers whose individual make-up and gambling conduct are similar. Compulsive gamblers, as a group, can be studied effectively using this approach; modern research indicates that common threads do exist in their emotional fabric.[1]

Most people who engage in forms of legalized gambling

are able to control and even enjoy it. The simple act of wagering does not make one a pathological gambler. Even regular or heavy gambling does not automatically indicate a problem; professionals are heavy gamblers who consistently win more than they lose. Compulsives, on the other hand, are heavy gamblers who seldom win. True compulsive gamblers are powerless to stop gambling until all their available resources are exhausted (Anderson 68). They are victims of an "uncontrollable impulse to bet" whether they win or lose (Wellborn 74). Gambling takes control of their lives to the exclusion of everything else, and they can't function without "staying in the action," even while putting "good money after bad" (Lesieur 13).

Gamblers Anonymous, a self-help organization for compulsive gamblers, is to problem gamblers what Alcoholics Anonymous is to alcoholics. The following quotations were taken from the files of Gamblers Anonymous. In them the reformed subjects describe the total lack of self-control that characterized their affliction:

> Terry A. "When I was at the blackjack table, my wife could have been home dying of cancer, and I could not have cared less."
> Marge W. "I stole vacation money from the family sugar jar. I spent every waking hour thinking about getting to the track."

Thomas J. "Gambling was the ultimate experience for me--better than sex, better than any drug. I had withdrawal tortures just like a heroin junkie." (qtd in Wellborn 73)

In 1980, the American Psychiatric Association put compulsive gambling on its list of pathological mental disorders (Hope 26). Though the problem existed long before the medical establishment chose to officially address it, their formal acceptance demonstrates the necessity of continued research. Representing the new attitude is Dr. Robert Custer, a psychoanalyst and former chief of mental health treatment services at the Veterans Administration. He started the first residential programs for compulsive gamblers in the United States at the VA hospital in Brecksville, Ohio.

Custer believes that as children compulsive gamblers were very energetic and active but didn't receive the attention from parents that other children of their type received (Wellborn 75). In some cases, this inattention was actual abuse, which caused them to begin adolescence with a lowered self-image. Later, gambling appealed to them as a way to increase their self-esteem and thus gain acceptance. A profile image of a compulsive in a recent <u>Psychology Today</u> article lends support to this theory. Charlie K "consistently failed to win the attention and affection of his father" (53).

Not surprisingly, modern research into the adolescent and young adult lives of compulsive gamblers has shown that their gambling activity started early, often in high school (Lesieur 87). Most compulsives gambled as youths and most were initiated through exposure to relatives who gambled. Interestingly, it has also been found that among compulsive gamblers men outnumber women four to one (Wellborn 75).

The concepts of self-image and self-esteem provide important insights into the playing behavior of compulsive gamblers. Compulsives become very emotionally involved in their gambling. They are loud and quick to vocalize their elation at winning or their disappointment at losing. Through this energized playing style, they attract attention to themselves and so reinforce their gambling identity. In card games, compulsives often criticize other players for "breaking up a good run" or "slowing down the game" and create for themselves a feeling of superiority and elevated self-worth in the presence of less experienced or novice players. Martinez calls compulsive gambling a "career organized around an identity" (39).

Custer loosely divides compulsive gambling careers into three phases: "winning, losing, and desperation." Initially compulsive gamblers win, probably because most compulsives have higher than average intelligence and choose to engage in gambling activity requiring some form of skill (Wellborn

75). Soon, however, the conscious moods that compulsive gamblers experience while playing become the focus of their attention; their playing drops off, and they start losing. Winning has become secondary to the mental and physical lift that is initiated by betting. Now compulsive gamblers start "chasing" bad bets and playing at each outing until their funds are totally exhausted. This leads to the final stage, desperation. By this time, the gambler may have lost job, family, and friends in an attempt to support the gambling habit. The gambler has "hit rock bottom" (Wellborn 74).

Thomas M. Martinez in *The Gambling Scene: Why People Gamble* explains in detail the conscious moods associated with compulsive gambling. These moods--known as risk-taking, here and now, fantasy, euphoria, and mysticism (54)-- are verified by others.

According to Martinez, gamblers usually say that they gamble to win money. In reality, many gamblers enjoy the "thrill and excitement" that risk-taking initiates. This excitement is often physically evident as a quickened heartbeat, a "tingling" sensation, or a general feeling of stimulation. Compulsive gamblers enjoy risk-taking for the previously mentioned reasons but want too much of a good thing. To create excitement, their betting becomes progressively heavier no matter how they are doing, eventually resulting in heavy losses.

Being involved in the "here and now," the second of the moods Martinez discusses, means giving a task full attention. Everything external to the immediate situation is blocked out for the "action":

> the preparation that goes into it, the setting up and "getting down" (getting a bet in) as well as coping with the consequences after the action is over.(Lesieur 14)

For a gambler to become compulsive, the here and now must be pleasurable (Martinez 57). Compulsive gamblers enjoy the here and now to forget problems. "This is the only place where I can relax. I close off the world when I sit down at the gaming table" (qtd.in Lesieur 88).

Involvement in gambling at the expense of reality leaves gamblers free to fantasize or dream. Martinez divides the gambler's fantasies into past, present, and future (58). In them subjects are always in a position of power, receiving praise from others. In past fantasies, the gamblers remember scenes in which they had little influence or effect and recreate them so that they become heroes (59). In the present tense gamblers imagine themselves as prestigious and daring in a romanticized environment, usually centered around gambling. One gambler "would imagine himself as an international gambler with international money backing him" (Martinez 59). Another fantasized a relationship with Marilyn Monroe while gambling (Lesieur 53). In the future, subjects become rich as the result of a lucky streak, and many people are around to acknowledge their new status (59).

Euphoria is a feeling of extreme and intense pleasure that for compulsive gamblers becomes a "peak experience" equivalent (Martinez 61). It is usually connected with winning a large wager. The shift from occasional to compulsive gambling is related to the intensity of the gambler's feelings of fantasy and euphoria. Feelings of euphoria are increased as more of the gambler's "fantasized self" becomes prominent in role-playing (Martinez 61). At this stage, subjects have committed a large part of themselves to gambling; time, money, job status, and personal relationships have all been sacrificed. But gamblers make these sacrifices willingly because gambling has become for them a "mystical" experience. Subjects "transcend" their immediate surroundings and experience feelings of heightened awareness. Self identity is expanded to include significance beyond the physical. Lesieur compares this stage to "opium addiction" (14); Martinez, however, finds it like "mysticism," a form of religious experience (62).

These feelings, though hard for the layman to understand, seem authentic descriptions of the moods that accompany increased involvement for compulsive gamblers. Little else seems to justify the horrendous play and abysmal betting patterns that characterize the compulsive gambler's playing technique. Compulsives often play while fatigued and often drink heavily while playing; both habits are cardinal sins to professionals. The moods of fantasy and euphoria keep the gambler close to the gambling environment. Gambling becomes a twenty-four-hour habit (Lesieur 15). Winning and losing have no influence on these feelings. To compulsives, how well they play becomes irrelevant; to continue playing is all that matters. By this time, the compulsive betting phenomenon known as "the chase"[2] has already begun to take shape.

"The chase" is actually a vicious cycle of betting that leads to utter financial ruin. Compulsive gamblers bet but lose. In an attempt to get even, they bet more money and so, usually, go deeper into debt. Refusing to accept a bit of bad luck and quit, as good professionals would, they become trapped in a downward spiral. As the gambling debt increases, the "resultant desire to resolve that debt by gambling increases" (Lesieur 1). The compulsive gambler is heading for the gutter; by chasing bad bets, the gambler begins to "bottom out."

Compulsive gamblers are now uninterested in anything but gambling and have become part of a social structure from which everything unrelated to gambling has been excluded. Subjects show an "overt hostility towards society" and become more withdrawn (Martinez 85). Subjects are, at this phase, "tapped out" financially. Some at this stage have already started stealing from family members or "hanging paper" (writing bad checks) to "stay in the action." Lying becomes commonplace and self-deception increases; they will stop at nothing to finance their habit.[3]

Compulsive gamblers keep telling themselves they'll quit while they are ahead or alter their playing styles, but they remain powerless to do anything but play until their money is gone. Only after they have reached this point does the hopelessness of their position begin to sink in. By this time, their families may be dissolved, they may have no friends and no job, and they may be resorting to crime to get more money. Now they begin to admit that they have a problem, renounce their behavior, and seek help.

> However, alone, this "abstinence" does not last, but is followed by a typical "relapse" pushing them even further into gambling. Only through groups like Gamblers Anonymous does help seem available (Lesieur 272-4).

Society has been slow in recognizing compulsive gambling addiction as a serious problem. Alcoholism and drug abuse have gotten the lion's share of public attention. The first government supported treatment program for compulsive gambling was not opened until October, 1979

(Greene 51). This was the Johns Hopkins University Compulsive Gambling Counseling Center, which is partly funded by the Maryland state legislature. It offers formal treatment programs designed to help private individuals who suffer from compulsive gambling disorders. Close-quartered work with groups of problem gamblers, like that at the Hopkins Center, offers the most comprehensive insight into the compulsive's peculiar character. Through a greater understanding of compulsive gamblers, more effective methods of treatment will be established. Studying compulsive gambling behavior in the light of psychological factors like personality and environment will lead to greater understanding of a serious social problem.

Notes

[1] An example of this type of research is a recent dissertation by Henry Richard Lesieur, which is based on interviews conducted with more than sixty compulsive gamblers. He begins with no initial bias, but after the extensive interviewing he is able to identify common patterns.

[2] The term _the chase_ was identified by Lesieur in his dissertation, and he has published a book using it as the title. Other slang terms used in the paper were taken from the dissertation, which reflects the language of compulsives. These include _get even_, _bottom out_, _tapped out_, _action_, and _getting down_.

[3] Lesieur traces this pattern of self-destruction where compulsive gamblers first turn to family members for money, then to legitimate funding sources, such as banks, then to bookmakers, loan sharks, gambling friends, and finally to crime to support their gambling--dealing drugs, pimping, embezzlement, theft.

Works Cited

Anderson, George. "Compulsive Gambling: Talking to the Experts: Views of R. Custer." *America* 3 Feb. 1979: 67-70.

Ashton, Nancy. "Gamblers: Disturbed or Healthy?" *Gambling Today*. Ed. David Lester. Springfield, IL: Thomas, 1979.

Commission on the Review of the National Policy Toward Gambling. *Gambling in America*. Washington, D.C.: GPO, 1976.

Greene, Johnny. "The Gambling Trap." *Psychology Today* Sept. 1982: 50-55.

"Hope for Victims of Another Addiction." *Futurist* Oct. 1981: 26

Lesieur, Henry Richard. "Compulsive Gambling: The Spiral of Options and Involvement." Diss., Michigan State U. 1980.

Martinez, Thomas H. *The Gambling Scene: Why People Gamble*. Springfield, IL: Thomas, 1983.

Weathers, Diana, et al. "Gamblers Who Can't Quit." *Newsweek* 3 Mar. 1980: 70.

Wellborn, Stanley. "Compulsive Gambling: A Spreading Epidemic." *U.S. News and World Report* 28 Jan. 1980: 73-75.

ABBREVIATIONS AND CONVENTIONS

Following is a short list of common abbreviations and symbols you may encounter when doing research. For additional symbols, see the *MLA Style Sheet*.

p., pp.—page, pages.

l., ll.—line, lines.

v., vv.—verse, verses.

vol., vols.—volume, volumes.

no., nos.—number, numbers.

cf.—compare.

n.—note, footnote.

c.—copyright; used when the date of a copyright is known but the date of publication is not.

c., ca.—circa, about; used in approximate dates (ca. 1888).

sic—thus; may be used after an obvious error in a quotation to indicate that the error was in the original; best used sparingly; when inserted in a quotation, should be enclosed in brackets.

n.d.—no date.

n.p.—no publisher.

n. pag.—no pagination.

ed.—editor, edited, edition.

trans.—translated by, translation.

rev.—revised

Graphs, tables, and other illustrations or tabulated inserts are imperative for many technical papers, and much complicated material is best shown in visual or tabular form. The writer should always consider whether a table or an illustration will not make the meaning clearer. Inserts of this sort should usually be labeled for ready reference in the text. Use *plate* to refer to a full page (Plate IX), *figure* for an illustration in the text (Figure 8), and *table* for a tabular or graphic arrangement (Table 3).

FOR STUDY
AND WRITING

A. A key to success in college is learning to use the library efficiently. Go to your library and familiarize yourself not only with the card catalog and reference desk, but with its special areas—a biography alcove, a business periodicals section, the film library, or a special collection of native American artifacts. If your library offers tours, take one.

B. In the reference section of the library locate a copy of the London *Times* or *The New York Times* (they are on microfilm) published the day of your birth and an edition of a local newspaper from the same day. Compare the headlines and lead stories. What happened the day you were born? What differences are reflected in the two newspapers. Write a short piece based on your findings.

C. Find the specific information requested in the following.

1. Using the card catalog, find the author, publisher, date, and place of publication of a book called *In the Shadow of Man.*
2. Using the same source, find out how many pages there are in a copy of James A. Michener's novel *Hawaii.*
3. Using the same source, look up a history of modern criticism by René Wellek. It is in several volumes.
4. Using the same source, find the title and publication details for the most recent book by Vladimir Nabokov in the library collection.
5. Using the same source, find a recent book about the Civil War.
6. Using *Reader's Guide,* locate an article printed in 1972 by Stanley Kripner and Richard Davidson, about what the Russians were doing with parapsychology.
7. Using the same guide, find a recent article on the efforts by *Greenpeace* to save endangered species.
8. Locate an article on Prince Charles and Lady Diana.
9. Using a standard encyclopedia, locate a brief biography of Jan Gaston Darboux.
10. Using *The New York Times Index,* find an article published in 1985 about Vietnam.

D. One good way to find a topic for a research paper is to pick a question and start looking for an answer to it. Select one of the following questions—or a question of your own approved by your instructor—and do enough preliminary investigation in the library to suggest to you the scope of the problem involved and the availability of material. Prepare three bibliography cards for items pertinent to the question. Then write a brief statement of your preliminary assessment of what would be involved in finding an answer or partial answer to your question.

1. What role did Henry Kissinger play in the improved relations between China and the United States?
2. What is the evidence for the existence of "Unidentified Flying Objects"?
3. What caused President Harding's death?
4. Was Mary Queen of Scots guilty of conspiring against Elizabeth?
5. Can bees distinguish colors?
6. What sort of law enforcer was Wyatt Earp?
7. Was Lizzie Borden insane?
8. Is the ballad "Frankie and Johnnie" based on a real event?
9. How did the Egyptians build their pyramids?
10. Do ants fight wars?
11. What is the origin of the legend that a toad has a jewel in its head?
12. What was the evidence presented to justify burning Joan of Arc at the stake?
13. What did Noah Webster think about spelling?
14. Did Adolf Hitler die in Berlin?
15. Has atomic testing had any effect on weather?
16. Has fallout from atomic testing had any effect on animal or plant life?
17. Was there a shot from a sniper before the National Guard opened fire on students at Kent State in 1970?
18. Did Columbus discover America?
19. Did Washington chop down a cherry tree?
20. How closely did Davy Crockett resemble the legends about him?
21. Is cancer becoming a young person's disease?
22. What was the Teapot Dome Scandal?
23. What was the role of H. L. Mencken in the Scopes trial?
24. How much scientific evidence is there for the existence of extrasensory perception?
25. How accurate historically is Shakespeare's portrait of Richard III?

E. The following represent the sources used by one student in writing a paper based on George Orwell's *1984*. The limited topic was mind control through word control. Write or type these in the proper form as they would appear on the Works Cited page.

1. A book by J. G. A. Pocock called Politics, Language and Time. The book was published by Atheneum in New York in 1971.
2. A book by Edwin Newman, Strictly Speaking, which was published by Bobbs-Merrill Company, Inc. in New York in 1974.
3. About Language, a book in its second edition, by Marden L. Clark, Soren F. Cox, and Marshall R. Craig. It was published in 1975 by Charles Scribner's Sons in New York.
4. An article by David A. Wiessler, Language Takes a Turn for Plusungood,

which appeared in the January 2, 1983 edition of U. S. News and World Report on pages 95 and 96.
5. A book, Politics, Language and Thought, which was published in Chicago by the University of Chicago Press in 1977. The author is David L. Laitin.
6. The book *1984* by George Orwell. This edition was published in 1949 by Harcourt in New York.
7. Of Bafflegab and Newspeak, an article by Allan Fotheringham, published in Macleans on January 16, 1984. The article appeared on page 56.

F. Once you have completed your research paper, evaluate your process. What was the most difficult part of the research? What was the easiest? What would you do differently next time? Have you learned any time-saving devices, special helps to remember in the future? Write these down so you will not forget the next time you do research.

17

Punctuation

> At this moment the King, who had been for some time busily writing in his notebook, called out "Silence!" and read out from his book "Rule Forty-two. All Persons more than a mile high to leave the court." Everybody looked at Alice.
> "I'm not a mile high," said Alice.
> "You are," said the King.
> "Nearly two miles high," added the Queen.
> "Well, I sha'n't go, at any rate," said Alice: "besides, that's not a regular rule: you invented it just now."
> "It's the oldest rule in the book," said the King.
> LEWIS CARROLL, *Alice's Adventures in Wonderland*

All languages are systems, or systems of systems, and most of them, including English, are in part conventional. That is, some customs of language have become so ordered and arbitrary that the reason behind a practice may be obscured in the rule that prescribes it. Even the "oldest rule in the book," however, may have good sense and good logic behind it. At worst it hardens as an accepted convention, a sort of truth by common agreement. At best it becomes a useful tool, and writers who use it skillfully can clarify their work.

USES OF PUNCTUATION

Punctuation usually helps the reader mainly by clarifying structure, but often it actually determines meaning. Compare:

If you want this job, when you are eighteen you must fill out this form.
If you want this job when you are eighteen, you must fill out this form.

Changing the location of the comma changes the meaning.
Anything as subtle and varied as language, however, can never be rigid, not even in punctuation. Styles differ in details, even from one newspaper or one publishing company to another. But there are practices common to most American publishers, codifications of accepted usage, and these are the basis of the guides that follow. You can probably find examples that do not conform to some of these. The following "rules," however, describe standard conventions you can safely follow in order to keep your writing clear.
In general, punctuation in English has three uses:

1. To Mark Off Sentences The most common use of punctuation is to mark the boundaries of sentences or independent clauses.

2. To Mark Minor Structures within a Sentence Punctuation works to preserve the flow from subject to verb to complement by setting apart any elements that interrupt the thought of the SVC pattern—nonrestrictive modifiers, parenthetic expressions, and the like. Most frequently, the comma, but also the semicolon, colon, dash, parentheses, and brackets may be used to mark these structures.

3. To Clarify Conventional Pattern Punctuation, most often commas, is used in a variety of ways, often arbitrarily, to clarify statistics, mark quotations, introduce lists.

END PUNCTUATION: PERIOD, QUESTION MARK, EXCLAMATION MARK

End punctuation, usually a period but sometimes a question mark or exclamation mark, indicates the end of a sentence and has some conventional uses. Following are common uses of end punctuation in English:

1. To End a Sentence A period marks the end of a sentence.

I can resist anything except temptation.

Problems occur if a period stops a group of words that is not a complete sentence, but only a fragment of a sentence, or if a period is omitted, creating a run-on sentence. (For a discussion of sentence fragments see chapter 6.)

2. *Exclamation* The exclamation mark indicates emotion or feeling. It is seldom used except in reporting conversation, particularly after exclamations like *Ouch!* or *Murder!* Some beginning writers try to liven their compositions with exclamation marks. The device seldom works—prose that must be emphasized with exclamation marks needs revision.

3. *Question* A question mark is used after a direct question, which often appears in a quotation.

> I asked her, "Will you go?"
> What are the reasons for her mother's antagonism?

An indirect question, in which the question is not stated verbatim but is part of a statement, is ended by a period.

> I asked her if she would go.

4. *Question within Sentence* The question mark is sometimes used after inserted interrogative material.

> Anyone who loves his country—and who does not?—will answer a call to duty.

Sometimes a question or a series of questions is included in a sentence, each ended with a question mark.

> The judge may very well ask these questions: When did you first meet the accused? How well did you know her? Did you see her on the night of the robbery?

Frequently a sentence like the above can be phrased more sharply with indirect questions.

> The judge may very well ask when you first met the accused, how well you knew her, and whether you saw her on the night of the robbery.

Notice in the first version that when a question mark appears at the end of a sentence, no period is used. Or notice:

> By Sunday I could stand no more, and I said, "Aren't you ever going to leave?"

Guide to Revision P1

END PUNCTUATION

Use appropriate end punctuation to close sentences or follow conventions. (See also chapter 6.)

ORIGINAL

He finally acknowledged that all people have an equal right to decent housing. Which was what I had been saying all along. [*Special circumstances might justify the unusual punctuation, but normally parts of the basic sentence pattern, or close modifiers of it, are best not segregated with end punctuation.*]

The question was whether Morgan would attack the center or make the long detour around Old Baldy and attack on the flank? [*The indirect question should be followed by a period. If the question were put directly, it would be followed by a question mark.*]

"Help," she screamed. "My dress, in the cogs."
[*A girl being dragged into power machinery may be excited enough to warrant exclamation marks.*]

REVISION

He finally acknowledged that all people have an equal right to decent housing, which was what I had been saying all along. [*With a comma replacing the first period the flow of the sentence is preserved, and when the end punctuation does appear it emphasizes the whole structure.*]

(1) The question was whether Morgan would attack the center or make the long detour around Old Baldy and attack on the flank.
(2) The question was this: Would Morgan attack the center, or would he make the long detour around Old Baldy and attack on the flank?

"Help!" she screamed. "My dress! in the cogs!"
[*The revision does not bolster weak prose; it makes clear at once the drama of the sentences.*]

5. Question as Request A request or command that for politeness is phrased as a question may conclude with either a question mark or a period.

Will you please sign and return the enclosed voucher? *or* . . . voucher.

Conventional Uses of the Period

1. Abbreviation In American usage the period appears after most abbreviations: P.M., Mr., pp., Ave., St., U.S.A., ibid., A.D. Any good dictionary will include abbreviations in the word list or in a special section.

The period is not used after letters standing for some widely used phrases which become cumbersome if written out: HUD, ZIP, POW, AFL-CIO, ICBM, ESP; after letters that represent scholarly or technical journals: PMLA, CA, MLR; after letters of radio stations: KLRB, WEAF, KATO; after MS (plural, MSS) for *manuscript;* certain unions and associations: WAA, AEF, NEA.

2. Ellipsis Three consecutive periods (. . .) make a punctuation mark known as the ellipsis, inserted in the place of material omitted from a quotation. When the omission comes after a completed sentence or completes a sentence, the end punctuation is retained so that four consecutive periods appear.

> Genius is the activity which repairs the decays of things. . . . Nature . . . insures herself.
>
> Ralph Waldo Emerson

Three periods mark an omission, a fourth period the end of a sentence.

THE SEMICOLON: PUNCTUATION BETWEEN INDEPENDENT CLAUSES, FUSED OR RUN-ON SENTENCES, COMMA FAULT OR COMMA SPLICE

The major use of the semicolon is to separate independent clauses combined in one sentence. We have discussed independent clauses, word groups containing a subject and verb and no function word to make them dependent (see chapter 6). Punctuation is needed to indicate the end of each independent clause. When the clause is written as a separate sentence, it is closed by a period or sometimes an exclamation mark or question mark. When independent clauses are combined within a sentence, several punctuation patterns are standard.

1. Semicolon with Independent Clauses Combined in a sentence and not joined by any function word, independent clauses are separated by a semicolon.

> We always like those who admire us; we do not always like those whom we admire.
> Humility is the most difficult of all virtues to achieve; nothing dies harder than the desire to think well of oneself.

2. Separation With Comma Before Coordinating Conjunction If independent clauses are joined by one of the coordinating conjunctions (*and, or, nor, but, for, yet, so*), they are separated by a comma preceding the conjunction.

> Statesmen are not only liable for what they say or do in public, *but* there is a busy inquiry made into their very meals, beds, and marriages.
> She fed all the peanuts to the elephant, and the monkey had to be satisfied with popcorn.

Notice that the second example illustrates how the comma may be necessary to avoid at least temporary ambiguity. Without the comma the reader would miss the structure of the sentence until coming to the second verb, thinking momentarily that the monkey had shared the peanuts. If the conjunction does not join clauses, however, no comma is used before it.

> Jack spent his mornings playing golf and his afternoons swimming.

The conjunction, *and,* connects *playing golf* and *swimming,* which are not independent clauses, and no comma is used.

3. Semicolon Before Conjunctive Adverb When the second clause is introduced by a conjunctive adverb like *hence, then, therefore, however, in fact, moreover,* etc., a semicolon separates the clauses.

> I do not have a taste for caviar; however, I should like to be rich enough to be able to develop one.

Notice that the conjunctive adverb is followed by a comma.

4. Commas with Short Clauses Short, closely related independent clauses, especially in series, may be separated by only a comma.

> The rain falls constantly, the river continues to rise.
> The camera rolls back, the boom moves out, the water ripples gently, and the only one now to make a move outside the lighted circle is the man with the little fog can and the fan.

Guide to Revision   **P2, Run-on, CF**

SEMICOLON: RUN-ON SENTENCES

Provide adequate punctuation to separate independent clauses.

ORIGINAL

The children tore the stuffed stockings from the mantel then they crept quickly back to bed.
[*The clauses can be made separate sentences, or separated with a semicolon (1); one clause can be subordinated (2); or one subject can be removed and the verb in the clause made part of a compound verb (3).*]

He had been, he said, a most unconscionable time dying, however, he hoped they would excuse it.
[*A conjunctive adverb* (however, moreover, therefore, then, hence) *is a modifier and does not obviate the need for a semicolon to separate the clauses.*]

Jack had been brought up on golf and tennis did not interest him.
[*The writer can supply a comma (1), or make one clause dependent (2).*]

Yesterday, having spent my last dime, I fasted, today, with a check from Uncle Harve, I gorged on steak.
[*Complicated clauses, containing commas within them, are joined here without adequate punctuation.*]

REVISION

(1) The children tore the stuffed stockings from the mantel; then they crept quickly back to bed.
(2) After the children had torn the stuffed stockings from the mantel, they crept quickly back to bed.
(3) The children tore the stuffed stockings from the mantel and then crept quickly back to bed.

(1) He had been, he said, a most unconscionable time dying; however, he hoped they would excuse it.
(2) He had been, he said, a most unconscionable time dying; he hoped, however, that they would excuse it.

(1) Jack had been brought up on golf, and tennis did not interest him.
(2) Since Jack had been brought up on golf, tennis did not interest him.

Yesterday, having spent my last dime, I fasted; today, with a check from Uncle Harve, I gorged on steak.
[*A semicolon is needed to point out the major division of the sentence.*]

5. *Semicolon with Complex Structures* When long or complex clauses, containing commas within them, are joined, a semicolon may be required before a coordinating conjunction to mark the main division in the sentence.

> Although the police had been ordered to keep everyone out of the building, they paid little attention to the back doors; and long before the rally was scheduled to begin, the big hall was packed with students.

Similarly, when items in a series or list are complicated and contain internal punctuation, the semicolon may be used to separate items (see p. 403).

COMMAS AFTER INTRODUCTORY MODIFIERS

The end of an introductory modifying clause is marked by a comma.

> After men come to like a sea life, they are not fit to live on land.
> When citizens assume a public trust, they should consider themselves public property.

Other introductory modifiers, especially if they are longer than four or five words, are followed by commas if the reader might otherwise have difficulty identifying the point at which the modifier stops.

> In matters of religion and politics, I believe that every person has a right to choose.

Even short modifiers are often marked with commas to ensure clarity.

> Above, the buzzards circled silently.
> In the morning, light filtered through the chinks in the ceiling.

Frequently the intended intonation provides a clue to punctuation. Consider:

> Meanwhile the dog ate our dinner.

Spoken, the sentence would probably carry a sharp rise in pitch on the first syllable of *meanwhile* and a pause after the word; a comma after *meanwhile* would enforce this intention.

> Meanwhile, the dog ate our dinner.

> *Guide to Revision* **P3**
>
> # COMMAS AFTER INTRODUCTORY MODIFIERS
>
> *Revise punctuation to mark the end of an introductory modifier.*
>
> | ORIGINAL | REVISION |
> |---|---|
> | Before we had finished eating the salad and the fish were snatched away. [*The reader momentarily thinks the salad and fish were eaten.*] | Before we had finished eating, the salad and the fish were snatched away. [*The comma stops the modifier after eating.*] |
> | By daylight, we could find our way. [*The comma does no harm, but the introductory modifier is short.*] | By daylight we could find our way. [*The comma is unnecessary.*] |
> | Accordingly I resigned. [*Though brief, the introductory element is set off in meaning.*] | Accordingly, I resigned. [*Accordingly would be set off orally; the comma is preferable.*] |

COMMAS WITH NONRESTRICTIVE OR PARENTHETICAL MODIFIERS

When modifiers limit closely, especially when they supply the information that identifies or distinguishes subject or complement, they are called restrictive and are not set off by punctuation. Modifiers not essential to the subject-verb-complement combination, which supply incidental information (as this clause does), are called *nonrestrictive,* and must be set off by punctuation. Compare:

> All the children who were in the front row received ice cream.
> All the children, who were in the front row, received ice cream.

First, read the two sentences aloud. As we read the first, we raise the pitch of the voice on *row* and tend to pause after it. As we read the second, we raise pitch on the main syllable of *children*, drop it on *row*, and pause after both *children* and *row*. That is, we distinguish restrictive and nonrestrictive in speech by intonation. We can tell which are nonrestrictive by thinking how they sound, and the punctuation helps us see how they should sound. The punctuation in writing reveals the meaning as the sound patterns do in speech. In the first sentence, both the sound and the punctuation show that, of all the children, only certain lucky ones, those in the front row, were treated. "Who were in the front row," without commas, is read as restrictive. It restricts or limits *children* to the group it names, specifies certain children; but the second sentence says that all the children received ice cream. The clause is nonrestrictive, as the commas indicate.

Sometimes, as in the sentences above, modifiers can be interpreted as either restrictive or nonrestrictive, but usually the modifiers make sense with only one kind of punctuation. A nonrestrictive modifier can be recognized because it can be dropped out of the sentence without distortion of the main meaning.

> The old house, badly out of repair, was hard to sell.

Omission of "badly out of repair" would not change the central idea of the sentence. But compare:

> An old house badly out of repair is no bargain.

"Badly out of repair" is required as part of the subject. Notice what happens if it is omitted:

> An old house is no bargain.

The meaning shifts; instead of questioning the value of a run-down house, it warns against buying any old house.

Except at the beginning or end of a sentence, nonrestrictive modifiers need commas both before and after them. Punctuation on only one side of an internal modifier is especially confusing because it separates essential parts of the main sentence as in the following:

> My grandmother, who still had a powerful voice went to the door and shouted.

The comma after *grandmother* marks the beginning of the nonrestrictive clause; but since there is no comma to mark the end of the clause, the first comma only separates the subject, *grandmother*, from its verbs. The commas should appear in pairs:

> My grandmother, who still had a powerful voice, went to the door and shouted.

Nonrestrictive modifiers include the following:

1. *Appositive Modifiers* A word or group of words that immediately follows another word or group of words and repeats its meaning is called an appositive. It is usually nonrestrictive and set off with commas.

> My brother, chairman of the board, opposed the stock issue.

"Chairman of the board" adds incidental information but is not essential to the subject-verb-complement pattern. Sometimes, however, an appositive does restrict the subject and is not separated.

> My brother John is chairman of the board.

John specifies which brother, restricts *brother.*

2. *Verbal Modifiers* Modifiers including a verbal are often nonrestrictive.

> The catcher, having played twelve innings, was glad to be taken out of the game.

Sometimes, however, verbal modifiers are restrictive, often defining a subject:

> The man standing on the corner is my uncle.

Standing on the corner is necessary to identify the man.

3. *Adjectives Following the Words They Modify* After the nouns they modify, adjectives are usually nonrestrictive.

> The three books, dirty and charred, were saved from the fire.

4. *Parenthetical Material* General modifiers of the sentence like *of course, that is, however, indeed, therefore,* or *in conclusion,* and expressions that interrupt a sentence to qualify or add incidental information are nonrestrictive almost by definition and are set off with commas.

> He decided, however, not to throw the pie.
> The cape, as the illustration shows, reaches nearly to the ground.
> Politicians, generally speaking, consider the desires of their constituents.

Parenthetical expressions that interrupt sharply or dramatically or that are not grammatically part of the sentence are sometimes set off by dashes or parentheses.

Guide to Revision **P4**

COMMAS AND NONRESTRICTIVE MODIFIERS

Revise to set off nonrestrictive matter, with commas before and after nonrestrictive modifiers within the sentence.

ORIGINAL	REVISION
I bought the material, that Mother had picked out. [*The modifier identifies or defines the material; it is restrictive.*]	I bought the material that Mother had picked out. [*The restrictive use of the modifier is clear without punctuation.*]
That evening which has always seemed the most terrifying of my life the dining room ceiling fell on us. [*The modifier is not essential; it adds incidental information and is nonrestrictive.*]	That evening, which has always seemed the most terrifying of my life, the dining room ceiling fell on us. [*The nonrestrictive modifier must be punctuated to set it apart from the main parts of the sentence.*]
We started running for the express station which was still several blocks ahead. [*The punctuation is accurate only if the clause identifies one station of at least two.*]	We started running for the express station, which was still several blocks ahead. [*In most contexts, the clause would be nonrestrictive.*]
The discussion is, indeed, silly. [*The punctuation is not wrong, but it probably sets off the modifier more than necessary.*]	The discussion is indeed silly. [*Probably the writer intends* indeed *to modify* silly *only, not to be parenthetical.*]
Aunt Agnes dyed her hair, painted her eyelashes, and plucked her brows although she always wore shoe-length dresses. [*The* although *clause had better be set off with a comma.*]	Aunt Agnes dyed her hair, painted her eyelashes, and plucked her brows, although she always wore shoe-length dresses.

5. *Final Qualifying Clauses* Qualifying clauses, especially when they begin with *although,* may be nonrestrictive even when they follow the main clause; they are then set off with a comma.

> Fools cause as much damage as criminals, although they are seldom punished.

When final clauses are restrictive, they are not punctuated, but even clauses beginning with *because* may be nonrestrictive.

> "Did you go to the picnic?" "I went, because I had to."

The modifying clause supplies additional information, not that required to answer the question.

COMMAS: PUNCTUATION IN A SERIES

Items in a series are separated by punctuation.

1. *Commas to Separate Items in Series* Commas separate words, phrases, dependent clauses, and sometimes very brief independent clauses when they are coordinated in a series of three or more.

> She announced that she was staying in bed until noon, that she was not cooking lunch for anybody, and that she would decide later about dinner.

Some newspapers do not require a comma before *and* (lettuce, endive and celery), but most publishers and writers of standard English prefer the comma before *and* (lettuce, endive, and celery) on the ground that the omission of the comma is occasionally confusing:

> Their menu includes the following: veal steak, roast beef, pork chops, ham and eggs.
> She purchased the following: veal, beef, pork, ham, and eggs.

In the first sentence the reader may be uncertain whether or not the eggs are fried with the ham.

If all the items in a series are joined by connectives, no punctuation is needed: "lettuce and endive and celery."

A combination like "bread and butter" within a series is treated as one element of the series.

2. *Commas to Separate Modifiers in Series* Consecutive modifiers that tend to modify individually rather than to combine to form a composite modifier form a series and are usually separated by commas. Compare:

The streetcar had badly constructed, old-fashioned seats.
The streetcar had grimy cane seats.

In the first, the adjectives seem to modify *seats* independently. As a rough test, insert the word *and* between them and see if the construction still pro-

---

Guide to Revision   **P5**

PUNCTUATION IN SERIES

Supply punctuation to separate items in a series.

ORIGINAL	REVISION
We distinguished highways, roads trails, streets and alleys. [*Commas are needed to separate all items.*]	We distinguished highways, roads, trails, streets, and alleys. [*A comma before the* and *is required in most formal styles.*]
The only available room was a dirty, vermin-infested, sleeping porch. [*Dirty and vermin-infested modify in series, but sleeping is not part of the series.*]	The only available room was a dirty, vermin-infested sleeping porch. [*Only the two items in series are separated; each of them modifies sleeping porch.*]
I canned dozens of gleaming many-colored jars of fruit. [*The modifiers are in series;* and *could sensibly be put between them.*]	I canned dozens of gleaming, many-colored jars of fruit. [*A comma should separate the items of the series.*]
The Council included the following representatives: President John A. Rickert, administration, Professor George P. Barrows, faculty, Avery Warren, student council, and Janice Worley, WAA. [*The commas alone do not adequately distinguish the two sorts of words in the series.*]	The Council included the following representatives: President John A. Rickert, administration; Professor George P. Barrows, faculty; Avery Warren, student council; and Janice Worley, WAA. [*Semicolons distinguish the main divisions of the series.*]

duces a familiar pattern. If it does, as in "badly constructed and old-fashioned seats," the modifiers are probably in series. In the second, however, *grimy* seems to modify all that follows it; the modifiers do not work independently in a series. "Grimy and cane seats" does not fill a familiar pattern for modifiers. As another rough test, reverse the order of the modifiers. Those in series can be logically reversed, "old-fashioned badly constructed seats"; those not in series cannot, "cane grimy seats."

Numerals and common adjectives of size, color, and age seldom appear in series: "twenty-four scrawny blackbirds," "two little girls," "a spry old man," "a pretty little girl."

3. *Commas to Separate Short Clauses* Short, closely related independent clauses, especially in series, may be separated by only a comma.

> The camera rolls back, the boom moves out, the water ripples gently.

4. *Semicolon When Items Have Internal Commas* The semicolon may substitute for the comma to divide items in a series or list when the items are complicated and contain punctuation within them.

> She told me that, in view of my prejudices, my poor health, and my interests, I never would be happy as a teacher; that I would find myself, at the end of the day, exhausted from policing dozens of squirming children; and that I would find my evenings, during which I hoped to practice music, given over to school plays, to the school band and orchestra, and to playing command canasta with the superintendent.

Semicolons separate the three dependent clauses. Since the sentence is long and involved, with commas inside the three dependent clauses, semicolons are needed to mark the main divisions.

COMMAS FOR CLARITY

A writer should use whatever punctuation may be necessary to avoid confusion. Usually awkward sentences should be revised, but sometimes, for emphasis, economy, or some other reason, a writer does not wish to revise, and a comma or two may effect a cure. Pope's famous dictum, punctuated as Pope did not write it, "Whatever is is right," would be at least momentarily disturbing. With a comma inserted, the meaning is clear: "Whatever is, is right."

> *Guide to Revision* **P6**
>
> # COMMAS FOR CLARITY
>
> *Insert a comma to clarify the construction.*
>
> **ORIGINAL**
>
> I told him to speak out out of turn if necessary.
> [*The unusual repetition of* out *becomes confusing without special punctuation.*]
>
> He looked up the words he had intended to say formed only by his lips.
> [*The sentence can be understood, but the reader's familiarity with the idea of looking up words leads to momentary confusion.*]
>
> An hour of lecture presumes two hours of preparation, an hour of laboratory none.
> [*Presumes is assumed between* laboratory *and* none.]
>
> **REVISION**
>
> I told him to speak out, out of turn if necessary.
> [*With a comma to separate the second* out *from the first, the structure becomes clear.*]
>
> He looked up, the words he had intended to say formed only by his lips.
> [*The inserted comma emphasizes that* words *is not the object of* look up.]
>
> An hour of lecture presumes two hours of preparation, an hour of laboratory, none.
> [*The comma makes the structure clear.*]

COMMAS SEPARATING STATISTICAL DETAILS

Commas can clarify various sorts of statistical detail:

1. Dates In general, commas are used between elements of a date. When a year is part of a date, it usually has commas both before and after it. Parts of a single element, such as the name of a month and the figure indicating the day, are not separated. With abbreviations, both a period and comma may be required.

They arrived by train at 10 A.M., Monday, January 9, 1967.
Tuesday night, July 6, 1820, the debate began.

In some styles, commas are omitted in brief indications of date: "In March, 1972, she . . ." or "In March 1972 she . . ." In the style used by the Armed Forces, and becoming increasingly popular generally, the day precedes the month and no comma is necessary: "11 August 1916."

2. *Addresses* Elements of addresses are similarly separated. When more than one element appears in an address, the last element is followed by a comma, unless the address is itself a separate unit, as in the address of a letter. Parts of elements, such as a street number and the name of the street following it, along with some code numbers, such as those in Zip Code, are not separated.

He gave 1162 West Avenue, Cleveland, Ohio 44100, as his address.

3. *Other Statistics* Commas separate parts of measurements, divisions of a whole, and other statistical details. The last element of a series of divisions, like parts of a book, is usually separated from what follows, but the last part of a series constituting a measurement is usually not.

He was six feet, eight inches tall.
The sentence appears on page 11, line 28, of the new book.
She must enter in Act III, scene 2, before the music begins.

Guide to Revision **P7**

COMMAS AND STATISTICAL DETAILS

Supply punctuation to clarify statistical information.

ORIGINAL

My new address is, 1905 West First Street, Hillsboro IA, 52630.

Mary was born January 4, 1962 in Chicago, at 1227 Second Avenue.

He cleared the bar at six feet four inches.

REVISION

My new address is 1905 West First Street, Hillsboro, IA 52630.

Mary was born January 4, 1962, in Chicago, at 1227 Second Avenue.

He cleared the bar at six feet, four inches.

INAPPROPRIATE OR EXCESSIVE COMMAS

Punctuation should clarify; sprinkled indiscriminately, especially when it separates closely related sentence elements, punctuation distracts or obscures. The mistaken notion that any pause in speech warrants a comma in writing is responsible for some excessive punctuation. Redundant punctuation includes the following:

1. *Separation of Main Sentence Parts* Punctuation that separates subject from verb or verb from complement may be especially misleading. Consider:

> Every book on the shelf, had been damaged.

The unnecessary comma separates the subject, *book,* from the verb. Without the comma the sentence reads more smoothly:

> Every book on the shelf had been damaged.

Putting a comma on only one side of a modifier has the same effect.

> The lamp that Wilbur made from discarded copper tubing, won a prize.

With a nonrestrictive modifier, commas would be needed on both sides. Here, since the modifier is restrictive, no comma is needed.

> The lamp that Wilbur made from discarded copper tubing won a prize.

2. *Unnecessary comma with* and The practice of using a comma before *and* in a series or between independent clauses should not be distorted into the notion that a comma always precedes *and*.

> Louise finally emptied the drawer, and found the ring.
> The Senator believed that the legislation was illegal, and that the bill would never pass.

The comma is not needed when *and* simply connects two verbs, like *emptied* and *found,* or when it connects two objects, *that the bill was illegal* and *that it would never pass.*

> Louise finally emptied the drawer and found the ring.
> The Senator believed that the legislation was illegal and that the bill would never pass.

3. *Unnecessary Comma Before Final Clause* A restrictive clause should not be separated even after a main verb.

> **Guide to Revision** **P8 No P**
>
> # UNNECESSARY COMMAS
>
> *Remove excessive or misleading punctuation.*
>
> | ORIGINAL | REVISION |
> |---|---|
> | The girl who had bought the high-heeled shoes, came wobbling back into the store. [*The comma on one side of a clause separates subject from verb.*] | The girl who had bought the high-heeled shoes came wobbling back into the store. [*The modifier is restrictive, and no punctuation is needed.*] |
> | My father, and John ran up the walk, and threw their arms around us. | My father and John ran up the walk and threw their arms around us. |
> | Mary was afraid, that someone else would wear a pirate costume. | Mary was afraid that someone else would wear a pirate costume. |
> | Of course, I looked in the drawer for the flashlight; but someone had taken it. [*The semicolon is acceptable, but the sentence would be clear with a comma.*] | Of course, I looked in the drawer for the flashlight, but someone had taken it. |

He asked to see the person, who had made the rule.

The comma would be appropriate with a nonrestrictive modifier, but the clause here is restrictive and should not be separated.

He asked to see the person who had made the rule.

THE COLON

The colon has two functions. It resembles in force the sign of equality in mathematics; that is, whatever comes before the colon is in at least one sense equal to what comes after it. But it also can mark a pattern of general to specific, introducing a specific instance of a more general statement:

John has one quality I admire: honesty.

The major uses of the colon are the following:

1. Series It is most frequently used to precede a series that has already been introduced by a completed statement, often containing the word *following* or *follows:*

> I find four kinds of people in adult education classes: those who come to meet people, those who are bored with their lives, those who have been sent by their employers, and those who are interested in the subject.

The colon is not needed, however, when the series immediately follows the verb as a group of complements. Compare:

> I find that the four kinds of people in adult education classes are those who come to meet people, those who are bored with their lives, those who have been sent by their employers, and those who are interested in the subject.

2. Independent Clauses The colon is occasionally used between independent clauses when the second part of the sentence has been introduced in the first:

> Two events occurred that spring to make Marie less happy in her new home: The mangy cat that had been her companion was hit by a car, and the low spot near the garage that became a fine mud puddle after every shower was filled and leveled.

The colon is unusual in this use, however, unless the second part of the sentence clearly repeats or clarifies the first.

3. Conventional Uses The colon also has certain conventional uses, notably after the formal address of a letter, in statements of time, in citations from the Bible, and in book titles:

> Dear Sir:
> 8:35 P.M.
> Genesis 5:1–3
> *Vanity Fair: A Novel Without a Hero*

Guide to Revision P9

THE COLON

Use the colon for its specialized purposes but not as the equivalent of a semicolon.

ORIGINAL	REVISION
The common silk dress goods are: raw silk, taffeta, crepe de chine, shantung, pongee, silk chiffon, silk organdy, satin, and silk velvet. [*The list is a complement and should not be separated from the verb it completes.*]	The common silk dress goods are raw silk, taffeta, crepe de chine, shantung, pongee, silk chiffon, silk organdy, satin, and silk velvet. [*The colon that breaks the continuity of the subject-verb-complement pattern is omitted.*]
In high school I competed in the principal sports, that is: in hockey, swimming, and basketball. [*The colon introduces a formal series; here* hockey, swimming, *and* basketball *are in apposition with* sports.]	In high school I competed in the principal sports, that is, in hockey, swimming, and basketball. [*The meaning is at once clear with a comma, and accordingly the lighter punctuation is preferable.*]
Many people try to come to Washington: After they get there they complain about the weather. [*The colon is no longer used as the rough equivalent of a semicolon.*]	Many people try to come to Washington; after they get there they complain about the weather.

THE DASH

The dash (—) is made with two hyphens on the typewriter and typed with no space on either side. Used with caution, dashes may mark any sort of sharp break, especially in an internally punctuated modifier:

Often had he recalled, in Asia, the drowsy verdant opulence of his home—those willow-fringed streamlets and grazing cattle, the smell of hay, the flowery lanes.

Dashes may also serve the following purposes: to give emphasis (sentence 1), to provide an introduction (sentence 2), and to summarize (sentence 3):

1. If he has any decency he will come and apologize—but has he any decency?
2. Of the thoughts that flashed through my mind one persisted—if I screamed, the children would wake up.

Guide to Revision   **P10 Dash**

USING DASHES

Use dashes for the purposes described above, but do not substitute them indiscriminately for other punctuation marks.

ORIGINAL

These discoveries,—evolution, relativity, and now atomic fission,—have given us a new conception of the world.
[*The commas are not necessary.*]

Knowing only the most elementary principles of chemistry—I should never have attempted the experiment alone—However—I set up the equipment—and got out the necessary materials—not knowing how explosive they were—especially in combination—
[*This is a jumble because the writer has not punctuated.*]

REVISION

These discoveries—evolution, relativity, and now atomic fission—have given us a new conception of the world.

Knowing only the most elementary principles of chemistry, I should never have attempted the experiment alone. However, I set up the equipment and got out the necessary materials, not knowing how explosive they were, especially in combination.
[*The dashes have been replaced by standard punctuation.*]

3. A brown, crusty turkey, fluffy mashed potatoes, jars of jam, pickles and olives, and mince and pumpkin pies—all these and more appeared before Linda, as if she were in a dream.

The dash also has conventional uses. It may be used before a citation at the end of a quotation. It is used in various kinds of informal tabular arrangements:

Humanities—fine arts, literature, language, philosophy
Social sciences—history, political science, sociology, economics

PARENTHESES AND BRACKETS

Parentheses and brackets are used to mark material that does not fit into the grammatical structure of the sentence but adds incidental information. Some of the uses are conventional.

1. Parentheses for Incidental Information Sometimes sentences or passages are not part of the main discussion but provide useful information. The material can be inserted in parentheses:

The statue bears this inscription: "To our bountiful lady, Margarita Fernandez." (Señora Fernandez was an Indian woman who married a Spaniard and at his death inherited his mining wealth.) It is an outstanding example of Spanish Baroque.

2. Parentheses in Formal Uses Parentheses have a variety of conventional uses. In this book, for example, parentheses enclose cross-references or examples inserted into sentences. They are used to enclose numbers or letters in an enumeration:

He cited reasons as follows: (1) No student had been allowed in the building in the past, (2) furniture was not well enough built to stand student use, and (3) students had adequate facilities without new quarters.

3. Brackets in Formal Uses Brackets are sometimes used for insertions within parentheses, to avoid the confusion of parentheses within parentheses. They also are used typographically to emphasize or set apart some material. Perhaps their most common use is to mark material inserted into a quotation to clarify it.

According to Coleridge, "The misfortune is that he [Tennyson] has begun to write without very well understanding what metre is."

Brackets indicate that the identification of *he* has been editorially inserted.

> *Guide to Revision* **P11 Parens**
>
> # PARENTHESES AND BRACKETS
>
> *Use appropriate parentheses or brackets.*
>
> | ORIGINAL | REVISION |
> |---|---|
> | He distinguished between the members of the family *Juniperus, Juniperus communis, Juniperus virginiana,* and the like, and the plants resembling juniper, such as retem, *Retama raetam.* [*The words separated by commas seem at first to be words in a series.*] | He distinguished between the members of the family *Juniperus (Juniperus communis, Juniperus virginiana,* and the like) and the plants resembling juniper, such as retem (*Retama raetam*). [*Parentheses clarify the sentence.*] |
> | To write, you need a sharp pencil and a quick mind (the first of which can be easily acquired). [*Clauses within a sentence are usually sufficiently set off with commas.*] | To write, you need a sharp pencil and a quick mind, the first of which can be easily acquired. [*The comma is sufficient; for a sharper break, a dash would be preferable to parentheses.*] |
> | We hold these truths to be *self-evident* (the italics, of course, are mine), that all men are created equal ... [*The parentheses imply that the inserted matter was part of the original and was there in parentheses.*] | We hold these truths to be *self-evident* [the italics, of course, are mine], that all men are created equal ... [*The inserted matter has been enclosed within square brackets.*] |

QUOTATION MARKS: PUNCTUATION WITH QUOTATIONS

In American English a quoted passage may be preceded and followed by double quotation marks. In British practice, only single quotation marks are used. Particularly in recent decades, words and passages that would formerly have been placed within quotation marks are frequently underlined in script and set in italic type when printed. At present, styles vary; for more on uses of quotation marks and italics see chapter 18.

Conventions concerning the punctuation of quoted material include the following:

1. *Direct Quotations* Words reported as conversation or words previously written or spoken are enclosed in double quotation marks:

> "Get out," she said.
> After his service in Vietnam, he agreed that "the paths of glory lead but to the grave."

Even a three- or four-word phrase taken directly from a source is distinguished by quotation marks:

> Perhaps the most pernicious effect of television is, as Marie Winn has stated, that it turns "the living into silent statues."

2. *Special Usages* The concept of quotation is sometimes extended to call attention to a way of saying something or to include short expressions that quote speech from a special level of usage and from a particular country, region, social class, or person.

> It was then the fashion for popular music groups to describe themselves as "Neanderthals," "zanies," or something else unpleasant.

The quotation marks are used because a quotation from some other speaking group is implied. Quotation marks are no longer generally used as indiscriminate apologies for slang or colloquial English. In most instances, the slang should be used without apology if it is appropriate and omitted if it is not.

3. *Indirect Quotations* Indirect quotations are not placed within quotation marks, but a few words within an indirect quotation may be quoted directly. Compare:

> *Direct:* In his quiet way, he said, "I am excessively annoyed with the hoodlums next door."
> *Indirect:* In his quiet way, he said that he was "excessively annoyed" with the hoodlums next door.

4. *Words out of Context* Quotation marks may be used to indicate that a word is used as a word, but italics increasingly serve this purpose (The noun "boy" is the subject) (see chapter 18).

5. *Titles* Quotation marks distinguish titles in two special circumstances: (1) when mechanical limitations, such as those in typesetting for a newspaper, make italics impractical; and (2) when a short work is to be distinguished from the larger work that contains it (see chapter 18).

Robert Frost's "Mending Wall" appears in *Poetry of America*.

6. *Quotations within Quotations* In American practice, single quotation marks enclose a quotation within a quotation:

The witness said, "I was just opening the door when I heard her scream, 'Drop that!' "

7. *Introductions to Quotations* When an expression like "he said" introduces a quotation, it is separated from the quotation by a comma:

I said, "I have always hated Pomeranians."

Sometimes a formal introduction to a quotation is followed by a colon, but the comma is not used before an indirect quotation:

I said that I had always hated Pomeranians.

8. *Position of Quotation Marks* Quotation marks appear before and after the quoted material. When a quotation runs for more than one paragraph, the mark of quotation begins every paragraph but closes only the last one. Long quotations may be printed without quotation marks, in smaller type and indented; typewritten, the passage may also appear without quotation marks, double-spaced and with each line indented.

9. *Quotation Marks and Other Marks* The position of a quotation mark in relation to other punctuation used with it is determined partly by logic and partly by arbitrary convention. Commas and periods are always placed inside quotation marks. Colons and semicolons are always placed outside. All other punctuation marks are inside if they punctuate only the quoted words, outside if they punctuate an entire sentence containing a quotation:

The rafters used a long handspike, which they called a "picaroon."
He asked me to open the "boot"; I did not understand.
"Are you ready?" I asked.
Do you know who said that "life is but an empty dream"?

Guide to Revision P12

PUNCTUATION WITH QUOTATIONS

Supply punctuation to distinguish direct quotations.

ORIGINAL

I am sorry, she said, but those weeds you are lying in are poison ivy.
[*Material quoted directly should be set off by quotation marks.*]

Thoreau said that most people lead lives of quiet desperation.
[*The latter part of the sentence is quoted directly.*]

I told her "she ought to stop wasting her time."
[*The quotation is not direct; the direct quotation was something like "You'd better stop wasting your time."*]

She said I was in a hassle and that I had blown my top.
[*Hassle and blown my top are quotations from the character's manner of speech.*]

An upright contraption, known as a "moon box", was used to show an artificial moon on the stage.
[*Commas go inside quotation marks.*]

"Are you afraid of the dark"? the child asked.
[*Since the question mark punctuates the quoted material, it belongs inside.*]

REVISION

"I am sorry," she said, "but those weeds you are lying in are poison ivy."

Thoreau said that most people "lead lives of quiet desperation."
[*The quoted matter has been placed within quotation marks.*]

I told her she ought to stop wasting her time.
[*The quotation marks have been removed, since an indirect quotation is not enclosed.*]

She said I was in a "hassle" and that I had "blown my top."
[*The characteristic words have been enclosed within quotation marks.*]

An upright contraption, known as a "moon box," was used to show an artificial moon on the stage.

"Are you afraid of the dark?" the child asked.

FOR STUDY AND WRITING

A. Supply appropriate punctuation and capitalization in the following sentences. The meaning may change with various punctuation.

1. Joseph Joubert is credited with the following some men find their sole activity in repose others their sole repose in activity
2. I said rats if they are eating the cake I don't want any of it
3. One avocado did not ripen I don't know why the other one did
4. A certain truck carries the following signs this truck stops for a red light or a red head backs up 25 feet for a blonde and courtesy is our motto
5. He was playing left end you say so you say he was playing left end is that it
6. He was the worst dean I ever heard of with the alumni his putting his whole Sigma Nu house on probation is still a favorite story
7. Two times two are four four times four are fifteen no four fours are sixteen or are they or is it is
8. So you think you're pretty good do you feel like taking off your glasses and settling this outside
9. The following have registered thus far Alice Melarkey Los Angeles Muriel Jones St. Louis Florence O'Brien Seattle Florence Schmidt Syracuse and Helen Adney Atlanta
10. A number of changes account for the movement of beef raising into the southeast wornout cotton lands heavily cropped for years will no longer raise a high-production crop successfully and meanwhile Texas ranchers finding they have insufficient pastures in this the driest year in a decade are glad to acquire additional grazing land in the eastern gulf states

B. Supply the missing punctuation in the sentences below, and correct inappropriate punctuation; where two marks of punctuation are required, be sure you put them in the proper order. Some sentences are well punctuated as they stand.

1. To distinguish the types of furniture, note the following: bamboo grows in sections and is hollow; rattan, a much stronger material, grows solid.
2. They had something they called a "booby-hutch," which was defined as "a carriage body put upon sleigh runners."
3. "They the Pueblo Indians make a kind of bread called guayave which the white people call a 'hornet's nest.'

4. I turned and ran toward the subway station,—or thought I did, for it was snowing so that I could not see,—then I bumped into someone.
5. Janice (a quiet girl who went out little) was eager to have dates.
6. Inside I saw: a cat, some kittens, and an old white-haired woman.
7. . . . the play's the thing
Wherein I'll catch the *conscience* the italics are mine of the king.
8. Maximillian had three courses before him he could try to become a genuine ruler of the Mexicans for the Mexicans; he could take his scraps of a French army and flee; or he could go on living in indolent luxury, which would probably be ended by a firing squad.
9. "The so-called Dixiecrats [dissident southern Democrats] hoped by this move to gain the balance of power."
10. Alice—the scrawniest little girl in our block—was growing up to be a beauty

C. Punctuate the following sentences, paying particular attention to punctuation of nonrestrictive and parenthetical modifiers.

1. Then she started talking about a tepidarium whatever that is.
2. The atoll a coral reef that barely broke the water was nothing to turn to for protection particularly in stormy weather.
3. Gladys who was the only daughter of a steel manufacturer used to make me angry and jealous showing off her new clothes.
4. She is the girl who won the 4-H scholarship.
5. After one hour saturate the curls with neutralizer for bleached, dyed, or overdry hair see instructions on the front of the folder.
6. What we called the "coasting hill" a long grade that wound past the cemetery and down through the schoolyard unfortunately crossed Lake Street at the intersection by the grocery store a crossing that was much used by shoppers on Saturday our only coasting day.
7. The sorority that my mother favored was the only one that showed me any attention.
8. In our school Beeson County High School most of the boys were interested in sports especially basketball and accordingly you did not ask whether a boy had anything in his head but only whether he was tall enough to hold his head six feet in the air.
9. The tailored suit which I had brought home with me from Hadley's Bazaar a department store in New York City hung on me like a Hindu robe but everybody admired the outfit I had made a simple little dress devised out of some coarse basket-weave that Aunt Lilly gave me.
10. That summer I was employed as assistant to the playground director in Jordan Park the same park in which the previous summer I had refused to take part in the group games.

D. The sentences below could be corrected by supplying adequate punctuation, but most of them would be improved by revision. Correct each by changing punctuation; then revise each by making one of the independent clauses dependent and compare the results.

1. It was cold and rainy outside, however, the house was warm and dry.
2. I was in the hospital during the time I was there I fell in love with the head nurse.
3. I never learned the multiplication tables for this reason I have always been slow at mathematics.
4. The clerk opened the bank door at the same time the three robbers pushed their way into the bank.
5. The team lost the final game of the tournament, for this reason we cried ourselves to sleep that night.
6. The wounded were evacuated by helicopter, they could not do this if antiaircraft fire was heavy, however.
7. I finished washing all the dinner dishes then Bob said he thought we might mop and wax the kitchen floor.

E. Insert the correct punctuation in the following. The sentences of the original are indicated by capital letters.

When I was in Cuernavaca Mexico on a vacation trip in July 1966 I heard a story of what became of one of Rivera's murals It seems that the proprietor of a fashionable restaurant ordered his walls decorated Since I do not wish to be libelous let us say that the restaurant was at 268 Morales Avenue which it was not The proprietor a small ingratiating excitable man considered various muralists interviewing them from the time he arose at 10 a m until he went to bed at 2 a m Finally he settled upon Rivera who was known to be fashionable with certain groups especially the foreigners The mural finished the proprietor awaited the approval of the dignified people in the town Members of the important old families who were eager to view the newest monument to local progress responded to his invitation. They came in holiday mood and looked they left enraged They had seen their own faces painted upon the bodies of gangsters robbers cutthroats and quacks With small ceremony and no delay at all they rendered their artistic judgment If those pictures stayed up the most important people would stay out What to do The proprietor loved his murals for they had cost him much money he loved his business for it had brought him much money So he paced the floor which was new and only partly paid for and tore at his trim carefully waxed mustache At that he had an idea and with deft strokes painted bushy whiskers sprightly goatees and respectable muttonchops upon the faces of the abused citizens Should he not reason that whiskers that would render a mayor unrecognizable would also make him genial and as a result might he not be expected to eat the restaurant enchiladas But the device that the proprietor's mustache inspired was more ingenious than successful The outraged citizens were more outraged than ever not only had the proprietor insulted them by calling them bandits but he had further and doubly insulted them by implying that they grew bad beards As for Rivera he threatened to shoot the proprietor for desecrating art Torn between art and the artist between his patrons and their patronage the bedeviled proprietor saved at once his sanity and his business by having the whole room replastered.

F. Look at several essays you have written. Which areas of punctuation seem to give you the most problem? Can you identify any patterns? Remember these during the editing phase of your next writing assignment.

18

The Writing System: Mechanics and Spelling

Customs may not be as wise as laws, but they are always more popular.
BENJAMIN DISRAELI

Customs, even the most foolish and most cruel, have always their source in the real or apparent utility of the public.
HELVETIUS

Languages existed as speech long before people invented any way of translating speech into writing. Writing systems, however, have existed for many centuries, evolving from cumbersome systems with pictures standing for ideas or words to more efficient systems with symbols or letters expressing individual sounds. With our English alphabet of only twenty-six letters we can write the more than half million words in the language. Other alphabets and writing systems exist—Greek, Hebrew, Arabic, Russian—but they all depend on general agreement about how the symbols apply—about which letters will be used to represent which sounds.

These agreements are not always logical or consistent—witness English spelling—and they are subject to change, but they are the basis of a series of "rules" about spelling, manuscript form, and other conventions. The rules are rules only in the sense that they record custom; they "have their source in the real or apparent utility of the public." But they are important because failure to observe them distracts a reader or editor, destroying at least part of the effectiveness of any writing.

MANUSCRIPT FORM

Any manuscript, whether submitted for publication, presented as a business report, or prepared to fill a class assignment, should be neat, standard in appearance, and conventional in spelling, capitalization, syllabification, and other mechanics. The following rules are standard and fit the requirements of almost any publisher or reader:

1. Typewrite or print with a word processor in black, or write in black or blue-black ink on standard size (8½- × 11-inch) paper, unruled for typing, and ruled for handwriting with standard measure ruling, not the narrow ruling sometimes used for notebook paper.
2. Write on only one side of the paper. Having to flip loose papers irritates a reader or editor, and in a manuscript of any length can lead to various confusions.
3. Double-space between lines of a typewritten manuscript. Most editors refuse to look at unsolicited copy that is not double- or triple-spaced. Keep typewriter type clean and use a well-inked ribbon.
4. Make handwriting legible, distinguishing clearly between capital and small letters, between *v* and *n*, *a* and *o*.
5. Leave generous margins on all sides of the paper—at least an inch and a half at the top and the left and an inch at the right and the bottom.
6. Indent about half an inch for each new paragraph—five spaces on the typewriter. In typing, leave one space after internal punctuation, two spaces after end punctuation.
7. Proofread all written work carefully. The reader sees what you wrote, not what you meant to write.

SPELLING AND SPELLERS

Spelling is not an index to intelligence; a "bad speller" may be a good student. But spelling is a relatively rigid writing convention, and a badly spelled letter or manuscript encourages a bad reception. Learning to spell is worth the trouble. Almost everybody can learn to spell—even in English—if the problem is tackled in a workable way.

To begin, if you have trouble with spelling, you might remind yourself that you have already learned a great deal, most of it without trying.

Students who have read enough to get to college have automatically collected a considerable body of words they spell accurately without thinking. Few people misspell *do* and *was*, although the spelling is not obvious from the sound. You have seen words like these hundreds of times and have developed a feeling for the English spelling system that will help you remember rarer words, or even guess the spelling of words you have never seen.

Furthermore, the English spelling system is not so confused as it might seem from the relatively small number of irregular examples that can be listed. As a written language develops, certain symbols, letters, get assigned to particular sounds. The sounds of /l/, /m/, and /b/, for instance, are almost always rendered by the letters *l, m,* and *b,* and most consonant sounds are similarly consistent. A common estimate is that 80 to 85 percent of the words in the language are spelled according to consistent patterns. You can handle the bulk of English words just by following patterns you have picked up from using the language.

But English spelling can be troublesome, partly because pronunciations have changed since spelling was established (see chapter 10). *Right, rite, write,* and *wright* now sound alike but are spelled differently because they were once pronounced differently. Some dialects today distinguish between words like *merry, marry,* and *Mary,* between *horse* and *hoarse*.

Spellings vary also because English has been one of the great borrowing languages (see chapter 10). Usually we have adopted the foreign spelling along with the borrowed term. Such spellings have changed slowly if at all, often while the pronunciations changed to something nearer the native sounds. Thus *colonel* and *reveille* retain French spellings but not French pronunciations. In formal usage *agenda* and *data,* adopted Latin plurals, are considered plurals, although they look like English singulars. Devising a system of spelling to get rid of such inconsistencies would not be difficult. Any body of linguists could do it. But getting everybody to agree to even a vastly better system would not be easy, and the spelling system, as it has grown with the language, is what we have.

The "Bad" Speller

In addition to the troubles that all spellers of English are heir to, an individual may have individual handicaps. We do not understand very well how minds work, but we know they work differently. Some work well with both sight and sound; some work well with one and not so well with the other. One of these is not necessarily better than another, but for spelling persons who might be called "eye-minded" have an advantage. When they write a word correctly, it looks right, since it duplicates the visual memory of the word. "Ear-minded" persons, on the other hand, are likely to remember how the word sounds but not what it looks like. They may conscientiously look up a misspelled word in the dictionary and write it correctly, may even write it several times. But they soon forget it, and have to look it up again. They go on looking up words and forgetting them, until they become discouraged and conclude that they are "bad spellers." Such spellers need not despair; they have only to do some deliberate learning. A more systematic approach to spelling, like the one described below, has cured many a "bad speller," and it will work for almost any student.

Curing Nonstandard Spelling

Spelling is an individual problem. No two people misspell in the same way, particularly those as advanced as college students. If you want to work on spelling, you need to find out which words you misspell and, if possible, why you misspell them. You should make a list of all words you have to look up in the dictionary and of all words you misspell in your writing, indicating any repeated errors. For diagnostic purposes, this repetition of errors is probably the most important. The lists should be drawn from as much of your normal writing as possible. The lists should record the actual misspellings but should also include a correction of each error. Diagnosis is likely to reveal that errors tend to be primarily of the same sorts—for instance, carelessness, not knowing the conventional letters for English sounds, or misspelling the same few words over and over. You may find several consistent types of errors. From the list, however, you can discover which of the following kinds of common difficulties need the most work:

1. *Carelessness* Carelessness is not a spelling problem at all, but it leads to many incorrect spellings. The main problem of the student who wrote the same word *damage, dammage,* and *damadge* in a brief paper was not misspelling. It was carelessness. The student had written fast, which is good; but had not edited the work afterward, which is bad. The readiest cure for carelessness is to force yourself to read over carefully everything you write and correct the errors.

2. *Habitual Misspelling* If your list includes mainly repeated mistakes in words like *receive, too, their, separate,* or *loose* for *lose,* you have a relatively easy problem. You have never learned the small number of common words with difficult spellings. You need to memorize them. They will be so few that you can afford to spend a little time on them and eliminate them forever. The best start is to look up the offenders in a good dictionary and learn a lot about each word. For most writers and most words, enough awareness should provide a cure. If you still have trouble you should think of a memory device—if you make it up yourself you will remember it better. For example, if you have trouble distinguishing *lose* and *loose,* you might notice that *lose* is related to *lost*—which no doubt you can spell—and that each has only one *s.* Or you might observe that *loose* is spelled like *goose,* and that any *goose* could spell *loose.*

3. Errors in Recording Sounds In a rough way, spelling records sound patterns, though not always obviously or consistently. If your lists include errors like *Scananavian* for *Scandinavian, athelete* for *athlete, preform* for *perform, pronounciation* for *pronunciation, tradegy* for *tragedy, thing* for *think, quanity* for *quantity, reglar* for *regular, cause* for *because, libary* for *library,* or *wend* for *went,* you are having trouble with sounds and their spellings. You can correct many of your errors by learning more precise pronunciation—the distinction between *prejudice* and *prejudiced,* for example.

4. Confusion of Similar Words Words cause trouble when they have the same sound but different meanings—*sight, site,* and *cite; to, too,* and *two; rite, write, right,* and *wright; led* and *lead.* The confusion of *of* for *have* (as in "He would *of* done it") is doubtless encouraged by pronunciation, since in many dialects *'ve,* the abbreviation of *have,* is pronounced like *of.* The following frequently cause trouble: *angle, angel; casual, causal; chose, choose; lose, loose; desert, dessert; canvas, canvass; accept, except; affect, effect; principle, principal.* Many of these spellings come from old forms, never modernized; *meet* and *meat* used to be pronounced differently and were spelled as they were pronounced. Some knowledge of etymology may help. For any one speller such words are likely to be few, so that the cures suggested in number 2 above will work; know a great deal about each word and think up a memory device if necessary.

5. Errors from Analogy or Etymology Spelling by analogy or etymology can help, but analogies may lead a writer astray, especially if they rest on false assumptions. One common misspelling is *definate* for *definite,* probably because of the large number of English words ending in *-ate.* The misspellings like *pronounciation* and *renounciation* result from the analogy with the corresponding verbs. The misspellings *Britian* and *villian* may reflect false analogy with many English words having *i* and *a* in this sequence, as in *Parisian, gentian, Martian.*

6. Confusion with Prefixes and Suffixes Numerous words cause trouble because they include a syllable, often a prefix or a suffix, that can be spelled in several ways or that differs but slightly from another syllable. Thus, *-ible* is confused with *-able,* and *-ents* with *-ence.* Some are illogical—or seem so—and must be learned if they give trouble, but many fit into patterns. The affixes *-able* and *-un* are native and tend to be used with native roots (*uneatable*). *In-* and *-ible* come from Latin and tend to be used with borrowed words (*inedible*). The suffixes *-ents* and *-ence* have different meanings; *-ents* is the plural of *-ent* as in *dependents* and *referents; -ence* may mark an abstract noun or a meaning that has grown from one, as in *dependence, reference.* The distinction between *-ance* and *-ants* is similar. Some affixes can be kept straight by careful pronunciation, *per-* and *pre-, ante-* and *anti-.* Further discussion of affixes is found in chapter 10.

7. *Confusions Involving Schwa* Especially in American English, when a vowel is unstressed it may become a *schwa*, which is a neutral sound, pronounced *uh*. Thus formerly *government* was pronounced with three distinct vowels, with the accent on the second syllable. When the accent moved to the first syllable, the last two vowels were reduced to schwas, if they did not disappear completely. Thus vowels in unaccented syllables may be pronounced alike. *Different* might as well be spelled *diffarunt*, *difforunt*, or *diffurunt*. One way to guess the spelling is to think of a related word having the stress on the syllable in question. Anybody who knows about automobiles will know the word *differential* and be able to guess that *different* is spelled with an *e*.

8. *Long and Short Vowels* Our alphabet has too few letters for vowel sounds, but the ancient device of recognizing "long" and "short" vowels helps. In many words, a short vowel is marked by doubling the following consonant (*better*), and a long vowel, by adding an *e* (*feel, mere*). The rule works frequently enough to be useful. One of the commonest misspellings is *writter* for *writer*. Anyone aware of the rule should see that the spelling *writter* would produce a word to rhyme with *bitter*, whereas what is needed is spelling to suggest a word rhyming with *biter*. There are a few special cases, such as *ck* which serves as *cc*, and the French spelling *qu*, which is often the equivalent of *kw*.

9. *Other Uses of Doubled or Silent Letters* A final consonant in an accented syllable having a short vowel is regularly doubled before an ending beginning with a vowel (*forgot, forgotten; omit, omitting; hug, hugged; slur, slurred*). In unaccented syllables the consonant is not doubled (*counsel, counseled; benefit, benefited*). Alternate forms (*traveller, travelling*) often occur but are discouraged in American spelling, which avoids unnecessary doubling. If the vowel in the syllable is long, a following consonant is not doubled (*ride, riding; eat, eaten*).

Final silent *e* is usually retained before an ending beginning with a consonant (*bore, boredom; love, lovely*) and dropped before an ending beginning with a vowel (*hate, hating; cure, curable*). Most exceptions fall into patterns. If the final *e* is preceded by a vowel, it is usually dropped regardless, to avoid an awkward sequence of letters (*true, truly; argue, argument*). It may be dropped if it might lead to mispronunciation when retained (*whole, wholly*). If the final *e* is used to indicate that a preceding *c* or *g* has the soft sound, that is, if it occurs before *a*, *o*, or *u*, it is retained (*notice, noticeable; courage, courageous*). In the United States, however, *judgment* is preferred to *judgement*, since the *d* is sufficient indication that the *g* is soft.

10. *Combinations:* y *with Endings;* i *and* e A final *y* regularly changes to *i* before an ending beginning with a vowel (*ally, allies; cry, cries; lucky, luckier*). Exceptions mostly stem from obvious reasons. If *y* is pre-

Guide to Revision **Sp**

SPELLING

Correct the misspelling, considering whether it suggests a fundamental spelling problem or violates a common spelling rule.

ORIGINAL

occured, refering, counsellor, begining, equiped, equippment
[*A final consonant in an accented syllable with a short vowel usually doubles before an ending beginning with a vowel.*]

ninty, lonly, guideance, leisurly
[*Final silent e is usually retained before an ending beginning with a consonant.*]

trys, happyest, appliing, applys
[*Final y usually changes to i before an ending beginning with a vowel.*]

beleive, decieve, frieght
[*To indicate the sound of e, i usually precedes e except after c.*]

REVISION

occurred, referring, counselor, beginning, equipped, equipment
[*It usually does not double when the syllable is unaccented or before an ending beginning with a consonant.*]

ninety, lonely, guidance, leisurely
[*It is dropped before an ending beginning with a vowel or to avoid an awkward sequence of letters.*]

tries, happiest, applying, applies
[*When the ending begins with i, the y does not change.*]

believe, deceive, freight
[*When the combination represents the sound of a, it is ei.*]

ceded by a vowel, it usually is not changed (*monkey, monkeys; destroy, destroyer*). If the ending begins with *i*, the preceding *y* is not changed (*fly, flying, flies; fry, frying, fries*). Proper nouns ending in *y* add *s* with no other change (*two Marys, all the family of Frys*). When *i* and *e* are combined to indicate the sound of *e*, the old rhyme reminds us "Put *i* before *e*/ Except after *c*." Thus we spell *relieve*, but *receive*. Among exceptions, the most common can be kept in mind by remembering the following sentence: "At his *leisure* the *sheik* will *inveigle* and *seize* the *weird* words *either* and *neither*." The standard spelling is *ei* when the symbol represents the sound of *a*, as in *weigh, neighbor*. In a few words having other sounds, *e* precedes *i*, as in *height, foreign, sovereign*.

11. Borrowed Terms   Terms borrowed from other languages may retain some of the spelling in the parent language. The most obvious come from Greek or French. In Greek words the sound represented by *f* is spelled *ph* (*physics*), the sound associated with short *i* may be spelled *y* (*physics*), the sound associated with *k* may be spelled *ch* (*chemistry*), and in combinations of *p* plus a consonant the *p* may be silent (*pneumonia, psychology*). These are common enough so that most users of English become accustomed to them. Likewise, French spellings are numerous, *-ette* meaning small, as in *dinette, majorette*, and *-ville* meaning town, as in *Nashville, Deauville*. Many terminal consonants are not pronounced in words from French (*depot, esprit de corps*). Some vowels in borrowed terms retain accent marks (*smorgasbord* or *smörgåsbord, soiree* or *soirée*).

Once you have a list of your common misspellings you are likely to see patterns in them and know what to work on. If you do not, your instructor will probably help you analyze your troubles. The trouble spots are likely to be few and easy to eliminate, once they are spotted.

CAPITALS

Whether or not we call capitalization a part of spelling, capitals help to identify words. The radio announcer who says, "We shall now listen to an angel recording," seems to be predicting a miracle if we assume he is thinking of a lower-case angel, but if he is thinking of an upper-case angel—"We shall now listen to an Angel recording"—he is merely announcing a record of a particular brand.

1. Sentence Capitals   The first word of a sentence begins with a capital. When a sentence is quoted within another sentence, it is also capitalized; but when a quotation is divided by an introductory expression, the second part is capitalized only if it is a complete sentence:

Mr. Wilde replied, "There is no sin except stupidity."

"A cynic," said Mr. Wilde, "is a man who knows the price of everything and the value of nothing."

2. Poetry   Traditionally each line of a poem begins with a capital, although much recent poetry does not follow the convention.

3. Proper Names   Proper names, abbreviations of proper names, and words derived from proper names are usually capitalized—names of people, places, languages, institutions, months, days of the week, historical events, etc.:

> World War I, Episcopal Church, Latin, the Declaration of Independence, Goucher College, the Midwest, the U.S. Navy

The names of the seasons are not capitalized, and names for points of the compass are capitalized only when they name a region:

> "They went west in the summer of 1869 because they had grown tired of the East and of Eastern traditions."

Names of relatives are capitalized when used like the person's name but not when used as common nouns:

> "My sister wanted Mother to give up her job."
> "My best friend brought her mother to the party."

4. Initials and Abbreviations See pp. 439-40.

5. References to Deity Nouns referring to deity are regularly capitalized; pronouns referring to Christian deities usually are, but usage varies. Pronouns referring to pagan deities are not capitalized:

> Jesus, Savior, the Holy Spirit, He gave His only begotten Son, Jupiter, Aphrodite

6. Titles The principal words of titles begin with capitals see pp. 440-41.

7. I, O *I* as a pronoun and *O* as an exclamation are capitalized.

The major problems concerning capitalization turn on the question, when is a noun a proper noun? Superficially, the answer is easy: a proper noun is a name. But when does a noun become a name? A river is named for Henry Hudson. Is it the Hudson River or the Hudson river? Does it flow through the Hudson River Valley or the Hudson River valley? There is a college on the bank of this river; is the president the President of Central College, since there is only one such president at a time, or the president of Central College, since presidents are of common occurrence? Are the subjects taught in this institution American literature or American Literature, History of the Americas or history of the Americas?

The confusions arise in several ways, but partly because every object on earth exists as an individual. Every pebble on the beach is a separate

Guide to Revision   Cap, lc

CAPITALIZATION

Correct dubious capitalization, considering whether the example reflects inadequate grasp of a basic principle.

ORIGINAL

During my Second Year in High School, I took American Literature, European History, Mathematics, french, and Home Economics, and a new course entitled social problems.
[*Terms like* high school *and* literature *are not proper nouns, even though the writer is thinking of only one school and one literature.*]

I went to the Library and read a copy of the Library.
[*The first* library *is not a proper noun; the second names a magazine and follows the rule for titles.*]

In the Autumn the ducks move South from Canada, and hunting is good in some parts of the west.
[*Names of the seasons are not capitalized.*]

REVISION

During my second year in high school, I took American literature, European history, mathematics, French, and home economics, and a new course entitled Social Problems.
[Social Problems *is capitalized because it is a title given to a course, not a description of the material in the course.*]

I went to the library and read a copy of *The Library.*
[*The revised form makes clear the nature of each library.*]

In the autumn the ducks move south from Canada, and hunting is good in some parts of the West.
[*A direction as a name is capitalized, but directions as such are not.*]

---

pebble, but one stone becomes the basis of a proper noun only if it is given a name, Plymouth Rock. This distinction usually answers the questions raised in the preceding paragraph. Conventional style is Hudson River, because that is the name of a particular geographical phenomenon, but Hudson River valley, because no such area has been officially designated and named. It is American Literature if that is the name of a course, American literature as the term for a subject. It is Dr. Jane Jones, President of Central College when it is a title, president of Central College as an identification.

Words derived from names and closely associated with them are usually capitalized. *American* derives from the name *America,* and although there are many Americans the word is capitalized. On the other hand, proper nouns that have become common nouns are not capitalized. *Chinaware* comes from China, but we no longer capitalize *china* in this sense. We capitalize *Sardinia,* because it is the name of an island, but not *sardines,* associated with it. If you are uncertain, consult a good dictionary.

COMPOUNDS, HYPHENS

When two words are used together to have a single meaning, they tend to combine in spelling, either as a single word or as a hyphenated word. The following examples illustrate how spelling differences signal differences in meaning:

> The redcap wore a red cap.
> The old stylebook was an old-style book.
> The fairyland lady rented a room and became a fairy landlady.

In speech we distinguish the uses by stress; we stress the first syllable of *redcap* because *redcap* is a noun, but *cap* in *red cap* because *red* is a modifier. Often we can see a kind of logical need behind the development of compounds. Presumably the black board in the front of a schoolroom was identified by its color so long that it naturally became a blackboard to distinguish it from any black board that happened to be around. But often no logic of any sort is observable. One can rationalize that *post office* has remained two words because there is no other meaning from which it has to be distinguished; but what of *courthouse?* There are, actually, no consistent principles for spelling compounds, but several tendencies in practice are general enough to be useful.

1. Compound Adjectives and Verbs When two words function as an adjective or a verb with a single meaning, they are regularly hyphenated:

> He was only six feet tall, but he made a seven-foot jump.
> One twentieth-century innovation was the pay-as-you-go tax plan.
> We hot-roll all the metal and double-rivet the joints.

Unless a compound adjective is formed from a word that has already become a single noun (*backhanded*), it is almost always hyphenated. When the first of two modifiers modifies the second, however, the modifiers are not hyphenated, especially if the first is an *-ly* adverb:

The widely advertised camera took poor pictures.
The wide-lens camera was easy to operate.

2. Compound Nouns With nouns consisting of components, practices are not consistent, and a dictionary is often necessary. When the second word of a compound noun is stressed, the compound is seldom written as a single word (*high water, club steak, back road* but *headwaiter*). Compound nouns are hyphenated only in special circumstances—especially when the first word of the compound is a possessive (*Dutchman's-breeches*), when the two words indicate parts of a joint idea with neither modifying (*secretary-treasurer*), and when a noun is joined to a word like *out* or *up* (*fade-out, slip-up*, but compare *fallout, breakdown, markup,* and *countdown* or *count-down*). Compound nouns stressed on the first word follow no consistent pattern, except that they tend to combine with continuing use, especially if there is possibility of a confusion of meaning with a noncombined pair of

---

Guide to Revision **Hy**

COMPOUNDS, HYPHENS

Hyphenate, join, or leave as separate words in accordance with modern practice, consulting a good dictionary if necessary.

ORIGINAL

The car sank hub deep in the recently-graded road.
[Recently, *which modifies* graded, *should not be hyphenated.*]

Our slow baked bread has been slowly-baked.

The alloy is rust, weather, and heat-resistant.
[*Alternatives preferably include the hyphen with each alternative.*]

REVISION

The car sank hub-deep in the recently graded road.
[Hub-deep *is hyphenated; two words join to form a modifier.*]

Our slow-baked bread has been slowly baked.

The alloy is rust-, weather-, and heat-resistant.

words (*highway, limestone, mailman, mailboat, iceman, coalbin, gaslight,* but compare *garbage man, mail car, ice pick, coal oil, gas mask*).

3. *Alternatives* If there are alternatives for the first element of a hyphenated compound, each of the alternatives may have a hyphen (*eight- and ten-paddle canoes, lower- and middle-income housing*).

4. *Prefixes* Typically prefixes like *mis-, non-, dis-, anti-,* and *pre-* join words with no separation, but most compounds with *self* are hyphenated (*self-defense, self-taught,* but *selfsame*). Hyphens sometimes separate a prefix ending with a vowel from a word beginning with the same vowel (*pre-eminent, semi-independent, re-elected,* but *co-ordinate* or *coordinate*). Hyphens separate *ex-* when it means "former" (*ex-president*), a prefix with a proper noun (*anti-Nazi*), and a prefix that leads to a combination that might be confused with another word (*re-cover* to distinguish from *recover*).

5. *Numbers* Compound numbers from twenty-one to ninety-nine are hyphenated. A fraction used as a modifier is hyphenated unless one element of it is already a hyphenated compound. Fractions used as nouns are usually not hyphenated:

> *twenty-seven* cattle, nine hundred and *ninety-nine,* a *four-fifths* majority, *four fifths* of the class, a *three-sixteenths* drill

In typewritten material, hyphens are used to join the figures in inclusive dates (*1790-92, 1850-1900*) and to join inclusive figures when these appear in tabular form (*500-1,000, 10,001-10,025*). In printed material short dashes are used to show ranges (*1790-92*).

PLURALS

English vocabulary is made up mainly of native words that have come from Old English, and words borrowed from other languages. Although Old English formed plurals in a variety of ways, most such nouns were reduced eventually to a single system, so that native words generally form their plurals by adding *s* or *es*. To form regular plurals, add *s* if the sign of the plural is not pronounced as a separate syllable (*boy, boys; regulation, regulations*). After a consonant, if the sign of the plural is pronounced as a separate syllable, add *es* (*grass, grasses; class, classes*); if the singular ends in *e*, add *s* (*house, houses; bridge, bridges*).

Some few nouns were not regularized in Middle English and retain archaic forms (*ox, oxen; deer, deer; brother, brothers* or *brethren; child, children*). For such words, consult a good dictionary. Words ending in *o* formerly regularly added *es* (*tomato, tomatoes; Negro, Negroes*), but words recently borrowed usually have only the *-s* ending in the plural (*radio, radios; banjo,*

> *Guide to Revision*   **Pl**
>
> # PLURALS
>
> *Use the standard plural form, distinguishing between plurals and possessives.*
>
> | ORIGINAL | REVISION |
> |---|---|
> | High over our heads we saw dozen's of vapor trail's from the plane's. [*The apostrophe is used with possessives, but not with regular plurals.*] | High over our heads we saw dozens of vapor trails from the planes. |
> | Be sure to dot your is and cross your ts. [*Numbers, letters, symbols, figures, and words out of context form the plural with 's.*] | Be sure to dot your *i*'s and cross your *t*'s. [*Notice also that italics show that the letters are used out of context.*] |
> | Mrs. Appleby brought all the little Applebies with her. | Mrs. Appleby brought all the little Applebys with her. |

banjos). For nouns ending in *y*, see pp. 425-27. In nouns having a final *f* or an *f* before a final silent *e*, the *f* is often changed to *v* before the sign of the plural (*wife, wives; loaf, loaves*), but there are many exceptions (*sheriff, sheriffs; belief, beliefs*). The spelling reflects the pronunciation.

 Words borrowed from other languages offer special problems. English speakers tend to keep a word relatively long in the form in which it has been borrowed. Eventually, if a word becomes common, it becomes Anglicized with a normalized plural. The change does not greatly affect the plurals of words from German, French, and Spanish, most of which form plurals with -*s*. Words from Latin and Greek, however, are somewhat complicated because they may retain endings from the complicated classical declensional systems. Latin words ending in *um* usually form the plural by changing the *um* to *a* (*datum, data; agendum, agenda*); *us* is changed to *i* (*focus, foci; cactus, cacti*); *a* is changed to *ae* (*alumna, alumnae*). Foreign words eventually acquire a plural form by analogy with English: that is, the plural ends in *s* or *es*. Thus, for a time, there are two current forms; *focuses* is now more common that *foci*. Sometimes foreign plurals are not recognized for what they are and are treated like singulars. Thus one hears "This data is unreliable," although *data* is plural and *is* is singular; and one hears "The committee made up its agendas," although *agenda* is already plural without the *s*. These expressions are becoming standard speech, but foreign forms are usually retained in writing.

Numbers, letters, and symbols become plural with the addition of *'s* (two 2's; a row of x's). Sometimes apostrophes are also used in the plurals of words spoken of as objects (*if's* and *and's*), but the current tendency is to form these plurals without the apostrophe (pros and cons; but me no buts). These are the only plural forms that use the apostrophe.

NUMBERS

In standard writing, numbers that can be expressed in two words are spelled out; thus, all numbers one hundred or below are usually spelled. Excep-

---

Guide to revision   **Num**

NUMBERS

Spell out all numbers that can be written in two words, except numbers in a sequence when one number cannot be so expressed; then write all numbers as numerals.

ORIGINAL	REVISION
1938 is remembered in our valley as the snowy year. [*A figure should not begin a sentence.*]	In our valley, we remember 1938 as the snowy year. [*The sentence is rearranged to avoid the initial figure.*]
The 4 of us moved into a little garden cottage at sixty-two Longfellow Avenue.	The four of us moved into a little garden cottage at 62 Longfellow Avenue.
He called out the following numbers: ten, sixty-four, a hundred, 256, 11,822.	He called out the following numbers: 10, 64, 100, 256, 11,822.

tions to this rule are frequently made in the interests of simplicity and clarity. If, for example, several numbers are used in a passage and some of them are large, all of them are written in figures.

> On a western highway, you pass through towns marked on the map with populations from zero up. Traveling east on Highway 80, you leave the San Francisco-Oakland metropolitan area, population 1,942,000, pass through Sacramento, 275,741; Verdi, 356; Mill City, 72; and Toy and Dad Lees, formerly 2, now 0, since the Lees have moved.

Some style sheets, including those of many newspapers, prescribe figures for all numbers above ten. Figures are regularly used in certain standard contexts: for street and room or apartment numbers in addresses (1238 Ralston Street, 14 West Twenty-third Street); to designate portions of a book (chapter 10, page 371); for dates (January 10, 1838); and for decimals and percentages when using words would become complicated (3.1416, 57%). Figures are not used to begin a sentence, and numbers are not written both as figures and as words, except in legal documents. For hyphenation in numbers see p. 432.

APOSTROPHES: POSSESSIVES, CONTRACTIONS

Following are the main conventions governing the use of the apostrophe:

1. *Possessives* The apostrophe is used as a sign of the possessive case. For singular nouns and indefinite pronouns and for a few plural nouns whose possessive form is pronounced with an added *s* or *z* sound, the possessive is spelled by adding an apostrophe and *s*: *Paul's temper, the cat's tail, anybody's opinion, the people's choice.*

For plural nouns ending in *s* the possessive is spelled by adding only an apostrophe: *the soldiers' rifles, the schoolgirls' idol, the horses' collars.* Nouns of specification in time, space, quantity, or value follow conventions for the apostrophe in the possessive, even though they carry no meaning of possession: *an hour's walk, a quarter's worth, at their wits' end.*

Exceptions are few. Singular nouns, especially proper names of more than one syllable, that end with an *s*, *sh*, or *z* sound may be spelled in the possessive with only an apostrophe, to avoid an awkward series of sounds: *Xerxes' army, Velasquez' painting, for conscience' sake, Frances's* or *Frances' earring, Keats's* or *Keats' poems.* In compounds and phrases, the last element takes the possessive form: *mother-in-law's visit, anyone else's rights, the King of England's crown.*

In expressions showing joint possession, only the last element takes the sign of the possessive: *Germany, France, and England's position; John and Robert's fight.* A possessive form for each of two or more coordinated nouns

Guide to revision **Apos, Poss**

POSSESSIVES AND CONTRACTIONS

Provide apostrophes to mark possessives or contractions.

ORIGINAL

When June went to North State Teacher's College for a years work, she found that the warm winds' there made her hair curl.
[*The apostrophe should be omitted from the proper name.*]

The Jones's dog chased the Macks's cat.
[*The sense indicates that plural possessives are required.*]

Youre supposed to pick it up by the back of it's neck.
[*The contraction* you're *requires an apostrophe; the possessive pronoun* its *does not.*]

The first spectrographic tests weren't directed toward detecting amino acids.
[*Contractions are avoided in formal writing and in the more serious sorts of informal prose.*]

The play does not adequately prepare the reader for the climax, and therefore the main scene isn't convincing.
[*The inconsistency with contractions—*does not *and* isn't*—suggests a shift in style.*]

REVISION

When June went to North State Teachers College for a year's work, she found that the warm winds there made her hair curl.
[*Year's, a noun of specification, requires the apostrophe;* winds, *a plural, does not.*]

The Joneses' dog chased the Macks' cat.
[*The apostrophe after the regular plural forms the plural possessive.*]

(1) You're supposed to pick it up by the back of its neck.
(2) You are supposed to pick it up by the back of its neck.

The first spectrographic tests were not directed toward detecting amino acids.

The play does not adequately prepare the reader for the climax, and therefore the main scene is not convincing.
[*The general tone of the sentence seems serious enough that contractions are probably inappropriate.*]

indicates individual possession: *Harry and Bert's bicycle* (they own it together), *Harry's and Bert's troubles* (each has troubles of his own). The double possessive, in which both the apostrophe or a possessive pronoun and *of* are used, is idiomatic in English: *a friend of my father's, a cousin of Ann's, a book of his.* The apostrophe is often omitted in proper names that have become established: *North State Teachers College, Clayton County Retired Actors Home.* Pronouns, including the possessive forms ending in *s* and *se*—*his, hers, its, ours, yours, theirs,* and *whose*—are possessives and do not have apostrophes.

2. *Contractions*   The apostrophe is used to indicate the omission of one or more letters or figures in contractions: *can't, isn't, o'clock, the Gold Rush of '49.* The apostrophe is especially important to mark a few contractions readily confused with possessive forms of pronouns not requiring apostrophes. Notice the following pairs:

Contractions	Possessive Pronouns
it's (it is)	its (The cat carried its kittens.)
they're (they are)	their (They ate their lunch.)
you're (you are)	your (Mind your manners.)
who's (who is)	whose (Whose little boy are you?)

Since they are primarily devices of speech, contractions like *I've* and *don't* are not appropriate in formal writing and are sometimes avoided in serious informal composition, partly because of the difficulty of using them consistently.

3. *Plurals*   Apostrophes usually are used to form plurals of letters, symbols, and words mentioned as words: *the 1920's, A's* (see p. 434).

4. *Dialect*   The apostrophe is used to indicate omissions in reports of dialectal speech:

"I rec'leck how y'r paw come courtin' like 'twar yestiday," she said.

Overuse of the apostrophe to record dialect clutters the page and confuses the reader. Writers usually mark only noticeable omissions to suggest pronunciation and do not attempt to record all variations.

ITALICS

The writing system uses two styles of letters, those drawn for relatively formal purposes and those written rapidly in a free-flowing hand, called respectively *roman* and *italic.* Commonly roman type is used as body type,

Guide to revision   Ital

ITALICS

Underline to indicate italic type in accordance with current practice.

ORIGINAL	REVISION
Soon, very soon, we shall start for *sunny California*, hoping to have the *time of our lives*. [*Overuse of italics for emphasis destroys the emphasis.*]	Soon, very soon, we shall start for sunny California, hoping to have the time of our lives.
After Professor Lovejoy's lecture, it became "de rigueur" to have read "The Road to Xanadu." [*Italics are preferable.*]	After Professor Lovejoy's lecture, it became *de rigueur* to have read *The Road to Xanadu.*
Man is the subject of the sentence. [*Italics should point to* man, *used out of context.*]	*Man* is the subject of the sentence.
The cartoon's caption was "It's N'Aimez que Moi, madam, don't love nobody but me."	The cartoon's caption was "It's *N'Aimez que Moi*, madam, don't love nobody but me." [*Foreign words are conventionally in italics.*]

the main type in which a book or periodical is printed. Italic type, indicated in typescript or handwriting by underlining, is used for special purposes. The following are the most common.

    1. Emphasis   Italics may be used for emphasis or contrast, as in "The President's spokesman—*not* the President himself—said you acted like a nincompoop." This device can readily be overworked, and good writers use it only sparingly, many not at all.

2. Foreign Terms   Italics are used for foreign terms not yet Anglicized, as *savoir-vivre, Weltschmerz.*

3. Words out of Context   Increasingly, italics are used for words out of context, that is, words used for themselves, not for their meaning or use in the sentence:

Hamlet is a noun; etymologically, *hamlet* means a little enclosed place.

Formerly, words used out of context were placed within quotation marks, and this practice is still acceptable in many style books, but italic type is becoming the standard means of indicating that a word is employed for itself, not for its meaning.

4. Titles   Increasingly, also, italic type is used for titles (see below). For the more complicated citations required in bibliographies see chapter 16.

ABBREVIATIONS

In general, abbreviations are avoided in writing, except in bibliographies, formal lists, compilations of statistics, tables, and addresses. There are a few exceptions: common forms of address when used with proper names (*Mr., Mrs., Ms., Messrs., Dr., Jr., Sr., Ph.D., LL.D., D.D., S.J.*; but not *Rev., Sen., Gov., Prof.,* or *Pres.* in formal writing); times of day (4:00 p.m. or 4:00 P.M.); *before Christ* and *anno Domini* when used with a date (B.C., A.D.), written with capital letters and printed with small capitals. The abbreviation A.D. precedes the date, and B.C. follows it. There are a few common standard abbreviations for informal, technical, or business writing (*cf., e.g., no., etc.*) and some government agencies (*NLRB, OPA, ICC, OEO*). Except in bibliographies, addresses, tables, and the like, the following are spelled out: names of states and countries (*California, United States*); details of publication (*volume, page, chapter*); addresses (*street, avenue, road*); months and days of the week (*December, Sunday*); business terms (*company, manufactured*); and other words not specifically excepted (*Christmas, mountain, fort, saint*). Characters or symbols used for *and* are not acceptable in standard writing.

In formal writing the titles *Reverend* and *Honorable* are considered adjectives. They are preceded by *the,* and followed by a designation like *Mr. (the Honorable Miss Prism).* When a name with a title like *Sir* or *Lady* is shortened to one name, the first name is used; Sir Winston Churchill is Sir Winston.

Guide to revision   **Ab**

ABBREVIATIONS

Use abbreviations only in accordance with standard practice.

ORIGINAL	REVISION
The pol. sci. assign. for Mon. is something about the U.N. meeting in N.Y.	The political science assignment for Monday concerns the United Nations meeting in New York.
Rev. McIntosh was in charge of the service. [*The abbreviation is used only in newspaper writing and some informal writing.*]	(1) The Reverend Mr. McIntosh was in charge of the service. (2) The Reverend Ira J. McIntosh was in charge of the service. [*Formally, both styles are acceptable.*]
Rome endured from 390 b.c., when it was sacked by the Celts, until 410 a.d., when it was sacked by the Germans.	Rome endured from 390 B.C., when it was sacked by the Celts, until A.D. 410, when it was sacked by the Germans.

TITLES

The title of a brief essay or other piece of student writing should be centered on the first page, separated from the body of the composition by a blank line if handwritten, and by at least four spaces if typed. Principal words, usually all except articles and short connectives, are capitalized, but a title at the head of a manuscript is not underlined or enclosed in quotation marks. Titles of long manuscripts are placed on a separate title page.

A general rule to follow is that the complete or long work is italicized in print—underlined when typed—and the shorter work or part of the whole is placed in quotation marks. The following illustrates:

<u>Underline</u>   "Quote"

a book   a chapter from a book
a collection of essays   an individual essay

The Writing System: Mechanics and Spelling 441

Guide to revision   **Titles**

IMPROPER FORM FOR A TITLE

Use standard form for a title.

ORIGINAL

"Confrontation on the campus"
[Except for titles within titles quotation marks and italics are not used in titles at the head of manuscripts.]

People will say we're in Love is one of the most popular songs from Oklahoma!

Robinson's poem Mr. Flood's Party appeared in the volume "Avon's Harvest," and was reprinted in COLLECTED POEMS.

REVISION

Confrontation on the Campus
[The first letters of all words are capitalized in titles except articles, conjunctions, and prepositions.]

"People Will Say We're in Love" is one of the most popular songs from *Oklahoma!*

Robinson's poem "Mr. Flood's Party" appeared in the volume *Avon's Harvest* and was reprinted in *Collected Poems.*

---

a novel	a short story
a collection of poems	a poem from a collection
a long poem (an epic)	any short poem
a periodical or pamphlet	an article from a periodical or pamphlet
a newspaper or magazine	an article from a newspaper or magazine
an album	a song
a movie, drama, or opera	a short feature
a television series	a weekly installment from the series
	a dissertation

WORD DIVISION

When a word will not fit entirely into the end of a line, it may be divided between syllables, with a hyphen at the end of the line marking the division. This is a way of keeping the right-hand margin even, and word processors and some typewriters can "justify" the lines—that is, adjust spacing between words so that all lines are the same length. But an uneven right margin is preferable to excessive dividing of words and often to the wide spacing sometimes produced on a word processor. In copy to be printed, hyphenation is uncommonly inconvenient, since the printer may not be sure whether the hyphen marks only the end of a line or the end of a line that breaks a hyphenated word. When necessary, words may be divided between syllables. Syllabification is complicated. In general, it follows pronunciation, and consonants attach to the vowels following them (*pa-per, re-gard*). Two consonants that represent two sounds go one with each syllable (*mis-ter, har-dy;* but *soph-o-more*). Prefixes and suffixes remain syllables by themselves (*ach-ing, ex-alt*), unless modern pronunciation has obscured a suffix (*chil-dren*). Double consonants are separated unless they are the ending of a word with a suffix (*rat-tle, swim-ming,* but *miss-ing*). Words of one syllable cannot be divided. Words should not be divided so that a single letter appears on either line. There are more rules and many exceptions; unless you are certain you should consult a good dictionary. When a word is divided, the hyphen appears at the end of the first line, not at the beginning of the second.

Guide to Revision   **Div**

WORD DIVISION

Divide words in accordance with standard practice, consulting a dictionary when in doubt.

ORIGINAL

If the division is doub
-tful, consult a dictionary.
They all left the commi-
ttee meeting early.

REVISION

If the division is doubt-
ful consult a dictionary.
They all left the commit-
tee meeting early.

FOR STUDY
AND WRITING

A. Correct mechanics in the following, noting any uses that would be acceptable in informal writing but inappropriate in formal writing.

I've just purchased in a 2nd hand book store a copy of *Appleton's Guide* to the United States for eighteen ninety-two. It's full of entrancing old things, but since for the past 8 or 10 years our Family has gone every Summer to the Adirondack mts., I was particularly interested in the description of those mts. The eds. point out that this section 30 yrs ago "was known even by name only to a few hunters, trappers, and lumbermen," but they're now able to give a detailed description of it. They correctly locate the area between L. Champlain and L. George on the East, and the St. Lawrence R. on the w. They also identify Mt. Marcy as the tallest mt. in the area, giving the measurement as five thousand three hundred thirty-four feet. They concede that this pk. is not so high as the Black Mts. of N.C., nor the White Mts. of N. Hampshire, but they point out that they're interspersed by more than 1000 lakes, the largest of which are more than 20 mls. long. These lakes're said to be infested with Trout weighing 20 lb. or more. Hunting was also A-1; for instance, the hunter could take woodcock from Sept. 1st to April thirtieth, & the fine for shooting game out of Season seems to have been only $25, which by our standards wasn't very high. The Publication also gave instrs. that a "lady's outfit" should include "a short walking-dress with Turkish drawers fastened tightly with a band at the ankle." Travel in the area was apparently done by boats, built a few ft. long, carried by the guides on their shoulders from lake to lake and from river to river.

B. Correct the faulty use or omission of italics, quotation marks, and capitals in the following:

Among the curiosities of literature and thought is the career of Lord Monboddo, a Scottish *baronet*, author of a book called Of the Origin and Progress of Language. He believed that human speech came from the speech of animals, and imported an *orangutan* into scotland, assuming that the animal represented *the infantine state of our species.* The *chimp*, as the animal was called, was presumably a representative of "Pongo pygmaeus" or Simia satyris. Lord Monboddo taught the animal to play the flute, after a fashion, but in Monboddo's words, he *never learned to speak.* The lord patiently tried to teach the animal to say "hungry" and "eat," but without success. The learned Journals of the day, periodicals like the Quarterly Review and Blackwood's Edinburgh Magazine, ridiculed poor Monboddo, publishing articles with titles like Misguided Jurist and *This Monkey Business*. Not until long after the publication of Darwin's Descent of Man did students of modern thought realize that Lord Monboddo had been ahead of his day. Among the milder satirists of the radical jurist was Thomas Love Peacock, who made genial fun of Monboddo and his Orangoutang by inserting into his book Melancourt, a satirical novelette, a certain sir Oran Haut-ton, whose name was of course a pun upon the french haut-ton, that is, high-toned.

C. In the following paragraph, identify the specified forms to fill the blanks:

[1]_____ [plural of *beekeeper*] have long been intrigued by their [2]_____ [possessive plural of *bee*] peculiar habits. A [3]_____ [possessive singular of *beekeeper*] year allows him some [4]_____ [form of *month* indicating extent] leisure, when he is likely to wonder what a [5]_____ [possessive singular of *bee*] mind is like, and spend long [6]_____ [plural of *evening*] reading [7]_____ [possessive singular of *Maeterlinck*] description of the social organization of the [8]_____ [plural form of *bee* in the possessive with *of*] and [9]_____ [possessive singular of *Fabre*] Entymology, available in [10]_____ [possessive singular of *Mattos*] translation. Maeterlinck, alone, provides a long [11]_____ [singular form of *evening* indicating extent] reading, or for that matter, several [12]_____ [plural form of *evening* indicating extent] reading, and raises curious questions. Why, for instance, with [13]_____ [possessive singular of *it*] reputation for industry, does a bee spend time on a sunny afternoon in what is called "play," when this time is [14]_____ [appropriate possessive singular of *it*] for the using? The beekeeper was likely to answer, "Why, indeed? [15]_____ [contraction of *they are*] strange [16]_____ [plural of *creature*] and [17]_____ [contraction of *there is*] no accounting for [18]_____ [possessive of *they*] doings." But [19]_____ [plural of *scientist*] work differently. The [20]_____ [possessive singular of *scientist*] method requires the collection and study of [21]_____ [plural of *datum*] that is, in the case of the [22]_____ [plural form of *bee* for the possessive with *of*], studying them when they are supposed to be at play. On any warm afternoon they can be observed in front of the hive in a sort of dance in the air, making figures like [23]_____ [plural of *s*] and [24]_____ [plural of *z*]. The beekeeper had assumed a few bees had become tired of industry, and danced around a little to feel better, but the [25]_____ [possessive plural of *scientist*] [26]_____ [plural of *record*] showed that these [27]_____ [plural of *bee*] were returning workers, laden with honey, who with a series of [28]_____ [plural of *signal*] were informing their fellow workers where they got the honey. In short, the supposed "play" is the [29]_____ [possessive singular of *bee*] way of giving directions, what might be called The [30]_____ [possessive plural of *honeybee*, form suitable for a title] Daily Market News.

D. In the passage below italicized words include several compounds. Which should be (1) combined into a single word, (2) hyphenated, or (3) left as they are? For each, decide whether the current form can be determined by the rule or must be sought in a dictionary.

> During the war in *Indo China,* a young *helicopter pilot* found himself in a *base hospital* and also in a *semi rigid plaster cast.* He was *thirty one* years old, *brim full* of energy, was *naturally curious,* and had a *ghetto born* horror of waste. He contemplated his cast with a *sadly jaundiced* eye. It was a *hand made* cast, intended to restrict his *inter costal* muscles, and it was *nicely calculated* to hold the *spinal column* while at the same time there was space enough to allow *abdomino thoracic* movement. In fact, by contracting his stomach muscles, he could enjoy a *side glimpse* of his own navel. There was enough space, he decided, to allow him to insert a *hen's egg.* He ordered a raw egg for his *mid morning* lunch, and proceeded to transform his cast into the equivalent of a *setting hen,* an *incubator cast,* if you will. That is, he tucked the egg under his cast, and it fitted nicely into his navel so long as he kept his *stomach muscles* contracted. But he was not a *mother hen* by nature. After *one day's* care, he relaxed and smashed the egg. He *back ordered* the egg, however, and was heard to remark, "I'll *mother hen* one of those things if I have to stay here until I've grown a *hen's nest* in my beard." Three weeks later he *hatched out* a little, downy, *baby chick.* He might, of course, have become a *duck incubator,* too, or started a *turkey flock,* even a whole *barn yard,* but he remembered that *turkey eggs* require a *five or six week* period, and he did not have room on his bed for a *duck pond.*

E. Dean Thomas Clark Pollock of New York University made an extensive summary of college spelling, for which he used nearly 600 reports from college teachers, listing 31,375 spelling errors, which included 4,482 different misspellings. Two salient facts emerge from this study: Most words are misspelled very seldom, and most of the misspellings occur with relatively few words. More than a third of all the words were misspelled only once, but the 27 words misspelled more than 100 times each accounted for 5,097 misspellings; that is, less than 1 percent of the words were involved in more than 16 percent of the errors. Similarly, the 417 words misspelled more than 20 times accounted for more than half the misspellings. The moral of all this is that most students who have trouble with spelling have their trouble with relatively few words, and learning to spell correctly may be easier than they think.

Following are the 308 word groups that account for 20 or more misspellings on the list, printed in the order of the frequency with which the words were misspelled.

th*ei*r	*exi*st	defi*ni*tely
th*ey're*	*exi*stence	de*fi*ne
th*e*re	*exi*stent	separate
t*wo*	*o*ccur	separation
t*oo*	*o*ccurred	bel*ie*ve
t*o*	*o*ccurring	bel*ie*f
rec*ei*ve	*o*ccurrence	
rec*ei*ving	defi*ni*te	*o*ccasion

lose
losing
write
writing
writer
description
describe
benefit
benefited
beneficial
precede
varies
various
category
embarrass
excellent
excellence
grammar
grammatically
repetition
consistent
consistency
prevalent
intelligence
intelligent
realize
really
led
loneliness
lonely
prefer
preferred
surprise
explanation
fascinate
immediate
immediately
interpretation
interpret
thorough
useful
useless
using

noticeable
noticing
probably
imagine
imaginary
imagination
marriage
prejudice
disastrous
hypocrisy
hypocrite
operate
planned
pleasant
athlete
athletic
challenge
fundamental
fundamentally
liveliest
livelihood
liveliness
lives
philosophy
speech
sponsor
unusual
usually
across
aggressive
article
disappoint
suppose
curiosity
curious
desirability
desire
knowledge
ninety
undoubtedly
optimism
permanent

relieve
religion
together
you're
familiar
suppress
where
politician
political
relative
scene
sophomore
guarantee
guaranteed
huge
indispensable
laid
length
lengthening
mathematics
remember
seize
several
substantial
tendency
whole
accompanying
accompanies
accompanied
accompaniment
hear
here
luxury
moral
morale
morally
phase
playwright
represent
schedule
source

capital
capitalism
certain
certainly
chief
interfere
interference
likeness
likely
likelihood
magazine
referring
success
succeed
succession
its
it's
privilege
environment
personal
personnel
than
then
principle
principal
choose
chose
choice
perform
performance
similar
professor
profession
necessary
unnecessary
began
begin
beginner
beginning
control
controlled
controlling
argument
arguing

passed
past
acquire
busy
business
Negro
Negroes
among
height
interest
origin
original
conscience
conscientious
accommodate
comparative
decision
decided
experience
prominent
pursue
shining
practical
woman
acquaint
acquaintance
exaggerate
incident
incidentally
effect
government
governor
prepare
recommend
appear
appearance
convenience
convenient
mere
opinion
possible
whose

author
authority
authoritative
basis
basically
before
conceive
conceivable
consider
considerably
continuous
dependent
extremely
finally
satire
careless
careful
condemn
maintenance
parallel
permit
weird
efficient
efficiency
friendliness
friend
fulfill
piece
temperament
carrying
carried
carries
carrier
happiness
response
further
laboratory
oppose
opponent
counselor
counsel
council

divine
fictitious
primitive
regard
roommate
story
stories
strength
accustom
forward
pertain
safety
satisfy
satisfied
sentence
theory
theories
tremendous
vacuum
view
accomplish
arouse
arousing
despair
guidance
guiding
ignorance
ignorant
magnificent
magnificence
narrative
obstacle
shepherd
simply
simple
straight
maneuver
mechanics
medicine
medical
miniature

mischief
proceed
procedure
achieve
achievement
controversy
controversial
all right
possess
possession
psychology
psychoanalysis
psychopathic
psychosomatic
analyze
analysis
equipped
equipment
affect
affective
rhythm
tries
tried
weather
whether
forty
fourth
criticism
criticize
apparent
sense
conscious
studying
ridicule
ridiculous
summary
summed
attended
attendant
attendance
coming
difference
different

hero
heroine
heroic
heroes
opportunity
paid
quiet
villain
accept
acceptance
acceptable
accepting
dominant
predominant
foreign
foreigners
independent
independence
particular
technique
transferred
discipline
disciple
humor
humorist
humorous
quantity
accident
accidentally
character
characteristic
characterized
propaganda
propagate
therefore
hindrance
approach
approaches
physical
advice
advise
entertain
influential

influence
significance
exercise
involve
leisure
leisurely
sergeant
subtle
Britain
Britannica
completely
dealt
divide
excitable
favorite
interrupt
perceive
persistent
reminisce
suspense
amount
approximate
curriculum
disease

especially
fallacy
financier
financially
meant
synonymous
themselves
them
amateur
attack
attitude
boundary
clothes
expense
fantasy
fantasies
intellect
irrelevant
laborer
laboriously
labor
later
license
medieval

naturally
noble
peace
sacrifice
strict
symbol
actually
actuality
actual
adolescence
adolescent
against
appreciate
appreciation
experiment
field
hungry
hungrily
hunger
omit
persuade
those
thought
tragedy
yield

F. When you receive a paper with a misspelling noted on it, enter this word in your journal or notebook along with the correct spelling. This can become a useful reference when you edit your writing.

Appendix A

Glossary of Usage

> *Good words are worth much, and cost little.*
> GEORGE HERBERT
>
> *"Whom are you,"* said he, for he had been to night school.
> GEORGE ADE

Good English is English that works. As we have seen, it is nonsense to assume that some expressions are absolutely good and some bad, that there is a "pure" or "correct" language constantly threatened with corruption. Language does not work that way. On the other hand, any expression gets part of its effect from the associations it provokes in a reader. The reader judges an expression by the company it keeps, connecting it with the people who customarily use it, linking it to different educational, occupational, or social settings. Terms like *standard, nonstandard,* or *colloquial* are among labels used to suggest how a word is likely to be received by a reader, but they are far from definitive. *Colloquial,* from Latin *loquor,* to speak, describes expressions appropriate for conversation or informal talk but not for edited writing. *Standard* is used to identify, in a broad way, the kind of language that is necessary for serious purposes, especially in writing. The following list selects expressions that frequently cause trouble and offers some guidance about when and where they are likely to be appropriate.

a, an The indefinite article was developed from *one* and retains some of its earlier meaning, usually having the force of *any*. Plural nouns, embracing all members of a class, and abstract and general nouns may require no article (*Americans* like *dogs, cats,* and *children*). Sound determines the spelling. *A* is used before words beginning with a consonant sound, even when a sound like /y/ is spelled with *e* or *u* (*a person, a history, a unit, a European*). *An* is used before words beginning with a vowel sound or a silent *h* (*an elbow, an hour*). Contemporary usage prefers *a* before a pronounced *h*, although *an historian* sometimes still appears.

a lot Informal for *many, much,* or *very much,* as in "*A lot* of students attended the lecture" or "I enjoyed it *a lot.*" Often written incorrectly as one word; revise for more specific diction.

above, below In common use as both adjective and noun, *above* refers to a preceding passage (in view of the *above* . . . The *above* conclusion . . .); *below,* used as an adjective, refers to what follows.

accept, except To *accept* is to receive; to *except* is to exclude. *Except* is also a function word to indicate an exception.
    He decided to *accept* the bribe. They agreed to *except* the controversial paragraphs of the motion. They all quit *except* Duncan.

actually Like *really,* frequently overworked as a broad intensifier.

A.D. Abbreviation of *anno Domini,* "in the year of (our) Lord"; used for dates after the birth of Christ when dates A.D. and B.C. could be confused. Being Latin, it preferably precedes the date (A.D. 43).

adapt, adept, adopt To *adapt* is to adjust, to make suitable. *Adept* means "skilled, proficient." To *adopt* is to accept or to take as one's own.
    The children *adapted* their habits to their new home. She is *adept* at typing. The resolution was *adopted.* He *adopted* the mannerisms of his teacher.

advise, advice The first is the verb, the second the noun (I *advise* you to listen to his *advice*).

adviser, advisor Both spellings are in current use; the *-er* spelling is perhaps more usual.

affect, effect *Affect* is a verb meaning "influence." *Effect* is usually a noun meaning "result," but it may be a verb meaning "cause" or "bring about."
    The weather does not *affect* her disposition. The weather has no *effect* on her disposition. The envoys tried to *effect* a compromise.

agenda A Latin plural, meaning "things to be done," with a singular, *agendum.* In English the word means "a list of things to be done" and has developed a new plural, *agendas.*

aggravate Used in formal English to mean "intensify" or "make worse." Used informally in the sense of *annoy* or *provoke.*

    Informal: The children *aggravated* her.
    Formal: The children *annoyed* her.
    Formal: The new ointment only *aggravated* the disease.

agree Idiomatically we agree *with* a person, *to* a proposal, *in* principle, *on* a course of action.

ain't Although *an't*, later *ain't*, was respectable in the eighteenth century, it is now frequently cited as an example of illiteracy, even though, as substitutes for *ain't I*, *am I not* is cumbersome and *aren't I* may sound pretentious.

alibi Formally used only in the legal sense, an indication that a defendant was elsewhere at the time of a crime; informally, "an excuse."

all (of) When *all of* precedes a noun, *of* can usually be dropped. When the construction precedes a pronoun, *of* must usually be retained (He could not bribe *all of* them with *all* the money in the world).

all right, alright *Alright* is a common and plausible misspelling for *all right* but is not accepted in standard usage.

allusion, illusion An *allusion* is a reference (an *allusion* to his earlier writings). An *illusion* makes a false impression, deceives (an optical *illusion*).

already, all ready *Already* is a single modifier meaning "before some specified time." In *all ready*, *all* modifies separately.

The team was *already* on the field. They were *all ready* for the kickoff.

all the farther (further) Common colloquially; *as far as* is standard.

alumnus, alumna An *alumnus* is a male graduate; *alumni*, the plural of *alumnus*, is usually used for groups including both males and females. An *alumna* is a female graduate; *alumnae* is the plural form of *alumna*. The contraction, *alum*, is not acceptable in standard English. The possible Anglicized plurals, *alumnuses* and *alumnas*, are nonstandard.

among, between The formal distinction that *between* is used for two and *among* for more than two has not been rigidly observed, at least informally.

The men divided the reward *between* Bob and me. The book records differences *among* [or *between*] synonyms.

amount, number *Amount* indicates a sum or total mass or bulk. *Number* refers to a group of which individual parts can be counted. It is a collective noun, singular when designating a unit, plural when designating individuals.

A *number* of friends were in the lobby. The *number* of his crimes is astounding. A large *amount* of wheat has been stored.

and which, and who Standard only when the following clause is coordinate with a previous clause introduced by *which* or *who*.

Nonstandard: That was the first car I owned, *and which* I expected to cut down for a racer.

Standard: The car, which was the first I ever owned *and which* I expected to cut down for a racer, was . . .

angle Colloquial for "point of view" but trite in expressions like "He knows all the *angles*," or "What's the *angle* on this?"

ante-, anti- *Ante-* means "before" as in *antedate*. *Anti-* means "against" as in *antiwar*.

anybody, any body; anyone, any one   Combine the words to make the pronoun form; separate if the first portion is a modifier.

> *Anybody* may come. *Any body* in the burning ruins . . .
>
> *Anyone* could do that. *Any one* infraction of the rule . . .

any more   Standard when used negatively (They do not live here *any more*) but suspect in a positive sentence (Deans are more tolerant *any more*).

anyways   Colloquial; prefer *anyway* or *anyhow*.

anywheres   Nonstandard; omit the *s*.

apt   See *liable*.

area   Overused, usually redundantly, to refer to a subject or discipline (He was a student *in* [not *in the area of*] agriculture). Not acceptable as an adjective meaning *local* or *community*, as in "Area citizens to vote Tuesday."

around   Informal when used for *about* (There were *about* [not *around*] a thousand people present).

as   Not standard as a substitute for *that* to introduce a noun clause (*I am not sure that I* believe you [not *I do not know as I* . . .]). *As* may be imprecise when used as a subordinating conjunction to indicate cause. In "As we were sitting on the beach, we had a good view of the race," *as* could mean "while," "when," "because," or "since." The more precise function word is usually preferable. For confusion of *like* and *as*, see *like*.

as (so) long as   Both are common except in expressions involving time or space; see *not . . . as* (The table is *as* [not *so*] *long as* the desk).

as to   Especially at the beginning of a sentence *as to* is standard English to emphasize or point out (*As to* the recommendations, the less said, the better). *As to* is usually awkward as a substitute for *about* or *of*.
> He spoke to me *about* [not *as to*] the nomination. He doubted *whether* [not *as to whether*] he should make any promises.

aspect   Overused as a blanket term.

at   Redundant in questions with *where* (see *where at*).

athletics   Plural in form, but often considered singular in number.

attribute, contribute   *Attribute* means "to trace to a cause" or "to credit to a source." *Contribute* means "to have a share" in something or "to give one's share."

auto   No longer much used as a colloquial shortening of *automobile*; *car* is a more common short form.

awful, awfully   Overworked as vague intensives: *awfully good, awfully bad*. Since the words are overused, their effectiveness is blunted. In formal English *awful* means "awe-inspiring."

bad   When used as subject complement, sometimes confused with the adverb *badly*; see chapter 8 (She felt *bad* [not *badly*] all day).

B.C. Abbreviation of *before Christ,* used to mark dates that could be confused with dates in the Christian era. It appears after the date (52 B.C.).

be The verb *be* or *to be* is made up of forms from several older verbs, and is thus irregular. It has the following forms: infinitive, *to be;* gerund and present participle, *being;* past participle, *been;* first person present in singular, *am;* second person present, *are* (*art,* used with *thou,* is archaic); third person present singular, *is* (*be* is preferred in relatively formal writing for the subjunctive or imperative: *if that be true; be thou me*); first and third person past singular, *was;* second person past singular and all past plurals, *were. Were* is also used in the subjunctive and conditional moods.

because Standard to introduce a modifier, not a noun clause; see chapter 7 (The reason I ride the elevator is *that* [rather than *because*] I am lazy. I ride the elevator *because* I am lazy).

begin Principal parts of the verb are *begin, began, begun.*

being as, beings as Nonstandard usage for *since* or *because* (*Because* [not *being as*] I lived here, I know what I am doing).

beside, besides Beside is used as a preposition, meaning ''by the side of.'' *Besides* may be an adverb or preposition, meaning ''in addition'' or ''except.''
   He had to sit *beside* the teacher. It was too late to go to the dance, and *besides* I was tired.

between See *among.*

blame Some writers still insist that formally at least ''He *blamed* me for it'' must be used rather than ''He *blamed* it on me,'' but the latter is used widely in educated speech and in some writing. ''He put the *blame* on me'' is not.

blond, blonde The feminine ending *e* of the French word is sometimes retained, with *blonde* used to refer to women; but *blond* is currently used for both sexes, and any distinction is disappearing.

break Principal parts are *break, broke, broken* (I must have *broken* [not *broke*] my glasses).

broke Used to mean ''out of money''; *broke* is not used formally; *financially embarrassed* as a substitute is trite and affected.

bunch Overused to mean ''group'' (A group [not *a bunch*] of students . . . A large amount [not *a bunch*] of material . . .).

burst, bust Standard principal parts are *burst, burst, burst. Bust* or *busted* in the sense of ''burst'' is nonstandard as is *busted* in the sense of ''bankrupt.''

but On the theory that *but* is a preposition when it means ''except,'' many writers have insisted that any pronoun immediately following it must appear in the objective case, but the nominative is widely used, especially as part of the subject (Nobody but *me* (or *I*) saw the crash).

but, hardly, only, scarcely Negative words are not used in standard English with another negative.
   He *had* [not *didn't have*] but one alternative. He *knew* [not *didn't know*] only one answer. I *hardly* [not *don't hardly*] think so.

but that, but what *But that*, and especially *but what*, have been condemned as redundant when used for *that* as a conjunction or as a relative pronoun, and even as nonstandard, but both are reputably used, as in the following from *The New York Times:* "There is little doubt but what Mr. Baruch's venture . . ." Most careful writers, however, avoid the constructions.

can, may In formal English, *may* refers to permission (Mother, *may* I go swimming?) and *can* to ability (I *can* swim across the pool). Informally, *can* is commonly used for both meanings, and even formally *can* sometimes refers to permission, to distinguish from *may* referring to possibility
    I *can* [I have permission to] go. I *may* [possibly I shall] go.

can't help but, can't hardly A double negative; see *but, hardly, only, scarcely* (I cannot help believing [not cannot help but believe] she is honest).

case Overworked in expressions like "in this *case*" or "in the *case* of."

censor, censure, censer To *censor* is to examine, especially to examine printed matter for possible objections. To *censure* is to reprimand or to condemn. A *censer* is a receptacle for incense, especially one used in religious ceremonies.
    Half the story was *censored*. The students condemned their treasurer in a vote of *censure*. Choirboys carried the *censers*.

certain Redundant in expressions like "this *certain* person" or "in that *certain* instance." *Particular* is preferable where *certain* could be ambiguous, meaning either *some* or *reliable* (*certain* examples).

character Redundant in expressions like "It was a problem of a very difficult *character*."

circumstances Currently misused and overused in jargonic writing; use a more exact expression (He was *in great difficulty* [not *in very difficult circumstances*]).

cite, sight, site To *cite* is to refer to. *Sight* means "view" or "spectacle." A *site* is a location.
    He *cited* an old legal document. The mountains below were a beautiful *sight*. We visited the *site* of the new building.

claim Overused as a blanket term.

complected A popular equivalent of *complexioned* in phrases like *dark-* or *light-complected*; generally considered dialectal or colloquial (She was *light-complexioned* [not *light-complected*]).

conscience, conscious *Conscience* is a noun referring to a sense of rightness. *Conscious* is an adjective meaning "awake" or "aware" or "active mentally" (Let your *conscience* be your guide. I was not *conscious* of his fear).

consensus A *consensus* is a general agreement; *consensus of opinion* is redundant.

contact Overworked as a verb synonym for *talk with, telephone, ask about, advise, inform, query, write to, call upon*.

continue on Redundant as a verb with a separable suffix; omit *on*.

could of Sometimes, because of its sound, mistakenly written for *could have* (He could have [not *could of*] looked up the word in the dictionary).

council, counsel, consul Council means "advisory board" or "group." *Counsel* means "advice" or, especially in law, "the man who gives advice." A *consul* is a government official.

    He was elected to the administrative *council*. The dean's *counsel* always made sense. She was American *consul* in Brazil.

couple Nonstandard as a modifier meaning "two" or "about two" (I gave him *two* [rather than *a couple*] dollars); used informally followed by *of* (*a couple of people*).

credible, credulous, creditable Something that is easy to believe is *credible*. A person easy to fool is *credulous*; a skeptical person is *incredulous*. An act that does someone credit is *creditable*.

cute Overworked colloquially as a vague way of expressing approval (He was an *attractive* [or *charming* or *pleasant* or *handsome* rather than *cute*] boy).

data Originally the plural form of Latin *datum*, often considered singular in colloquial usage but still plural in formal English (*These* [not *this*] data confirm [not *confirms*] the theory). *Strata* and *phenomena* are plurals of the same sort. The Anglicized plural *datas* is not standard.

date A useful neologism, now generally considered standard, meaning "appointment" or "to make an appointment," or "the person with whom an appointment is made," especially if the appointment is social and with a person of the opposite sex. *Current American Usage* says it "occurs in informal standard writing, especially that dealing with teen-agers and their social relationships."

deal Currently overworked as a vague slang term for any transaction or arrangement or situation. A more specific term is preferable. *A great deal of* is loosely used as an equivalent of *many* or *much*.

definite, definitely Overworked as vague intensifiers in expressions like "a definitely fine party."

different from, different than *From* is idiomatic when a preposition is required; *than* introduces a clause. British usage is *different to*.

disinterested, uninterested Although now used interchangeably, the two words allow for a useful distinction in meaning, with *disinterested* meaning "impartial" and *uninterested* meaning "lacking interest" (The judge was *disinterested* but not *uninterested*).

do A verb with so many uses that it may appear where it cannot function idiomatically (Everyone has an ambition to *fulfill* [rather than *do*]). When *do* acts as a substitute to avoid repeating a verb, it must refer clearly to an identifiable antecedent. Compare:

    Unclear: He expresses the revolt against bondage and the desire to be free. His argument centers around the possibility to *do* so.

    Revision: He speaks of *revolting* against bondage and being free. His argument assumes the possibility of *doing* so.

The revision provides *revolting* as an antecedent for the substitute *doing so*, making it parallel in form and position. *Do* sometimes functions as an intensifier (He may be stupid, but he *does* have good manners). Like any device for emphasis, this one is easily overworked (I *do so* want you to be my friend), suggesting the conversation in Victorian novels.

don't   Contraction of *do not*, common in conversation but in writing not standard after *it*, *he*, *she*, or a singular noun (It *does not* [or *doesn't* in conversation, not *don't*] seem wise).

doubt   *Doubt that* implies a negative; *doubt whether* (informally *doubt if*) assumes that there is room for doubt.
I *doubt that* he will come [presumably he will not]. I *doubt whether* he will come [probably he will not, but he may].

drag   Standard past forms are *dragged* (He *dragged* [not *drug*] the body into the closet).

due to   Like *owing to* or *on account of, due to* was originally an adjective modifier (The delay was *due to* the icy roads). Its use adverbially is not generally accepted as standard English, although it has long been common in introductory adverbial phrases. (*Due to* unavoidable circumstances, the delivery has been delayed). *Because of* is the preferable adverbial idiom (*Because of* [not *due to*] the icy roads, the bus was late).

each and every   Used in legal documents and common in officialese, but redundant and needlessly pompous for most uses.

each other, one another   Some careful writers distinguish, using *each other* to refer to only two and *one another* to refer to more than two.

effect   See *affect, effect*.

either, neither   Usually singular in number (see chapter 9 and *each other*) and used to designate one of two, not one of more than two (*Any* [not *either*] of the three books has the information).

enthuse   Colloquial but overworked for *be enthusiastic* or *make enthusiastic*.

equally as   A wordy confusion of *as good as* and *equally*.
My cake was *as good as* Sue's. The cakes were *equally* [not *equally as*] good.

etc.   Abbreviation for *et cetera* meaning "and so forth" or "and the like"; appropriate only when statistics or lists justify abbreviations. *And etc.* is redundant; *et* means "and."

everybody, everyone   Historically, these words are the equivalent of *every individual*, relying on the earlier use of *body* as a synonym for *person* (If a *body* meet a *body*, comin' thro' the rye). Thus traditionally the words are singulars and require singular verbs and reference words. Formal writing would require singulars (*Everybody* considers *his* or *her* own best interest). In modern usage both words frequently have plural force (*Everybody came*), and hence plural verbs and reference words are common in conversation and in some informal writing. *Every one* is usually followed by *of* (*Every one of* them is guilty).

exactly Currently popular as a meaningless word. The person who asks "*Exactly* what is poetry?" probably does not want to be told "exactly," even if he or she could be.

except See *accept*.

expect Colloquial in the sense of "suppose" or "suspect" (I *suppose* [not *expect*] that his paper is finished).

extra Nonstandard in the sense of "unusually" (The coffee was *unusually* [not *extra*] good).

fact, the fact that Often overused as a roundabout way of saying *that*. (He was aware *that* [not *of the fact that*] everybody disliked his plan).

factor An overused blanket term.

famed Used for *famous* or *well known*, *famed* usually suggests journalese or amateur writing.

farther, further A distinction, not universally made, prefers *farther* as the comparative form of *far* in expressions involving space, and *further* to mean "in addition." Modern dictionaries recognize the interchangeable use of the two words.

fellow Colloquial when used as a synonym for *man, friend, person*.

fewer, less *Fewer* is used in distinctions involving numbers, of individual items, *less* in relation to value, degree, or quantity.

There were *fewer* than ten students. The receipts were *less* than the expenditures.

field Overworked and often redundant when used to refer to a realm of knowledge or subject (He was an expert *in* [not *in the field of*] chemistry).

figure Colloquial for *think, expect, suppose, conclude, believe* (I did not *expect* [not *figure*] the course to be difficult).

fine Nonstandard as an adverb (She sang *well* [not *fine* or *just fine*]).

fix In standard English a verb meaning "make fast" and, more recently, "repair." The word is nonstandard as a noun meaning "predicament" and as a verb meaning "intend" or "prepare" (I was *fixing* to go). It has many colloquial uses, most of them less precise than alternatives.

He was *fixing* breakfast. She was getting *fixed* up for the party. The alderman *fixed* his traffic ticket. He wanted me to *fix* his hair.

folks Colloquial for *people* or *relatives*.

formally, formerly *Formally* means "in a formal manner"; *formerly* means "previously."

We had to dress *formally* for the party. She was *formerly* a singer.

funny Overused and imprecise as a synonym for *strange, odd, unusual, perplexed*. A more exact word is preferable.

get, got Useful verbs and the basis of many standard idioms, but also used in many colloquial and slang expressions. (The song *gets* me. The pain *got* him in the back. Better *get* wise.) Used to mean "must" or "ought to," *got* is colloquial and usually redundant (We *must* [or *have to*, not *have got to*] finish by evening).

good An adjective, not to be confused with *well*, the corresponding adverb (The car runs *well* [not *good* or *pretty good*]).

good and Nonstandard as an intensive (He was *very* [not *good and*] angry.

gotten Alternative form for *got* as past participle for the verb *get*.

guess Dictionaries record *guess* in the sense of "believe," "suppose," "think," but some writers restrict it to colloquial usage.

had better, had best, you'd better These are standard idioms for the more formal *ought* or *should* (You *had better* [more formally *ought to*] talk to the instructor). "You *better* talk to the instructor" is colloquial.

had of Nonstandard for *had*; see also *could of* (I wish he *had* [not *had of*] told me).

had ought, didn't ought, hadn't ought Nonstandard redundant forms for *ought* or *should* (He *ought not* [or *should not*, not *hadn't ought to*] say that).

hang Principal parts of the verb are *hang, hung, hung*, but to refer to death by hanging, they are *hang, hanged, hanged* in formal English (We *hung* the new picture. The murderer was *hanged*).

hardly See *but, hardly, only, scarcely*.

he, him See *I, me*.

he or she, he/she See chapter 11.

healthful, healthy A distinction often not observed restricts *healthful* to "conducive to health" and *healthy* to "possessing health."

heap, heaps Not common in standard written English in the sense of "a great deal."

heighth Common misspelling for *height*.

his, him, their, them In written formal English possessive forms are used before a gerund (The principal was not amused by *their* playing poker in class). Sometimes a distinction in meaning is involved. Compare:
He saw *him* [or *Alfred*] drinking sloe gin. He disapproved of *his* [or *Alfred's*] drinking.

hisself Nonstandard for *himself*.

honorable Used as a title of respect, mainly for people holding a political office. It is usually preceded by *the* and used only with a full name (*The Honorable John H. Jones* or *The Honorable Mr. Jones*, not *Honorable Jones* or *the Hon. Jones*).

hopefully The use of *hopefully* to mean "One hopes" or "It is to be hoped," though widespread, is sometimes regarded as uneducated and should be avoided.

however *However* tends to modify a whole predication if it appears initially in a clause, but thereafter it modifies the preceding word or structure; see chapter 8.

human Originally an adjective, *human* is now often used as a noun meaning "human being."

I, me, he, him, she, her, we, them In standard English the subject forms (*I, he, she, we, they*) are used as subjects of a clause, even when in a compound (Jim and *I* [not *me*] made the first team. I promised that *he* [not *him*] and Nancy could divide the lunch). Subject forms are also used in formal written English after a linking verb (It was *I* who finally spoke. The real victim is *she*.). Colloquially "It's *me*" is common. Formally subject forms appear also in comparisons after *than* or *as* (She is older than I [am]), but objective forms are common informally. Objective forms (*me, him, her, us, them*) are standard for objects of verbs or prepositions and subjects or objects of verbals. A tendency to overcorrect produces infelicities with pronouns in objective positions, especially in compounds, and the result sounds pretentious or affected.

> He told my wife and *me* [not *I*] that the tickets were ready.
> We never liked the Broadnicks, neither *her* [not *she*] nor her husband.
> Just between you and *me* [not *I*], no hair ever got that color naturally.
> The manager promised *us* [not *we*] boys the new apartment.
> The man sitting in front of John and *me* [not *I*] kept his hat on.

idea A handy word that careless writers readily overuse. A more exact word is often preferable.
> My *purpose* [not my *idea*] is to become a nurse. The *theme* [not the *idea*] of the book is that crime never pays.

if, whether *If* implies uncertainty; *whether* implies an alternative. *If* is not used with *regardless*.

> *If* he will trust me, I shall tell him. I shall tell him, *whether* or not he believes me.
> Even though [not *regardless if*] she is a doctor . . .

imply, infer To *imply* is to suggest a meaning; to *infer* is to draw a conclusion from evidence.
> The attorney *implied* that the witness was lying. The jury *inferred* that the attorney was trying to discredit the witness.

in, into *In* implies rest or motion within a restricted area; *into* is preferable to indicate motion from outside to the inside.
> She lives *in* town. We drove *into* town.

in back of Redundant; prefer *behind*.

in regards to Nonstandard; use *in regard to*.

individual Originally an adjective, *individual* is loosely used, and often overused, as a synonym for *person*. As a noun, the word is best used to emphasize the singleness or separateness of an item or person (Students are not merely names in a card file; they are *individuals*).

infer See *imply*.

inferior than Nonstandard; use *inferior to*.

ingenious, ingenuous *Ingenious* means "having or giving evidence of resourceful intelligence." It can be used of either persons (*an ingenious strategist*) or things (*an ingenious device*). *Ingenuous* means "naively frank." It is used only of persons and of things closely associated with them (*an ingenuous proposal*).

inside of Redundant as a compound preposition; omit *of*.

in terms of Overworked as a useless filler in sentences such as "What is new *in terms of* the theatre?" Omit it.

invite A verb. Not acceptable as a substitute for *invitation* (I asked Joe for an *invitation* [not an *invite*] to the dance).

irregardless Nonstandard; use *regardless*.

is when, is where, is because See chapter 7.

it Although sometimes convenient, usually to be avoided in impersonal constructions, especially in locutions like "*It* says in the book . . . ," in which *it* seems to have an antecedent but does not; see chapter 9.

its, it's *Its* is the possessive form of *it*. *It's* is the contraction of *it is*.

it's me, it is I *It's me* is common informally; in written form, except in recording conversation, *It is I* is standard; see *I, me*.

kind, sort Singular words, which formally can be modified only by singular demonstrative adjectives, *this* or *that*. Plural forms, *those kinds* or *these sorts*, are used, and colloquially *kind* and *sort* are commonly treated as if they were plural (*these kind*).

kind of, kind of a Colloquial as the equivalent of *somewhat, rather*.

lay For confusion of forms of *lay* and *lie*, see *lie*.

lead, led *Lead* is the present tense of the verb. Because of the identical pronunciation, the past tense, *led*, is often misspelled *lead*, the name of the metal (He *led* [not *lead*] the horse to water).

less See *fewer*.

let, leave Both are common in a few idioms (*leave* [or *let*] it alone), but in other idioms, especially when the verb carries a sense of permission, *let* is standard (*Let* [not *leave*] them stay. *Let us* [or *let's* not *leave us*] go soon).

liable, apt, likely Interchangeable informally, but often distinguished in careful writing. Strictly, *liable* means "responsible for" or "subject to." *Apt* means "has an aptitude for." *Likely* means "seems probable."

She is not *likely* [rather than *liable* or *apt*] to tell her teacher. He is *liable* for the damage he caused. Marie is an *apt* pupil.

lie, lay Three pairs of similar verbs have been so thoroughly confused in dialect and nonstandard usage, and even in literate conversation, that many people have trouble distinguishing between them in meaning and spelling, particularly in their uses with separable suffixes. See also *rise-raise* and *sit-set*.

Lie (*lay, lain*), intransitive, but usually modified or combined with a suffix like *down*, indicates that the subject occupies a position.

The book *lies* on the table. The book *lay* on the table yesterday. The book *has lain* on the table in the past.

Lay (*laid, laid*), transitive except for a few special uses (The hens *lay* well; *Lay* on, Macduff), means *place* or *put* and now appears mainly in a variety of special contexts (see a dictionary).

He *lays* brick in his spare time. The men *laid* their plans carefully. The soldiers *have laid* down their arms.

like, as In formal written English *like* is used only as a preposition (He ran *like* a deer), and *as* and *as if* are conjunctions (He ran *as if* he had seen a ghost). Informally, however, the distinction is disappearing (He looks *like* he could use some sleep). The confusion has perhaps aggravated a tendency to overcorrection, misusing *as* as a preposition (He ran *as* a deer). Sometimes the distinction is useful to specify the meanings (He slipped into the house *as* a thief and He slipped into the house *like* a thief, He cried *as* a baby and He cried *like* a baby). In general, college writing requires limiting the words to their formal functions (*As* [not *like*] I said, the meeting is canceled).

line Jargon or slang or redundant in certain current uses.

He sells books [not *Selling books is his line*]. I want to buy something *similar to* [not *along the lines of*] the dress in the window. He was *deceiving her* [not *handing her a line*].

literally An antonym, not a synonym, of *figuratively*. The student who wrote "I was *literally* dead when I got in" did not say what he or she probably meant.

loan Now generally accepted as a synonym of *lend*; many careful writers, however, use *loan* only as a noun and prefer *lend* as a verb.

locate Provincial as a synonym for *remember* or *take up residence*.

loose, loosen, lose *Loose* is usually a modifier but may be a verb meaning "to unfasten." *Loosen* is a more common verb with meanings related to those of *loose*. Confusion with the quite different verb *lose*, "to mislay" or "to be deprived of," may lead to misspelling.

lot(s) of Colloquial as a synonym for *many*.

love Imprecise and sometimes affected as a synonym for *like*.

mad Colloquial in the sense of "angry." Use *angry* or a more exact word like *vexed, furious, annoyed*.

math Clipped form of *mathematics*, not appropriate in formal writing.

may An auxiliary verb, past tense *might*, expressing possibility or likelihood or permission; see also *can, may*.

It *may* rain tomorrow. The application *may* be considered this week.

might of Use *might have* (see *could of*).

mighty As a synonym for *very*, not acceptable in formal English, although common in speech in some areas (She was a *very* [not *mighty*] pretty girl).

moral, morale *Moral* is a modifier, concerning the preference of right over wrong; *morale* is a noun suggesting good spirits and a healthy attitude.

George Washington was a *moral* man. The victory improved the soldier's *morale*.

more than one Logically plural, sanctioned by custom as singular except when the meaning clearly requires a plural verb.

More than one man is eager to marry her. If there are *more than one* apiece, they should be divided equally.

most Nonstandard as synonym for *almost*. (I am home *almost* [not *most*] every evening).

muchly Nonstandard; use *much*.

must Currently overworked as a noun.

myself Perhaps to avoid choosing between *I* and *me,* or from a sense of modesty, many speakers use the reflexive rather than the personal pronoun, but the form is not standard in formal writing.

Henry and *I* [not *myself*] decided to remodel the boat. They invited Anne and *me* [formally not *myself*] to the luncheon.

nature Redundant in certain current expressions (The job was *difficult* [not *of a difficult nature*]).

neither Used of two; see *either*.

neither . . . nor Used as correlatives (She could *neither* set up her experiment *nor* [not *or*] conduct it).

nice Colloquial as a synonym for *affable, agreeable, amiable, congenial, considerate,* and so on through the alphabet. Prefer a more exact word. Carefully used, *nice* means "precise," "exact," "discriminating."

nice and Colloquial as an intensive (The coffee was *pleasantly* [not *nice and*] hot).

none As a subject, *none* takes a singular or plural verb depending upon the meaning intended.

not . . . as Some writers have objected to this construction, preferring "He is *not so* [rather than *not as*] dull as his younger brother." Either is generally considered acceptable.

nothing, none After *not* these produce a double negative, not standard in English (She didn't do *anything* [not *nothing*] about it).

nowheres Nonstandard; omit the *s*.

of Often better omitted when used with another preposition (He was running *inside* [not *inside of*] the stadium). Confused with *have*. See *could of, might of*.

off of, off from Redundant and nonstandard; use *off*.

on Sometimes redundant with dates (I shall see you *Tuesday* [rather than *on Tuesday*]).

on the part of Often a clumsy equivalent of *by*; see *part*.

one Used in English in impersonal constructions, although it sometimes seems stiffly formal. Replacing *one* or *one's* with *he* or *his* is now considered sexist (see chapter 11).

only For the position of *only*, see chapter 8.

-orama, -orium Faddish suffixes overused in various advertising coinages: *seafood-orama, lubritorium* (for a service station).

out of Prefer *out* (*out* the door; not *out of* the door).

outside of Redundant as a compound preposition (*outside* the barn, not *outside of* the barn). *Outside of* is colloquial in the sense of "except" (He failed all his examinations *except that in chemistry* [not *outside of chemistry*]).

outstanding Overworked as a vague modifier.

over with Colloquial as a synonym for *done, finished with, ended, completed.*

overall Useful as a synonym for *general*, but currently overused; accurately used in a phrase like "the *overall* length."

part, on the part of Often used in wordy writing.

> Wordy: There was some objection, *on the part of* the administration, to the moral tone of the skits.
>
> Revised: The administration objected to the moral tone of the skits.

party Not usually acceptable in composition as a synonym for *person*; used in legal papers (*party* of the first part) and by telephone operators (I have your *party* on the line).

past, passed *Past* is the modifier or complement, *passed* the verb form.
His troubles were *past*. She had *passed* all the tests.

per-, pre-, pro- Three prefixes, borrowed from Latin. They are related to such English words as *fare, far,* and *for,* and they share in some of the meanings preserved also in their English cousins. *Per-* means "through," as in *percolate* and *perforate,* preserving the idea of movement as in *fare. Pre-* means "before," as in *pre-Columbian, pre-eminent,* preserving the idea suggested in *before. Pro-* means "for" or "forth," as in *projectile, pro-administration,* observable in the expression "being *for* somebody or something."

phenomena Plural; the singular is *phenomenon* (compare *data*).

phone Informal; in formal composition use *telephone. Phone up* is redundant; formally use *telephone, call on the telephone*; less formally, *call up.*

picture Currently overused in expressions like "I gave them the whole *picture.*" More specific writing provides the cure (I told them why I needed five dollars).

piece Nonstandard in the sense "a short distance."

plan on Redundant and colloquial in some uses (*plan to go* not *plan on going; plan to see,* not *plan on seeing*).

plenty Not acceptable as an intensive (*excellent*, not *plenty good*).

point Overworked as a blanket word (He had many admirable *characteristics* [not *points*]).

poorly Used in some dialects, not in formal writing, in the sense "in poor health."

prejudice A noun, not to be confused with *prejudiced*, a modifier (He was *prejudiced* [not *prejudice*] against John).

presence The noun form corresponding to *to be present* (The chairman requests your *presence* on the platform); to be distinguished from *presents*, plural of *present*.

principal, principle *Principal* can be a modifier meaning "first in importance" (I answered his *principal* objections), or a noun naming somebody or something first in importance (a high school *principal*, the *principals* in the fight). *Principle* is always a noun.

The law of the conservation of matter formulates a fundamental *principle* in physics. Machiavelli has been accused of having had no *principles*.

prof Slang when used as a common noun (I like the course but not the *prof*). Acceptable in journalistic and informal writing as an abbreviation with a full name (*Prof. George B. Sanders*, but *Professor Sanders*). Best formal style requires that *professor* be written out in all titles.

proved, proven *Proved* is the only form having a historical foundation, but *proven* is also commonly accepted. The verb *prove* is often used carelessly of statements that are not proved; often *suggest, imply,* or *indicate* would be more accurate.

providing In older usage, not admitted as a synonym of *provided*, a conjunction meaning "on the condition"; common in modern usage.

put across Blanket term for *explain, prove, demonstrate, expound, argue, make clear, establish,* and the like.

quite Generally accepted, although often unnecessary, in the sense of "entirely" (*quite* dead, frozen *quite* to the bottom); colloquial in the sense "somewhat," "rather" (*quite* cold, *quite* a big job).

raise For confusion of forms of *rise* and *raise*, see *rise*. *Raise* is now generally accepted as a synonym of *rear* in the sense "bring to maturity," but many writers prefer *rear* when referring to human beings.

rate Currently overused and misused; slang in some usages (He does not *rate* with us).

re In the sense of "about," used for formal purposes only in legal documents and skeletonized commercial writing.

real Colloquial as an intensive (It was a *real* nice clambake). Use *really, very,* or a word expressive enough to need no intensive.

really A useful word frequently overused and misused so that it clutters sentences. It is redundant in a sentence like "It was *really* true."

reason is because See *because* and chapter 7.

reason why Usually redundant (The *reason why* I like to swim . . .); omit *why*.

reckon Dialectal and inexact as a synonym for *believe, suppose, assume*.

regard, regards Often overused. *Regards* is nonstandard in constructions like *in regards to*.

relate to Colloquial expression not appropriate in standard English. "Professor Johnson really *relates to* her students" could be revised to "Professor Johnson *understands* her students."

respectfully, respectively *Respectfully* means "in a respectful manner" (*respectfully* submitted); *respectively* means "in the specified order," "severally" (The balloons were identified as 4b, 5a, and 2g, *respectively*).

Reverend Used in standard English with the first name or initials of the person described or with the title Mr. (see chapter 18); in formal usage preceded by *the* (*The Reverend* William Dimity, *The Reverend* W. L. Dimity, *The Reverend* Mr. Dimity).

right Informal as an intensive in expressions like *right away*; prefer *immediately, at once, promptly*, and the like. A localism in the sense of *very*. (It was a *very* [not *right*] good fight).

right on In the sense of perfect or excellent, nonstandard at this writing.

rise, raise The two verbs are frequently confused. *Rise* (*rose, risen*), intransitive, often combined with suffixes like *up*, indicates that the subject moves.

He *rises* before dawn. He *rose* before dawn yesterday. He *has never risen* before dawn in his life.

Raise (*raised, raised*), usually transitive, but (John opened the betting, and Tom *raised*), indicates that the subject acts on something, making it rise or appear.

He *raises* his hand when he wants to talk. The committee *raised* a new issue. His salary *has not been raised* for a year.

said Pseudo-legal affectation as a modifier; if necessary, use *this, that, these,* and the like (Having rejected *the motion* [not *said motion*], the committee adjourned).

same As a pronoun used with *in, same* is sometimes useful in legal documents, but sounds affected in most writing (Having made his bed he must lie *in it* [not *in same*]).

scarcely Not to be used with another negative. (There *was scarcely* [not *was not scarcely*] any butter).

seem A useful word, often misused or overused, especially as a qualification in constructions like "it would *seem* that" (The evidence *suggests* [not *would seem to suggest*] that Shakespeare was once a schoolmaster).

seldom ever Redundant; omit *ever*.

set For confusion of forms of *sit* and *set*, see *sit*.

setup Slang in the sense of "an easy victory," and currently overused in jargonistic writing to mean anything related to organization, condition, or circumstances, as in "I liked the new setup."

shall, will The verbs *shall* and *will* are troublesome because they have a troubled background. In Old English *shall* and *will* were not signs of the future; the word for *shall* meant "ought to" and the word for *will* meant "willing to," "to be about to." These meanings have been preserved in *should*, which implies obligation, and *would*, which implies willingness. But *shall* and *will* became indications of the future, just as words with the same meaning today (I am about to go; I have to go) are becoming future forms. For hundreds of years little effort was made to distinguish between *shall* and *will* as auxiliaries, and users of English apparently never have had any deep-rooted feeling for a distinction between them—a fact that may account for the distinction's being difficult. In the eighteenth century, a popular grammarian laid down rules for the use of *shall* and *will*, and most handbooks of usage since then have repeated his rules—though a few have turned them exactly backward. At present, most people, especially in America, pay little attention to these rules. Partly because contractions (*I'll, we'll*) are so common in speech, *will* is used in all persons in most informal situations. A few people, however, attach great importance to the arbitrary distinction between the words, and the following rule is still observed in some formal English: In the first person, use *shall* to denote simple futurity, *will* to denote determination and purpose; in the second and third persons, use *will* to denote simply futurity, *shall* to denote determination and purpose. In general, *should* and *would* also follow this rule, except when the use would interfere with the basic meaning of these two words, *should* implying duty, *would* implying willingness.

I *shall* consider each of the arguments. I predict that the people *will* reject the offer.

shape Colloquial in the sense of *condition, manner*. (She was *well trained* [not *in good shape*] for the tournament).

should For distinctions between *should* and *would*, see *shall, will*.

should of Mistaken form of *should have;* see *could of*.

show Slang as a synonym for *chance, opportunity;* colloquial as a synonym for *moving picture, play*.

show up Not standard in either the sense *arrive* (Jim did not *show up*) or the sense *expose* (He is no gentleman, and Mary *showed him up*.)

sic See page 385.

sit, set The two verbs are frequently confused. *Sit* (*sat, sat*), intransitive except for a few uses, especially with suffixes like *out* or *with* (She *sat* out the dance; she *sits* a horse gracefully), indicates that the subject occupies a place or seat or is in a sitting position.

He *sits* by the window. He *sat* by the window last week. He *has sat* there for a year.

Set (*set, set*), transitive except for a few uses (The sun *sets* in the west; the hens are *setting*), means *place* or *put*, often varied in combinations with words like *off, up,*.

He *sets* the lamp on the table. They *set up* the new organization yesterday. Finally they *have set out* on their journey.

situated Often used redundantly (The house was *in* [not *situated in*] the tenement district).

she, her. See *I, me*.

situation Wordy and jargonistic in expressions like "the team had a fourth-down situation."

size Not generally accepted as a modifier (*this size of dress,* not *this size dress*).

so Avoid excessive use of *so* to join independent clauses; see chapter 9.

so as Not to be confused with *so that*; see chapter 9.

so long as See *as long as*.

some Not standard to indicate vague approval (It was *an exciting* [not *some*] game).

somebody's else The sign of the possessive appears on the last word; see chapter 18. Use *somebody else's*.

sometime, some time One word in the sense "occasion," "some other time"; two words in the sense "a period of time."
    Come up to see me *sometime*. The repairs will require *some time*.

somewhat of *Somewhat* is most commonly an adverb (They were *somewhat* slow); *somewhat of* is not a standard idiom.

somewheres Nonstandard. Omit the *s*.

sort See *kind*.

sort of, sort of a Both are clumsy and colloquial as modifiers.
    I was *rather* [not *sort of*] tired. He was *an amateur* [not *sort of* a plumber].

speak, speech The difference between the vowels in the verb *speak* and the noun *speech* generates many spelling errors.

state Currently misused as a loose equivalent of *say, remark, observe, declare*. Carefully used, to *state* means "to declare in a formal statement."
    The board *stated* that the coach's contract would not be renewed.
    The coach *said* [not *stated*] that practice would be postponed until 4:30.

stationary, stationery *Stationary* is a modifier meaning "not movable" or "not moving"; *stationery* is a noun meaning "writing materials." They can be distinguished by remembering that l*etters* are written on station*ery*.

such Overused as a vague intensive (It was a very [not *such* a] warm day).

suit, suite *Suit*, the commoner word, can be either a verb (suit yourself) or a noun (a tailor-made *suit*). *Suite*, only a noun, has several specialized uses (The ambassador and his *suite* occupied a *suite* of rooms).

suspicion A noun, not appropriately used to supplant the excellent verb *suspect*.

sure Colloquial as an intensive (He was *certainly angry* [not *sure sore*]).

take and Redundant and nonstandard in most uses (He *whacked* [not *took and whacked*] the hornet's nest).

take sick A regionalism not generally accepted in formal English; prefer *become ill* or *sick* or a more exact expression.

terrible, terribly Overused and misused; colloquial as general intensives (She is a *terribly* sweet girl) and as blanket words signifying anything unpleasant (I had been vaccinated and felt *terrible*).

terrific Recently misused and overused as a general synonym for *large, impressive, dramatic, significant, dexterous,* or *important,* it can now scarcely be used in its standard meaning, "causing terror."

that Like *who* and *which, that* is often unnecessary to introduce a clause (*Everybody knew* [*that*] *he had failed*). Omission is confusing, however, when it causes temporary misreading (Mr. Chamberlain *forgot that the umbrella* [not *forgot the umbrella*] had been torn). For reference of *that,* see chapter 9.

that there Nonstandard; omit *there.*

that, which Both *that* and *which* are used as relative pronouns. *That* is the oldest of the relatives and can be used to refer to either persons or things; *which* does not refer to persons. A recent distinction, perhaps prescribed in an attempt at neatness, specifies *that* to introduce restrictive clauses and *which* and *who* to introduce nonrestrictive clauses. The distinction has never been common, even in formal writing, but many writers distinguish between *that* and *which* on this basis.

the The definite article regularly identifies something as previously mentioned or as distinct from others in its class.

> I saw a man and a woman standing by the ticket office. *The* man was eating cotton candy.
>
> He lost his eye in *the* accident I was telling you about.

Since *the* usually refers to something previously mentioned, its use to introduce a noun new to the context may be confusing.
> When we arrived, the park seemed deserted. *A* [not *the*] man was sitting alone on a bench near the entrance.

their, there, they're Commonly confused in spelling. *There,* which can be remembered by its similarity to *where,* means "in that place" (Lie *there,* Nipper). *Their* is the possessive of *they. They're,* the contraction of *they are,* is not acceptable in formal composition.

these Should be avoided as a substitute for *the;* see *this.*

these kind, these sort See *kind.*

they For the colloquial use of *they* to refer to people or society, see chapter 9.

this Like *the, this* as a determiner indicates that the noun it precedes has been previously mentioned (On our way home from Sunday School, *a* [not *this*] man came up to me and took my hand, and then *he* [not *this fellow*] said . . .). For reference of *this,* see chapter 9; for *this* as a symptom of inadequate subordination, see chapter 8.

this here Nonstandard; omit *here.*

tho A variant spelling of *though* not preferred for formal composition.

those Colloquial as an intensive with no reference (He looked back fondly on *his* [not *those*] old college days).

thusly Affected or nonstandard for *thus.*

to, too, two Distinguish the function word *to* (*to* the game, learn *to* read) from the adverb *too* (*too* sick, *too* hot), and the number *two* (*two* seats on the aisle).

toward, towards Alternative forms; *toward* is more common in the United States.

trait Redundant in *character trait*; use *trait* or *characteristic*.

try and *Try to* is preferred in standard English.

type In formal English, *type* is a noun or verb, although colloquially it is often an adjective as in *a ranch-type house* (*This type of research* [not *this type research*] yields results).

unique For the use of *unique*, see chapter 8.

up Useful in verb sets, *up* can frequently be separated from the verb, but often the sense is clearer and the construction smoother if *up* is kept close to the verb (He *made up his mind,* not He *made his mind up*).

used to The *d* is elided in speech but not omitted in writing (We *used to* [not *use to*] go to the beach every summer).

used to could Nonstandard for "used to be able."

wait on Except in the sense of "serve," *wait for* is idiomatic (We have been waiting *for* [not *on*] you to arrive).

want for In most constructions the *for* is redundant (I *want* [not *want for*] you to meet her).

ways Colloquial for *way* to mean "distance" (It was a long *way* [not *ways*] to the road).

we For the editorial and impersonal *we* as subject, see chapter 2.

weather, whether Frequently confused in spelling with *whether* (I asked him *whether* or not we could depend upon fair *weather*).

well An adjective in the sense "in good health," "cured" (The patient is now recovered and is quite *well*); an adverb corresponding to the adjective *good*, but not to be confused with it; see chapter 8 (She played her part *well* [not *good*]. The blueprints look *good* [not *well*]).

what Nonstandard as a relative pronoun (I liked the places *that* [not *what*] he recommended). *What all* occurs in some dialects (*What all* they do I have to do), but *all* is redundant.

when Avoid the *when*-clause in a definition; see chapter 7.

where Nonstandard or colloquial when substituted for *that* (I noticed in the paper *that* Senator Jones is a candidate for re-election [not I see by the paper *where* Senator Jones is up for re-election]).

where at In most constructions, omit the *at* (*Where* is he? [not *Where at* is he? or *Where* is he *at*?]).

whether See *if*.

which For *which* after *and*, see *and which*; for the use of *which* to refer to human beings, see *that*; for *which* and *that*, see *that, which*.

while In Old English, *while* (spelled *hwil*) meant a period of time, as it still does in a phrase like "in a short while," and most subsequent meanings preserve the idea of time. For centuries, *while* was most commonly used as a relative conjunction to indicate that the time in the subordinate clause is the same as that in the main clause (*While* I broil the chops, you might set the table). Presumably this use developed a concessive conjunction, the equivalent of *although* (*While* Father disapproved of the damage an off-road vehicle might do to the ecology, he hated to deprive us of having a good time). Read with the traditional meaning of *while,* that the one action took place while the other took place—and presumably only at that time—the sentence is confusing and even nonsensical. Recently, another use has appeared, in which *while* serves as a coordinating conjunction, the equivalent of *and* (Jenkins will run in the relay, *while* he also competes in the javelin). This sentence, likewise, will be nonsense to many careful readers, although such uses are now common in sports writing and in some other areas.

who, whom Logically, relative and interrogative pronouns take their form from their use in their clause—*who* for a subject or subject complement, *whom* for an object. When the words occur out of the usual subject-verb-complement order, however, users of the language do not always make the case distinction. Compare:

> I asked him *who* he thought he was hitting.
> I asked him *whom* he thought he was hitting.

In these sentences the pronoun functions as the object of *was hitting;* formal written usage would require *whom.* Since the pronoun is the first word in its clause, however, in the subject position, speakers tend to use *who,* the subject form. Formal writing might require:

Whom did Tom invite? *Whom* do you see? I don't know *whom* he is taking to the party.

Informally, *who* is common in such sentences. *Whom* is used consistently when the pronoun immediately follows a preposition. (I wasn't sure to *whom* [not *who*] I was speaking). Concern for correctness with such pronouns often causes exaggerated deference to *whom* and becomes more disturbing than informal neglect for the case distinction. Notice the following:

Who [not *whom*] does he think he is? I met the woman *who* [not *whom*] everyone said would win the election. I asked him *who* [not *whom*] he was.

who's The contraction of *who is.*

whose English no longer has a possessive form for *which. Whose,* the possessive of *who,* is now regularly used to avoid the often cumbersome *of which,* even though *who* is usually restricted to reference to people (I do not like a ring *whose setting* [compare *the setting of which*] reminds me of snakes).

will For the distinction from *shall,* see *shall, will.*

wire Informal for either *telegram* or *telegraph.*

-wise Overused as an informal suffix for almost everything (The meal was good *tastewise*). The use readily becomes absurd.

without Nonstandard as a substitute for *unless.* (I will not stay *unless* [not *without*] you raise my wages).

wood, woods In the United States either is acceptable as a synonym of *forest.*

worst kind, worst way Not acceptable in the sense "very much."

worthwhile Overused blanket word.

would have Often awkward (If they *had* [not *would have*] tried harder . . .).

would of Mistaken form of *would have* (see *could of*).

you To be used with caution in impersonal constructions.

you-all Informal Southern form as the plural of *you;* not acceptable for formal composition.

Appendix B

Revising an Essay Using the Guides to Revision

Even though you have have revised carefully, your instructor is likely to suggest corrections and changes for your paper, using the symbols in the list below which refer to the Guides to Revision throughout the book. When you find a reference symbol or abbreviation on your paper, you can find on the list a page reference that will lead you to a guide suggesting a revision. This guide is a summary of fuller discussions in the chapter in which it appears. If the brief guide does not explain the instructor's suggestion adequately, study the chapter in which the guide appears before making your revision.

You should note that profitable revision often requires more than correcting misspelled words or changing punctuation. For example, the mark *Coh* in the margin tells you that part of your paper lacks coherence or continuity. The mark suggests that you strengthen ties between ideas. Study chapter 4 to which the mark refers you, and rewrite the passage so that it holds together. If the mark *Sub* appears, you need to refer to the guide in chapter 8 which suggests improving sentence structure by using subordination. You may need to combine sentences, reducing a clause to a phrase or a single word. The selection below has been marked with the abbreviations in the list.

474 Revising an Essay Using the Guides to Revision

Wordy   The public is fooled every day by a <u>variety of many kinds</u> of people ranging from the glib medicine man to people working for <u>high geared</u> political machines. *Hy*

Agr   The <u>inteligence</u> of these people <u>vary</u> widely. *Sp*

The people they fool are often

CF   more <u>inteligent</u> than the<u>y, however,</u> their *Sp*

skills are so great that they overcome

Sp   even the <u>inteligent</u> man. <u>Inteligence</u> is *Sp*

Sp   not acquired, but <u>knowlege</u> can be acquired, *Dev*

(due to) man's ability to learn. | Salesmen

Sub   often (state) as fact information about *Coh*

their products. Often these are untrue.

This opening for a paper is not promising, and frequent errors in structure and mechanics have been marked. To correct them, you would need to find the page reference for each abbreviation and refer to the appropriate Guide to Revision. You would discover that *Wordy* indicates wordiness and repetition and refers you to a short guide in chapter 11. *Hy* indicates faulty hyphenation discussed in chapter 18. *Agr* refers to agreement of subject and verb or pronoun and antecedent and is discussed in chapter 9. The fourth sentence is marked *Dev*, a reference to chapter 3, which suggests revision to improve development of ideas. *Due to* in the same sentence is circled with no mark in the margin. The circle suggests that you look up the marked expression in the Glossary, Appendix A.

ALPHABETICAL LIST OF CORRECTION SYMBOLS REFERRING TO GUIDES TO REVISION

		Page
Ab	Faulty Use of Abbreviations	440
Adj	Improper form for Adjective	182
Adv	Improper form for Adverb	182
Agr	Lack of Agreement of Verb and Subject or Pronoun and Antecedent	215

Revising an Essay Using the Guides to Revision 475

		Page
Apos	Omission or Misuse of Apostrophe	436
Cap	Error in Capitalization	429
CF	Comma Fault, see P2	395
Coh	Coherence	90
Colon	Faulty Use of Colon, see P9	408
Conc	Inadequate or Inappropriate Conclusion	122
Conj	Misuse of Conjunction	200
Dash	Misuse of Dash, see P10	410
Degree	Inappropriate Degree of Modifier	190
Dev	Inadequate Development of Ideas	56
Div	Improper Division of Words at End of Line	442
Eq	Inaccurate Equation with *To Be*	155
Expl	Overuse of Sentences with Expletive	158
Frag	Inappropriate Use of Sentence Fragment	143
Gloss	Refer to Expression in Glossary, Appendix A	
Hy	Misuse of Hyphen or Inaccurate Compounding	431
Intro	Inadequate or Inappropriate Introduction	120
Ital	Lack of Italics or Misuse of Italics	438
lc	Misuse of Capital Letter rather than Lower Case	429
Mod	Misplaced or Dangling Modifier	188
NoP	Inappropriate or Unnecessary Punctuation, see P8	407
Num	Improper Form for Numbers	434
P	Improper Punctuation	389–416
P1	End Punctuation	392
P2	Run-on Sentence, the Semicolon	395
P3	Comma after Introductory Modifier	397
P4	Comma with Nonrestrictive Modifier	400
P5	Punctuation in Series	402

		Page
P6	Comma for Clarity	404
P7	Comma and Statistical Details	405
P8	Inappropriate or Unnecessary Comma	407
P9	The Colon	408
P10	The Dash	410
P11	Parentheses and Brackets	412
P12	Punctuation with Quotations	415
Paral	Lack of Parallelism in Coordinate Structures	175
Pass	Overuse of Passive Sentences	162
Pers	Inconsistency in Person	40
Pl	Inaccurate Plural Form	433
Poss	Inaccurate Formation of Possessive	436
Pred	Implausible Predication	150
Prep	Inaccurate or Unidiomatic Use of Preposition	202
Ref	Unclear Reference of Pronoun to Antecedent	206
Run-on	Sentences Run Together Without Proper Separating Punctuation	395
Shift	Shift in Structure	156
Sp	Incorrect Spelling	426
Sub	Inadequate or Misleading Subordination	179
Subj	Ineffective Choice of Sentence Subject	137
Tense	Inconsistency in Tense and Point of View	47
Titles	Improper Form for a Title	441
Tone	Inappropriate or Inconsistent Tone	44
Trans	Inadequate Transition	115
Trite	Trite Expression, Cliché	250
Usage	Inappropriate Usage	255
W	Inappropriate or Inaccurate Choice of Words	237

		Page
Wordy	Excessive Wordiness	248
WRef	Unclear Reference of Words	209
¶	Unclear or Inappropriate Paragraphing	85

If a word in a paper is circled, look it up in the Glossary, Appendix A.

Index

a, an, 451
Abbreviations, 439-40
  for investigative paper, 385
above, below, 451
Abstract words, 240-42
accept, except, 451
Actor as subject, 135-37
actually, 451
A.D., 451
adapt, adept, adopt, 451
Addresses, punctuation in, 405
Adjectives, 180-84
  compound, 430-32
  degree, 189-91
  in *-ly*, 181
Adverbs, 180-83
  degree, 189-91
  in sentence pattern, 133-34
advice, advise, 451
adviser, advisor, 451
affect, effect, 451
agenda, 451
aggravate, 451
agree, 452
Agreement, 209-16
  with alternative subjects, 212-13
  with collective nouns, 212
  with compound subjects, 212-13
  identifying subject, 213-14
  with indefinite pronouns, 211
  with linking verbs, 213-14
  nouns that refer, 214-16
  in number, 210-16
ain't, 452
alibi, 452
all (of), 452
all ready, already, 452
all right, alright, 452
all the farther (further), 452
allusion, illusion, 452
alumnus, alumna, 433, 452
among, between, 452
amount, number, 452
Analogy
  as development, 65-66
  as evidence, 291
Analysis, 15-16
  for organization, 96-101
  to refine a topic, 25-26
  of style, 328-29
and, to begin a sentence, 198-99
and which, and who, 452
angle, 452
Anglo-Saxon language, 220-22
ante-, anti-, 452
Antecedent
  agreement with, 210-15
  pronoun, 203
anybody, any body, anyone, any one, 453
any more, 453
anyways, 453
anywheres, 453

478

Apostrophe
  in contractions, 437
  with dialect, 437
  in possessives, 435-37
Appositive modifiers, 399
apt, 461
area, 453
aren't I, see *ain't*, 452
Argument, 279-98
  appeals, 280
  strategies, 282-87
Argumentation, 58
around, 453
Arrangement, 3, 95-123
as, 453
aspect, 453
at, 453
athletics, 453
attribute, contribute, 453
Audience, 32-34
  and the student, 33-34
  and the writer's voice, 34-37
auto, 453
awful, awfully, 453

bad, 453
bad, good, 181
bad, well, 181
B.C., 454
because, 454
begin, 454
being as, beings as, 454
beside, besides, 454
between, 452
Bibliography
  cards, 347-49
  working, 346-47
blame, 454
blond, blonde, 454
Borrowed words, spelling, 427
Borrowing in language, 223-24
Brackets, 361, 411-12
Brainstorming, 20-21
break, 454
broke, 454
bunch, 454
-burger, as suffix, 229
burst, bust, 454
but, 454
  to begin a sentence, 198-99
but hardly, only, scarcely, 454
but that, but what, 455

can, may, 455
can't help but, can't hardly, 455
Capitals, 427-30
Card catalog, 341-42
case, 455
Case, pronoun, 204-5
censor, censure, censer, 455
certain, 455
character, 455

Characters, writing about, 325-27
Circular argument, 298
circumstances, 455
Citation, parenthetical, 362-63
cite, sight, site, 455
claim, 455
Classification, 96-97, 99-101
  as development, 66-67
Clauses, 140-41
  coordinating, 167-68
  dependent, 140-41
  independent, 140-41
  subordinate, 140-41
Clichés, 250
Clustering, 19-20
Coherence, 86-91
  continuing a subject, 88
  repetition of ideas, 87
  in sentences, 196-216
  transitional words, 89-90
  word order and, 89-90
Collective nouns, 212
Colloquial English, 252-53, 450
Colon, 407-9
  with quotations, 361
Comma fault, splice, 168, 393-96
Commas
  before *and* or *but*, 394-95
  for clarity, 403-4
  between clauses, 168
  excessive, 406-7
  with introductory modifiers, 396-97
  with nonrestrictive modifiers, 397-401
  in series, 401-3
  with statistical details, 404-5
Commitment and response, 74-76
Commitment-response units, 75-76
Comparative degree of modifier, 189-91
Comparison
  definition by, 285
  as development, 67-69
  faulty in sentence, 173-75
  parallelism in, 173-75
  in writing about literature, 331-32
complected, 455
Complement, 139-41
  object, 139-41
  in sentence pattern, 132-41
  subject, 139-41
Composing process, 3-12
Compounding, 228
Compounds, 430-32
Computer
  and research, 342
  and revision, 12
Conclusions, 121-23
Concrete words, 240-42
Conjunctions, 198-201
  coordinating, 198-99
  correlative, 199
  subordinating, 199-201
Conjunctive adverbs, 199
  joining clauses, 168

Index 479

position of, 186–87
punctuation with, 394–95
Connotation, 240, 242–43
conscience, conscious, 455
contact, 455
Contexts and meaning, 240
continue on, 455
Continuity
  passive for, 161
  subordination and, 178–80
Contractions, 437
Contrast as development, 67–69
Conventions for investigative paper, 385
Coordinating conjunctions, 198–99
Coordination, 97–101
  in sentence, 134, 166–75
Correctness, 251–53
Correlative conjunctions, 199
could of, 456
council, counsel, consul, 456
couple, 456
credible, credulous, creditable, 456
Cumulative sentence, 265, 267–68
cute, 456

Dangling modifiers, 185–88
Dash, 409–11
date, 456
Dates, punctuation in, 404–5
datum, data, 433, 456
Deadwood, 246–49
deal, 456
Deduction, 292–98
definite, definitely, 456
Definition
  as development, 63–64
  methods of, 282–85
Degree of modifiers, 189–91
Denotation, 240, 242–43
Description, 57
Development, 52–69
  adequate, 54–57
  by analogy, 65–66
  by cause and effect, 65
  by classification, 66–67
  by comparison and contrast, 67–69
  by definition, 63–64
  by example, 62–63
  by extended incident, 62–63
  and forms of discourse, 59–60
  by instances, 60–62
  by process analysis, 66
  specific, 54–57
Dialect, 251–53
Dialogue paragraphing, 82–83
Diction, 235–55
Dictionaries
  making of, 231–32
  use of, 230–33
different from, than, 456
Direction in meaning, 249
Discourse, forms of, 57–60
Discussion, 303–5
disinterested, uninterested, 456
Diversion, as response, 74
do, 456
Documentation, 361–64
don't, 457
Double possessive, 437

Doublespeak, 243–44
doubt, 457
drag, 457
due to, 457

each and every, 457
each other, one another, 457
Economy in diction, 246–49
effect, 451
either, neither, 457
either, or, 199
  agreement with, 212–13
Ellipsis mark, 361–393
Endnotes, 364–65
End punctuation, 390–93
enthuse, 457
Enthymeme, 293–98
equally as, 457
Equations
  false in sentence, 151–55
  in frame sentence, 154
etc., 457
Ethics in persuasion, 280–81
Euphemism, 243–44
everybody, agreement with, 211
everybody, everyone, 457
Evidence, 287–91
  fact and opinion, 288–89
  testing, 289–91
exactly, 458
Examinations, 305–11
  analyzing questions, 307–9
  preparing for, 306–7
  writing essay answers, 309–11
except, 451
Exclamation mark, 391–92
expect, 458
Expletive, 157–59
Exposition, 58
  strategies for, 60–69
extra, 456

fact, the fact that, 458
Fact and opinion, 288–91
factor, 458
Fallacies in logic, 289–91, 294–98
famed, 458
farther, further, 458
fellow, 458
fewer, less, 458
field, 458
Figurative language, 244–46
  in literature, 329–31
figure, 458
fine, 458
fix, 458
Focusing, 26–29
  devices for organization, 111–13
  thesis sentence, 26–28
folks, 458
formally, formerly, 458
Formal style, 271
Form in literature, writing about, 327–28
Forms of discourse, 57–60
Fragment, sentence, 141–44
Frame sentence, 154
Freewriting, 18–19
Function words, 196–203
  and grammar, 129
funny, 458

General and specific, 53
Generalization, 287–88
General words, 241–42
Gerund, pronoun before, 459
get, got, 458
good, 459
good, as predicate adjective, 181
good and, 459
gotten, 459
Grammar, 127–44
  dictionary information, 232–33
  English, 225–26
  function words, 129
  inflection, 129
  privilege of occurrence, 130
  word order, 129
guess, 459
Guides to revision, 12, 473–77

had better, had best, you'd better, 459
had of, 459
had ought, hadn't ought, 459
hang, 459
he, him, 460
he, she, it as subjects, 39
healthful, healthy, 459
heap, heaps, 459
heighth, 459
his, him, their, them, 459
hisself, 459
home, derivation of, 225
honorable, 439, 459
hopefully, 459
however, 459
humor, 459
Humor, and tone, 43
Hyphens
  in compounds, 430–32
  with numbers, 432
  in word division, 441–42

I, as subject, 38
I, me, 140
I, me, him, she, her, we, them, 460
idea, 460
if, whether, 460
imply, infer, 460
Impromptu essays, 309–11
in, into, 460
in back of, 460
Indention for paragraphing, 76–78
Independent clauses, ways to join, 168
individual, 460
Indo-European language, 220–22
Inductive reasoning, 287–91
inferior than, 460
Infinitive, split, 187
Inflection and grammar, 129
Informal style, 271
ingenious, ingenuous, 461
in regards to, 460
inside of, 461
in terms of, 461
Interview, 340–41
Intransitive verb, 128
Introductions, 116–20
Invention, 3, 52–69
Investigative paper, 338–85
  sample, 370–84
invite, 461

480 Index

Irony, 272-73
irregardless, 461
is because, 153-54
is when, 153-154
it, 461
 as dummy subject, 149-50
 as expletive, 157-59
Italics, 437-39
 with words out of context, 439

Journal, for recording ideas, 20-24

kind, sort, 461
kind of, 461

Language, 219-33
 borrowing, 222-24
 dialects, 224
 growth and change, 225-26
 history, 219-30
 Indo-European, 220-22
 native words, 227-28
lead, led, 461
less, 458
let, leave, 461
Letters
 application, 315-16
 forms and conventions, 312-15
Lexicographer, 230-31
liable, apt, likely, 461
Library, use of, 341-49
lie, lay, 461
like, as, 462
line, 462
Linking verb, 138
 and predicate complement, 181-82
literally, 462
Literature
 personal response to, 332-33
 writing about, 321-35
loan, 462
locate, 462
Logical fallacies, 289-91, 294-98
loose, loosen, lose, 462
lot, for *many*, 451
lots of, 462
love, 462

mad, 462
Malapropism, 238
Manuscript form, 421
math, 462
may, 462
Meaning
 in literature, 323-25
 and word choice, 236-40
Mechanics, 420-42
Metaphor, 244-46
 trite, 250
Middle term in syllogism, 296-98
might of, see *could of*, 456
mighty, 462
Modification in sentence, 175-79
Modifiers
 dangling, 185-88
 economy in, 247-48
 limiting, 183
 misplaced, 185-88
 movable in fixed position, 184-86
 sentence, 181

squinting, 185
and word order, 182-91
moral, morale, 462
more, with modifiers, 189-91
more than one, 463
most, 463
 with modifiers, 189-91
muchly, 463
must, 463
myself, 463

Narration, 57
nature, 463
neither, 457
 agreement with, 212-13
neither, nor, 199, 463
Newspaper indexes, 342-44
nice, 463
none, 463
 number of, 211
Nonrestrictive modifiers, 397-401
Non sequitur, 294-98
not . . . as, 463
Notebook
 reader's, 23-24
 writer's, 20-23
Notes
 and plagiarism, 356-57
 taking and preserving, 349-54
number, 452
Number, and agreement, 210-15
Numbers, 434-35
 hyphen with, 432

Object
 complement, 139-41
 hidden, 151
 implausible, 151
 of verb, 132-41
Observing, as prewriting, 16-17
of, 463
off, of, 463
Old English language, 220-22
on, 463
one, 463
only, position of, 183-84
on the part of, 463
-orama, -orium, 464
Organization, 95-123
 ascending or descending order, 102
 chronological, 101-2
 focusing devices, 111-13
 logical, 103
 spatial, 102
 strategies for, 101-3
Outline, 104-11
 conventions in, 107
 form, 106-7
 and revision, 109-11
 sentence, 109
out of, 464
outside of, 464
outstanding, 464
overall, 464
over with, 464

Paragraphs, 73-94
 appropriate, 83-85
 coherence in, 86-90

and commitment-response units, 76-78
 conventional, 82
 dialogue, 82
 guide to revision, 85
 standard and expository, 79-82
 unity in, 84-85
Parallelism, 169-75
 in comparisons, 173-75
 completing patterns, 172-73
 and style, 266-67
Paraphrase, in notes, 351-54
Parentheses, 411-12
Parenthetical modifiers, 397-401
Parody and style, 268-70
part, on the part of, 464
party, 464
passed, past, 464
Passive sentences, 159-63
per-, pre-, pro-, 464
Period, 390-93
 in abbreviations, 393
Periodical indexes, 342-44
Periodic sentence, 265-67
Person, 37-40
 consistency in, 40
 and pronouns, 38-40
 and voice, 37-40
Persona, 32
Persuasion, 279-98
 appeals, 280
 ethics and, 280-81
 strategies for, 282-87
phenomena, 464
phone, 464
picture, 464
piece, 464
Plagiarism, 354-57
Plan of book, 13
plan on, 464
plenty, 464
Plot, writing about, 327
Plurals, 432-34
 foreign, 433-44
 of numbers, 434
point, 464
Point of view, consistency in, 45-47
poorly, 464
Possessives, 435-37
Post hoc ergo propter hoc fallacy, 290
Postponed subject, 157-59
Predicate adjective, 133, 140
Predicate nominative, 133, 139-41
Predication, 147-63
 implausible, 150
Prefixes, 228-30
 and spelling, 424
prejudice, 465
Preposition, 201-3
 at end of sentence, 202-3
Prepositional phrase, 201
presence, 465
Prewriting, 3-12, 15-30
 asking questions, 24-25
 brainstorming, 20-21
 clustering, 19-20
 freewriting, 18-19
 observing, 16-17
 remembering, 17-18
 using a notebook, 20-24
principal, principle, 465

Privilege of occurrence, 130
  in predication, 148
Process, composing, 3–12
Process analysis as development, 66
prof, 464
Pronouns
  form and reference, 204–5, 460
  indefinite, 205–7
  person, 38–40
  reference, 203–7
  relative, 201
  and voice, 38–40
Pronunciation, 232
  and spelling, 422, 424
Proper nouns, capitals with, 428–30
Proposition in argument and persuasion, 281–82
proved, proven, 465
providing, 465
Punctuation, 389–415
  for clarity, 403–4
  between clauses, 393–96
  end, 390–93
  excessive, 406–7
  after introductory modifiers, 396–97
  with nonrestrictive material, 397–400, 410–12
  with quotations, 412–15
  in series, 401–3
  with statistical details, 404–5
  uses of, 390
Purpose
  and voice, 34–37
  the writer's, 32
put across, 465

Question mark, 391–93
Questions, as prewriting, 24–25
quite, 465
Quotation marks, 412–15
  with other marks, 414–15
Quotations
  punctuation, 412–15
  in research writing, 360–61

raise, 465
rate, 465
re, 465
Reading
  as prewriting, 23–24
  and style, 273
real, 465
really, 465
Reasoning and writing, 279–98
reason is because, 153–54, 454
reason why, 465
reckon, 465
Reference
  patterns of, 203–5
  pronoun, 203–7
  word, 207–9
Reference books, 344–46
Refutation in argument and persuasion, 288
regard, regards, 465
relate to, 466
Relative pronoun, 201
Remembering as prewriting, 17–18
Repetition as response, 74
Research, 341–57
  for writing on literature, 333–34

respectfully, respectively, 466
Résumé, 316–18
Return, as response, 74
reverend, 439–40, 466
Revision, 3–12
  and development, 54–57
  guides to, 12, 473–77
  outlining for, 109–11
  in paragraphing, 83–84
  of research paper, 357–58
  for style, 273–74
Rhetoric, 2–3
  communication triangle, 2
  parts of process, 3
Rhythm in sentences, 264
right, 466
right on, 466
rise, raise, 466
Run-on sentences, 393–96

said, 466
same, 466
scarcely, 466
Schwa, 425
seem, 466
seldom ever, 466
Semantics, 238–40
Semicolon
  between clauses, 168, 393–96
  in series, 403
Sentence
  actor-action-goal, 135–37
  basic, 130–34
  complement, 132–41
  cumulative, 265, 267–68
  fragment, 141–44
  length, 262–64
  periodic, 265–67
  rhythm in, 264
  subject, 132–37
  variety, 262–64
  verb, 132–39
Sentence modifier, 181
Series, punctuation in, 401–3
set, 467
setup, 466
Sexism
  and pronoun agreement, 211
  and usage, 253–55
shall, will, 466–67
shape, 467
She, her, I, me, 140
Shifts in structure, 155–56
should, would, see *shall, will*, 466
should of, 467
show, 467
show up, 467
sic, 385
sit, set, 467
site, 455
situated, 467
situation, 467
size, 468
Slanting words, 242–43
so, 468
so as, 468
some, 468
somebody's else, 468
sometime, some time, 468
somewhat of, 468

somewheres, 468
sort of, sort of a, 468
Sources for material, 340–49
speak, speech, 468
Specific and general, 53
Specification, as response, 74
Specific words, 241–2
Spelling, 421–34
  changes, 225
  common errors, 445–49
Split infinitive, 187–88
Squinting modifier, 185
Standard English, 252–53, 450
state, 468
stationary, stationery, 468
Style, 3, 260–74
  analyzing, 328–29
  appropriate, 270–73
  characteristics of, 261–62
  in investigative paper, 353–59
  natural, 273–74
  parody and, 268–70
  varieties of, 270–73
Subject
  choice of, 134–35, 148
  complement, 139–41
  dummy, 149–50
  forgotten, 149
  in sentence pattern, 132–37
Subject for research, 339–40
Subject-verb-complement (SVC), 132–34
Subordinating conjunction, 199–201
Subordination, 97–101
  inadequate, 179
  in sentence, 131, 166–67, 175–91
such, 468
  reference of, 208
Suffixes, 228–30
  and spelling, 424
suit, suite, 468
Summary, in notes, 351–54
Superlative degree of modifier, 189–91
suspicion, 468
SVC pattern, 132–34
Syllogism, 292–98
  middle term in, 296–98
Synonyms, 240
Synthesis, 15–16

take and, 468
take sick, 468
Technique, writing about, 327–28
Tense
  consistency in, 45–47
  sequence, 46
  in writing about literature, 334–35
terrible, terribly, 468
terrific, 468
that, 469
  in noun clause, 153–54
that there, 469
that which, 469
the, 469
their, reference with, 204
their, there, they're, 469
Theme, writing about, 323–25
there
  as expletive, 157–59
  reference of, 208
these, 469

Thesis and subject, 340
Thesis sentence, 26-28
they, 469
this, 469
  reference of, 205-8
this here, 469
tho, 469
those, 469
thusly, 469
Titles, 414, 440-41
to, too, two, 469
to be, 454
  in equations, 151-55
  overuse of, 139
Tone, 32, 41-44
  appropriateness, 42-44
  consistency in, 42-44
Topic sentence, 78-79
Topics for writing, 25-26
  limiting, 25-26
toward, towards, 469
trait, 470
Transitional words and coherence, 89-90
Transitions, 113-16
Transitive verbs, 138
Tricolon, 266
Triteness, 250
try and, 470
type, 470

Understatement, 272
unique, 189
up, 470

Usage, 251-55
  levels of, 252
  sexism and, 253-55
  varieties, 252
used to, 470
used to could, 470

Verbs
  development, 226
  intransitive, 137
  linking, 138
  merged, 138
  in sentence pattern, 132-39
  with separable suffix, 138
  transitive, 138
Vocabulary
  building, 226-30
  four types, 227-28
  prefixes and suffixes, 228-30
Voice
  the writer's, 32-40
  writing about, 325

wait on, 470
want for, 470
ways, 470
we, editorial, 38
weather, whether, 470
well, 470
well, good, 18
what, 470
when, 470
where, 470
where at, 470

whether, 460
which, 470
  reference of, 205-7
while, 470-71
who, agreement of, 214
who, whom, 471
who's, 471
whose, 471
wire, 471
-wise, 471
without, 471
wood, woods, 471
Word choice, 235-55
Word devision, 441-42
Word groups, to extend SVC, 133-34
Wordiness, 246-49
Word order
  and grammar, 129
  and modifiers, 182-91
Word reference, 207-9
Words
  borrowed, 236
  native, 236
Works cited, 365-70
Works cited page, style for, 367-70
worst kind, worst way, 472
worthwhile, 472
would have, 472
would of, 472
Writing system, 420-42

you, 472
  as subject, 39
you-all, 472